Visions of the City

For my mother and father

Visions of the City

Utopianism, Power and Politics in Twentieth-Century Urbanism

David Pinder

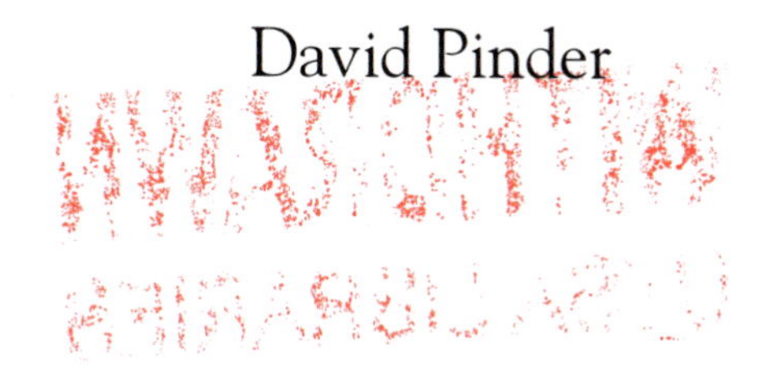

NEW YORK

Published in the USA and Canada in 2005 by
Routledge
Taylor and Francis Group
270 Madison Avenue
New York, NY 10016

Routledge is an imprint of Taylor and Francis Group, LLC.

Published by arrangement with Edinburgh University Press, Edinburgh, in 2005.

Typeset in 10.5/13.25 Adobe Goudy
by Servis Filmsetting Ltd, Manchester, and
printed and bound in Great Britain.

Cataloging-in-Publication Data is available from the Library of Congress.

ISBN 0 415 95310 3 (hardback)
ISBN 0 415 95311 1 (paperback)

Contents

Preface

This book is about utopian visions of the city during the twentieth century. It focuses on attempts to imagine cities differently, and to change radically their spaces and social relations. In addressing this theme, I have turned to past utopian endeavours to imagine and build better cities. This is in the belief that there is much to learn from some of these struggles, much also to sustain a sense of hope and possibility in the present. This is perhaps especially important in recent times when hope has all too often been under threat, and when glimmers of other possibilities can seem all too faint. There is no doubt that contemporary urban problems can seem overwhelming in a global context and that dreaming of utopias can seem wholly inadequate. Talk of utopianism might seem to many people inherently dangerous, given the long history of disasters and oppressive schemes that have resulted from previous plans in its name. To others its emphasis on desire, dreams and imagination may at times see far-fetched or even a distraction compared with hard pressing practical concerns. Yet addressing past forms of utopianism can be valuable. This is not only for thinking critically about their profound influence on conceptions of cities, and for understanding more fully why it is that utopian visions have so often been denounced as misguided, authoritarian or dangerous. It is also because, in spite of such disasters, a utopian impulse remains necessary in my view for confronting the challenge of creating better futures through its emphasis on exploring possibilities and what could be. A utopianism for the present, furthermore, cannot afford simply to ignore or discard past visions; it needs to come to terms with those histories, and may indeed find ways of using them as it forges its own poetry with different futures in mind.

Cities have, of course, long been the subjects of utopian imaginations and hopes for better futures. They have frequently been portrayed as the crucibles for potential enlightenment, democracy and freedom, where city air was famously said to make one free. At the same time cities have been depicted in dystopian terms as hellish places and the focus for fears, despair and apocalyptic scenarios. The tension between these two sides runs through urban imaginations in western culture. This book does not attempt to provide a survey of utopian visions, but instead cuts a particular line into this field, focusing on selected cases of utopianism within twentieth-century western Europe. These include both mainstream visions that have had considerable impact on the architecture, planning and construction of cities, and those from within the modern avant-garde that are more marginal, although they have been attracting increasing attention recently. Although many of these visions remained imaginary and never found built expression, that does not mean they are unworthy of attention; far from it, since their significance extends in many other ways, in questioning reality, in influencing conceptions of space, in expressing desires for alternatives, in harbouring the seeds for other interventions. Attending to previous alternatives is indeed vital in opening senses of possibility, and in challenging histories based on the linear unfolding of ideas that have been officially sanctioned where history appears as written by the victors. Although this book focuses on specific cases, it may therefore be seen as part of a wider interest in exploring alternative visions and practices from the past, including so-called 'failures', so as to read aspects of modern urbanism 'against the grain'.

How and why the different utopian visions in this book focused on cities and urban space are questions central to the book. It is worth emphasising in this regard that my interest is in the spatiality of cities, where cities are understood not as 'things' reducible to their buildings and physical forms, but as spaces that are socially produced and that are dynamic, open and interconnected. This is important for recognising that the struggles over cities discussed here involved the contestation of practices and processes that are not confined to a bounded conception of a city as such. The urbanists, artists, writers and activists discussed in these pages nevertheless all attached importance to intervening in cities and urban spaces for political and social ends, in recognition of the ways in which society is spatially constituted. Their aims were to change society as well as space. Through the book I have tried to stay close to the original materials and activities through which their utopian visions were articulated. In doing so, I hope to have retained at least some of the inspiring qualities that I have found in many of these materials, even if in a form far disconnected from the interventions themselves. One of my hopes for the later chapters on the situationists in particular is that they might encourage readers who are not already familiar with the writings and practices of that group to explore them further themselves, and make use of them for their own ends. Recognition should be given in this regard to all those who have done so much to ensure the availability of original situationist texts over the years, especially before the recent upsurge of interest in the group. Those publishers, translators, activists and more recently website designers deserve considerable credit. My indebtedness to other writers in this field and especially to the many architectural and planning historians who have so richly discussed Ebenezer Howard and Le Corbusier will also be apparent from the notes, and ought to be acknowledged directly.

The book has been with me for a long time and the personal debts that I have accumulated over the years are too numerous and deep to acknowledge adequately here. I would particularly like to thank Linda McDowell for her enthusiasm and support as my supervisor when the materials here had an earlier life as a doctoral thesis at the University of Cambridge. Her ability to create a stimulating and supportive environment for graduate students was greatly appreciated, as has been her interest and help since then. I am grateful to those who helped me to get started, in particular Mark Billinge, Stuart Corbridge, Philip Howell and the late Graham Smith; to Stephen Tommis whose teaching and bookshelves (especially early editions of *Antipode*) first opened my eyes to radical geography; and to all those colleagues who contributed to a lively graduate school. Early on, Alastair Bonnett and Sadie Plant both responded enthusiastically and generously to my initial enquiries. I would like to thank Constant for his generosity as well as inspiration; and Trudy van der Horst and Victor Nieuwenhuys for their kind help. I am grateful to Constant, Donald Nicholson-Smith and the late Ralph Rumney for sharing interesting thoughts on the situationists.

I received considerable help from the staff at a number of archives and libraries. They include those at the Haags Gemeentemuseum in the Hague, in particular Elmar Groen; the Rijksbureau voor Kunsthistorische Documentatie in the Hague, especially Jan Teeuwisse, Marcia Zaaijer and Hans Wijgergangs; the International Museum for Social History, the Stedelijk Museum, and the University Library in Amsterdam; the Silkeborg Kunstmuseum in Silkeborg, especially Dorte Andersen and Troels Andersen; the Museum of Modern Art in New York; the Tate Gallery Library, and the Victoria and Albert National Art Library Museum, in London; the Hertfordshire Archives and Local Studies in Hertford; the Fondation Le Corbusier in Paris; and Liliana Dematteis of the Archivio Gallizio in Turin. I have also relied on the British Library, the Cambridge University Library, the Hartley Library in Southampton, and the Queen Mary Library in London. I am indebted to those who helped with translations, especially Jany Keat and James Simpson. Many thanks also to Edward Oliver for his efficient help with images. I would like to acknowledge the support of the UK Economic and Social Research Council for funding the original research from which this stems; Sidney Sussex College, Cambridge, for additional support; and the Faculty of Science at the University of Southampton, and the Faculty of Law and Social Sciences at Queen Mary for subsequent help with travel.

Colleagues and graduate students at the University of Southampton and now Queen Mary, in London, have provided much appreciated support. At Southampton Alison Blunt and Jane Wills were always encouraging and stimulating as colleagues and friends, and I have learned a huge amount from teaching and talking with them. I am also especially grateful to Kristie Legg and Steven Pinch. Moving to East London has been inspiring for thinking and writing about cities, and it has been made all the more pleasurable by the presence of an exceptional group of geographers and friends with whom I have often discussed these materials, in particular Catherine Nash, Miles Ogborn and Bronwyn Parry, as well as (having made the same journey) Alison Blunt and Jane Wills. Students on the MA Cities and Cultures and my undergraduate course on urbanism at Queen Mary have contributed by engaging with many of the ideas, often in remarkably fresh and interesting ways. I am grateful to them as well as to the organisers and participants of many seminars and conferences who have provided opportunities to try out and discuss parts of the book. For invitations that sparked off new connections or thoughts, or for helpful comments on earlier drafts or for other kinds of assistance, I thank in particular Elza Adamowicz, Guy Baeten, Iain Borden, Felicity Callard, Denis Cosgrove, David Crouch, Anna Dezeuze, James Duncan, Derek Gregory, David Harvey, Gerry Kearns, Roger Lee, Loretta Lees, Doreen Massey, Chris Philo, Steve Pile, Alan Read, Jenny Robinson and Sophie Watson. Some of the materials have been aired in different forms elsewhere, and I am grateful to the editors, referees and publishers of those essays, in particular Routledge for permission to expand on a much shorter version of Chapter 4 that appeared as 'Modernist urbanism and its monsters', in Thomas Mical (ed.), *Surrealism and Architecture* (London: Routledge, 2005), pp. 179–90. Certain passages of other chapters also draw in more limited ways on essays previously published as: '"Old Paris is no more": geographies of spectacle and anti-spectacle', *Antipode* 32 (2000), 357–86; 'In defence of utopian urbanism: imagining cities after the "end of utopia"', *Geografiska Annaler* 84B (2002), 229–41; 'Inventing new games: unitary urbanism and the politics of space', in Loretta Lees (ed.), *The Emancipatory City?* (London: Sage,

2004), pp. 108–22; and 'Utopian transfiguration: the other spaces of New Babylon', in Iain Borden and Sandy McCreery (eds), 'New Babylonians', *Architectural Design* 71.3, 15–19.

I am very grateful to John Davey for his editorial advice, interest and patience. His thoughtful engagement with the ideas and his encouragement have been greatly appreciated, and I am sorry for keeping him waiting for so long. I further would like to thank two anonymous readers of an earlier version of this manuscript for helpful comments and support; Anna Oxbury for her skilful copy-editing; and James Dale, Ian Davidson and everyone else at Edinburgh University Press for their excellent work on the text. Particular thanks go to friends for sharing joy and a utopian spirit over the years. Much of what is at stake within these pages has come most alive for me through being walked and explored with them. Pam Cox has been a great friend since my interest in the themes of this book began, and she has helped me in numerous ways including through many discussions about its contents. For helping me to see things differently while wandering through cities and for many other insights, I thank Sam Gibson, Graham Jeffery, Jany Keat, Val Rose and Deirdre Williams. Through them and other friends, who have been wonderfully encouraging and inspiring, and who have contributed in so many important ways, writing this book has always felt much more than a scholastic exercise. I treasure their generosity, love and reminders of remarkable things too easily overlooked here and now. All my thanks go especially to my parents and family for their love and support; the book is dedicated to my parents.

London

Illustration credits

The author and publishers gratefully acknowledge the following individuals and organisations for permission to reproduce copyright materials. The author has made every effort to contact copyright holders, but the publisher would be grateful to hear about any errors or omissions so that they can be rectified in future editions of the book.

Aart Klein/Nederlands fotomuseum – 6.2
Archivio Gallizio, Turin – 5.1, 6.7, 6.8, 6.9
Constant – 6.1, 6.10, 7.1, 7.2, 7.3, 7.4, 7.5, 7.6, 7.8, 7.9, 7.10
FLC/ADAGP, Paris and DACS – 3.1, 3.2, 3.3, 3.4, 3.5, 3.6, 3.7, 3.8, 4.5, 4.6, 4.7, 4.8, 4.9
Brian Goodey – 1.3, 1.4
Hertfordshire Archives and Local Studies – 2.5, 2.6
The New York Times Co. – 4.2
Queen Mary Library, University of London – 1.2
Rebel Press, London – 8.1
Marcus Schubert, Toronto – 4.4, 4.11, 4.12

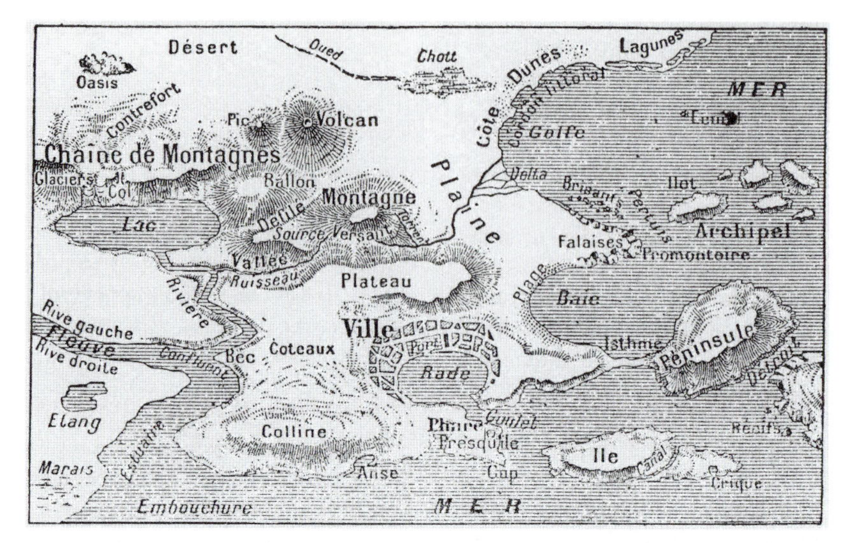

Figure 1.1 Map from Gilles Ivain (pseudonym for Ivan Chtcheglov), 'Formulary for a new urbanism', *Internationale situationniste* 1 (June 1958).

CHAPTER 1

Introduction

Utopia has been discredited, it is necessary to rehabilitate it. Utopia is never realised and yet it is indispensable to stimulate change.

Henri Lefebvre[1]

'Change life!' 'Change society!' These precepts mean nothing without the production of an appropriate space.

Henri Lefebvre[2]

An urban adventure

'Everyone will live in his own personal "cathedral", so to speak,' declared Ivan Chtcheglov in 1953. 'There will be rooms more conducive to dreams than any drug, and houses where one cannot help but love. Others will be irresistibly alluring to travelers.' In his manifesto entitled 'Formulary for a new urbanism', written under the pseudonym of Gilles Ivain, he set out a 'new vision of time and space'. Among other proposals he called for the invention of 'new, changeable decors', and for the construction of cities bringing together 'buildings charged with evocative power, symbolic edifices representing desires, forces, events past, present and to come.'[3] At the time Chtcheglov was nineteen years old and part of a small band of young revolutionaries who had announced their presence in Paris during the previous year by breaking away from the Letterist Movement to found a splinter group called the Letterist International.[4] Although his statement was not published until some years later, it was one of the first documents to be adopted by its members.

The manifesto's visionary qualities expressed the Letterist International's critical attitude towards capitalist urban life and its opposition to the current social and political constitution of cities. But the text spoke not just of what existed at the time and what the group contested, it also invoked what its members believed was *possible*. It gave vague but tantalising glimpses of riches that, in their opinion, *could be* obtained but were currently suppressed by dominant social relations and ideological apparatuses. According to Chtcheglov, an awareness of such possibilities in the mid-twentieth century had become obscured by what he called the 'banalization' of city space, and the hypnotic effect of modern commodities and labour-saving devices. He argued that the realm of production and conveniences – 'sewage system, elevator, bathroom, washing machine' – had overstepped an initial aim of alleviating material cares and had now 'become an obsessive image hanging over the present'.[5] 'Presented with the alternative of love or a garbage disposal unit, young people of all countries have chosen the garbage disposal unit,' he raged. The urban landscape itself, which once might have seemed a charged and poetic realm, had become a closed field, drained of mystery and passion.[6]

In an effort to break out of this state he proposed a radical programme for transforming urban spaces. At the heart of this was an effort to re-imagine the city and to think about how its geographies might be changed and reconstructed in line with different needs and desires. In part, he suggested, this required a transformation of urban consciousness. It was not enough to appeal to abstract notions of 'the imagination', though, since in his view '[o]ur imaginations, haunted by the old archetypes, have remained far behind the sophistication of the machines.'[7] He therefore argued that it was necessary to renew people's understandings and perceptions of their environments, to expand senses of social and political possibility by 'bringing to light forgotten desires and by creating entirely new ones', and by 'carrying out an *intensive propaganda* in favour of these desires'. This included working with and developing resources from the past as well as the realm of the unconscious, for as he put it: 'A rational extension of the old religious systems, of old tales, and above all of psychoanalysis, into architectural expression becomes more and more urgent as all the reasons for becoming impassioned disappear.'[8]

With its sweeping tone and visionary language, Chtcheglov's text shares characteristics often associated with utopian tracts and avant-garde manifestos. However, unlike many utopian thinkers, Chtcheglov did not propose ideal plans or formal spatial representations for the reconstruction of the environment. Rather, he stressed that his vision of time and space was a provisional statement, oriented towards experimentation, and that it needed to be developed through interactions with present urban conditions before it could be used as the basis for future constructions. While he acknowledged the evocative power of certain existing urban areas and their potential for providing a sense of original conceptions of space, he emphasised the importance of experimenting with architecture and spatial forms in the city as a way of challenging conceptions of the environment. 'Architecture is the simplest means of *articulating* time and space, of *modulating* reality, of engendering dreams', he wrote. With the rise of relativity in all spheres of life, and with the establishment of an increasingly mobile and machine-based society, architecture can be 'a means of experimenting with a thousand ways of modifying life, with a view to a mythic synthesis'.[9]

Chtcheglov's text raises issues at the heart of this study. In condemning the degradation of the city and urban life, and attempting to outline how they might be imagined differently and transformed, his writing is imbued with a utopian spirit. Through imaginative projection, he attempts to expand what is regarded as a possibility and explore what cities might be. A similar impatience with aspects of the present and a desire to bring about radical spatial and social change marks the pages that follow. This book is about the utopian search, as expressed by Chtcheglov, for an other space and society. The twentieth century was replete with manifestos demanding new cities and urban environments, and the fact that Chtcheglov calls for a new urbanism is hardly remarkable in itself. A distinctive aspect of his text, though, is the way in which he poses the question of change. He closely links changes in urban space with changes in urban life and implies that the transformation of one is bound up with the transformation of the other. He thus effectively calls for a new approach to the geographies of everyday life. Such a concern with everyday life and urban geography, and with thinking how they might be mutually transformed, threads through the study. So too do a number of other questions raised by Chtcheglov's text that include: In what senses might utopian visions such as this be regarded as revolutionary? Of what wider geographical imaginations and political projects are they a part? How do they differ from competing conceptions of urban space, including more dominant forms of utopian urbanism? And what might the relevance of such projects be now for those studying urban areas, and those seeking to engage critically with and to change urban space and society?

Underground visions

A prominent part of my study is concerned with the radical movements that formed the background to Chtcheglov's essay, especially the group that was founded several years after it was written, the Situationist International (SI). This group brought together activists, artists and writers from all over western Europe and beyond during the 1950s and 1960s in an attempt to contest the changing conditions of the post-war world and ultimately to bring about revolution. The situationists published 'Formulary for a new urbanism' under the pseudonym of Gilles Ivain in the opening issue of their journal *Internationale situationniste* in June 1958.[10] The essay was accompanied by an imaginary map of a landscape by the sea that showed a variety of physical features – lagoons, bays, plains, hills, volcanoes – in the manner of an illustration in a children's book that, in classical utopian fashion, spoke of no place in particular (figure 1.1). In giving Chtcheglov's work a significant place in their journal five years on, the situationists showed their recognition of its inspiring and visionary qualities. Several members, including Guy Debord and Michèle Bernstein, had been colleagues with Chtcheglov in the Letterist International (LI) during the early 1950s and had then adopted the text as an important document. Chtcheglov did not make it into the situationist group himself. By the time the letterists came together with two other organisations, the International Movement for an Imaginist Bauhaus and the London Psychogeographical Association, to form the SI in July 1957, he had long left their ranks. He was expelled three years previously along with several others of the so-called 'old guard' in the LI, in his case for supposed 'mythomania' and 'delirium' and lacking in 'revolutionary consciousness'.[11] The publication of Chtcheglov's essay in the journal was therefore important for highlighting the significance of his ideas for the situationists and their immediate predecessors as he set out a crucial set of issues that the groups would develop. The SI further acknowledged this later when they accorded him the status of 'member from afar', referring to his role in the origins of the movement as 'irreplaceable, both in its first theoretical endeavours and in its practical activity'.[12]

When Chtcheglov's text appeared it was accompanied by other writings on the situationists' fledgling revolutionary programme. There were discussions of art, cinema and youth rebellion. A strident tone was established with dismissals of the dissent of the American Beat Generation and the British Angry Young Men. An essay introduced an activity that the situationists believed should be central to new forms of art and politics, the 'construction of situations'. This involved breaking down artistic specialisms and consciously and collectively creating moments, settings and ambiences of everyday life. 'As opposed to all the regressive forms of play,' they argued, 'it is necessary to promote the experimental forms of a game of revolution.'[13] In later years the journal continued to range widely. Among the issues addressed were urbanism, modes of political organisation and representation, the problems of Stalinism and discourses of the left, and international political struggles including those in Algeria, China and Vietnam. The situationists critiqued the alienating and image-saturated conditions of the post-war era. They insisted on confronting them as a totality and to this end employed the concept of the 'spectacle'. They argued that the conditions of 'the society of the spectacle' necessitated new means of resistance and contestation, and they advocated autonomous struggles against hierarchical power in all its manifestations.[14] One of the SI's tasks, argued Debord in 1963, was to contribute to the 'theoretical and practical articulation of a new revolutionary contestation'. But he stressed that this action was part of a 'unitary approach' and that it had to be combined with the SI's simultaneous manifestation as an 'artistic avant-garde' and as 'an experimental investigation of the free construction of daily life'.[15]

The group's theoretical and political framework was indebted to Marx and Hegel, and had significant connections with strands of western Marxism. The SI also positioned itself in relation to earlier twentieth-century avant-garde groups. At the foundation of the group in 1957, Debord acknowledged the significance and constructive possibilities of earlier avant-gardes, especially dada and surrealism. He believed, however, that the initial radicalism of the avant-gardes around the 1920s had since been lost and he therefore called on the SI to surpass these preliminary efforts and to develop a truly revolutionary critique of everyday life and space.[16] Early on the situationists argued that they were 'of a nature different from preceding artistic avant-gardes. Within culture the SI can be likened to a research laboratory, for example, or to a party in which we are situationists but nothing that we do is situationist . . . We are partisans of a certain future of culture, of life.'[17] Throughout its existence the SI remained a small, tightly organised and internationally diverse group with the number of members at any one time being around ten to twenty. By the time it was officially disbanded in 1972, seventy individuals had participated from sixteen different countries.[18] It was this evolving band of people that produced the journal and a range of texts and works that included paintings, graphics, films, maps, models and plans as well as interventions in cultural and political arenas through events, political agitations and situations. Despite its deliberate avoidance of most 'official' media channels – the SI declared that it was 'interested not in finding a niche in the present artistic edifice, but in undermining it' and that it was 'in the catacombs of visible culture'[19] – it became increasingly well known in the late 1960s, especially after its involvement in the revolts in Paris in May 1968.

For the situationists and their avant-garde associates, a key task for radical political action lay in changing cities and social space. From Chtcheglov's 'Formulary for a new urbanism' on, they approached urban space through a commitment to revolutionary change. They understood that attempts to change urban spaces had to go beyond narrow conceptions of design, architecture and planning, being critical of these fields as specialist activities that conceptualised space as a terrain to be shaped by experts. For them urbanism was not reducible to planning but incorporated political questions about everyday life and urban culture. They addressed the production of space as part of the process of revolutionising socio-spatial relations, as a necessary component in any radical transformation of everyday life. In this sense they shared Lefebvre's conviction signaled in the second of the quotations at the head of this chapter – one that has also been at the heart of radical geography, and one that continues to need to be asserted – that to change society and life it is necessary also to transform space.

Utopian spaces past and present

This book explores aspects of the situationist project. My interest in the situationists, however, is part of a wider concern with utopian visions of cities, one that ranges beyond the group's activities to address other episodes of utopianism in twentieth-century western Europe. The concept of utopia, derived from Thomas More's famous text of that name in 1516, traditionally refers both to somewhere good and to nowhere. The double meaning is contained within the word itself, which plays on the Greek compounds *eu-topos* (a happy or fortunate place) and *ou-topos* (no place). The term is often associated with visions of other worlds, outlined through literary or other art forms. Utopia has also played a vital role in social and political thought and activism from across the spectrum, relativising present conditions by transcending their limitations in the name of a better world elsewhere or yet to come. Questions of space and place are important to the definition of utopia, as the roots of the term demonstrate. The connections between utopian thought and the city have been particularly significant, with fantastic urban visions running through social and artistic imaginaries and often being part of dreams of social transformation. Utopian thought is replete with names invoking glittering city images from the Heavenly City, New Jerusalem, the City of the Sun, on to the Garden City and Radiant City of more recent times. Cities have more generally often been viewed as sites of potential freedom, in tension with countervailing perspectives that cast them at the same time as centres of alienation, despair and dystopian nightmares.[20]

The visions of cities addressed in this book were all driven by a desire to change urban spaces radically. They confronted the conditions and problems of cities of the time and sought to produce spaces conducive to different ways of living. One characteristic of the visions discussed, however, is that for the most part their instigators insisted that they were not utopian, at least where that term is used in the common colloquial way to mean 'unrealisable' or 'impractical' and as belonging to a distant future or to the realm of fantasy. Rather, they asserted that the transformation they imagined *could* be realised if certain changes were set in motion. They proposed the possible nature of what they envisaged and indeed its necessity for producing a better world. Their concern with avoiding the description 'utopian' was in part due to the narrow standard definitions of that term, something that I discuss further below. But it also came from an effort to sidestep the pejorative connotations of utopian, where ideas and practices are sometime labeled that way by opponents seeking to impute that they do not require serious attention. As Karl Mannheim once pointed out, 'the representatives of a given order will label utopian all conceptions of existence which *from their point of view* can in principle never be realised.'[21] In nevertheless referring to these visions as utopian, I will be deliberately displacing the automatic equation of that term with impossible fantasy, arguing that such a definition of utopianism is inadequate. Not least this is because one of the most productive functions of utopianism lies in challenging prevailing definitions of the possible and the impossible. The utopian visions considered here expressed a desire for radical change that engaged directly with current spatial and social relations, and in so doing they sought to expand senses of what is possible.

The early parts of this study turn back to influential utopian visions of cities that emerged during the late nineteenth and early twentieth centuries, a particularly intense period of utopianism. The background to these urban visions lies in rapid urbanisation and socio-economic and cultural transformations associated with modernity in western Europe, and experiences of upheaval and continual change. A range of modernist and avant-garde groups emerged that took a visionary stance, exploring what Edward Timms refers to as 'an "unreal city" located between the extremes of hope and dread, between a distant Utopia and imminent Apocalypse'.[22] The significance accorded to the figures of utopia and apocalypse in modernist literature and art, and the oscillation between them in some cases in the same works, was symptomatic of the contradictory nature of many people's experiences of modernity. On the one hand, the unleashing of industrial and technological forces and the transformation of social and political landscapes seemed to sweep away traditional notions of order and stability, and threatened to plunge human life into chaos and confusion. This fed into images of collapse and demonic destruction. But on the other hand, it expanded human possibilities and appeared to reveal people's vast and rich creative capacities. With the establishment of new systems of production and technology, the old world was shaken and a new one seemed within reach.[23]

From the ferment of utopian imaginings of those years, I focus initially on two contrasting prominent approaches. The first is associated with the garden city movement and the work of Ebenezer Howard around the turn of the century. The second is connected with elements of the so-called modern movement and especially the urban schemes of Le Corbusier in the 1920s and 1930s. In their different ways the protagonists proposed ideal cities as a means of confronting 'disordered' spaces and of establishing a new order. They viewed urbanism as a means of changing – or saving – societies, and they had a considerable influence on urban thought and planning in Europe and North America, helping to shape urban imaginations and cities themselves in many parts of the world, especially after the Second World War. These approaches have now attained canonical status in the narratives of what Leonie Sandercock terms 'mainstream planning history'.[24] As such they have exerted a powerful hold on common understandings of modern urbanism, even if the utopianism of their original visions has often been sidelined. In my account it is the relative familiarity of these narratives that I want to work with and against. To begin with, reconsidering their original arguments, positions and proposals is important for regaining a sense of the utopian positions they took in confronting modern urbanism, as they developed polemical and contentious stances on cities against many orthodoxies of the time as well as against existing conditions. It is worth remembering these oppositional qualities even if the plans later fed into construction projects that were driven by quite different aims.

Despite the differences between these strands of utopianism, however, what particularly concerns me is their common focus on spatial and social ordering, and the political implications of their approaches to the 'problem' of order. This theme remains undertheorised in mainstream planning histories, which have often been reluctant to address such political issues, although it has increasingly been brought to light by developing critical planning perspectives informed by Marxism, feminism and postcolonialism. Addressing the theme is an important part of dismantling myths of value-neutrality in planning and making visible what Sandercock calls its '*noir*' side, in this case opening up perspectives on other sides to the utopian spaces that involve forms of regulation and control.[25] Interrogating utopian visions in this way is not to deny their emancipatory intent, nor the laudability of the desire to change cities for the better. It nevertheless draws out the politics of their visions that were often masked by claims of being neutral. My aim is further to unsettle understandings of the projects by connecting them with other contemporaneous currents of utopianism, especially from within the avant-gardes. Modernism always contained contested ideals about what the geographies of cities might be, with these ideals being sites of struggle. In addressing this theme, my focus moves from the surrealists in the 1920s and 1930s, who engaged in direct exchanges with modernists such as Le Corbusier, to the activities of the situationists and associated groups in the 1950s and 1960s, who confronted the legacies of such thinking and charted their own utopian routes. When the letterists and situationists started to develop their utopian approach, they attacked in particular visions of the modern movement that were then having considerable influence on architecture and planning, and they connected critiques of functionalism and rationalist urbanism to wider concerns with transforming urban geographies.

Much has been written about critical reactions towards modernist and utopian urbanism in Europe and North America. Since the 1970s it has frequently gone under the sign of the 'postmodern'. What have less often been addressed are other utopian currents from within modernism and the avant-gardes that were similarly opposed to dominant notions of modernist planning but that were driven by different visions of what cities and urban life might be. Until relatively recently these have been marginalised in discussions of histories of urbanism and restricted notions of the modernist city have often been constructed, in part to lend critical force to claims about the postmodern. In exploring different currents within modernist and avant-garde movements, my account connects with increasing interest in challenging such erasures and researching the plurality and heterogeneity of modernisms, which extends across disciplines and which has important effects on theorising the field of 'the modern' generally. This includes work on the historical geography of modernity where that has drawn out the geographical imaginations of modernist movements in recognition of the way that, in the words of Derek Gregory, the 'characteristically modernist gesture was to *disrupt* narrative sequence, to *explode* temporal structure, and to accentuate *simultaneity*'. For in many of those movements there was a belief that the 'vertigo of the modern', to use the phrase Gregory cites from the surrealist Louis Aragon, 'could be figured through an exploration of its spatiality'.[26] It has also involved research more specifically in architectural culture that, after years of neglect, has been bringing into focus different inter-war and post-war tendencies within and in critical relation to the modern movement, among them various 'anxious modernisms'.[27] As part of this there have been significant historical recoveries of urban visions from the perspectives of women, ethnic minorities and other marginalised groups, through the development of 'insurgent planning histories' against 'official' stories of planning, and putting the lie to claims, for instance, that modern urban planning has only 'founding fathers' and almost no comparable 'founding mothers'.[28]

It should be noted that my choice of subjects in this book does nothing in itself to displace the male-dominated and Eurocentric focus of standard narratives of modernist and avant-garde urbanism. But I want to suggest that engaging with those modernist and avant-garde approaches is still an important means of questioning those narratives as well as their influences and challenges, and of opening up the contested nature of modernist urbanism to trace out the potentialities of past interventions. In addressing different historical tendencies, it is helpful to recall Peter Bürger's famous if not uncontroversial argument distinguishing between modernist and avant-garde movements. This is not least to counter the vague ways in which the term avant-garde is often bandied around. Bürger argues that although both modernists and the avant-gardes posed critiques of modern bourgeois society, their theoretical positions and roles were distinct. Whereas modernism challenged styles, techniques and modes of representation, the avant-gardes launched attacks on aestheticism and the institutions of art themselves, and were characterised by attempts to break down the boundaries between art and everyday life. He describes the emergence of the early twentieth-century avant-gardes, especially dada and surrealism, as marking a period in which art entered a stage of self-criticism, with attempts to use art to intervene in everyday life, to change life through artistic practices.[29]

Bürger, however, notably ignores post-war avant-garde activities associated with, among others, the letterists and situationists. His assessment of the repetitive nature and inevitable failure of post-war 'neo-avant-gardes', condemned to remain in the shadow of the original historical movements, is typical of what was for a long time a widespread sidelining of these groups. An unfortunate effect has been the tendency to overlook the distinctive ways in which they addressed the changing conditions and possibilities of their times and spaces, including their 'renewed *putting in question* of the avant-garde', which involved a critical encounter with the legacies of earlier movements and attempts to rework the concept of avant-garde itself.[30] Recent years have nevertheless seen a belated flourishing of interest in the situationists among other post-war movements. After the SI's demise in 1972, the group remained the subject of considerable attention within certain radical political, artistic and 'underground' circles, but it was rarely the subject of sustained historical or academic discussion, with Sadie Plant noting in 1990 the 'spectacular neglect' that had surrounded it.[31] Studies since then, however, have been writing the SI into histories of the twentieth century in a variety of ways. With the growth of interest, Tom McDonough now refers to the 'spectacular' reception of the SI and calls for it to be superseded by critical and historical interpretation.[32] Others worry on the contrary about the depoliticisation of the group's ideas within much of the recent scholarly literature, with Erik Swyngedouw referring to 'the strange respectability of the situationist city in the society of the spectacle'.[33] The recent interest in the group is all the more striking given how its revolutionary utopianism contrasts so obviously with the prevailing social and political climate where, as Lefebvre notes in the first epigraph at the head of this introduction, utopia seems to have been 'discredited'. But I want to suggest that, in this context, exploring situationist demands alongside the visions of earlier groups is not only of historical concern in developing understandings of utopian urbanism; it is also significant politically for confronting claims about the 'end' of utopia and tracing out other paths. For all the increasing 'respectability' of situationist ideas, the critical charge of situationist positions here remains prominent; current conditions may even be allowing aspects of them to attain new force.

In the wake of utopia?

Lefebvre's remark quoted above about the discrediting of utopia came in a conversation towards the end of his life, as he looked back over the adventures of a century that his own life had almost spanned. His sense that the events of the century had led to a waning or even ending of utopia is commonplace. Notwithstanding recent historical interest in utopias, especially in museum and academic arenas, there is a sense that any discussion of utopianism today is occurring, as it were, 'after utopia'. Many critics have viewed this favourably: they have pointed to the long trails of catastophes and horrors to which utopian plans have led, and have argued that utopianism has been too often driven by authoritarian ideals, and too closely associated with totalitarianism, and that its demise should therefore be welcomed. But as well as those taking a stance against utopianism who are part of a long tradition of hostility to utopian thought, there are also those – often more sympathetic to the field – who have been arguing that the concept of utopia has become fundamentally problematic. According to a number of authors we have been living in the 'twilight of utopia';[34] it is felt that 'utopia has clearly weakened – whether fatally we cannot say';[35] it is claimed: 'The "End of Utopia" is a concept that seems to suit our contemporary experience of society and politics on the world scale.'[36] The close of the twentieth century, argues Susan Buck-Morss, witnessed the passing of the very idea of mass utopia. This was the collective dream that drove the modernisation process in both its capitalist and socialist forms, and that 'dared to imagine a social world in alliance with personal happiness' as it 'promised to adults that its realization would be in harmony with the overcoming of scarcity for all'. That dream is ending, she writes, and with it the dreamworlds that chacterised both 'east' and 'west' as they opposed each other during the Cold War.[37]

A rhetoric of being 'in the wake of utopia' also runs through discussions specifically about cities. There is a widespread feeling that utopian urban projects belong to a previous age, as remnants of hopeful but naive thought, as depleted husks unable to respond to current demands. Related to this is reluctance among many critics addressing urbanism to pose questions about alternative futures, to consider how urban processes and forms might be radically different. 'Unfortunately the sclerosis apparent in our cities also reigns in our heads,' writes David Harvey. 'No one believes any more that we can build that city on a hill, that gleaming edifice that has fascinated every Utopian thinker since Plato and St Augustine. Utopian visions have too often turned sour for that sort of thinking to go far.'[38] He discusses this in relation to changes in processes of urbanisation and forces of capital accumulation, uneven spatio-temporal development and patterns of migration, and presents a number of scenes from current urban worlds that are being forged out of such processes. They range from capitalist cities in the west marked by job losses, stark inequalities, concentrations of impoverishment and increasingly stressed physical and social fabrics, to the enormous and distinct problems and challenges associated with rapid urbanisation in the global south. The dynamic nature and sheer scale of such issues threaten to elude current conceptual apparatuses as does the apparent intractability of the social problems. 'For many,' notes Harvey, 'to talk of the city of the twenty-first century is to conjure up a dystopian nightmare in which all that is judged worst in the fatally flawed character of humanity collects together in some hell-hole of despair.'[39]

Apocalyptic cityscapes thus cast terrifying shadows on urban narratives and haunt much contemporary discourse. 'If the city was once spoken of as the harbinger of enlightenment, the "New Jerusalem",' writes one commentator, 'it is now the incubus of discontent and the living proof of societies' failures to care adequately and equitably for all their members, and to construct efficient and ecologically sound environments.'[40] Meanwhile, remaining strands of utopian urbanism often appear in the form of neoliberal visions of the market, as an ideal realm of free exchange and consumer satisfaction, running smoothly with flows of money and commercialised desire; or as spaces of 'utopic degeneration', to use a term that Harvey borrows from Louis Marin. By that phrase Harvey means spaces such as commercial renewal projects, shopping malls and other urban spectacles that are disconnected from wider transformative projects, turned in on themselves, no longer intent on radiating outwards in that transformative move that was central to utopian conceptions of the modernist urban structure. They are unable to offer 'alternatives' save those provided by 'the conjoining of technological fantasies, commodity culture, and endless capital accumulation.'[41] Fundamental concerns arise in this context about the difficulty of thinking cities against the grain of dominant capitalist imaginaries.

At issue is what Kevin Robins identifies as 'a profound and long-term crisis of the city and of urbanity'. In recent years, he argues, 'there has been a kind of imaginative collapse: what was once driven by vision and energy is now drained of affect. The utopian has collapsed into the *banal*. We do not plan the ideal city, but come to terms with the "good enough" city.' He connects this in particular to what he calls 'the exhaustion and crisis of the modernist vision and programme'.[42] As Robins recognises, caution is necessary when discussing claims about 'the end of utopia', 'the death of the urban vision', and the like. Such declarations have a familiar ring, not least from the way there has been proliferation of claims about the end of this or that aspect of the cultural and political landscape in recent times. It is therefore important to consider carefully what is said to be coming to an end and what forms, trajectories and interests are involved. It is also worth remembering that, as Andreas Huyssen points out, obituaries for utopian thought have frequently been written and rewritten, and he suggests that during the twentieth century 'the discourse of the end of utopia is as endemic to the utopian imagination as its visions of other worlds, other times, or other states of mind.'[43] Nevertheless, the situation evoked by Robins and others clearly contrasts with the earlier decades of the twentieth century when there was a profusion of utopian programmes, projects and manifestos devoted to imagining urban spaces differently and transforming cities. As the dust settles from the collapse of many of those projects, it would seem that it is not only their assumptions that are often being swept away, but the question of utopia as such. In such a climate, writes Fredric Jameson, 'the question of Utopia would seem to be a crucial test of what is left of our capacity to imagine change at all.'[44]

Although the rejection of many utopian approaches to urban questions is understandable and even a positive development, being based on an assessment of past failures and a principled opposition to their authoritarianism, it need not entail a retreat from utopianism in its entirety. Indeed, such a retreat can have disturbing political and cultural consequences, associated with a narrowing of critical thought and diminishing sense of possibility. It also fails to recognise other voices that stem from different perspectives and positions, and that continue to develop forms of utopianism that dream of transforming the present. Among the most significant over the last thirty years or so in Europe and North America have been those associated with social movements, especially with feminism. In refusing to give up on utopianism I agree with Lefebvre when he argues that, although utopia might seem discredited, it should not be abandoned and even that it is 'indispensable to stimulate change'. The following chapters are similarly underpinned by a commitment to retaining the concept of utopia and to countering the motto that has become depressingly well ingrained into contemporary consciousness after being a talisman of the Thatcher government, and gaining force in many discourses of globalisation, that 'there is no alternative' to the present social and spatial order. In returning to specific utopian projects from earlier periods of the twentieth century, I therefore seek to open up further discussion about utopianism and urban space, and to re-direct attention to issues of imagination and radical urban change. Rather than echo a retreat from utopianism, I examine different approaches and practices – their visionary qualities, their critiques of geography, their engagements with urban space – as well as their struggles over what the modern city might be. And in later chapters in particular, I explore other currents of utopianism opposed to those associated with modernist urbanism in the belief that, if attended to and read in certain ways, they might help to challenge some of the closures frequently surrounding understandings of urbanism, as well as to encourage a dissident and utopian spirit in the present. 'Utopia?', Lefebvre once remarked, as if anticipating the incredulity of his readers when faced with his favourable use of the term. 'Yes indeed,' he continued; '*we are all utopians*, so soon as we wish for something different and stop playing the part of the faithful performer or watchdog.'[45]

Utopia, desire and the city

Before turning to the utopian visions of cities themselves, it is necessary to discuss briefly some broad issues about defining utopianism. Part of the problem with the concept of utopia lies in its traditional definitions, which have often fixed it around notions of an ideal state or blueprint for a perfect future. Against this it is imperative to reconceptualise utopia and utopianism in more open ways. When Thomas More coined the term in his *Utopia* of 1516, he used it to designate an imaginary society with its own political constitution. The contrast between the conditions of this society and those of sixteenth-century Europe was highlighted by the organisation of the text, which started with a critical dialogue addressing social problems in England in the first part, followed by a description of Utopia as 'the best state of a commonwealth' in the second (figure 1.2).[46] Perhaps not surprisingly, given that it was the original source for the term 'utopia', More's text still exerts considerable influence on how the word is commonly understood and used. In particular, utopia is frequently seen as an imaginative projection of a new place or state. Like More's island, this place is closed off from the present, lying in another space or time as the embodiment of a social and political ideal. The ambiguity of the word is thus retained as it refers to a good place that is nowhere in the present known world.

Figure 1.2 The island of Utopia by the Dutch painter Ambrosius Holbein, from Thomas More's *Utopia, Book II* (1563 edition). Courtesy of Queen Mary Library, University of London.

A first common approach to defining utopia is to focus on content.[47] The emphasis is on what constitutes the 'good society', in the sense of the projected ideal social-spatial arrangement. As a general definition this is beset with difficulties, though, due to the obvious diversity of opinions about what is a desirable state and to the variation in modes of construction. Even More's text complicates such an approach. While the book contains a formal presentation with programmatic connotations, as its subtitle 'A truly golden handbook' suggests, the long-standing debates surrounding the work testify to its enigmatic and multi-layered character. This includes speculative and satirical qualities, an engagement with political debates of the time, and a frequent undercutting of readers' assumptions through wordplay and puns, including one on the name of the fictional traveller who tells of the island of Utopia and its people, Raphael Hythloday, which in Greek implies 'expert in nonsense'. A second common way of defining utopia is in terms of form. Here attention most often centres on utopia as a literary genre, which More's book is seen inaugurating. The distinguishing feature of this genre is its exploration of the good society, often through a fictional journey to another place or time where the text is composed like a tour. The visitor is thus guided around the spaces of the new society before returning home to recount what she or he has learned. The traveller's experiences may also be worked through a narrative to reveal the society's organisation, laws, and social and spatial relations. Again, however, defining utopia exclusively as a literary form is too restrictive, for the concept also been important for social thought and for artistic and political practice, and an approach that is unable to address that fact is inadequate.[48]

A third approach to utopia is in terms of its function. The focus here is on what utopia is for and how it works for particular purposes. Debates typically pivot around whether it enables or discourages social change and how it does so. Utopias might be seen as escapist or compensatory, distracting attention from the repressive state of existing social conditions. Alternatively they might be regarded as ideals that direct change in a particular direction. Utopias can also function as social and political criticism, raising questions about or satirising the present. The very break with the present that they enact can help to disrupt dominant assumptions about the organisation of society, and to point to other possibilities or desires. They can thus be subversive, forcing recognition that particular social arrangements are not natural or eternal but that they could be different, and they can play an important role in opening up new ways of thinking about possible futures, stimulating demands for action and informing political practice. This stress on function has been particularly prominent within Marxism where there has been criticism of the reactionary role of utopias, including from Marx and Engels themselves, but also a more positive engagement with the term among writers such as Lefebvre, Herbert Marcuse, Ernst Bloch and more recently Fredric Jameson. Bloch is among those who have done most to recover the concept of utopia as a central category for modern Marxism in his wide-ranging studies and reconceptualisation of utopianism as an 'anticipatory consciousness' and a 'principle of hope', situated at the level of everyday life.[49]

In what follows I lean towards this last approach. As Ruth Levitas argues, though, none of content, form or function can in themselves provide an adequate general means for defining utopia. Each one points to important elements but is too limited on its own and is unable to account for the diversity of utopian thought and its changing historical and geographical manifestations. It is therefore necessary to adopt a broader analytic definition of utopia that draws on theorists such as Bloch to recognise that *desire* is a central issue, where utopia is understood as an expression of a desire for a better way of being and living.[50] It is a desire that moves beyond the limitations of aspects of the present, seeking spaces and worlds that are qualitatively different from what exists. This can take many different forms, and have different content and functions. These differences are important for specifying particular modes of utopia and utopianism. But rather than searching for a single definition based on one of these categories, a more inclusive approach encompasses them and enables a consideration of how they change and interconnect, and also how they relate to material conditions at particular times and places. My own concern here is particularly with the connections between the desire of utopia and cities, where it is striking how often that desire is articulated through the figure of the city itself. Some critics have even suggested that 'Utopia and the image of the city are inseparable',[51] and have made a distinction between Arcadia and utopia, arguing that utopia is 'primarily a vision of the orderly city and of a city-dominated society'.[52]

The association between utopia and the city has been traced by Lewis Mumford back to the Ancient Greeks, who thought of the ideal state and political community as a city. Although Plato did not discuss its physical environment in detail in his *Republic*, he projected his ideal commonwealth in the spatial form of a rationally ordered and hierarchically organised city-state, which looked more towards the example of Sparta than that of Athens. The relationship between the polity and the physical form of the city was given further substance by Aristotle. Mumford proposes that these influential visions were not simply products of Hellenic speculation but that they reflected earlier ties between utopia and the city, which had been realised in the archetypal ancient city in Egypt and Mesopotamia. In those societies, according to Mumford, the city actually *was* utopia; it was the very first utopia, being created by a king acting in name of a god, and being established as a sacred place, initially through the construction of a temple and surrounding walls, with an intrinsic relation to the cosmic order. It was this coming together of the royal, the religious and the cosmic that differentiated the city from other kinds of settlement and made it what it was: 'something "out of this world", the home of a god'. As he puts it, 'the city itself was transmogrified into an ideal form – a glimpse of eternal order, a visible heaven on earth, a seat of life abundant – in other words, utopia.'[53] Mumford thus draws attention to an event from before Plato's *Republic*, regarded as the Greek text that has most influenced discussion of ideal cities in the west. He suggests that this ancient image has continued to haunt utopian thinkers from More to Etienne Cabet and Edward Bellamy.

Whatever is made of Mumford's claim, it highlights a theme that will be taken up in my consideration of utopian spaces of the early twentieth century: the concern with authority and processes of ordering. This is indeed a theme that has been central to many traditional utopias that have been figured around the power of a king or authority figure, and have sought to project an ideal order, depicting that power and order as being embodied in, and constituted through, a particular *spatial* order. In More's book, for example, Utopia was established after being invaded by King Utopus whose first act was to create the island as a defined, self-contained unit, by organising the digging of a channel by the indigenous population to separate it from the mainland. The space was then carved up and ordered to reflect the rationalism that was meant to underpin the polity, with a series of 'spacious and magnificent' cities that were rigorously planned and geometric. 'If you know one of their cities,' notes the traveller Hythloday, 'you know them all, for they're exactly alike, except where geography itself makes a difference.'[54] Despite More's lack of descriptive detail, it is apparent that Utopia has a rigid spatial form. Each city has a population of six thousand families and is integrated with the countryside, being referred to as a *civitas* or city-state. There are fifty-four in all, which are at least twenty-four miles apart. A hierarchical arrangement is established by the capital Amaurot – the 'dark' or 'shadowy' city – that is almost square. It is subdivided like the others into four equal districts, with streets that are twenty feet apart, and quarters with regular houses and gardens placed in a manner that reproduces the form of the city (figures 1.3, 1.4).

The importance More attaches to ordering and to the maintenance of a harmonious space finds parallels in much utopian thought about cities in the European tradition. An emphasis on architectural form and spatial arrangement as components of the good society characterised the ideal cities of Renaissance Italy. In cases such as Filarete's imaginary city of Sforzinda (1460) and Tommaso Campanella's City of the Sun (1602),

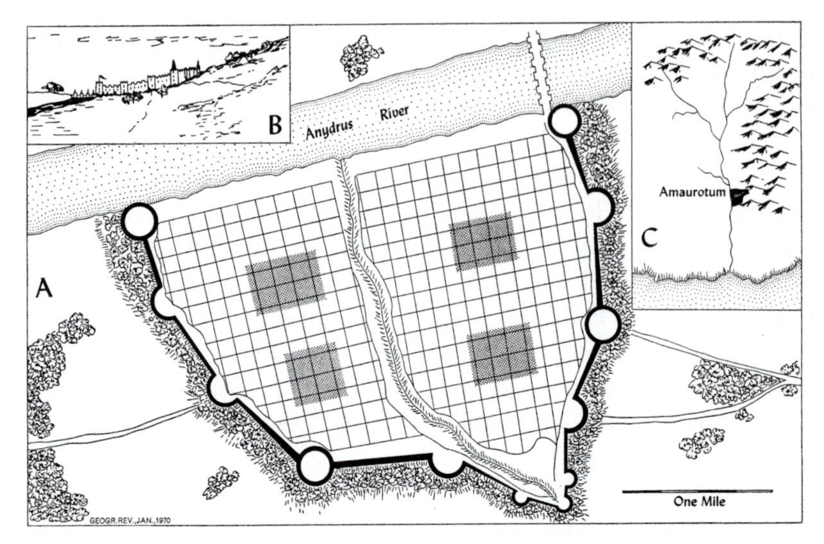

Figure 1.3 The city of Amaurot, in Thomas More's Utopia. As drawn by Brian Goodey, based largely on More's descriptions. The drawings show (A) the site plan, (B) the possible elevation, and (C) the situation of the city in relation to the drainage system. Market areas in the city are shaded. From Goodey, 'Mapping "Utopia": a comment on the geography of Thomas More', *Geographical Review* 60 (1970). Reproduced courtesy of the author.

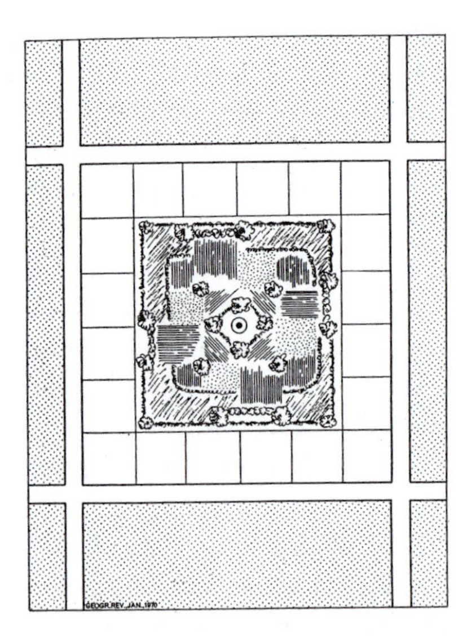

Figure 1.4 A plan of a city block in Amaurotum. Each block in the city is identical and contains a large garden. As drawn by Brian Goodey based on More's descriptions; from Goodey, 'Mapping "Utopia": a comment on the geography of Thomas More', *Geographical Review* 60 (1970). Reproduced courtesy of the author.

geometric forms featured strongly in their attempts to establish the true principles of order as a means of bringing about harmony and beauty in society, and to establish cities as self-sufficient entities that embodied an ideal order, defined against a surrounding untamed nature. Many utopian thinkers in the Enlightenment again focused on cities and architecture, often through grand plans that embodied rationalist and reformist principles, and in critical dialogue with new political and industrial concerns. Claude-Nicholas Ledoux, for example, developed a series of plans for an industrial city of Chaux (1804) that were informed by his belief that the industrial process had a central role to play in aesthetic terms and as the main principle of order for the good society. His city 'could be said to be a monument erected to the *Utopia of the Enlightenment*', suggests one commentator. In his view it was '[m]ore than a utopian city', and it might be understood as 'Utopia itself imagined in stone, or even a museum in which the utopian dreams of the epoch are realised in an architectural representation and organised in a spatial whole'.[55]

Traditional urban utopias are therefore not only typically characterised by an emphasis on architectural form, geometric designs and rigid spatial order; they also have a related concern with control, regulation and modes of surveillance. These latter elements are seen as crucial in maintaining harmony and the ideal state. In More's Utopia, inhabitants have 'to live in full view of all' to ensure hard work and respectability. As Hythloday puts it in the book: 'there is no chance to loaf or kill time, no pretext for evading work; there are no wine-bars, or ale-houses, or brothels; no chances for corruption; no hiding places; no spots for secret meetings.' Inhabitants also have to obtain permission before wandering beyond the city's walls, with the warning that: 'Anyone who takes upon himself to leave his district without permission, and is caught without the prince's letter, is treated with contempt, brought back as a runaway, and severely punished.' The gender-specific language in the last quotation seems deliberate, since he adds: 'Anyone who wants to stroll about and explore the extent of his own district is not prevented, provided he first obtains his father's permission and his wife's consent.'[56] Ledoux's royal saltworks at Arc-et-Senans (1773–9) also conveyed a powerful sense of order and surveillance. While the 'vigilant eye' that oversaw the factory grounds in the form of the director's house – known as the *temple du surveillance* – was largely a symbolic effect, since trees sheltered workers from the director's sight, an interest in a disciplinary apparatus nonetheless accompanied his concern with workers' welfare and reform. Surveillance took on a more implicit form through a 'hierarchy of relays', as workers watched over each other in the manner of a self-policing, and as the ideal city was constructed 'according to the laws of a geometric system that united the powers of sight with those of spatial order'.[57]

These characteristics raise questions to be considered in relation to utopian thinking in more recent times, namely to what extent are attempts to establish order and socio-spatial regulation essential components of utopian urbanism? Is the drive to create a 'pure', enclosed and controlled realm a necessary characteristic of the utopian space? Must utopian attempts to create a new urban space repress complexity, diversity and ambiguity? Or are other understandings of utopianism possible, other routes that challenge dominant conceptions and suggest different ways of engaging with urban spaces? The questions further connect to another major theme that is central to my study, and that is the respective emphasis on space and society in utopian urban projects. In More's Utopia, the regulation of space was bound up with the maintenance of a harmonious social and moral order and vice versa. A striking feature of much modern utopian thought, however, has been a tendency to separate space and society, to disaggregate them, and to privilege one or the other. Space is marked off as a distinct realm as if it were the preserve of specialists such as architects and planners, while social dreams are pursued with a relative neglect of geographical constitution. 'Most utopian proposals lose track of either space or society,' argues the urbanist Kevin Lynch. 'There are brilliant spatial fantasies which accept society as it is, and social utopias which sketch a few disconnected spatial features, in order to add colour and semblance of reality.'[58]

There has therefore apparently been a frequent division between utopian thinkers primarily interested in questions of social and physical space, who have designed ideal cities, architectural fantasies and so on, and those mainly concerned with imagining social change. A number of commentators have sought to highlight this difference by making a formal distinction between what they call the 'ideal city' and 'Utopia' proper. The former, supposedly having more in common with the plans for geometric layouts drawn up during the Renaissance, 'was often conspicuously indifferent to the social system to which it gave shelter', according to Reyner Banham, whereas the latter 'is often obsessional about the proposed social system, but not too concerned about architectural form'.[59] The distinction relates to one made more recently by David Harvey between what he calls 'utopias of spatial form', which give a central role to those spatial concerns, and 'utopias of social process', which are projected outside the constraints of spatiality, and which effectively ignore qualities of space and place. By the former category, however, Harvey does not mean utopias that are simply 'indifferent to the social system'. Rather, he refers to those that project an ideal spatial order as means of securing social processes and history, so that 'the dialectics of social change – real history – are excluded, while social stability is assured by a fixed spatial form.'[60] More's text is a classic example of this, as are the schemes of many utopian thinkers such as Campanella and Ledoux onwards to figures of the twentieth century. These discussions and distinctions therefore raise another set of important questions about different utopian projects that will be taken up in what follows. Do utopian projects emphasise changing spatial forms? Do they centre on social relations? How do they envisage the connections between the two? Earlier I mentioned arguments by many geographers in recent years along with Lefebvre and the situationists, that the transformation of everyday life requires the transformation of everyday space and vice versa. How these issues are addressed is of crucial political as well as historical significance.

Outline of the chapters

My study begins with forms of utopian thought in western Europe that addressed spatial and social issues through their projections of new cities in the late nineteenth and early twentieth centuries. Chapter 2 is concerned with what I call 'restorative utopias', considered primarily through the ideas of Ebenezer Howard and the garden city. Chapter 3 focuses on 'modernist calls to order', mainly through the urban visions of Le Corbusier. These chapters explore how utopian visions were developed to confront cities and reorder their spaces and social life. I particularly focus on this ordering process and argue that, rather than viewing the utopian spaces simply as positive projections founded upon ideal principles, as they are often presented, they should be examined in relation to their other sides, that is in terms of what they sought to control and repress. My account in addition moves away from the common tendency to view the spaces as the disembodied products of rationalist enterprises, instead centring on how they worked through regulatory practices that were bound up with political conceptions of the world, and how they were repositories of desires, dreams and fears. These themes are developed further in Chapter 4 through a focus on Le Corbusier's encounters with New York in

1935, where I seek to destablise the pure spaces of his utopian plans by setting them back into contact with contemporaneous oppositional tendencies within the avant-garde. With reference to surrealism, in particular, I explore how that movement contained a counter-current of dreaming and utopian urban thought.

The remainder of the book moves from the surrealists to concentrate on other dissident utopian spaces, specifically those of the situationists and their avant-garde associates. Chapter 5 addresses the critique of urbanism developed by the letterists and situationists from the 1950s, including their attacks on earlier utopian visions as well as their attempts to explore alternative possibilities within existing urban spaces. Underlying their practices was a vision of urban space as a potential realm of freedom, play and the creative unfolding of life. Their association with Lefebvre was important here, and their dialogue with him threads through much of this discussion. Chapter 6 explores the situationists' utopian visions for the transformation of cities and urban life further through the concept of 'unitary urbanism'. My focus is on the early manifestations of what they called this 'great game', especially in debates with Lefebvre and in the practices of artists that played an important role at the beginning of the situationist movement, in particular the Dutch artist Constant. Chapter 7 turns to the fullest attempt associated with the situationist movement to explore imaginatively the utopian spaces of unitary urbanism, Constant's New Babylon. This provocative urban vision was developed by Constant from the late 1950s to the early 1970s through an array of art works, constructions and writings, both within and subsequently beyond the SI after his resignation from the group. In tracking the development of New Babylon in relation to the situationists and beyond, I draw out tensions and difficulties within their approaches, some of which are at the heart of those found in utopian thought more widely. In Chapter 8, in conclusion, I reflect on the paths taken and their implications for rethinking histories of modernist urbanism as well as for the prospects for a utopianism today committed to changing urban spaces and society.

When I embarked on the study, I sometimes thought of it as part of a 'counter-history' of utopian visions of the modern city. Such a history, I imagined, differed from mainstream histories of urban utopias by telling of projects that consciously cut against such schemes, and that rejected hegemonic understandings of space and time. For a number of reasons I am now more wary of claims about an 'alternative' or 'counter-hegemonic' tradition. Part of my interest in returning to utopian visions connected with the modern movement is to explore complexities of modernist utopian schemes as well as to question their supposed stability in terms of how they were caught up in what they sought to oppose. Common connections between modernist and avant-garde groups that were otherwise in conflict with one another are also apparent, something to which I will return in the last chapter. But if caution is therefore required, I still work with the concept of counter formulations. This is in part because the avant-garde groups themselves projected their ideas in opposition to other approaches, but also because the term underlines the contested character of utopian and modernist thought about the city, and the way that these fields contained clashing currents.

In turning to the situationists' ideas and activities in later chapters, I do not hold them up as providing a ready-made 'alternative' utopianism, which is somehow just waiting for a call to arms, or a model that needs only to be dusted off, wheeled out and put into action to guide those struggling against dominant representations of space and powerful interests. Nor do I suggest that they can be projected onto the problems of the present without due regard to the historical rootedness and range of their activities. Such projections collapse differences in social and political contexts and can only be bought at cost to understandings of what is distinctive about the situationists' engagements with their own circumstances, something that was one of the problematic features of some earlier Anglophone literature on the group.[61] To set the situationist project up as an object of reverence is to be swayed by what one former member of the group has criticised as 'those absurd hagiographical impulses which mystify the [SI]'.[62] It is to turn the group into what another critic has called an 'Occult International', complete with a 'transcendental doctrine of revolution that sprung fully formed from the heads of a few privileged individual "geniuses"' rather than occupying a position that was necessarily 'a product of the conditions of its time'.[63] But if it is important to avoid such mystification and situate the group's positions in their contexts, I will also argue that elements of the situationist project remain relevant and that working with them now can have significant effects of a theoretical and political kind. Their vibrant energy and insights still reach across the decades to encourage dissident attitudes and put into play radical demands on the present. It is for this reason that I want to avoid hagiography while, at the same time, resisting a too smooth adaptation of 'situationism' as a packaged entity into the academic realm.[64]

There is certainly something strange about exploring the politicised ideas and practices of the situationists within intellectual debate. The paradox involved in describing the group's revolutionary attempts to change society in a manner that removes them from that context is often noted. Critics frequently portray this as a form of 'recuperation', a term used by the situationists themselves to refer to the ways in which radical perspectives become accommodated and turned around to support the reproduction of dominant relations of power. In presenting the SI, I do have a degree of unease. This is less to do with the perception of automatic recuperation as such – after all, the situationists are now increasingly part of more mainstream debate, meaning that their ideas and practices are already in wider play – and more to do with the manner of this reception, and the risk of eliding the distinctiveness of the situationists' positions and ideas. At its worst it can lead to a reduction of the group's project to an anaemic form of theorisation, so that it becomes nothing more than part of what Derek Gregory has referred to critically as 'a theoretical work-*out* – a super-circuit around the most advanced theoretical exercise machines'.[65] But there is nothing inevitable about this. Discussion of situationist ideas need not be a formulaic exercise; it can and indeed should involve much more than that for, as the situationists themselves demonstrated, such ideas *matter*: they are connected to forms of practice, and they constitute what Gregory calls 'bloody theory', which is 'both embodied and transgressive'.[66] What this underlines is the importance of thinking about the kind of account to be produced and its purposes, and about what might, in turn, be inspired – not only intellectually but also politically – by an encounter with the SI.[67]

It is not nostalgia that draws one back to the projects discussed here; nor is it the prospect of consolation, the chance to revive spirits wearied by contemporary political cynicism by dipping into warming streams of earlier utopian visions. The dreams of urban liberation that follow certainly need to be understood in their historical context. But what is striking in particular about many of the visions addressed later in the book some half century on is their continuing power to challenge, to provoke, to displace assumptions about what cities are for and what they might become. It is certainly true that a study of the situationists such as the one presented here will miss out much of what the group and its projects were about. It is also the case that I cannot provide any easy assurances in relation to a question once posed by the critic Irving Wohlfarth, originally with reference to another subject but one that might be adapted here. 'How, then,' he asks, 'can we, the assembled suppliers, avoid setting up a culinary [SI] to the jaws of the culture industry?'[68] His question will therefore be left hanging, as both an issue of concern and a warning. But if the problem of the co-optation or recuperation of certain radical positions seems all too apparent in the early twenty-first century, and if the prospects of thinking 'otherwise' about urban futures often seems increasingly bleak in our period of the 'posts-' (with its declarations of being post-avant-garde, post-utopian, post-modern and so on), then I think we might do well also to consider something else: that is, the potential transformative and disruptive effects that can still be mobilised by returning to projects that were part of earlier utopian avant-gardes, and by working with – and allowing ourselves to be confronted by – their claims.

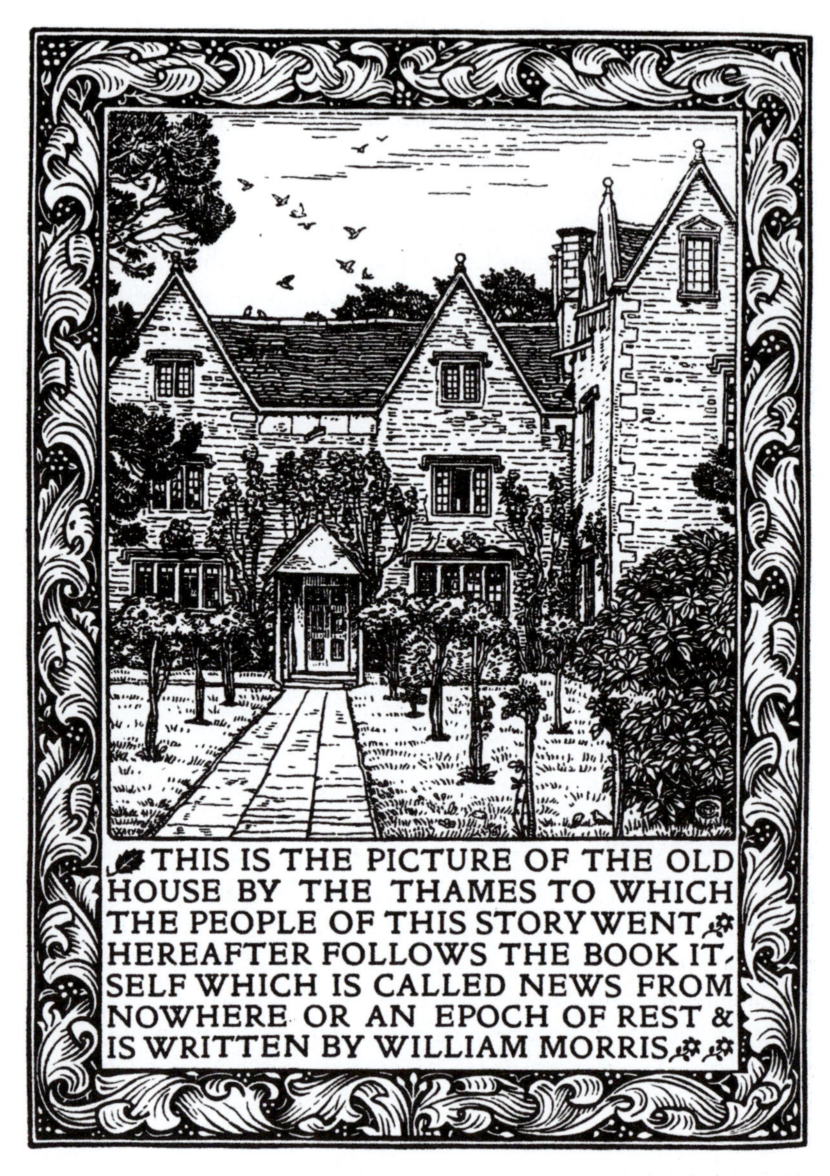

THIS IS THE PICTURE OF THE OLD
HOUSE BY THE THAMES TO WHICH
THE PEOPLE OF THIS STORY WENT
HEREAFTER FOLLOWS THE BOOK IT-
SELF WHICH IS CALLED NEWS FROM
NOWHERE OR AN EPOCH OF REST &
IS WRITTEN BY WILLIAM MORRIS

Figure 2.1 Frontispiece from William Morris, *News from Nowhere: or, an Epoch of Rest, Being Some Chapters from a Utopian Romance* (1893). By C. H. Gere, as designed by Morris.

CHAPTER 2

Restorative utopias

New cities well planned and thought out because the needs of all will be considered, will displace the cities of today which are chaotic, disorderly, untidy because founded in selfishness. These new cities will be as remarkable for the freshness of their air as are our modern cities for their unwholesomeness . . . cities bathed with country air, encircling and encircled by open fields and made bright and sparkling with flowing water.

Ebenezer Howard[1]

Utopian awakenings

William Guest awakens – or is this still a dream? – shortly before the beginning of the twenty-second century and finds that London has been transformed. Much of the city is almost unrecognisable to him. The main street through his neighbourhood of Hammersmith no longer teems with people. It has disappeared, and instead he sees a 'teeming garden' accompanying each of the houses. The construction of these buildings is along medieval lines and, when combined with the costumes of the inhabitants, they almost make him feel that he has returned to the fourteenth century.[2] As he explores the area, he emerges from fields to come upon a mass of architecture that 'was not only exquisitely beautiful in itself, but it bore upon it the expression of such generosity and abundance of life that I was exhilarated to a pitch that I had never yet reached'.[3] Relying on the guidance of his companion, Dick Hammond, he progresses on foot as if 'a visitor from another planet'. He discovers that the Houses of Parliament have been converted into a storage place for manure. Trafalgar Square has now become an open space with an orchard. Meanwhile, the shops in Piccadilly are now run by children and require no money, and instead of a large-scale factory they find a Banded-workshop where people voluntarily gather to make craft products. Later, Hammond summarises his view of the changes to the English landscape. 'England was once a country of clearings amongst the woods and wastes, with a few towns interspersed,' he recalls. 'It then became a country of huge and foul workshops and fouler gambling-dens, surrounded by an ill-kept, poverty-stricken farm, pillaged by the masters of the workshops. It is now a garden, where nothing is wasted and nothing is spoilt, with the necessary dwellings, sheds, and workshops scattered up and down the country, all trim and neat and pretty.'[4]

The scenes are from William Morris's classic novel or 'utopian romance' of 1890, *News from Nowhere, or an Epoch of Rest* (figure 2.1) Through the figure of William Guest, Morris envisages the sweeping away of the cramped streets and slums of large cities and their replacement by beautiful towns and villages with fields and gardens. His fantasy is marked by a longing for a more harmonious and environmentally balanced world, where alienation has melted away and where money, property and central government have all been abolished. Influenced by romantic and Marxist sensibilities, it describes a society reborn through a process of socialist revolution where the blight of industrial capitalism has been consigned to the past, and where old industrial enterprises have been replaced by a decentralised system based on craft production, use values, and work determined by need and pleasure. The year before writing his book, Morris had complained about the 'sickening hideousness' of bourgeois London. In his view, 'other ugly cities may be rougher and more savage in their brutality, but none are so desperately shabby, so irredeemably vulgar as London.' He had also made clear his belief that underlying this ugliness was a legalised form of class theft, from the poor by the rich.[5] Earlier he had once further referred to 'the spreading of the hideous town' and had dreamed instead 'of London, small and white and clean', with the 'clear Thames bordered by its gardens green'.[6] His belief that architecture should be able to inspire passion and intense feelings is in evidence in his utopian text, particularly in relation to new buildings whose exuberance he contrasts with the neo-classicism that he hated. Also finding clear expression is his conviction that a socialist revolution should involve a change in both the landscape and in social relations.

Morris's text was part of a much wider outpouring of utopian ideas in the late nineteenth and early twentieth centuries that found expression through not only imaginative literature but also many of the arts and the fields of architecture and planning in Europe and North America. The vogue for utopias in the late nineteenth century has been connected in particular with widespread concern at the sense of threat and upheaval associated with laissez-faire capitalism, and the desire to present an ordered alternative.[7] The city played an important role in much utopianism as a source of inspiration and also a target for critique and dreams of radical change. Strands of utopian thought emerged in response to urban problems and challenges, in direct contestation of facets of the contemporary city. Confronting commentators at the time was not only the vast scale of urban expansion in the nineteenth century, with cities apparently 'flooding' into surrounding areas. The population of London, for example, increased more than fivefold during that century to reach in excess of five and half million, and by the century's close the growth curve seemed to be pointing ever upwards. Of related concern were also the enormity and depth of urban problems as reformers, social surveyors, moralists and other critics exposed concentrations of poverty and destitution in cities along with issues of overcrowding, inadequate sanitation and high mortality rates. Fears about the social consequences of these conditions and 'the city of dreadful night' were rife and they often spilt over into an already familiar rhetoric about the city as a sprawling hellish place or as a 'Great Wen', to use William Cobbett's famous phrase likening London to a giant cyst. There was also speculation about the threats posed to bourgeois order by physical degeneration and the 'biological decline' of the population, along with potential political unrest and insurrection. In addition there was considerable discussion about the impact of urbanisation on the countryside and on rural ways of life, and about the prospects for land reform and improvements in rural welfare.[8]

In this chapter and the next, I draw out two influential broad utopian approaches to cities that emerged from these intense fears and debates of the late nineteenth and early twentieth centuries. Both of these approaches emphasised spatial concerns, asserting the importance of changing urban space as a means of constructing a different and better future. Both also came to have a profound impact on the discourses and practices of modern planning, and on the spatial and social landscape itself. In this chapter my focus is on 'restorative utopias', in so far as they responded to the upheaval of the modern city by projecting a new spatial form that was intended to restore and shore up values about urban settlement, community, order and harmony. Aspects of this approach find voice in Morris's dream. In thinking about how the foul and dark urban spaces of industrial capitalism might be replaced by a garden landscape that would provide the setting for a new civilisation, he was joined by numerous critics who also opposed the disorder associated with urban expansion and industrialisation. Many of them adopted anti-urban positions and, in so doing, joined a long tradition, especially in Anglo-Saxon countries, that is driven by a myth of the country as a source of the 'organic' and 'natural' society, defined in opposition to the city that is depicted as corrupt, as exploitative and as undermining existing notions of order. Rarely far away is the whiff of ideas about pastoral perfection, of a golden age or arcadia that stretches back to classical antiquity and that hankers after the idea of a pre-industrial harmony between humans and nature. However, the strand of utopianism addressed in this chapter did not see itself as anti-urban as such. Rather, it claimed to be opposed to the current state of cities as it looked towards a different mode of urban living, one that would be more integrated with the country and closer to nature. In recoiling from aspects of the crowded city with its dirt and noise and uproar, it searched for an alternative urbanism that still valued aspects of city life.

While Morris provides an important cue for this utopian approach, my primary focus is on the vision developed by Ebenezer Howard and the garden city movement. Howard believed that countering urban problems should involve reconstructing not only the built environment but also the very fabric of civilisation. Despite the modest origins of Howard's proposals and his initial position as an outsider to architectural, planning or governmental circles, the influence of his ideas has been extraordinary, reaching across many parts of the world. He wrote only one book in his lifetime, originally published at his own expense in 1898 as *To-Morrow: A Peaceful Path to Real Reform*. A revised edition appeared four years later under the now familiar title, *Garden Cities of To-Morrow*. According to Lewis Mumford, the book 'has done more than any other single book to guide the modern town planning movement and to alter its objectives'.[9] Peter Hall assigns its author a role as 'the most important single character' in his intellectual history of urban planning and design during the twentieth century, and portrays his garden city concept as 'overwhelmingly the most important response to the Victorian city'.[10] By returning to Howard's utopianism, my reading critically addresses the themes of restoring order, harmony and balance in spatial as well as social terms. These have implications for wider understandings of utopian urbanism and they will be taken up further in relation to other modernist utopian visions in the following chapter.

The vision of Ebenezer Howard

Howard reacted strongly against what he described as the 'crowded, ill-ventilated, unplanned, unwieldy, unhealthy cities' of the late nineteenth century. 'These crowded cities have done their work,' he declared; 'they were the best which society largely based on selfishness and rapacity could construct, but they are in the nature of things entirely unadapted for a society in which the social side of our nature is demanding a larger share of recognition.'[11] He registered the continuing growth of cities and their 'flooding' outwards as a terrible disorder, and he depicted the 'unhealthy' cities as 'ulcers on the very face of our beautiful island'.[12] Organic and medical metaphors frequently appear in his denunciations of existing cities. He thus quoted with approval the judgement on London by Lord Rosebery, speaking as Chairman of London County Council: 'Sixty years ago a great Englishman, Cobbett, called it a wen. If it was a wen then what is it now? A tumor, an elephantiasis sucking into its gorged system half the life and the blood and the bone of the rural districts.'[13] Yet Howard's judgements on cities were not unremittingly negative. He often spoke of his pride in London as his birthplace and was enamoured of the social possibilities of urban living and the opportunities presented by cities in terms of work, leisure and culture. Recalling his return to London as a young man on holiday while living in Chicago in 1874, he spoke of his thrill at mounting an omnibus and riding through the crowded city where a 'strangely ecstatic feeling' possessed him. At the time lacking the consciousness of social problems and divisions in the city that later inspired his campaigning for change, he stated: 'There flowed through every nerve of my body from head to foot as it were streams of electricity . . . The crowded streets – the signs of wealth and prosperity – the bustle – the very confusion and disorder appealed to me, and I was filled with delight.'[14]

Howard was born in London in 1850. He trained as a stenographer and described himself as an inventor, not a planner. An early influence on his thinking was another popular utopian novel, Edward Bellamy's *Looking Backward* that was published in 1888. Its vision was very different from Morris's *News from Nowhere*. Indeed, Morris strongly opposed Bellamy's book when it appeared and partly wrote his own text against it.[15] Bellamy similarly used the narrative device of a man falling asleep and waking up to find himself bewildered by the changes that a city has undergone, this time Boston in the year 2000. He portrayed a socialist society of the future based on centralised management and planning, where industry is run under a government-owned trust employing an industrial army, and the city is like an efficient and regimented machine. Smoky chimneys have been banished as have poverty and social disorder. Collective interests outweigh the 'excessive individualism' of the past. Technology is harnessed to create an ordered landscape that features broad boulevards, parklands, trees, fountains, statues, and vast public buildings of an unparalled architectural grandeur.[16] When Morris reviewed Bellamy's book, he attacked its mechanisation and what he saw as its repressive managerial organisation. However, Howard's initial reaction was much more favourable. He remembered the impact vividly as he read the book 'at a sitting, not at all critically' and 'was fairly "carried away" by the eloquence and evidently strong convictions of the author'. As a result he recognised 'the splendid possibilities of a new civilisation based on service to the community and not almost exclusively on self-interest', and became determined to put the ideas he had been developing as part of the London-based middle-class Radical movement into action with the intention of realising that civilisation.[17] He also remarked on the significance of the book for his socialist beliefs, stating that one result was 'to give to my imagination . . . a very vivid sense of the evanescence of the present forms of the instruments of production and distribution and their almost entire unsuitability and inadaptability to a new order. The chief illustration of this evanescence which forced itself upon my attention was our great cities, especially London.'[18]

Howard helped to get Bellamy's book published in England and established discussion groups devoted to its ideas. In time Howard came to question what he saw as the authoritarianism of Bellamy's ideas and criticised their emphasis on nationalisation and centralisation. In this he sympathised with Morris's position. When Howard later directly compared the texts by Bellamy and Morris in a talk in 1909, he stated that he found the latter's book 'charming to contemplate' and noted how its alternative communist vision as a 'great Brotherhood' was 'far less rigid in its relationships [than Bellamy's], far sweeter and far more truly human'. Yet he was puzzled as to how life could be led so luxuriously in Morris's utopia with so little evidence of modern technology, law and organisation.[19] Ultimately Howard valued the approaches taken by both of these 'prophets', as he called them. While he likened Bellamy's orderly systematic approach to that of a mechanic or an administrator and law giver, he referred to Morris's depiction of society as that of a poet, full of imagination who cherished freedom and viewed work in terms of its potential for joyous creativity. Howard claimed that, despite their differences, they were brought together by something more essential. That was their shared emphasis on the force of love. In his view, each book gave different expression to this force but it was this that ensured social cohesion in their respective utopian visions and that gave unity and harmony of purpose through unselfishness.[20]

This attempt to reconcile apparent opposites and restore a balanced position was a familiar Howard manoeuvre. His approach typically involved trying to bring together perspectives, to supercede antagonisms and to establish harmonious balance and order. Howard's early enthusiasm for Bellamy's vision nevertheless was indicative of his concern with rationality, modernity and technology that remained with him throughout his life. He did not turn away from cities and industrialisation, as is sometimes implied by critics, nor did he take refuge in a simpler medievalism. Instead, he sought to find what he defined as 'modern' solutions, and in so doing he showed considerable faith in the powers of new technologies and the principles of social reform. 'What Is may hinder What Might Be for a while, but cannot stay the tide of progress', he wrote.[21] Confident of the place of his proposals in relation to historical trends, he argued that contrary to common opinion the large cities in Britain were no longer modern. 'Each generation should build to suit its own needs', he asserted, and in his view these needs were running counter to those that existing cities could accommodate. Embellishing on the image of the 'tide of progress', Howard drew an analogy between large cities and the nineteenth-century stage-coach, and he appealed to his readers to consider the fact that the cities might be no more permanent in their present form than the stage-coach system had been at the moment that it was about to be replaced by the railways.[22] Elsewhere he compared his proposals with the early development of the railways as he reiterated the progressive nature of the garden city scheme as an enterprise that might start on the small scale and face many difficulties but that could enable a radical transformation of the social and physical landscape, becoming 'the stepping stone to a higher and better form of industrial life'.[23]

Smokeless, slumless cities

One of Howard's central concerns was the overcrowding of large cities. When he presented his ideas in both versions of his book, he opened with a catalogue of criticisms from writers around the beginning of the 1890s about overcrowding and the 'tide of migration' fuelling urban expansion. He believed it necessary to stem this flow of people and attract them back to the country through the construction of new towns that would be 'bright and fair, wholesome and beautiful'.[24] Presenting the characteristics of urban life and of rural life as two 'magnets', with lists of their different advantages and disadvantages, he proposed an alternative third magnet that was meant to combine the best features of both (figure 2.2). 'Town and country *must be married*,' he declared in a famous line, 'and out of this joyous union will spring a new hope, a new life, a new civilisation.' The 'town-country magnet' was meant to overcome an 'unholy, unnatural separation'. His claim about transcending this division and restoring 'naturalness' was underpinned by a metaphor of female and male difference, as he proposed that 'As man and woman by their varied gifts supplement each other, so should town and country.'[25]

Howard thus asserted that his programme was not anti-urban but rather based on a 'balanced' way of living, as his original terms for the garden city of 'Unionville' or 'Rurisville' were meant to imply.[26] This involved building anew on fresh ground. He wrote: 'Order and beauty rather than chaos and ugliness: the needs of the whole people rather than *the supposed* interests of a few will be the governing elements in determining the ground plan of the city.'[27] The broad outlines of this plan are well known. The settlements would each cover 1,000 acres with a permanent greenbelt of 5,000 acres, and contain at most 32,000 people. They would be circular, divided into six equal wards by the boulevards with a functional separation between land uses (figure 2.3). Howard suggested that they would further form clusters of six cities of similar size, along with one central city of 58,000 people, collectively constituting a polycentric Social City. His vision of this 'Group of Slumless, Smokeless Cities' was most fully articulated in the original text of *To-Morrow* (figure 2.4). He dropped the diagram from subsequent editions, however, as he imparted a practical air through discussing the 'correct principle of a city's growth'. He argued that, as each garden city grew and reached its limit, another city should be established in the region, ensuring the preservation of the city's boundaries along with the surrounding countryside. While he acknowledged that the scheme would require legislation, he presented the driving force as a growing demand for the benefits of such a 'beautiful group of cities'.[28]

Howard never claimed originality for the garden city's component parts and referred to it in a chapter title as a 'unique combination of proposals'. His concern with separating zones while unifying city and country recalls

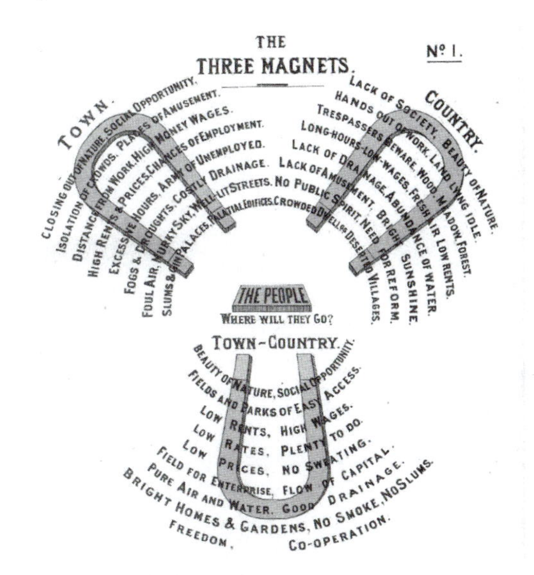

Figure 2.2 Ebenezer Howard, The Three Magnets. From Howard, *To-Morrow: A Peaceful Path to Real Reform* (1898).

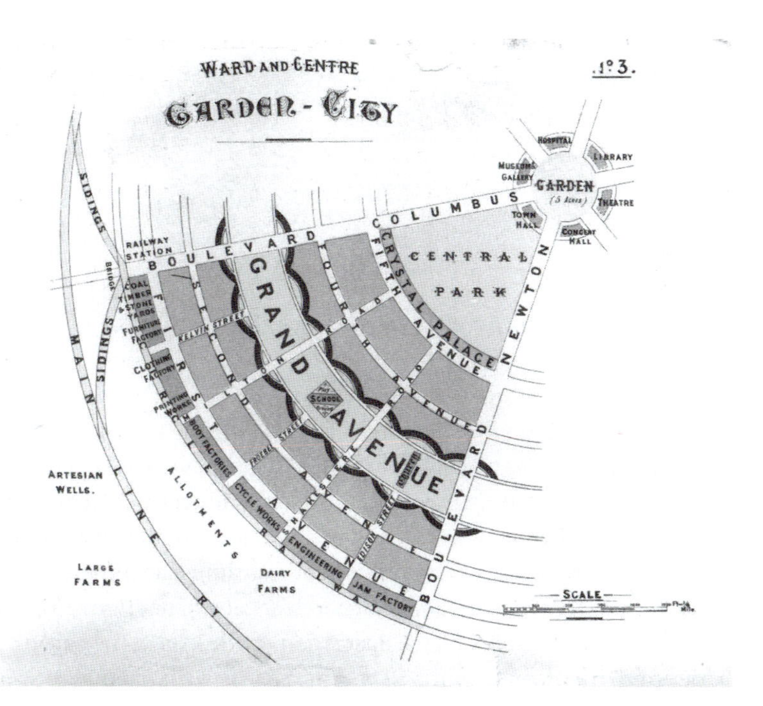

Figure 2.3 Ebenezer Howard, Ward and Centre of the Garden City. From *To-Morrow* (1898).

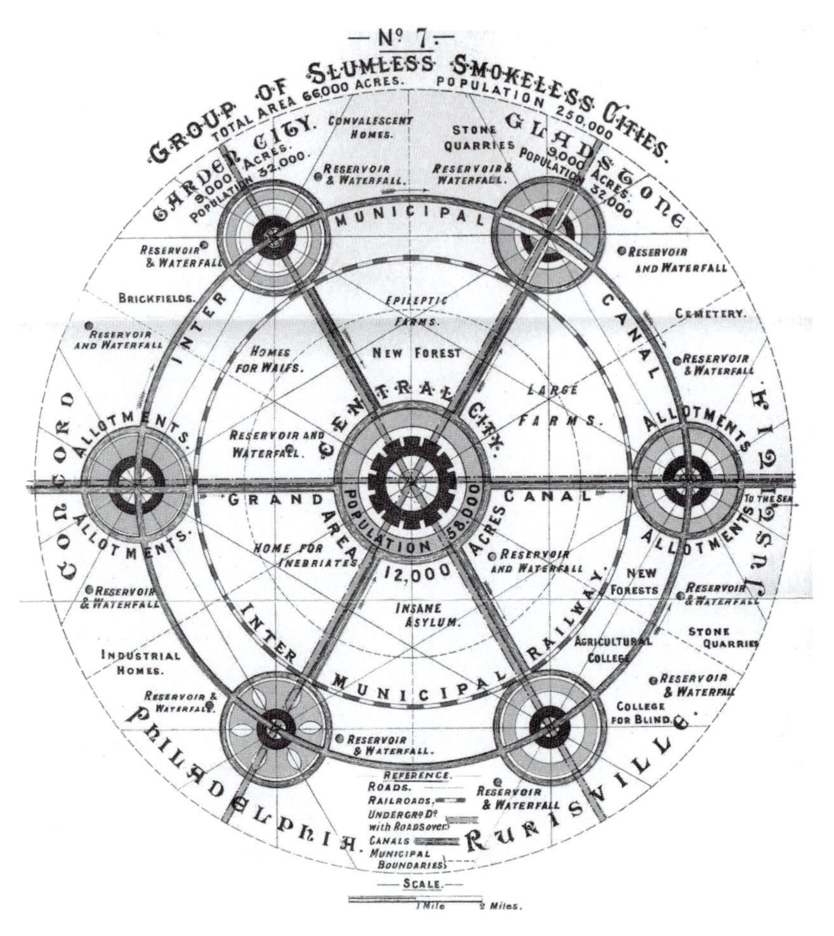

Figure 2.4 Ebenezer Howard, The Social City. From *To-Morrow* (1898).

earlier utopian visions. These include Thomas More's *Utopia* and Johann Valentin Andreae's *Christianopolis*, as well as Claude Nicolas Ledoux's ideal city and Charles Fourier's proposals in the early nineteenth century for a *phalanstère* for communal living and a 'new industrial world'. Howard indeed referred to More as being among several thinkers – others included William Morris, John Ruskin and the anarchist geographer Peter Kropotkin – who only narrowly failed to give expression to the idea of the garden city. In a speech to the London Spiritualist Alliance, he went so far as to suggest that the garden city idea 'exists in the spiritual atmosphere which envelopes and pervades the lives of us all', and that his own role was only that of a messenger.[29] Among direct influences on him were plans by social reformers involved in sanitary and social science in England around the mid nineteenth-century. Howard attached considerable significance to Benjamin Ward Richardson's *Hygeia: A City of Health* of 1876. This model city was dedicated to the reformer Edwin Chadwick and it gave a central role to light and clear air in its assault on disease-ridden spaces. Richardson aimed to separate functions and to keep factories, sanitation works and slaughterhouses away from the town. He also sought to abolish underground rooms that he associated with 'loathsome' residences and 'savage children', and to situate kitchens on upper floors with perfect lighting 'so that all uncleanliness is at once detected'.[30] One of Howard's first attempts to describe his garden city came in an essay from around 1891 entitled 'A city of health and how to build it' that he sent to Richardson.[31]

Howard further cited the urban plans of another influential nineteenth-century social reformer, James Silk Buckingham. The latter had been influenced by Robert Owen's utopian socialism but had sought to distance himself from what he termed the 'evils of communism' in favour of 'the benefits of association'. Buckingham, like Richardson, asserted the need for adequate light, air and drainage along with the removal of 'unhealthy' and 'disagreeable' activities from the city in a scheme that linked concerns about health with those about morality.[32] His ideal town of Victoria in 1849 was regularly arranged with concentric squares, radial streets and strict zoning with a population of no more than ten thousand. All means of 'intoxication' were prohibited. As with many utopian plans, everything would be visible as he promised that with 'the entire absence of all wynds, courts, and blind alleys, or *culs-de-sac*, there would be no secret and obscure haunts for the retirement of the filthy and the immoral from the public eye'.[33] Howard acknowledged the resemblances with his own scheme especially in terms of its outer form, although he pointed out that he had not seen Buckingham's proposals until he had progressed far with his own. He also distanced the 'inner life' of his garden city from the 'rigid cast-iron organisation' that held together Victoria, although he shared concerns about intoxication and the 'demon drink'.[34] Howard nevertheless took up reformist principles about spatial organisation and environmental design in his proposals, and he shared the earlier confidence of these reformers that his vision would be realised. 'Utopia itself is but another word for time,' Richardson had stated, 'and some day the masses, who now heed us not, or smile incredulously at our proceedings, will awake to our conceptions.'[35]

The 'master key' to socio-spatial reform

Howard stressed the importance of utopianism for enabling urban and social change, and specifically for building the kind of socialism to which he was committed early on. He stated 'it is essential to have an ideal showing us the direction in which we should move.'[36] In developing his vision, he gave a central role to space. He insisted that everyone should have 'ample space in which to live, to move and to develop', and this became a point of critique of the existing order as well as a guiding principle of his alternative.[37] He therefore presented the garden city as a new spatial form through which new social arrangements and relationships could develop, as the city acted as both a means for social change and an example to encourage further change in the future. It was through the medium of a new city that he imagined a new social order and civilisation. Re-ordering the city was a means of re-ordering society, as he cast his vision of cities as both the symbol and materialisation of a more balanced, co-operative and 'healthy' society. If his vision was utopian, though, it was not meant for distant time or place, nor for a society that had already been transformed. He intended it to be of immediate utilisation and as a means of bringing about 'real reform' as the title of his original book made clear.

Howard argued that land should be brought into the ownership of the whole community and that rents should flow back into communities to be used to finance public services. He therefore argued that garden cities should be established on these principles, placing the interests of the community above those of private landlords who would in due course cease to exist. His aim was that the cities would embody the values of a more just and equitable social order, and that they would set in train a process of social reform that would ultimately be a means of superseding the class conflicts of capitalism. The building of the new settlements and the restoration of people to the land was to be the '*Master Key*', he believed, helping to unlock the door to the new order.[38] This order would be neither capitalist nor state socialist, as they were then understood, but would consist of decentralised and locally managed commonwealths characterised by 'freedom' and 'co-operation', terms shown as underpinning the town-country magnet in the Three Magnets diagram. In developing his ideas about land reform, Howard drew on a largely English tradition of reform and dissent and especially the work of Herbert Spencer, Thomas Spence and Henry George.[39] He was also influenced by the anarchist movement and in particular the work of Kropotkin.

When the *Times* newspaper in London reviewed Howard's book, it opined that the 'only difficulty is to create [such a city]; but that is a small matter to Utopians'. According to Howard, this reaction was 'pretty general'. Not surprisingly he rejected it, pointing out: 'I never regarded the difficulties as small, but set myself to face them and to seek to get others, far more influential than myself, to face them also.'[40] Howard gave considerable attention to practical questions of business and political support, presenting his ideas in part as a guide to building a garden city in the present, hence the long sections of his book devoted to financial considerations and attempts to justify the soundness of investments. If successful, he hoped this city would act as a beacon for further efforts in the future and help to bring about a wider transformation by force of example. Most importantly the experiment was meant to break up interests of property and capital, and to unite and inspire workers, bringing them together as a group with the owners of capital and of agricultural land and thus creating a broad-based force for change.[41] Howard had little faith in the parliamentary system, describing it as 'the great friend of vested interests'.[42] His campaigning therefore bypassed it as he brought together industrialists, financiers and other sympathisers with the aim of raising awareness in the belief that 'the city which was pictured so vividly in my own mind must be pictured more or less vividly by many.'[43] A number of people also took the message on the road including Elizabeth Howard, who played an important role in organising her husband's activities until her death in 1904. The Garden City Association was founded in 1899 and within three years it had a membership of 1,300 that included twenty-three MPs and the industrialists George Cadbury, Joseph Rowntree and W. H. Lever. Its establishment of the Garden City Pioneer Company Ltd was succeeded in 1903 by the First Garden City Company, which began work at Letchworth in Hertfordshire. Preparations for another city at Welwyn followed in 1919. Through these developments some of Howard's ideas gained concrete form but they also took on a different complexion.

In his determination to construct garden cities, Howard recognised the need for flexibility. Although his spatial designs for the garden city gave a simplified and universalising cast to his vision, he discussed how the geometric diagrams would need to be reshaped according to the specific location and circumstances. In captions added to the 1902 edition of the book he therefore noted that the 'plan must depend upon site selected', and stressed that they should not be seen as immutable blueprints but were '*merely suggestive, and will probably be much departed from*'.[44] He later further remarked that 'my friends and supporters never regarded this book [*Garden Cities of To-morrow*], any more than I did, as more than a sketch or outline of what we hoped to accomplish.'[45] More fundamentally, however, the social commitments of his vision also shifted over the years. In particular, he moderated much of the radical rhetoric apparent in some of the drafts of his texts and diagrams from the late nineteenth century. In drafts of the Three Magnets diagram such as one from around 1892, for example, Howard referred to 'Individualistic – Socialism' and 'Freedom not Regimentation', before changing this to the more inclusive sounding 'Freedom' and 'Co-operation' (figure 2.5). He also dropped rousing calls such as 'Go up and possess the land!' in a draft of his diagram of the 'Ward and centre of the garden city' (figure 2.6). Further alterations came with the new version of his book in 1902, for which sections were rewritten and the Social City diagram removed. The change of the book's title to *Garden Cities of To-Morrow* was itself significant, with Hall noting how this 'was perhaps catchier, but it diverted people from the truly radical character of the message, demoting [Howard] from social visionary into physical planner'.[46] These changes were symptomatic of the direction that the garden city movement took as Howard sought greater practical influence, and as his movement became increasingly dominated by business people rather than workers to whom he also appealed.

When building work started at Letchworth, numerous compromises were made to ensure financial support and to rein in costs. A significant addition also came with the architects appointed for Letchworth, Raymond Unwin and Barry Parker. They reworked Howard's geometric plans to pursue notions of organic unity and co-operation that looked back to traditional design and the example of the medieval village. Influenced by Morris and the Arts and Crafts movement, and later by the Viennese urbanist Camillo Sitte, they helped to imbue the garden city with a longing for integration and wholeness and for a strongly rooted community. In returning to the example of the medieval village, Unwin and Parker found a favourable expression of what they called 'a small corporate life in which all the different units were personally in touch with each other, conscious of and frankly accepting their relations, and on the whole content with them'.[47] Commenting on issues of co-operation, harmony and a hierarchical village life, they pointed with admiration to the way that, 'Every building honestly confesses just what it is, and so falls into its place.'[48] Their plans reduced the densities envisaged by Howard as they aimed to counteract the overcrowding and the unregulated growth of

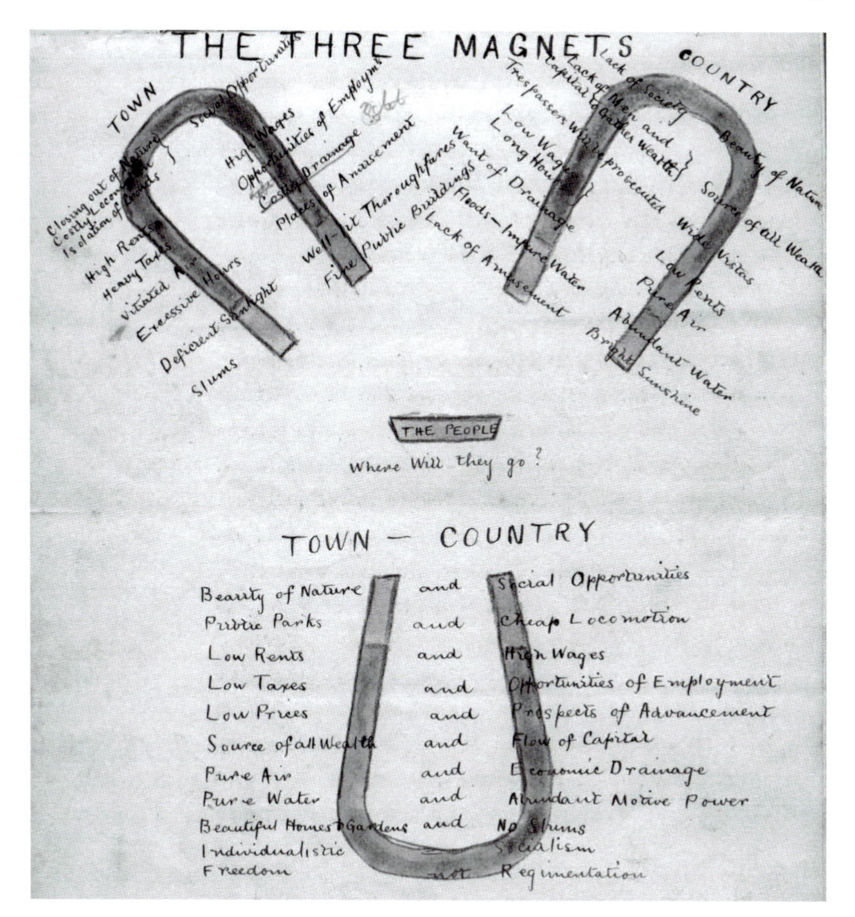

Figure 2.5 Ebenezer Howard, unpublished early draft of the Three Magnets diagram. From typescript of *To-Morrow*, around 1892, in the Howard Papers, D/Eho/F1/13. Reproduced courtesy of the Hertfordshire Archives and Local Studies.

existing urban areas, and to create a synthesis of visual and social elements so that the view could again induce a feeling of order, with the village 'an animate symbol' and the middle ages 'the historic standard' (figure 2.7).

Unwin and Parker's mythologising of the past conflicted with Howard's rational vision, even if the latter was apparently supportive of their designs. Their work sounds 'a note of nostalgia for a vanished stability not heard in Howard', according to Robert Fishman, bringing 'to prominence an element in the Garden City that had hardly existed in Howard: the fear of the great city and its social turmoil, the desire to discard the burdens of progress and return to the simple life'.[49] Standish Meacham connects their

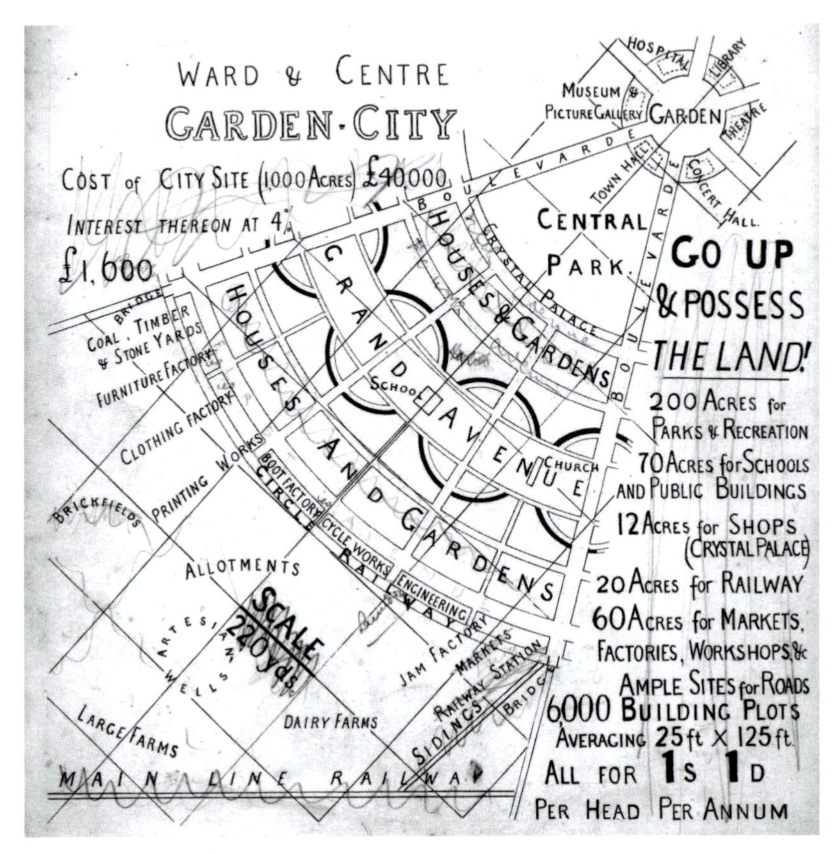

Figure 2.6 Ebenezer Howard, unpublished version of the Ward and Centre of the Garden City. Undated draft, from the Howard Papers, D/EHo/F1/18. Reproduced courtesy of the Hertfordshire Archives and Local Studies.

stance to a conservative and anti-urban Englishness that he argues was a hallmark of the early garden city movement, and that he contrasts with the sources and imagery of Howard's ideal city.[50] Unwin and Parker's contribution did not involve a total retreat to the past, though, for there was a more progressive element to some of their architectural schemes with an emphasis on purity and simplicity of design. They also shared Howard's interest in co-operative housekeeping arrangements, which had been a focus of earlier radical community experiments by the Owenites and socialist-feminists. They produced designs for quadrangles where domestic work was re-organised on a communal basis and co-operative projects were first introduced to Letchworth in the form of Homesgarth in 1909–13, a quadrangle in which Howard lived for a time. Howard

Figure 2.7 Village Street, Kersey. Illustration from Raymond Unwin, *Town Planning in Practice: An Introduction to the Art of Designing Cities* (1909).

described it as a response to 'the domestic servant question' as well as to 'woman's labour problem', caused by the waste of women's abilities and energy under current social relations. He believed that it was a practical solution 'at once lessening the drudgeries, and setting free the energies of women'. Although currently small scale, he asserted the possibility of extending this beyond the middle classes to the working classes, claiming that this experiment had 'wrapped up within it part of the germ of a new and brighter – a juster and a happier social order – an order too, in which woman will play a far larger part than she plays to-day'.[51]

In the early twentieth century the influence of Howard's garden city vision grew substantially, with interpretations and translations of his ideas along with other versions of the garden city concept appearing in a range of countries including the United States, France, Germany, Japan, Russia and Australia.[52] Elements were also taken up within the regional city tradition, notably by Patrick Geddes and Mumford.[53] However, the term garden city lost its distinctive edge and social conviction. In a letter to a newspaper in 1919, Howard complained that the 'loose use' of the term in England was preventing proper recognition of the 'supreme importance' of the only real garden city of the time, that of Letchworth. It was this city, he claimed, that was preparing the way 'for a real and splendid solution of the housing problem, the traffic problem, the health problem, the labour problem'. He also claimed that the project about to be initiated at Welwyn would 'give the whole world a lesson in the art of city building which it cannot fail to understand, and to yet further develop and improve upon'.[54] That year the renamed Garden Cities and Town Planning Association duly advanced a formal definition of the 'Garden City' but it was already apparent that even in the cases of Letchworth and Welwyn, Howard's aim of social transformation had been subsumed under the drive to gather sufficient support for attaining relatively limited planning objectives. 'The Garden City movement, therefore, gradually lost its commitment to social change and became a city planning movement in the narrow sense,' notes Fishman. 'The sponsors of Welwyn Garden City no longer claimed to be initiating a revolutionary transformation in English society: their hope was to create one new community which would be clean, compact, and close to nature.'[55] A similar point is made by Stephen Ward who argues that 'the social reformism of the garden city idea was quickly converted into an environmental reformism which was in turn technicalized and dissembled to form part of the emergent professional practice of town planning.'[56]

Biologically sound cities and bodies

The garden city therefore became increasingly associated with a mode of urban planning within existing capitalist relations rather than a vehicle for deeper social and spatial change. The influence of the garden city movement on the field of planning, and specifically on the emergence of the new town movement as government bureaucracies sought to reorganise urban and regional systems, is well documented.[57] Its 'historical tragedy' is also widely recognised, in the sense that its commitment to a new way of living and to a path to 'real reform' became diverted into a version of 'prosperous suburbia', where it has even been held responsible by one recent critic for opening 'the floodgates for a new, far more nefarious breed of suburbia which came to swamp inter-war Britain'.[58] Many of the problems associated with the garden city can be seen in this manner as stemming from the social processes that were mobilised in the effort to realise its forms. This points to the difficulty that David Harvey identifies with attempts to build utopias based on spatial forms more widely, where constructing that form depends upon compromising and working with restrictive sets of social processes, most often the agency of capital accumulation or the state. Harvey therefore makes the pertinent point that the 'failure of realized utopias of spatial form can just as reasonably be attributed to the processes mobilized to materialize them as to failures of spatial form *per se*.'[59] Nevertheless, further questions need to be asked about the utopia of the garden city itself in terms of what made it so conducive to existing powerful interests, and what enabled its appropriation for ends that might seem antithetical to its more progressive elements. In need of closer critical attention in particular are the modes of ordering and sorting within its utopian conception of urbanism. These constitute another side to the garden city, I want to suggest, one that meshes more neatly with the needs of capital and the state than might be supposed from Howard's stated intent.

Howard and his supporters often appealed to natural principles and laws to legitimise the garden city as a 'healthy' and 'organic' form. In so doing they frequently portrayed existing urban problems in bodily terms as a kind of physical deformation, as 'ulcers' or the result of sickness. Giving a talk in Edinburgh in 1908, for example, Howard called on his audience to tend carefully to that city as a living organism 'to whose well being you shall minister, with patient thought, with loving service, removing every stain and blot and sore which now defaces its fair beauty'.[60] Howard also emphasised laws governing organic growth. He implied that, by setting limits on town size, urban areas should not transgress their boundaries when growing but rather should multiply in the manner of biological cells. 'A town, like a flower, or a tree, or an animal, should, at each stage of its growth, possess unity, symmetry, completeness,' he wrote, 'and the effect of growth should never be to destroy that unity, but to give it greater purpose, not to mar that symmetry, but to make it more symmetrical.'[61] In Mumford's view, this development of organic concepts was Howard's greatest contribution to urban thought. Mumford claimed that they brought to the city 'the essential biological criteria of dynamic equilibrium and organic balance', and for him Howard's 'genius was to combine the existing organs of the city into a more orderly composition based on the principle of organic limitation and controlled growth'.[62] This was meant to allow the maintenance of unity and coherence within a context of urban expansion, and to set out processes that, in contrast to those behind unregulated growth, were 'purposeful, goal-seeking, self-limiting'.[63]

One of the consequences of the use of organic and biological concepts by Howard and his supporters was that it allowed them to *naturalise* their projects and to present them as working for the good of the whole. In particular, it enabled them to identify problems in terms of a disturbance to the balance of the organism, and to portray their schemes as forms of health care or medicine to restore the city's health. It was a means of depoliticisation whereby problems rooted in the social production of urban space were dissimulated to appear as ailments that required the guiding light of a new urban vision to be resolved. In a similar way to classical political thinkers who depicted civil disorder as a sickness, and who proposed that a restoration of the right balance and hierarchy would bring about the recovery of the organism (the polis), so too here the re-establishment of a healthy balance and harmony was seen as the key to enabling the recovery of the city and of urban society. The way in which Howard figured tending to the city's life and body varied. At times it appeared in terms of a relationship between a parent and child. He also took up a phrase from George Bernard Shaw about 'nursing a site', suggesting that this was especially fruitful for thinking about the location for a new garden city. 'To nurse a site surely implies that the site to be nursed should be an underdeveloped site but one capable of healthy growth under the care of its kindly nurse,' he stated. Stretching this naturalising metaphor further, he added that 'the site to be nursed should not only be one in the early stage of infancy', nor should it be 'a puny undersized infant', but rather 'one which may be developed into the stature of a perfect organism – in other words into a real municipality'.[64]

In his vision of a well-structured and biologically sound urban body, Howard gave a critical role to circulation. He stressed the need for a scientific system of flows within and between his garden cities. These were based around systems of railways, canals and reservoirs that he depicted in the networks and routes criss-crossing his diagram of the Social City. This concern relates to the longer historical significance given to circulation for the health of cities in conceptions of urbanism. Urban planners began to emphasise the importance of circulation in this manner during the eighteenth century. Influenced by William Harvey's discoveries early in the century before about the circulation of blood in the human body, they started to model the traffic system on the blood system of the body so that streets came to be viewed as 'veins' and 'arteries'.[65] Movement was held to be essential for a healthy urban environment with air, water and waste having to be kept in constant motion. Circulation became an increasingly important concern for urban policy during the nineteenth century. The hygienist movement in particular focused on differentiating elements in urban space and ensuring their circulation. An incessant flow of water was necessary for washing the body of the city and removing waste matters, the brisker the better argued Edwin Chadwick in 1842;[66] and Benjamin Ward Richardson proposed the daily washing of the streets in his model town of Hygeia to clear away accumulations of dirt and mud.[67] When the English hygienist F. O. Ward proposed a system of urban sanitation in 1852 he based it on the principle of 'Circulation instead of stagnation', and in the process explicitly drew a connection with Harvey's theories.[68]

As Didier Gille comments, in such texts circulation is associated with health and sanitary welfare, while stagnation is connected with disease. But more than those links, which were a ritual expression of hygienism, he discusses how circulation became constructed as a principle in itself, opposed to stagnation that consequently became the ill to be addressed. Around this basic opposition, a range of other terms could gather including those imputing moral qualities. It was implied that the improvement of flows and the opening up of previously closed and 'stagnant' districts to the 'cleansing' power of circulation would enable their purification at a number of levels, not least raising their sense of moral purpose.[69] More generally, a formula emerged that shaped conceptions of urban space: 'whatever was part of circulation was regarded as healthy, progressive, constructive; all that was detached from circulation, on the other hand, appeared diseased, medieval, subversive, threatening.'[70] It is thus not surprising to find Howard, in an appendix on 'Water supply' in the original version of *To-Morrow*, discussing how the water networks could be used for cleansing, transportation and other functional and leisure uses as well as being harnessed to generate power (figure 2.8). He emphasised that it is 'most important that the water should be kept in a constant state of circulation, and submitted as much as possible to the action of air and light' so that it could contribute to the production of a space that is characterised by 'health, brightness, cleanliness, and beauty'.[71] As Gille suggests, continual circulation is here valued beyond the physical activities it enables: it is associated with what is progressive, good and beautiful. The invocation of physical beauty was common too in more general discussions of a new urban order by Howard and many other supporters of the garden city. As with those presenting ideal cities in the Renaissance, Howard visualised this in terms of circular and geometric designs, but he further implied that the beauty of the new cities was an expression of the ethical qualities of the reformed socio-spatial order. It was based on social and communal values.[72]

The idea of 'the gardening state' has a particular critical resonance in this context. Zygmunt Bauman uses the term when he discusses how the metaphor of the garden has been used to sort out 'weeds' in a given population to create a productive society. He quotes the example of the progressive writer H. G. Wells – a member, incidentally, of Howard's Garden City Association – who asserted the urgency of 'replacing disorder by order', and who argued that the socialist should be like a scientist in seeking 'to make a plan as one designs and lays out a garden, so that sweet and seemly things may grow, wide and beautiful vistas open, and weeds and foulness disappear'.[73] Such metaphors are not innocent, nor are they political neutral, for they have material effects. They have power in attempts to delegitimise an 'uncultivated' present state, to sort out matter 'out of place', to separate and classify and order.[74] It is interesting to consider in this light the associations between the conception of good planning articulated by Wells and the attempts by Howard and others associated with the garden city movement to project a well planned city, despite Howard's own opposition to bureaucratic control. This is evident especially around questions of the urban body and the threat of national

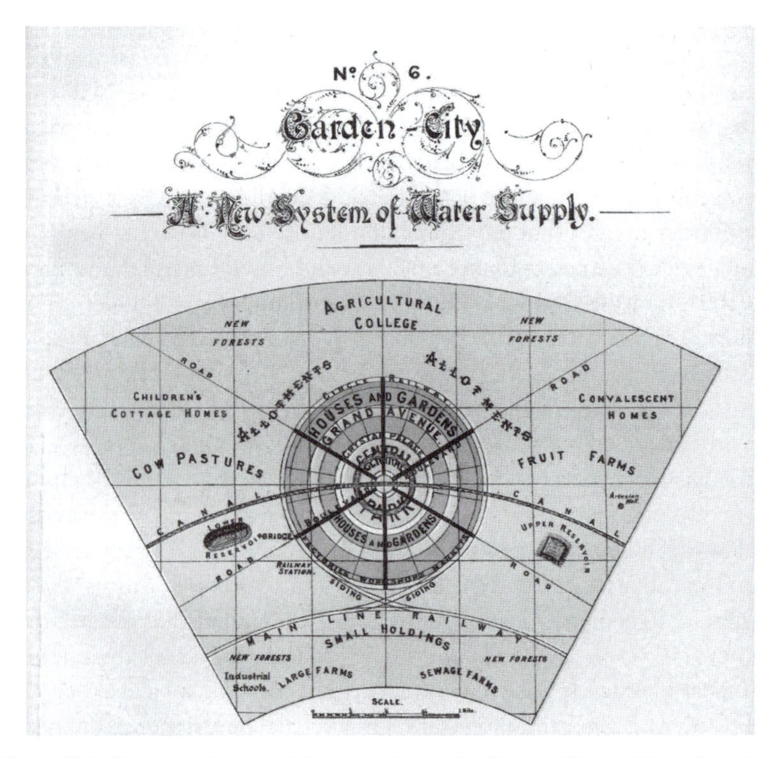

Figure 2.8 Ebenezer Howard, Water supply and the Garden City and Rural Belt. From *To-Morrow* (1898).

physical degeneration, where the potential of the garden city to counter the latter problem was widely seen as one of its strengths.

Early in his book Howard quoted Dean Farrar's fear about the consequences of city growth on the population, where he claimed that 'great cities tend more and more to become the graves of the physique of our race.'[75] Many people rallied to the cause of garden cities with similar fears in mind. The *British Medical Journal* lent its support to the garden city idea in 1903, around the time when the national debate about physical degeneration reached its height.[76] Mumford too later claimed that 'so organic, so deeply biotechnic, was [Howard's] whole conception that the sort of city he projected was precisely the kind whose population will be biologically capable of reproducing itself and psychologically disposed to do so.'[77] It was these qualities that further attracted advocates of eugenics to Howard's ideal city, as eugenic science became influential within reformist movements and social hygienism. The journal *The Race Builder* therefore promoted garden cities in 1906 as a means of 'purifying men's blood by bringing them back into invigorating touch with the soil and quickening their minds by social contact in a friendly atmosphere'.[78] Howard, it should be noted, did not discuss eugenics explicitly himself in either version of his book. However, the eugenic aim of classifying the population and excluding certain social groups from propagation found expression in his diagram of the Social City (figure 2.4). In the open space between the urban areas, in the midst of his vision of a group of 'Smokeless, slumless cities', separate asylums and homes are marked to house elements of the population that are shut out from the cities themselves: the 'insane', 'epileptics', 'inebriates', 'waifs', and the 'blind'.[79]

Securing space

By considering what kind of order Howard's garden city aimed to establish, it is therefore possible to render more visible other sides to its projected ideal, including those based around what is excluded, eliminated because it is deemed disorderly. These have much to tell about the desires and anxieties of the approach. Thinking critically about such visions is not to deny that they addressed deeply pressing urban problems on issues of public health, social inequalities and housing conditions. They certainly aimed to bring about radical improvements in those realms and that consciousness remains vital. But it does involve questioning the political implications of their conceptualisations of the city as well as whose interests were supposed to be restored in their reassertion of 'natural' order, balance and harmony. In relation to questions of gender, for example, despite Howard's experiments with co-operative housekeeping and challenges to traditional ideas about domestic work, patriarchal assumptions are apparent behind the garden city ideal. Critics have argued that garden cities upheld a notion of a nuclear family based around a working man with a dependent wife and children, with the Matrix group of architects and critics asserting that garden cities 'perfectly express the ideology of women as keepers of the domestic sphere in the "natural" setting, unsullied by the noise, grime and ugliness of the urban environment.'[80]

Elizabeth Wilson argues more generally that, despite its claims to bring together the best aspects of both town and country, the garden city ideology was essentially anti-urban and it proposed 'a sanitised utopia, with the obsessional, controlling perfectionism that characterised all utopias'. Further, she states that it was as a sanitised and controlling vision that the garden city became 'a dominant model of how all good cities should be'.[81] Jane Jacobs adopted a similar position in her famous attack on utopian urbanism in her book *The Death and Life of Great American Cities* in 1961. She lambasted Howard along with other utopian visionaries for their attempt to prescribe how spaces should be created according to abstract principles, which neglected the intricate reality of existing urban life especially on urban streets. 'As in all Utopias,' she commented in relation to Howard's proposals, 'the right to have plans of any significance belonged only to the planners in charge'. His ideal small, self-sufficient towns were in her view 'really very nice towns if you were docile and had no plans of your own and did not mind spending your life amongst others with no plans of their own'.[82] Both Wilson and Jacobs might seem too sweeping in their attacks on Howard given his suspicion of centralised planning and his stated concern with co-operation and with the provisionality of his plans. Yet if they appear to conflate his ideas with wider targets, they importantly draw attention to the will to sanitise and control that lies behind the garden city vision, and that connects it to a longer history of urban utopias.

Howard drew on a range of earlier utopian visions that included Thomas More's *Utopia*, as has been discussed. What my discussion also suggests is that Howard's garden city vision is framed by many of the same concerns of those traditional utopian schemes with spatial ordering, regulation and control. In the previous chapter it was noted how More emphasised a rigid spatial order and attendant systems of discipline and surveillance as a means of maintaining Utopia's harmonious moral order.

Throughout More's discussion of Utopia he emphasises containment and exclusion, with the city being surrounded by a turreted wall and a ditch, except where the river serves as a moat, and with the island itself having a fortified coast and a treacherous entrance to the bay. The island is presented as a unified and harmonious space, with boundaries and lines being essential for preventing contamination and ensuring its 'purity'. Internally its harmony is maintained through regulation and surveillance, with the inhabitants always being on display in a manner that demands respectable behaviour. The space is defined against an external world, which is consequently devalued as its 'other', allowing that outside space to be depicted as suitable for colonisation and exploitation. As Jennifer Burwell points out, Utopia as a self-contained body thus resolves its internal contradictions by converting them into contaminations, which are externalised and kept at bay through the strengthening of boundaries. She connects the procedure with traditional utopias more generally, with their focus on projecting an ideal spatial form.[83] It similarly underpins Howard's vision of harmonious and stable settlements, which have strict limits on size and secure boundaries to prevent contamination.

It should be stressed that, when considering Howard's vision as a utopia, there are openings to different and more libertarian perspectives. In saying this it is necessary to insist that, contra the comments by Wilson and Jacobs above, utopias need not always be about authoritarianism and controlling perfectionism. A more critical perspective on utopian form can be suggested by returning to William Morris, one of the utopian 'prophets' praised by Howard. Morris's utopian depiction of a transformed society in *News from Nowhere* should be understood in terms of his critical intent and alongside his other socialist writings. Morris once praised Thomas More's *Utopia* for its powerful critique of society and read it as an ideal vision that was informed by the author's protests against the brutalities of early 'Commercialism', his condemnation of the destruction of peasant life in England and his ability to see 'deeper into its root-causes than any other man of his own day'.[84] While this interpretation of the work is debatable, Morris's own utopia was likewise set against the iniquities of its time and in particular against alienating work and industrial capitalism. It was connected to a socialist movement seeking to respond to the conditions of nineteenth-century London. The great longing that pervades its pages, and the desire for a different kind of future that is embodied therein, give the text a richness and potential subversiveness of function that is more profound than some criticisms of its pastoralism suggest.

Morris was in fact wary about proposing utopian visions and stressed that his book, like all literary utopias, should not be taken literally as a blueprint or plan for the future. To do so could be potentially damaging politically for it was necessarily a partial view, he noted, and could not hope to answer everyone's wants and desires. As he put it the year before the publication of his utopia, an individual's 'vision of the future of society . . . must always be more or less personal'.[85] This did not entail the acceptance of total relativism but rather an acknowledgement that there was a real danger in believing that one vision could provide the ideal form for all aspects of society. Morris also recognised that authors constructed their ideas of utopia from within a particular context, from within the very conditions that they proposed to change. For that reason too they could not envisage a perfect future that was not at least in part shaped by the values of the less than perfect present that needs to be changed. This was apparent in his own utopia, in particular in its stance towards discussions of gender roles and the agency of women. Morris nevertheless believed that the creation of imaginary utopias could be valuable as a potential source of inspiration and hope, especially through the function of articulating and educating desire.[86]

In approaching the garden city as a utopia, it is necessary similarly to acknowledge its particularities and situatedness within discourses and debates at the time. It is also important to explore the ways in which it embodies desires transgressive to the role that it has played as a narrow conception of spatial planning. Particularly significant here are its elements of anti-authoritarianism drawn from anarchist perspectives and especially from the work of Kropotkin, whom Howard once described as 'the greatest democrat ever born to wealth and power'.[87] These perspectives inform Howard's interest in decentralisation and in co-operation as underpinning the attraction of the garden city. Returning to the anarchistic sides of the garden city vision as well as its emphasis on unity, love, co-operation, and unrealised possibilities of social development might in this manner work in a critical mode beyond its function in supporting existing capitalist and patriarchal social relations. It might encourage exploration of the potentialities of modern urbanism as well as what is missing from current perspectives in terms of living arrangements, land ownership, relationship to nature and so on through what Harvey refers to as 'imaginative spatial play'.[88] This is interesting for attending to sides of Howard's utopianism that have been downplayed in other depictions of his legacy for urban planning, and in potentially complicating contemporary appeals to Howard's ideas in debates about 'green' and 'sustainable' cities, or in versions of 'new urbanism'.[89] It can further critical perspectives on the uses to which his legacy has been put.

At the same time, however, the most enduring aspect of Howard's utopia has been as a mode of ordering and planning space. Howard's proposals have proved conducive as means of tying in the future through a pre-established spatial form, where planning procedures and protocols are the main means of realising that form. This is not only about the distortion of his ideas, I have argued, but also relates to the form of the utopianism itself. There are again parallels here with the literary utopias by Bellamy and Morris that Howard read so avidly, and that so inspired his early thinking. Despite Morris's more libertarian stance and objections to the repressive centrally planned utopia proposed by Bellamy, his own depictions of a transformed England in *News from Nowhere* as 'all trim and neat and pretty', and his vision of London as 'small and white and clean', are also fairly stifling. There is much about his depiction of a future society that is reactionary, representing what Wilson calls 'a retreat from modernity and a nostalgia for patriarchalism'.[90] Chris Ferns is less dismissive but similarly critical of the regressive impulses of Morris's utopia and its emphasis on 'a paradise regained'. In a thoughtful discussion of its ambiguities and contradictions, Ferns explores the sense of stasis that pervades Morris's vision, which he argues is based on a 'return to an old, organic harmony between humanity and nature', where time and struggle have come to an end in an 'epoch of rest'.[91] He suggests that this in part comes from its reliance on a narrative model that is associated with earlier utopian texts from the Renaissance, one that was shared with Bellamy, and one that was used primarily to articulate dreams of order. In his view, Morris's utopia can therefore, along with Bellamy's, be referred to as 'Looking Backward'.[92] In a similar manner, Howard's garden city remains within the frame of traditional urban utopias whose dreams of spatial order sought to fix space and time as a means of establishing harmony and 'natural' balance. Howard's attempt to restore urban settlement and community likewise depends upon forms of restriction, control and the creation of pure space. Howard's proposals have therefore typically taken on a closed cast and become associated less with social reform or free play than spatial order. In this way they have significant connections with the otherwise contrasting influential utopian visions of cities associated with the modern movement in the early twentieth century, as will be seen in the next chapter.

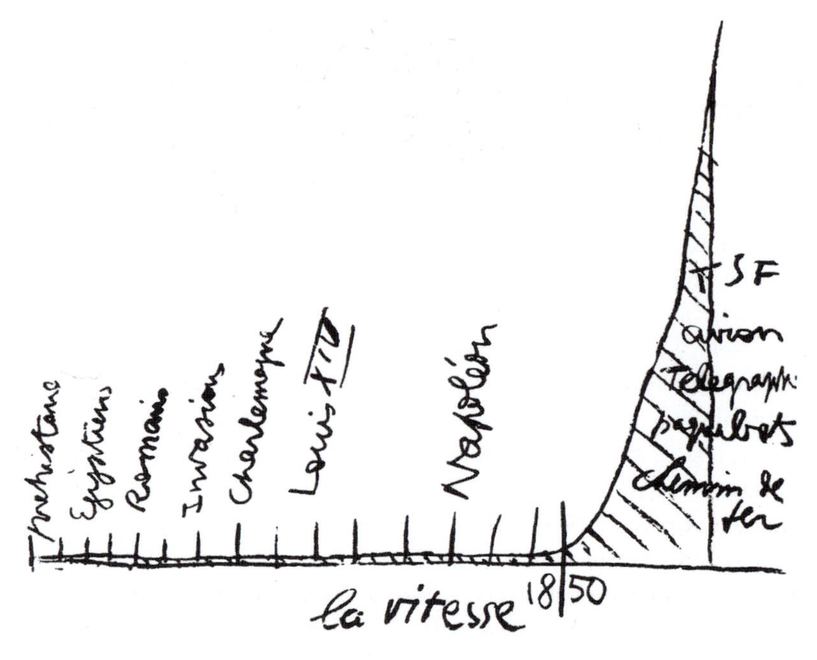

Figure 3.1 'Speed': sketch by Le Corbusier from a lecture in Buenos Aires, 14 October 1929. © FLC/ADAGP, Paris and DACS, London 2004. From the left: prehistory, Egyptians, Romans, invasions, Charlemagne, Louis XIV, Napoleon, railways, ocean liners, telegraph, aeroplane, TSF (radio) (as trans. in *Precisions*, 1987, p. 147).

CHAPTER 3

Modernist calls to order

Modern life demands, and is waiting for, a new kind of plan, both for the house and the city.

Le Corbusier[1]

Architecture and City planning!
We must equip the machine age!
We must use the results of modern technical triumphs to set man free.

Le Corbusier[2]

Time and space died yesterday

'We stand on the last promontory of the centuries!' declared Filippo Tommaso Marinetti in 'The founding and manifesto of futurism' in 1909. 'Why should we look back, when what we want is to break down the mysterious doors of the Impossible? Time and space died yesterday. We already live in the absolute, because we have created eternal, omnipresent speed.'[3] Few artists or architects embraced the feeling that life in the early twentieth century was accelerating and becoming more dynamic with as much vigour as the Italian futurists. Few, too, were as emphatic in their attempts to dramatise the sense of rupture and to draw clear lines between the past and the new era. They announced their enthusiasm for among other attractions speed, revolt, danger, roaring cars and war. Their emphasis on motion, mechanisation and an energising disorder was profoundly urban as they celebrated shipyards, railway stations, factories, bridges, locomotives and other city scenes. Their view of the city as the setting for a changed life runs through many early futurist manifestos and artworks, with the authors of the 'Manifesto of the futurist painters' pointing to the importance of 'the frenetic life of our great cities' and 'the exciting new psychology of night-life' for painting and a living art.[4] Architecture was understood as part of the group's cultural experimentation, being addressed in terms of explorations in painting, sound and movement. 'When we talk about architecture, people usually think of something static; this is wrong', noted Carlo Carrà. Instead, he referred to dynamic architectures such as those produced by the futurist musician, Pratella, or those found 'in the movement of colours of smoke from a chimney, and in metallic structures, when they are expressed in states of mind which are violent and chaotic'.[5]

A more substantive focus on architecture and urbanism within the movement came with the work of Antonio Sant'Elia and his visionary drawings for the *Città Nuova* of 1912–14. These depicted multi-levelled buildings, towers, power stations, and interlinked transport services as parts of an architecture that aimed to break with tradition and to draw inspiration from 'the elements of the utterly new mechanical world we have created'.[6] Dynamism and speed were key preoccupations. 'We have lost the sense of the monumental, of the heavy, of the static; we have enriched our sensibility by a taste for the light, for the practical, the ephemeral and the swift', stated Sant'Elia in the 'Manifesto of futurist architecture' in 1914. He created geometric forms and also urban planning schemes that combined architectural elements into a centralised entity. 'We must invent and rebuild the Futurist city like an immense and tumultuous shipyard, agile, mobile and dynamic in every detail,' he asserted, before adding that 'the Futurist house must be like a gigantic machine.'[7] A closing section of the manifesto added by Marinetti asserted the necessity for impermanence and transience in relation to architecture and for the constant renewal of the urban environment, with the command: 'EVERY GENERATION MUST BUILD ITS OWN CITY.'[8]

The futurists heralded the utopian urbanism that is my focus in this chapter. This approach contrasts with the tradition discussed in the previous chapter in a number of respects. It is inspired by new technologies and industrial processes and aligns itself with the means of modernisation. Rather than turn away from modern cities and their centralised power, it enters directly into their disruptions and energy and seeks to produce new spaces out of the maelstrom. It draws on a pro-urban tradition and takes its cues from the factory, the motor car, the steamship, the aeroplane – symbols of speed, energy and mechanical efficiency. It also makes much of breaking with the past, announcing the new, and looking to the present and future. More generally it embraces the transforming energy of the machine, seeing it as a symbol for the new age cutting across national boundaries and fields of interest, and as having the potential to enable liberation as well as to wreak devastation. The background to this utopianism again lies in rapid urbanisation in the late nineteenth and early twentieth centuries and attempts to confront urban problems. It is also bound up with a range of modernist experimentations and explorations of cultural forms, which engaged affirmatively with shifts in consciousness and transformations associated with experiences of modernity. Yet the utopianism addressed in this chapter is characterised less by the chaotic impulses of the Italian futurists, with their troubling politics at times imbued with fascistic and misogynistic tendencies, than by attempts to confront the upheavals of the city to construct a new rational landscape fit for a new human subject. Its main protagonists are from the field of modern architecture and what is often referred to broadly as the 'modern movement', and it is informed by new construction techniques and the use of materials such as glass, steel and reinforced concrete. It is above all marked by attempts to channel, direct and tame the powerful flows unleashed by a new era, to call to order what otherwise might overwhelm human life.

Crucial to the emergence of this strand of utopianism was the extraordinary flowering of modernist and avant-garde activity in early twentieth-century Europe. Referring to the 'furore of experimentation' in modernism that reached a period of great intensity around 1910–15 across a range of intellectual and social fields, David Harvey suggests: 'It is not hard to conclude that the whole world of representation and knowledge underwent a fundamental transformation during this short space of time.'[9] Harvey's discussion situates modernist thinking in its material context, exploring how it can be understood in dialectical relation to crises of modernity and to political-economic developments that challenged common understandings of space and time. Other commentators have similarly discussed the crucial nature of this period for modernist practice, even though they have often been more wary about identifying the origins of cultural change in this way. According to Henri Lefebvre, the years around 1905 were marked by a dramatic 'mutation' and a new emphasis on discontinuity as the shape of modernity and modernism began to emerge with greater clarity, ushering in a period of intense cultural activity.[10] In later accounts he repeatedly returns to the events of these years and refers to 1910 as a key date signifying a moment when 'a certain space was shattered': when apparently stable referents and codes gave way, including those tied to Euclidean and perspectival space that had been developed from the

Renaissance as embodied in philosophy and also in philosophy of the city, and when new ways of experiencing and thinking about space and time emerged.[11]

After the First World War an emphasis on newness and reconstruction, although of course one marked deeply by the devastation of that conflict, characterised a so-called 'heroic' phase of modernism. Attitudes towards art and politics in this period were also profoundly affected by the Russian Revolution. The dadaists railed against what they saw as the inherent barbarism of capitalist society, exposing the complicity of art in the inhumanities of war, and expressing their contempt for ideals of progress as they mocked contemporary values and new technological imagery. Others, however, advocated a constructive utopianism. At times this took fantastical forms, as in the dreams of glittering crystal towers and a glass-lined 'alpine architecture' by the German expressionist Bruno Taut. He proposed sparkling crystal structures that would be the basis for decentralised communities in the countryside and he praised glass for its connotations with purity and the cosmic. His ideas about returning to the land were influenced by Peter Kropotkin and Ebenezer Howard, and his interest in the latter's garden city was part of a wider mood at the time such that, according to one critic, Howard's plans were being taken up with 'fanatical intent' in certain circles in Berlin and Dresden.[12] The utopian architectures of many expressionists such as Taut were based in radical and often anarchistic politics, and their influence went beyond fantastical and impassioned dreams, informing for instance the early work of the school most prominently associated with the modern movement, the Bauhaus.

Founded in Weimar in April 1919 under the directorship of Walter Gropius, the Bauhaus initially drew on Arts and Crafts principles to address ideas about craft guilds and the potential for a unified system of workshops embracing all branches of craft and design. Marinetti had earlier dismissed the work of William Morris and John Ruskin, denouncing the latter's 'morbid dreams of primitive rustic life' and his 'hatred of the machine, of steam and electricity'.[13] Those working at the Bauhaus viewed them more positively, however, finding them along with the Deutsche Werkbund conducive for thinking about the social responsibility of architects and designers, and about methods for working and teaching. Under Gropius there was also a strong expressionist component in the early Bauhaus that found a clear voice in early proclamations for the school. In a text published in the same month as the school's opening, Gropius called for the collective creation of a 'new building of the future' that will 'one day rise towards the heavens from the hands of a million workers as the crystalline symbol of a new and coming faith'.[14] His vision was matched by a woodcut on the cover by Lyonel Feininger that showed a 'cathedral of the future', meant to represent the 'cathedral of socialism' towards which they were striving.

This position subsequently came under attack. 'We need "machines for living in" instead of cathedrals,' wrote Oskar Schlemmer, in a letter in June 1922, and he argued 'let us turn away, therefore, from the middle ages and from the concept of craftsmanship' and set sights on 'objective objects which serve specific purposes'. In his diary that same month he described the moves as: 'Turning one's back on utopia.'[15] With important changes in staff, along with a shift in Gropius's own work, the Bauhaus moved in a new direction. A lecture by Gropius in August 1923 entitled 'Art and technology: a new unity' provided a key slogan for the new sensibility, and marked what one critic describes as 'a public emergence of a man purged of medievalizing craft-romanticism and Utopian dreams'.[16] The Bauhaus henceforth sought a greater reconciliation between craft design and industrial enterprises, and a closer engagement with mechanisation and techniques of mass production; and in this way the school's thinking about space became tied to industrial practice and to research on architecture and urbanism, as it took up what Lefebvre identifies as its 'historic role' connected specifically to the production of space. 'It was thus no longer a question of introducing forms, functions or structures in isolation,' writes Lefebvre, 'but rather of mastering global space by bringing forms, functions and structures together in accordance with a unitary conception.'[17]

This chapter is concerned not with 'turning one's back on utopia', however, but rather with turning towards it in the spirit of reconstructing the modern city. My focus is on prominent forms of utopian urbanism envisioned by Le Corbusier during the 1920s and 1930s. In critically engaging with modernist calls to order through his projects, I do not want to imply that they can stand for the 'modern movement' as a whole. The term modern movement, if it is to have any value at all, must be recognised as heterogeneous with multiple geographies and histories, and with varied networks and connections. Different perspectives and stories are of course to be gained from addressing the groups mentioned above as well as many others, including the Russian avant-gardes, whose diverse experiments around the time of the Russian Revolution represent some of the most remarkable utopian interventions in modern architecture and urbanism. Intense arguments raged over different positions and approaches within the modern movement, especially in terms of their politics. Le Corbusier nonetheless occupies a critical position in histories of utopian urbanism, not least due to his immense influence on architecture, planning and the city. Peter Hall, for example, writing as an implacable critic rather than admirer, remarks that the practical effects of his urban schemes have been 'at least as immense as those of Howard's rival vision', and 'their impact on twentieth-century city planning has been almost incalculably great'.[18] Le Corbusier's utopian perspectives compare and contrast with those of Howard in many interesting ways. They also resonate with wider proposals by CIAM (Congrès Internationaux d'Architecture Moderne), which was founded in 1928 as a loose-knit but prominent platform for modern architecture, and in which he played an influential role. The issues raised by his utopianism therefore demand attention in terms of this influence and also in relation to wider debates about utopian urbanism.

Le Corbusier and the spirit of construction

Le Corbusier repeatedly attacked the 'disorder' of large cities, arguing that the task of transforming their spaces was urgent. Sharing Howard's opposition to the industrial city in its current form, he employed the kind of hyperbolic language that had been mobilised in justifying the need for garden cities. 'The city is crumbling; it cannot last much longer; its time is past', Le Corbusier wrote in 1925. He claimed that 'the Great City, which should be a phenomenon of power and energy, is to-day a menacing disaster, since it is no longer governed by the principles of geometry.'[19] In a medical language that he often deployed in various ways, he asserted that 'Paris is sick', that its 'heart and lungs are mortally sick', and that the '*centres of our towns are in a state of mortal sickness, their boundaries are gnawed at as though by vermin*'.[20] Along with many architects involved with CIAM, he sought to change urban space as a means of instituting wider social change. They claimed that it was through architecture and planning that current urban and social crises could be resolved. Properly conceived and organised, architecture could ensure the deliverance of society from forces threatening its existence, including those of political upheaval. When Le Corbusier therefore turned at the end of his book *Towards a New Architecture* of 1923 to his famous and much debated formulation 'Architecture or Revolution', he proposed the reply: 'Revolution can be avoided.'[21]

Le Corbusier was born as Charles-Édouard Jeanneret in 1887, in the

Swiss town of La Chaux-de-Fonds. His early studies of housing were influenced by the garden city movement but, as with many prominent early interpreters of Howard's ideas in France, he was more interested in the ideas of Raymond Unwin and Barry Parker and their designs for Hampstead than the underlying principles of social reform. Jeanneret settled in Paris in 1916 and adopted his new name four years later.[22] He remained based in that city for the rest of his life, wrestling continually with 'the problem of Paris' in a relationship described by one critic as an 'explosive mixture of love and animosity, of enthusiasm and revolt'.[23] Le Corbusier launched himself into debates about post-war reconstruction at a time when the housing crisis was especially acute in Paris. A contemporary report designated half of the population of the Département of the Seine badly housed, and the Municipal Council in 1919 identified seventeen *îlots insalubres* (unhealthy blocks) in which high tuberculosis mortality rates demanded urban renovation.[24] Le Corbusier argued that urban problems were rooted in a failure to come to terms with the demands of industry and the 'machine age'. He frequently drew attention to the consequences of industrialisation and mechanisation for urban life, to the speeding up of the world and increases in traffic, and to the ways in which this posed new dangers as well as opportunities. If the coming of the railway engine had set the world in motion, he stated, of particular significance for cities now was the automobile, replacing horses with horsepower units and multiplying the potential speed of travel many times over (figure 3.1). Yet the current structure of city centres was such that congestion, inefficiency and danger to pedestrians were inevitable. Having been built up over centuries according to what he termed 'the Pack-Donkey's Way', where houses were built gradually along winding tracks, European cities lacked 'arteries' and had only 'capillaries', meaning that any further growth in these cities threatened 'sickness and death'.[25]

It was not just a 'readjustment' that was now needed, Le Corbusier wrote, employing a word that he once used to describe the task at hand when faced with today's cities before quickly catching himself and dismissing it as 'too tame'. Instead, 'It is the possibility of a great adventure that lies before mankind: the building of a whole new world.'[26] His emphasis was neither on reverting to romanticised notions of the past – 'What is the good of regretting the Golden Age!'[27] – nor on turning away from existing cities. In contrast to Howard, Le Corbusier's early projects exalted the centralised power of great cities and aimed to increase the densities of city centres while at the same time pursuing what might seem to be the irreconcilable goals of decongesting the centre, improving traffic circulation and increasing the area of green and open spaces.[28] Having been initially ambivalent about the scientific management ideas of F. W. Taylor – he described Taylorism in a letter to his friend William Ritter in 1917 as 'the horrible and ineluctable life of tomorrow' – he came to see them as crucial in the post-war drive for social renewal, and he proposed an architecture and urbanism that would be in tune with mass production, having absorbed lessons about standardisation and industrialisation while also being imbued with the utopian promise of that 'great adventure'.[29]

In this manner Le Corbusier's formulation 'Architecture or Revolution' might appear not as a disparagement of revolution as such but as a claim about the significance of changing architecture and urban space as a radical act, as something that extends into the heart of social, cultural and political conditions. Fredric Jameson suggests that, 'Le Corbusier's seemingly antipolitical stance can be reread as an *enlargement* of the very conception of the political, and as having an anticipatory kinship with conceptions of "cultural revolution".'[30] This reading would align Le Corbusier with the belief of many CIAM architects that by breaking radically with present conditions at the level of both the cityscape and individual buildings it was possible to transform everyday life. For these architects, new architectural forms, conceived of as elements or 'cells' within a wider vision of change, could challenge perceptions of urban space and traditional patterns of behaviour, and 'conduct' new experiences and ways of living outwards into the surrounding space and social life through a process of 'radiation'. The utopianism of the procedure lay not only in the vision of spatial and social transformation that underpinned it but also in the proposed connections between architectural change and social change, whereby the latter was to be instituted by the former that contained within it a social programme.[31] But if Le Corbusier's formulation of 'Architecture or Revolution' might therefore be open to radical readings, it also implied new forms of control where the proper use of architecture and planning *circumvented* a radical change of social relations. Other critics therefore argue that he was in many respects conservative rather than avant-garde in the proper political sense of that term, in that he was concerned mainly with the position of the architect rather than sublating that privileged role in socially transformative activity.[32] The politics of Le Corbusier's urban schemes were certainly also a point of considerable contention among critics during the 1920s, as will shortly be discussed.

Spatial purification

Clean up, reorder, purify: the themes famously ran through Le Corbusier's writings and utopian urban projects from the early 1920s. They underpinned the rigidly zoned space he presented as 'A Contemporary City for Three Million People' in 1922. At the centre stood the transportation interchange and twenty-four skyscrapers that would house the 'seat of power' and the city's 'brains', while surrounding the towers were residential blocks for the elite (figure 3.2). Densities in the centre reached 1,200 people per acre but due to the use of the towers ninety-five per cent of the ground area was open space and parkland. A geometry, static order and classification of functions characterised the whole socio-spatial structure. When commentators portrayed it as a city of the future, Le Corbusier reiterated the *contemporary* part of the title and insisted that it had immediate relevance and that it was of its time. He exhibited the plans again in 1925 at the Pavillon de l'Esprit Nouveau for the Exposition Internationale des Arts Décoratifs et Industriels, where he also displayed his notorious 'Voisin Plan' for the radical reconstruction of Paris. This proposed to destroy around two square miles of the historic city centre north of the Seine and replace it with eighteen cruciform skyscrapers for the business and administrative elite, accompanied by luxury apartments and open space (figure 3.3). He depicted the project as 'a frontal attack on the most diseased quarters of the city' and as a 'means of regaining possession of the eternal centre', with the skyscrapers providing space for around 500,000–700,000 members of the business and administrative elite.[33] In sweeping clean the old 'junk' of the city that lay like a 'dry crust' on the soil, it would preserve only selected monuments and historical relics, with the claim that they would be enshrined in their new setting and the past would thereby be '*rescued*'.[34] Alongside the grand urban projects Le Corbusier presented a model of a 'residential cell' that demonstrated his belief in the connections between planning, architecture and the equipment of the home, being characterised by clean lines, smooth walls, unencumbered space, a clear use of colours, a flood of light, and the replacement of 'furniture' with mass produced domestic 'equipment'.

These early schemes were informed by Le Corbusier's involvement with purism, developed in collaboration with Amédée Ozenfant. Writing with Ozenfant, Le Corbusier argued for a rational and logical approach to culture based on universal laws and a new cultural synthesis. Their understanding of purism, presented in publications that included the journal

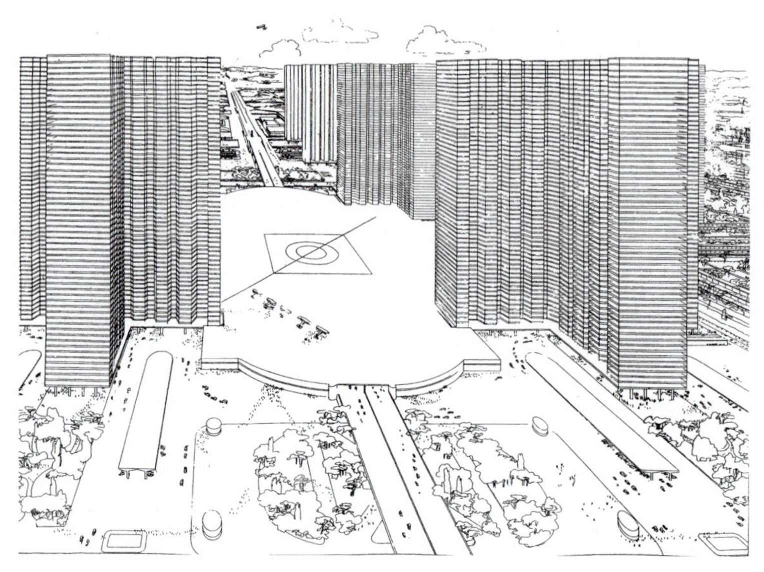

Figure 3.2 Le Corbusier, A Contemporary City for Three Million People, 1922. Line drawing of the central station and skyscrapers, with tracks for fast motor traffic passing under the aerodrome, FLC 30850. © FLC/ADAGP, Paris and DACS, London 2004.

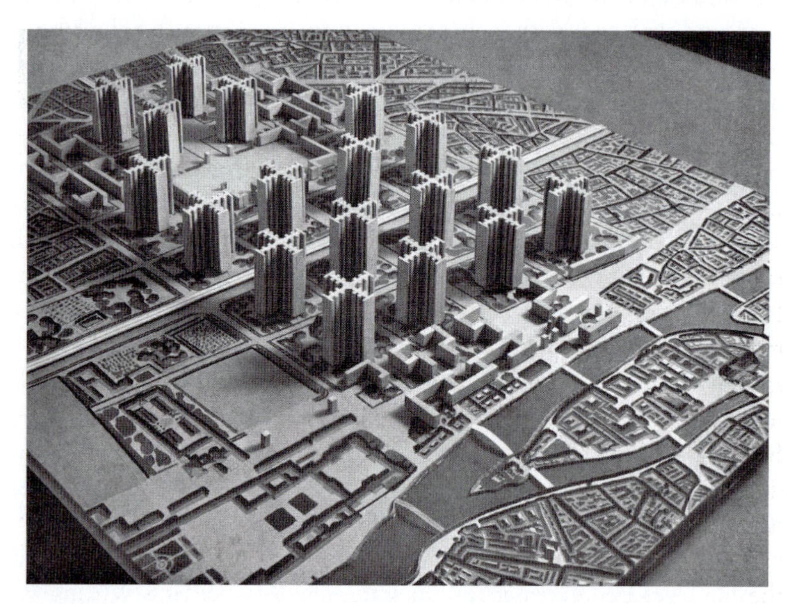

Figure 3.3 Le Corbusier, Voisin Plan for Paris, 1925. Scale model exhibited in the Pavillion de l'Esprit Nouveau. © FLC/ADAGP, Paris and DACS, London 2004. 'In the name of the beauty of Paris, you say "No!" In the name of the beauty of Paris I maintain, "Yes!"' (Le Corbusier, *The Radiant City*, p. 207).

l'Esprit Nouveau that they launched with Paul Dermée in 1920, are part of what the critic Kenneth Silver terms a 'straightening up after the Great War' at a time when there was wider concern gathering pace in France for a *rappel à l'ordre*.[35] The artist was seen as a *constructeur* within a wider social and political discourse of restorative action, bringing together painting, sculpture and architecture with the last of these fields providing an over-arching sense of logic and order. The purist images produced by Le Corbusier and Ozenfant are a testament to their concern with clarity and visually defined geometric form, and contrast strongly with cubist experiments. In place of the latter's interest in 'indeterminacy, simultaneity, the mutability of time and space', notes Silver, the purists provided a sense of stability and durability, producing 'images with a freshly starched spiritual and moral rectitude, showing the certainty and direction of "the great collective current"'.[36] Le Corbusier and Ozenfant associated the phrase 'the great collective current' with the Great War, which they even gave certain 'healthy' connotations for French life in referring to it as the Great Test (*la Grande Épreuve*).[37]

In their essay on 'Purism' in 1920, Le Corbusier and Ozenfant criticised cubism's depiction of objects for over-emphasising accidental aspects and even creating 'arbitrary and fantastic forms'. Instead, they argued for 'the necessity of a reform, the necessity of a logical choice of themes, and the necessity of their association not by deformation, but by *formation*'.[38] They distanced themselves in particular from those who revelled in the flux and speed of modernity such as the futurists. In an essay on 'The right angle', which contains one of Le Corbusier's few direct references to the futurists, Le Corbusier and Ozenfant contrasted the orthogonal as a sign of the permanent, and as a key component of their understanding of the structural law of things, to the oblique as a sign of the unstable, variable and passing moment, and as a guiding motif of futurism and expressionism. 'Futurism's race toward the fugitive moment would shipwreck the crew in the nothingness of the *movement*,' they asserted. 'Impressionism, Futurism, and Expressionism are all forms of expression that avoid the fact of creation – durable, humane, and compatible with plastic work.'[39] Sant'Elia had earlier written of the futurist house as a 'gigantic machine', but he meant by this something different from Le Corbusier's infamous conception of the house as a 'machine for living'. Sant'Elia used the phrase to evoke notions of speed, movement, noise, power, excitement and an intense sensory experience, whereas Le Corbusier's endorsement of the machine was part of an orderly conception of architecture and urbanism.[40] For the latter, the machine was a symbol of a geometric, efficient, precise, powerful and reassuringly dependable creation that, in its perfection, also embodied an order of beauty.

The 'purity' of the vision proposed by Le Corbusier and Ozenfant in their early texts spoke of the need to restore 'a unified scopic regime', to use Martin Jay's term, one that was in keeping with their vision of a new disciplined society that they believed should lead the country out of the war-torn era.[41] In France more generally after the First World War the *rappel à l'ordre* had a strong classicising and moralising tone. As Romy Golan emphasises, much of it was imbued with a nostalgic regionalist strain that put the emphasis on a *re*turn to order, on the recovery of a sense of identity closely connected to the land in which images of the peasant and the countryside played a prominent role.[42] But as Golan further points out, while it was this regionalism that held the commanding positions in the French section of the Exposition des Arts Décoratifs et Industriels Modernes in 1925, it was a relatively marginalised contribution by Le Corbusier and Ozenfant in the form of their Pavillon de l'Esprit Nouveau that set out the essential components of Le Corbusier's utopian vision of the city in that decade and that produced a manifesto that was a critical event in the history of modernist urbanism.

Water-tight formulae

A key moment illuminating Le Corbusier's conception of urban ordering as well as the desires and anxieties that lay behind it took place in the streets of Paris. In the foreword to *The City of Tomorrow* of 1925, Le Corbusier recalls taking a walk on the Champs Élysées one autumn evening shortly after he wrote his text and being struck by the fury of the traffic around him and by the threat of being 'a possible sacrifice to death in the shape of innumerable motors'. (He returns to the threat in a more detached way in a later chapter, where he refers to newspaper reports and cartoons about traffic problems and accidents in Paris.) The scene contrasts with the glee with which Marinetti reports in his 'The founding and manifesto of futurism' on speeding in his car and flirting with death, and on crashing in a ditch to emerge dirty, torn but joyful. Having established the sense of danger, however, there is a sudden switch in the tone of Le Corbusier's account. He now immerses himself in the scene and celebrates the forces around him:

Motors in all directions, going at all speeds. I was overwhelmed, an enthusiastic rapture filled me . . . the rapture of power. The simple and ingenuous pleasure of being in the centre of so much power, so much speed. We are part of it. We are part of that race whose dawn is just awakening.[43]

The leap in this passage, with its move from the personal experience of 'I' to an immersion in a collective 'we', and with its dramatic embrace of the power of a new society ('We have confidence . . . We believe in it'), has been brilliantly analysed by Marshall Berman. For Berman, Le Corbusier's account in essence signifies a shift from the person in the street, a figure familiar from the poetry of Charles Baudelaire and other modern writers and artists, to an incorporation into the power of the new age by becoming the person in the motor car. The scene thus presages a view that will inform the paradigms of twentieth-century modernist urban planning: the perspective of the highway, and of attempts to transform the old corridor street with all its interminglings and encounters into a clearly segmented zone that Le Corbusier calls '*a machine for traffic, an apparatus for its circulation*'. From that magic moment on the Champs Élysées, writes Berman, 'a vision of a new world is born: a fully integrated world of high-rise towers surrounded by vast expanses of grass and open space – "the tower in the park" – linked by aerial superhighways, serviced by subterranean garages and shopping arcades.'[44]

It is also revealing, though, to consider how Le Corbusier characterises the power of that Parisian scene in the lines that immediately follow those quoted by Berman. He describes it as 'a torrent swollen by storms', 'a destructive fury'. It is 'a kind of cataclysm' and 'something utterly abnormal', he states, and its force threatens to carry all before it: 'The torrent can no longer keep to its bed.' It is in the light of the dangers posed by this power, which Le Corbusier associates with the impact of industrialisation, that he dismisses piecemeal strategies and remedies for dealing with the city. He likens them to 'improvised barrages', put up in haste and terror by inhabitants of villages attempting 'to dam a torrent swollen by storm, which is already carrying destruction in its menacing swirl'.[45] Le Corbusier's reaction helps to explain his decision to leave aside small-scale initiatives and to identify so completely with the forces described, to seek a voice within the movement and traffic. But it also underlines his concern to establish order. Le Corbusier's continual emphasis on setting out a plan, a design and a means of regulation may be understood against the background of this desire for liberated power and energy but also this fear of a terrible flood. It is not surprising, therefore, to find him later extolling the importance of constructing '*a theoretically water-tight formula*' for the fundamental principles of urban planning.[46] Only resolute principles immune to leakage can provide a means of coming to terms with the opportunities of the present as well as the threats of the 'chaos', 'magma', 'torrents', 'sweeping invasion', 'confusion', 'submersion', and the like that he returns to repeatedly in the book. Elsewhere, he locates the need for ordering energies in terms of saving people from the destruction brought about by the first wave or 'floodtide' of the machine age. On the one hand, there is again the thrill of immersion as he refers to 'the propulsive force of the age we are living in' and claims: 'If only we allow ourselves to be carried away by that force we shall be strong; otherwise we shall moulder away, we shall rot.' But on the other hand, there is also the move to establish principles and order. 'We must control the machine age,' he argues; 'place man above the machine; restore order by means of city planning and architecture; use that order to re-establish the play of harmonious energies released by *labours of love*: happiness!'[47]

What is so feared in these passages is the transgression of boundaries, the failure of things to keep to their place, the flow that bursts its banks and sweeps away everything before it. But there is also the excitement at the idea of immersion, of being part of the torrent that seems to presage a new future. To find a way of opening up urban spaces to transformative flows and speed, and thus of guarding against rot, as well as a means of channelling the currents, and thus of ensuring against confusion and loss of control – these are presented as key tasks for the city planner. In seeking to establish a 'water-tight formula', Le Corbusier's early writings and plans make frequent appeals to spatial laws that are meant to be beyond the contingencies of current conditions. Of particular importance is geometry. Zygmunt Bauman has described geometry as 'the archetype of modern mind', with the grid as 'its ruling trope', and many modernist artists of the early twentieth century believed that geometric forms embodied rational as well as ethical values.[48] Le Corbusier discussed the production of 'pure geometry' in terms of abstraction and distancing from the body, suggesting that the geometry of human creations such as a violin and chair that have close contact with the body are less pure than creations further removed, such as a town. For him the ordered geometric landscape was an object of desire and he presented it as a source of security and happiness. The more exact the order of the landscape is, he suggested, the more happy and secure will the human subject feel.

Part of the attraction of geometry lay in its purity: it was meant to be a mark of a 'civilised' society that had progressed away from the sensuous tactility of ornate decoration and towards an order of perception based more on an intellectual and visual appraisal of the world, with an accent on the abstraction of form and harmony of proportion. It was part of a sensibility that rejected superfluities and was concerned with clearing and cleansing to attain an 'essential' that was assessed by a steady gaze. The attraction of geometric order further lay in its fixity, with 'the eternal forms of pure geometry' seeming to provide a reassuringly stable presence within a context not only of a chaotic nature but also of social change and speed.[49] Despite the importance Le Corbusier ascribed to speed – he viewed it as 'a brutal necessity', and asserted that 'the city which can achieve speed will achieve success'[50] – there was also a defensiveness about his assertion of geometric order. Indeed, one critic suggests that the geometric forms that Le Corbusier posits as the origin of building were connected with an attempt to endow buildings with 'that aura of reliability that seems to protect against time', and even with finding 'a refuge from the terror of time';[51] another claims that, 'Out of his fears for the destruction of civilisation, Le Corbusier fashioned an image of the modern city which would have the immutable stability of a Renaissance church.'[52]

If the institution of geometry and spatial order was associated with security and purpose, however, then conversely the lack of geometric order was perceived as threatening, as causing actions to become incoherent and directionless. The great city was now a menacing disaster, Le Corbusier wrote, *because* it was no longer governed by geometric principles. Anxiety, even horror resulted from their absence. This was apparent in Le Corbusier's reactions on viewing parts of Paris from the air. Referring to an aerial photograph in *The City of Tomorrow* that looked down vertically on a district of the city made up of buildings averaging seven stories high, he demanded: 'Is this a picture of the seventh circle of Dante's Inferno?' He added: 'Alas no! It shows the terrible conditions under which hundreds of thousands of people have to live.' He wrote of the shock when faced with such a bird's-eye view, of how it was like 'a blow between the eyes'. On the facing page he reproduced a different aerial view showing the Champs Élysées district with the straight lines of its boulevards. But despite describing this as 'incomparably superior', Le Corbusier still complained that it was the result of 'drift and opportunism' and a 'dreadful' and 'shocking' sight, and he held up the pair of images as 'denunciatory photographic documents'.[53]

Le Corbusier's critique depended upon his ability to extract himself from the city's grasp, to use the view provided by aeroplane to distance its confusion and 'reveal' its lack of order. The significance of the bird's-eye view in inaugurating a distinctly modern consciousness of space was something that he frequently referred to as he portrayed high flight as a tool of enlightenment. (Late in his life he remarked, 'For years I have been using an eye that is 30,000 feet above the ground!')[54] His vision of geometric order, presented during the 1920s in the proposals for the Contemporary City and the Voisin Plan, was usually rendered through line drawings. These were composed from a position outside the city, typically in plan form or in perspective from a position on high, again as if in an aeroplane swooping above the towers. Their juxtapositions with photographs from existing cities were designed to highlight the order of his plans in opposition to the disorder of the present, and to spark a change of perception whereby the city might be seen anew. Le Corbusier thus placed his 'solution' of the Voisin Plan over part of the first aerial photograph of Paris to demonstrate the districts to be demolished and those to be constructed in their place (figure 3.4). Dwelling on the contrast, he wrote: 'instead of a flattened-out and jumbled city such as *the airplane reveals to us for the first time*, terrifying in its confusion . . . our city rises vertical to the sky, open to light and air, clear and radiant and sparkling.'[55] He also employed juxtapositions of plans to contrast the order of his own ideal geometric schemes with present city layouts. The antagonistic relationship established in the graphics, where the geometric space demarcated the area to be cleared for the new construction to proceed, was demonstrative of the will to negate that accompanied Le Corbusier's ideal of creation: its order was projected onto the supposed jumble of the old city with the promise of sweeping away the differences accumulated in space to enact a new beginning in time.[56]

A related source of anxiety was rooted in the opaque, shadowy character of the urban spaces that he sought to rise above. Michel Foucault once noted how a fear haunted the late eighteenth century, 'the fear of darkened spaces, of the pall of gloom which prevents the full visibility of things, men and truths'.[57] The generalisation of attempts to institute a Benthamite panopticism discussed by Foucault might seem to reach an apogée in Corbusian schemes. Le Corbusier reacted especially violently against what he called in his article 'The street' of 1929 the 'murky canyons' of traditional corridor streets, describing feelings of being 'plunged in eternal twilight' where the 'sky is a remote hope far, far above'.

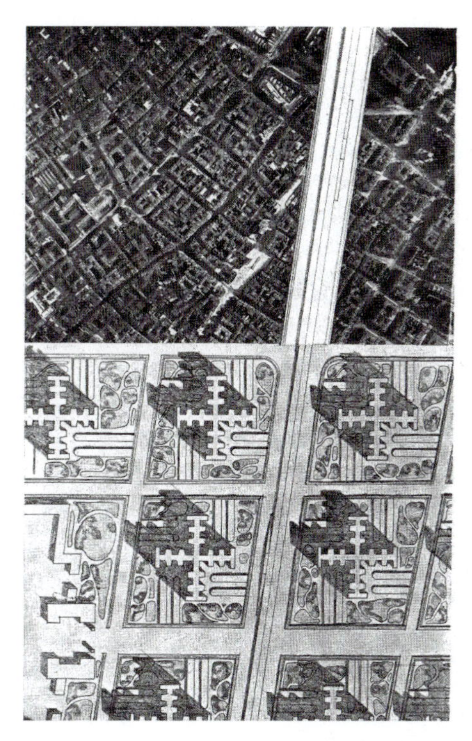

Figure 3.4 Le Corbusier, aerial photograph of Paris with drawing of the Voisin Plan, 1925. The 'solution' shows the districts to be demolished and those to be constructed in their place, with images reproduced to the same scale. © FLC/ADAGP, Paris and DACS, London 2004.

Despite recognising the street's appeal as a site of Balzacian drama and spectacle, he argued that, with its narrowness, gloom and the crowds pullulating along its length, 'when all is said and done we have to admit it disgusts us.' It was not only the murk that appalled him, but also the mingle-mangle of the street, the muddle of bodies and the threat of touching of strangers (figure 3.5). The components of his 'up-to-date' street were depicted as a glittering scene in contrast to the present. In lyrical mode he referred to standing on the lawns under the shade of trees and looking up 'through the charmingly filigreed arabesques of branches out into the sky', towards the city's 'widely-spaced crystal towers', with its 'translucent prisms that seem to float in the air'.[58] He later wrote: 'The city of light that will dispel the miasmas of anxiety now darkening our lives, that will succeed the twilight of despair we live in at the present, exists on paper. We are only waiting for a "*yes*" from a government with the will and determination to see it through!'[59]

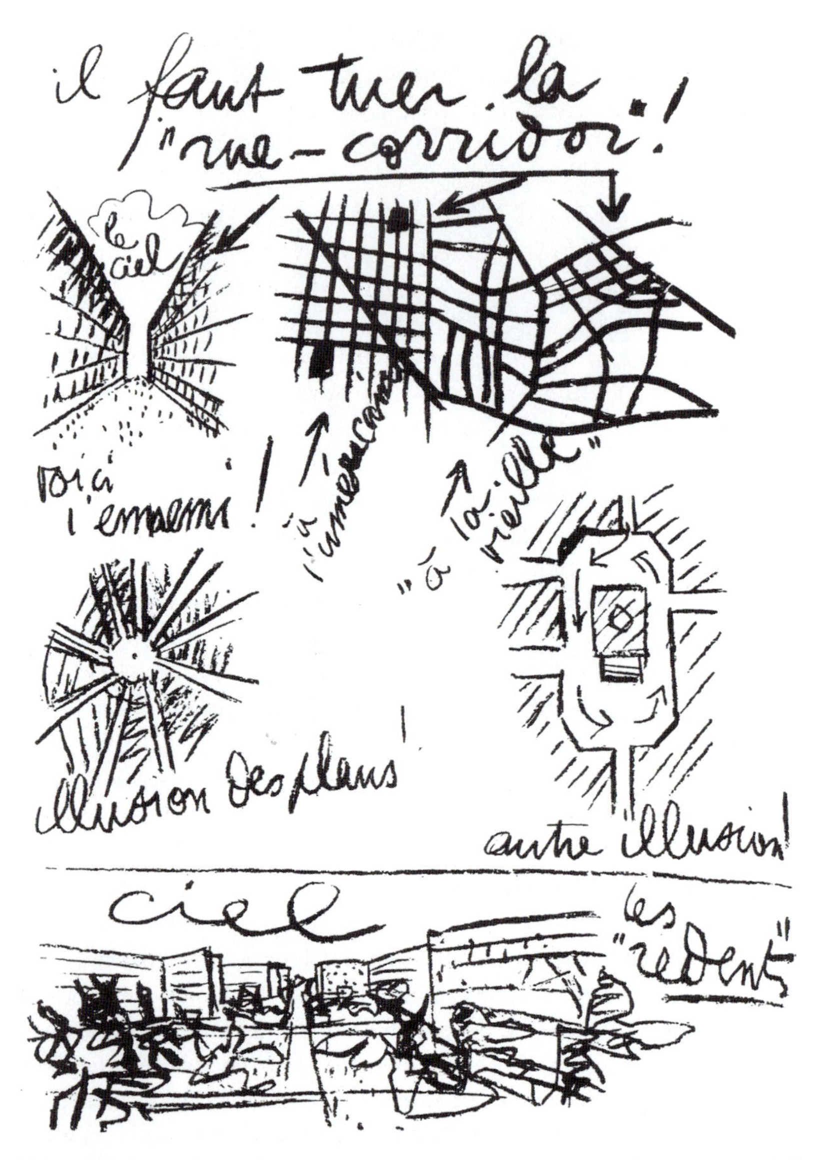

Figure 3.5 Sketch by Le Corbusier for a lecture in Buenos Aires, 18 October 1929. © FLC/ADAGP, Paris and DACS, London 2004.

From the top:
the 'corridor street' must be destroyed!
the sky / here is the enemy/ American style / 'old-fashioned'
the illusion of plans! another illusion!
sky / zigzag buildings

(as trans. in *Precisions*, 1987, p. 171)

Such visions of translucent constructions and spaces bathed in light point towards the theme of transparency that became a standard principle of modernist architecture in the early twentieth century. Light and openness were here part of a therapeutic modernism, one that took up the language of hygiene and, as Anthony Vidler puts it, looked towards a space that would be cleansed of all mental disturbance.[60] The demand for light can be related back to earlier fears about the opaqueness of the industrial city especially among reformers of the mid-nineteenth century, and to the concerns that middle-class commentators and investigators had about spaces that were inaccessible to their gaze. A paucity of sunlight and ventilation had been connected with ill-health and disease, especially since the establishment of the miasmic theory of contagion. But as Felix Driver has discussed, such conditions were also connected with *moral* disease and disorder, hence the overwhelming obsession among commentators of the time, often characterised by a mix of fear and fascination, with 'hidden recesses, narrow turnings, dark alleys and shadowy corners'.[61] Le Corbusier's fears about the gloom were themselves intertwined with fascination, and it is important to attend not simply to the application of light in his schemes but to the ways in which the interest in illumination operates alongside his concern with darkness and obscurity. It is the associations between transparency and obscurity that demand attention, as Vidler points out elsewhere in an interesting discussion of 'dark space' in relation to the utopian architect Etienne-Louis Boullée. In Vidler's view the radiant spaces of modernism, including Le Corbusier's urban plans for a city of light, 'should be seen as calculated not on the final triumph of light over dark but precisely on the insistent presence of the one in the other'.[62]

The importance of visualisation in the construction of a 'proper space' within these utopian schemes is nonetheless apparent, as exemplified in Le Corbusier's desire for an aerial view. Michel de Certeau provides an influential critical discussion of the 'atopia-utopia of optical knowledge' and its aims of 'surmounting and articulating the contradictions arising from urban agglomeration'.[63] Acknowledging the potential delights of the view from on high, he discusses how it lifts one's body above the clasp of the streets, above the rumble of differences and the mass of the crowds of the kind that Le Corbusier reacted so strongly against. From there one is like an 'Icarus flying above these waters', de Certeau states, who 'can ignore the devices of Daedalus in mobile and endless labyrinths far below'. He suggests that a common scopic drive lies behind many attempts to set the city at a distance and attain a panoramic view. But rather than associate this perspective with a superior way of knowing, he argues that it transfigures the subject into a voyeur while setting up the city itself as an inert object or text. The force of this becomes apparent when he remarks that the 'voyeur-god', created by the fiction of the panorama-city, 'knows only cadavers'.[64] With this image the visual-based knowledge of surveyors and cartographers is associated with death; and from this, as Christopher Prendergast comments, 'it would seem plausible to construe the view from on high as animated as much by an impulse to annihilate as by a will to administer.'[65]

Urban surgery

Given the contentiousness of Le Corbusier's urban vision outlined in his plans of the 1920s, it unsurprisingly came under fierce criticism. Le Corbusier's Contemporary City was attacked by a number of critics as the product of leftist ideology and a thinly veiled communism. But it was also criticised in communist newspapers in France as an agent of capitalism and as counter-revolutionary, for failing to address questions about the identity of those who would control the centralised means of administration. Answering critics at the end of *The City of Tomorrow*, Le Corbusier portrayed his interests as being technical rather than political. He argued that it was sufficient to describe his buildings as 'Administrative Services' and 'Public Services'.[66] In putting forward these claims he continued a line of utopian thought associated especially with Henri de Saint-Simon, who had envisaged a new society based on industrial principles and administrated by an elite strata of *industriels*. Like Ebenezer Howard, Le Corbusier further depoliticised his procedures through his use of organic and biological metaphors. He argued that the city's body should be investigated scientifically followed by the use of 'physic' or 'surgery'. He believed that the survival of cities had long depended upon the actions of 'surgeons who operate constantly', and he referred with admiration to Haussmann's reconstruction of Paris as involving 'the most startling operations' and 'surgical experiments' and as giving the city 'a powerful dose of medicine'.[67] To emphasise the need for drastic procedures he likened present piecemeal demolition and reconstruction in parts of central Paris to 'the nodes of a cancer which have been allowed to settle around the heart of the city, and will end by stifling it'.[68] As Susan Sontag has pointed out, the use of the metaphor of cancer in political discourse commonly acts as 'an incitement to violence' and 'encourages fatalism and justifies "severe" measures'.[69] Indeed, Le Corbusier followed the point by arguing that physic or medical solutions were now unable to resolve fundamental problems at the city's centre and instead radical surgery must be applied.[70]

Through this approach Le Corbusier presented urban plans as a means of curing the city and restoring its health. Only the judicious hand of the planner would resolve problems, so it was claimed, with the planner appearing as a 'doctor of space'. Appeals to natural principles and laws legitimised new utopian conceptions of the city. As discussed in the previous chapter, the use of such language involves a series of mystifications. It diverts attention from the critical analysis of space in favour of more reactionary schemes based on the damaging idea that, in the words of Lefebvre, 'the modern city is a product not of the capitalist or neocapitalist system but rather of some putative "sickness" of society.'[71] Le Corbusier nevertheless continued to assert the urgency of this surgery through the 1930s, when he was at times almost breathless in his haste to alert readers: '*PARIS IS IN DANGER!*' Having declared his love for the city and its vitality, he turns to his fear that it is 'racked with disease' and yet there is: 'No Colbert to prescribe for it, no surgeon to operate. Not even a diagnosis!'[72] Like Howard he saw himself as proposing 'proper' remedies and thus as being in contrast to those urban practitioners who were later dismissed by Lewis Mumford for applying 'poultices, salves, advertising incantations, public relations magic, and quack mechanical remedies until the patient dies before their own failing eyes'.[73] Writing to Le Corbusier in 1936, the Soviet architect Mosei Ginzberg thus declared: 'You are the finest of the surgeons of the modern city, you want to cure it of its ills whatever the cost.' However, he identified Le Corbusier as essentially wanting to preserve the existing social order. Behind Le Corbusier's intent to cure the city was the desire to 'keep it the same as capitalism made it'. Ginzberg contrasted this with architects in the Soviet Union, arguing that the latters' critical diagnoses of the modern city led them to want to complete its destruction and build a new kind of socialist settlement.[74]

To tackle the sickness of cities and promote a healthy alternative, Le Corbusier shared Howard's concern with circulation. This was especially from the late 1920s when he ventured the 'outrageous fundamental proposition: *architecture is circulation*'.[75] The significance Le Corbusier attached to this theme relates to its longer historical importance in conceptions of urbanism and to the way that modernists took further earlier arguments about movement and circulation as underpinning a healthy urban environment. The importance given to increasing water usuage and to plumbers in the civilising of cities – Adolf Loos around the turn of the century even called the plumber 'the first artisan of the state' and 'the first billeting officer of culture', who was 'the pioneer of cleanliness'[76] – was connected with changing understandings and medical discourses of the city. It related to the supersession of older models of circulation associated with the 'organic city' towards models based on 'bacteriological' terms, as medical discourses informed concerns with improving health through technological developments and networks.[77] Le Corbusier therefore followed other planners in valorising movement as a means of preventing stagnation and even as a principle of life. He contended: 'Movement is the law of our existence: nothing ever stands still, for if it does it begins to go backwards and is destroyed, and this is the very definition of life.'[78] A key step for him lay in differentiating matters and removing obstacles, as he believed that traffic should be classified according to type, function and speed, with intermixed streets being replaced by machines of circulation arranged in distinct channels. Le Corbusier viewed uncontrolled flows as posing a danger not only to the individual body but also to the body of the city. A graphic in *The Radiant City* illustrating 'The death of the street' played on the medical connotations of circulation as well as its meaning as 'traffic' to register the sense of threat (figure 3.6).

Le Corbusier argued in response that it was necessary to establish 'the correct bed for that new fluid of the modern era: the automobile'.[79] He sought to organise fluidity by drawing upon the 'laws of water', suggesting that traffic was like a river, beholden to the same laws, and that automobiles were like boats that must have ports or harbours for docking. The association of water with cleansing further distinguished these routes from the old street, which he believed 'poisoned' houses bordering it.[80] Le Corbusier also likened plans for traffic networks to anatomical drawings and sketches in biology textbooks, and he developed his biological conceptions through a series of schemes that culminated in his complex traffic system termed the '7 Vs' (*voies de circulation*). This was employed at Chandigarh in his plans for the capital of the State of Punjab in India from 1951, where he asserted that the scheme acted in the city plan 'as the blood-system, the lymph system and the respiratory system act in biology. In biology these systems are quite rational, they are different from each other, there is no confusion between them, yet they are in harmony.'[81] As with Howard, Le Corbusier's overriding concern in his vision of a healthily circulating space with biologically sound cells was a desire for wholeness, harmony and the regeneration of the body, both of the city and of

This crossroad represents a fresh development in the history of mankind: death on tap; or at least a permanent threat of it.

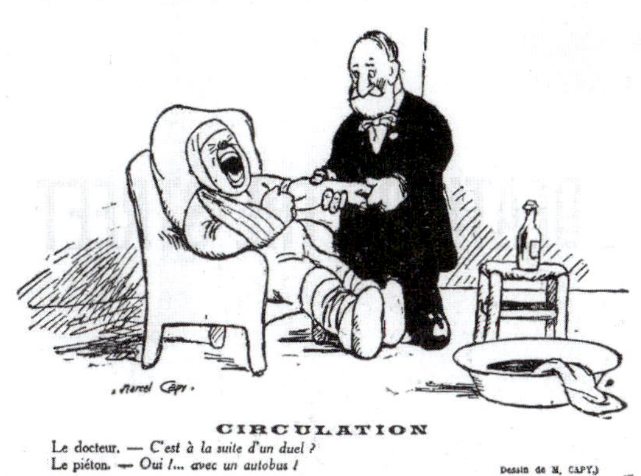

CIRCULATION
Le docteur. — C'est à la suite d'un duel ?
Le piéton. — Oui !... avec un autobus !
Dessin de M. CAPY.

Thank you, Capy!

TRAFFIC (CARTOON BY M. CAPY)
Doctor: *Were you involved in a duel?*
Pedestrian: *Yes, with a bus!*

Figure 3.6 The problem of circulation: photographic collage from Le Corbusier, *The Radiant City* (1935). © FLC/ADAGP, Paris and DACS, London 2004.

the human subject. If the human subject had been disturbed by the first machine age, then the second rationally planned era would see a rebirth, Le Corbusier claimed, with '*the formation of a serene soul in a healthy body*'.[82]

Political authority and the plan

Le Corbusier's argument that he was a modern technician or doctor and therefore above political concerns was nevertheless undermined by the very construction of his texts. In *The City of Tomorrow* this occurs most strikingly through the painting on the final page that shows Louis XIV commanding the building of L'Hôtel Royal des Invalides with a plan held out before him (figure 3.7). Below this Le Corbusier wrote 'Homage to a great town planner', and noted: 'This despot conceived immense projects and realised them. Over all the country his noble works still fill us with admiration. He was capable of saying, "We wish it," or "Such is our pleasure".'[83] The reproduction of the painting is not 'about' architecture or planning as those fields are presented in the preceding pages but rather, as Dennis Crow comments, it is 'an allegory on the use of political authority to "get things done"'. It is 'a rhetorical exercise in honouring this authority', as well as an allegory of the planning process that depends upon the exercise of political authority to organise such things as finance, labour and control over land.[84] Crow's discussion is part of a wider consideration of the textual strategies in the book, in which he suggests that the figures of the text constitute a 'revelatory collage' – a term suggested by Gayatri Spivak – 'which is folded into the argument, but exceeds it at every turn'.[85] Le Corbusier's own recognition that the reproduction of the painting might be misunderstood is shown by a note in the original French edition of the book, stating that the image should not be taken as indicative of support for the right-wing monarchist party, Action-Française.

Le Corbusier's work underwent a period of reassessment around 1929–30. Whether or not he made a decisive break with the purist-machinist vision during the first half of the following decade as some critics have suggested,[86] a more organic and lyrical quality became apparent, including in his building projects, which engaged more closely with specific sites and began to employ 'primitive' and exposed materials, and in his paintings that incorporated biomorphic forms and human figures. In 1930 he wrote of turning away from 'the architectural revolution', in the belief that this had now been achieved, and focusing instead on the 'hour of *Great Works*' that he saw beckoning.[87] He devoted considerable energy

Figure 3.7 'Homage to a great town planner': painting of Louis XIV commanding the construction of the Hôtel des Invalides. From Le Corbusier, *Urbanisme* (1925). © FLC/ADAGP, Paris and DACS, London 2004.

to his new preoccupation of planning and to propagandising his schemes through international tours and lectures. Many of his plans over the coming decade related to his utopian conception of the Radiant City, which he exhibited in its initial form at CIAM III in Brussels 1930 and published in 1935. This was an 'ideal type' that Le Corbusier developed alongside site-specific projects in places that included Rio de Janeiro, Geneva, Antwerp, Stockholm, Paris, and especially the French colonial context of Algiers, a city for which he produced six uncommissioned proposals (Plan Obus) in 1932–42. In that last context his colonising ambitions to clear a site and construct anew took on particular violence, as they were posed in direct relation to Islamic culture and to French interests celebrating the colonial occupation of Algeria.[88]

Le Corbusier was also influenced by experiences and discussions on his journeys to South America in 1929, and Russia in 1928–30. Breaking with the concentric designs and the spatial segmentations according to class positions that had characterised the Contemporary City, he followed a more process-oriented and egalitarian approach that had an openness and

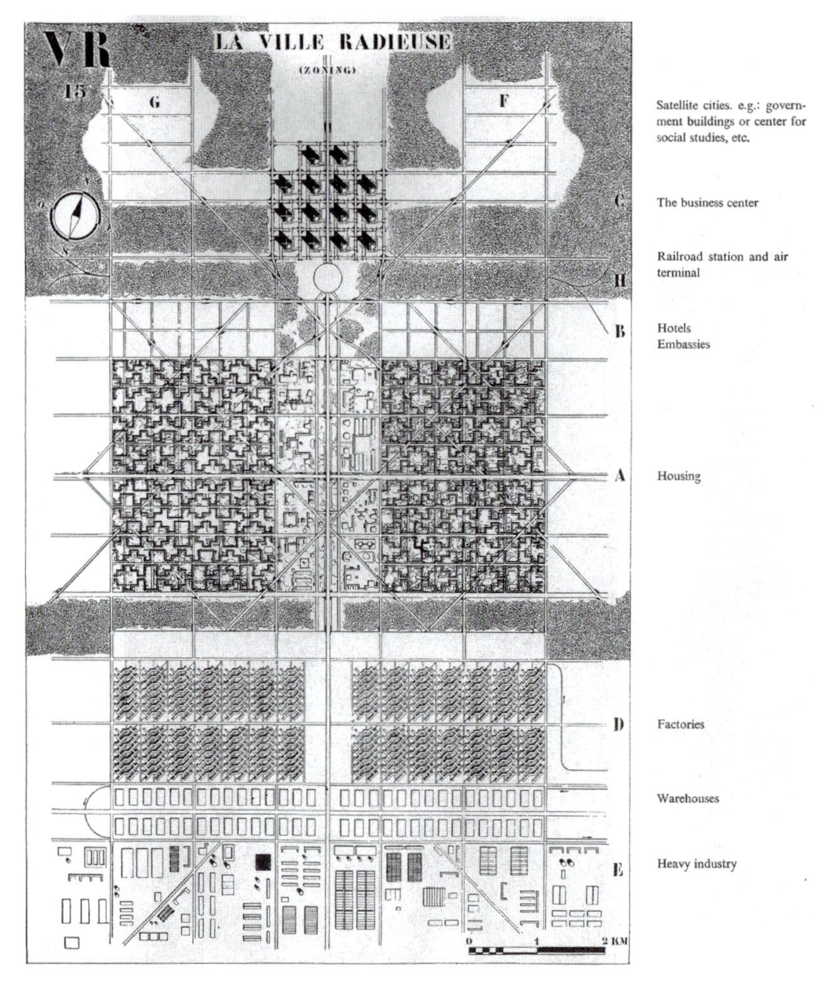

Figure 3.8 Le Corbusier, The Radiant City Plan, 1930, FLC 24909. © FLC/ADAGP, Paris and DACS, London 2004.

fluidity oriented on a 'heliothermic axis', which allowed change and potentially indefinite growth, but also a formal basis on an articulation between a mechanical grid and a natural order. The latter was suggested by an analogy he drew with the human body, starting with the business and administration centre as the head (figure 3.8). The housing unit designs continued to address the fundamental relationship between the individual and the collectivity, echoing Fourier's utopian phalanstery in their attempts to realise an integrated structure based on co-operatively organised communal facilities and devoted to enhancing collective happiness. It seems likely that Le Corbusier was also influenced by Howard's co-operative housing schemes, having studied them early in his career. The culmination was his 'Unité d'habitation', built in Marseilles in 1947–52 to house 1,600 people compared with the 1,800 of Fourier's scheme.

Throughout the Radiant City proposals, Le Corbusier emphasised the 'basic pleasures' of sun, space and greenery and he referred to the result as the 'Green City'. He dismissed current garden city schemes as 'a pre-machine-age utopia' and as an 'illusory solution' or 'palliative'. He claimed that, among other detrimental effects, such schemes led to 'an enslaved individualism, a sterile isolation of the individual' and 'the destruction of social spirit'. But highlighting the green credentials of his own ideas he stated that 'instead of *horizontal garden cities*, we have created *vertical garden cities*', and that the 'vertical solution has all the advantages'.[89] Le Corbusier's criticisms came at a time when the French government was seeking to ease the pressure on the capital by developing *cités jardins* (garden cities) in the Paris region. In establishing sixteen during the inter-war years, government officials acknowledged the inspiration of Howard and the garden city movement in Britain. As early as 1919, however, Henri Sellier noted as director of the HBM (Habitations à Bon Marché) office in the Département de la Seine that the plans would not follow Howard's formulation but would rather pursue a more limited objective of building ensembles as a means of decongesting Paris and its suburbs, and of showing developers that it was possible to provide decent quality dwellings for workers.[90] Le Corbusier's dissatisfaction with the government's measures and with the slow pace of public housing construction, which was particularly badly hit by the economic depression in 1931, became bound up with his growing disillusionment with capitalism and the money economy.

From the late 1920s Le Corbusier sought an alternative basis for his urbanism in regional syndicalism, a loosely defined political movement that was opposed to contemporary capitalism and parliamentary democracy. While it could take on different guises across the political spectrum with its proponents typically seeking to go beyond left and right, it involved a neo-corporatist technocratism or *planisme*. This advocated the election of a multi-layered administrative hierarchy constituted by professional associations or *syndicats* based on people's trades, to provide an 'organic' social body and to ensure 'expert' direction of the economy. Authority remained a recurrent theme in Le Corbusier's writings and he gave this an explicitly patriarchal cast as he lamented the lack of a 'head' and a 'father' to guide France. 'Authority must now step in,' he wrote, 'patriarchal authority, the authority of a father concerned for his children.'[91] In syndicalism he found a means of articulating this so that the 'despot' for whom he claimed people were yearning could be seen not necessarily as an individual 'man', a single authority figure like a king or administrator, but as *a fact*: 'A PLAN'. It was the '*correct, realistic, exact* plan' that was meant to provide the solution to existing problems and to pave a route for the exertion of patriarchal authority, acting as 'a tyrant, a tribune of the people'.[92] This conception of planning did not entail a simple imposition of top-down rule, he claimed, since it should involve mass participation through a 'pyramid of natural hierarchies'. Ideally he looked towards a situation where grass-roots interests would mesh with those established by the administrative elite. He aimed to synthesise the interests of the individual and the collectivity, and of freedom and order, hence his assertion in his book *The Radiant City* that the 'keystone of the theory behind this city is the *liberty of the individual*', while he dedicated the volume as a whole to 'AUTHORITY'.[93]

Such an approach was in keeping with the dualistic patterns that recur in Le Corbusier's thinking, and his tendency to favour a play of opposites and dialectical modes of argument in terms of both his architecture and his theoretical statements. A similar complexity is apparent in his attempt to combine aspects of Saint-Simonian and Fourierist philosophy in the Radiant City and thus to synthesise what have long been seen as antagonistic traditions of utopian thought.[94] He was now more willing to concede that his approach could be labelled 'revolutionary' so long as that term was taken to mean a constructive attempt to change urbanism and society according to a plan. He indeed referred to the Radiant City as 'a key to a social and economic revolution', thus echoing Howard's notion of the 'Master Key'.[95] But it was notable that Le Corbusier excluded mechanisms for the democratic political control of the urban and social system, and he again insisted that the plans were 'not politics' but were a 'rational and poetic monument set up in the midst of contingencies'.[96] The authoritarianism of this version of syndicalism became increasingly bold during the 1930s as his frustration with democracy, like that of many other so-called 'non-conformists' in France at the time, became more intense; and his search for a basis for authority led him from an association with proto-fascist elements among the *planistes*, to contacts with Mussolini and Fascist Italy and later involvement with the Vichy government in France.

It is clear, then, that when considering Le Corbusier's claims to be taking a technical or surgical rather than a political stance, and his statements about setting out the rules and formulae for a modern conception of planning, it is necessary to consider the underlying ideologies at play and the ways in which notions of political authority are being deployed or obscured. In many ways the utopian visions introduced in this chapter and the last seem quite different, even directly competing. Their divergences have been underlined by the fierce criticisms that have sometimes been traded between their respective advocates, with commentators often lining up in favour of one or the other. Besides their contrasting attitudes to the 'great city' and to ideal urban forms, they have different approaches to authority. Howard had connections with radical and reformist circles in late nineteenth-century London, and with decentralist and community-centred ideas. In contrast Le Corbusier, like many modernist architects, gave a central role to experts, planners and administrators and sought to elevate their roles along with that of the rational plan as a guiding force. As has been seen, Le Corbusier's own search for authority took him from syndicalism to the Vichy government and he was not alone among the great modernist architects in seeking accommodation with authoritarian regimes. Despite the differences between Howard and Le Corbusier, however, there are also significant similarities in their approaches to space. Both focus on what de Certeau calls the 'Concept City'. They employ a utopian urbanistic discourse that is concerned with the production of its own space, demanding the realisation of a spatial and social order through the construction of a regulated and structured urban space, *un espace propre* that is rationally organised and 'pure'.[97] As such both can be described as *dreams of urban order*, claiming in their different ways to express 'the spirit of modernity'.

Their approaches are powerful exemplifications of what Bauman identifies more generally as modernity's concern with the concept of order and most particularly with order *as a task*. Bauman argues that with the collapse of the divinely ordained world, order and chaos were conceived as '*modern* twins'.[98] Order became something to be reflected upon, questioned, debated. It became a matter of design and action as existence came under the effects of forms of administration, management and engineering. But he emphasises how this order was defined in terms of its 'other': chaos and disorder. The search for order therefore involved a vigilant struggle against chaos, an attempt to master and control unordered existence and to eradicate ambivalence. By being defined against chaos, humanly created order was always unstable and provisional, and required constant practice to sustain it from internal disintegration and external threats. It depended upon continual attempts to purify its inner realm and to establish boundaries and borders to mark its outer edge. An impossible and infinite task, the elimination of the 'scandal of ambivalence' and the threat of under-determination and contingency nevertheless became one of the key *focii imaginarii* of social order according to Bauman, a point of struggle with the present and a site of projected movement towards a different future. Ambivalence became '*the waste of modernity*', appearing as the failure of attempts to classify and institute a 'proper' order.[99] This concern with order and with the threat of disorder has been enacted with particular violence through processes of colonisation, in efforts to impose modernity on supposedly 'uncivilised' others'.[100]

What de Certeau terms the Concept City is part of this process, a subject constituted through practices of administration by 'ministers of knowledge'. He suggests that as the elements and functions of the city are differentiated, classified and redistributed, the production of space demands an expulsion of all that does not fit in with the order and a clearing away of 'the "waste productions" of a functionalist administration'. The practices of administration and elimination go hand in hand, as classification and ordering entail the removal and repression of 'pollutions' that would compromise the integrity of the produced space. For de Certeau, the Concept City is therefore 'simultaneously the machinery and the hero of modernity'.[101] Similarly for utopian urbanists such as Le Corbusier and Howard, the Concept City was a form of 'machinery' and a 'heroic' goal. Confronted with the transgressive space of the modern industrial city where many previously assumed boundaries were being disrupted, and where codes of space and time were revealed to be not just contingent but also liable to be shattered, they proposed their utopian plans as a response. Through their schemes they aimed to bring about a higher synthesis underpinned by 'individual liberty' and 'collective forces' (Le Corbusier) or 'freedom' and 'co-operation' (Howard). But in both cases, as has been discussed, it is important to question *whose* interests are supposed to be restored through establishing socio-spatial order. In both cases, as has also been argued, the search for order was fraught with difficulties and shot through with desires and anxieties. In the next chapter I explore these desires and anxieties further, focusing more closely on Le Corbusier's confrontations with the modern city and specifically New York during the 1930s. Rather than codifying his schemes as fixed forms, my intention is to question his dreams of urban order by reconnecting his ideas with those of other avant-garde groups at the time who were opposed to such conceptions of the city, and who engaged with urban spaces to different ends. These latter avant-gardes developed their own strands of utopianism, which I take up in what follows.

Figure 4.1 S.S. *Normandie* arriving at New York Harbour, 1935. Photograph by Fairchild Aerial Surveys, Inc. Courtesy of Library of Congress, Prints and Photographs Division, LC-USZ62–90162.

CHAPTER 4

Dreams of cities and monsters

Utopia as representation defines a totalitarian power, an absolute, *formal* and abstract power.

Louis Marin[1]

In fact, only society's ideal nature – that of authoritative command and prohibition – expresses itself in actual architectural construction. Thus great monuments rise up like dams, opposing a logic of majesty and authority to all unquiet elements . . . The fall of the Bastille is symbolic of this state of things. This mass movement is difficult to explain otherwise than by popular hostility towards monuments which are their veritable masters.

Georges Bataille[2]

Between two journeys

In October 1935 Le Corbusier travels west from Paris to New York. He has long been fascinated by Manhattan, its vertical structures an obvious reference point for his own plans for a 'machine age' city, but this is his first visit, for a lecture tour organised by the Museum of Modern Art. On his third day in the city, he gives a talk at Radio City in the recently constructed Rockefeller Centre, broadcast to more than fifty stations in the United States, in which he describes his initial feelings on arriving. When his liner the *Normandie* stops at Quarantine, he sees 'a fantastic, almost mystic city rising up in the mist'. As the ship moves forward, 'the apparition is transformed into an image of incredible brutality and savagery.' But he adds: 'This brutality and this savagery do not displease me. It is thus that great enterprises begin: by strength.'[3] He claims to be greeted relatively coolly, but newspapers and magazines show considerable interest in his visit and several latch onto his early comment on Manhattan's skyscrapers. 'Too small? – Yes, says Le Corbusier; too narrow for free, efficient

LE CORBUSIER SCANS GOTHAM'S TOWERS

The French Architect, on a Tour, Finds the City Violently Alive, a Wilderness of Experiment Toward a New Order

The City of the Future as Le Corbusier Envisions It.

By H. I. BROCK

THE citizen of the French Republic who is known as Le Corbusier—he was born Jeanneret and his given name is Charles-Edouard—is just now paying his first visit to America and has had his first eyeful of the man-made miracle which is New York. In circles where disputing about art is a major sport, Le Corbusier is identified as the founder and public exponent of the mood in architecture which has been labeled the International Style and which certain stiff conservatives insist does not look like architecture at all.

The basic principle of this style is to regard the architect's function as primarily one of household efficiency engineering. His job is to furnish human creatures with a convenient "machine for living in." As stated, the principle applies specifically to the family dwelling. But it applies also to the multiple arrangement of buildings which takes care of the composite employments and the complex human activities of a city where great numbers of people must live and most of them attend to business.

Since the modern dwelling and the modern city have each new demands to meet, since each has at command a service of machinery and materials which no dwelling and no city has ever had before, Le Corbusier and his school begin by discarding traditions and dismissing prejudices which would perpetuate formulas of building evolved from conditions of life that have ceased to exist.

* * *

THE rough idea is that the machine age, with its vast concentrations of population and its prodigious accumulation of mechanical devices for quantity production and for mass movement of goods and men, has created problems which the older architecture is incompetent to solve. The new architecture must face these problems squarely and find a solution on a sound mechanical basis, let the chips of academic estheticism fall where they may.

New York City, for example, is planted thick with skyscrapers—filing cases of millions of human beings at work or stowed away for the night. The streets of New York are jammed with automotive vehicles engaged in distributing the quantity-production output or moving these millions of people about, back and forth between home and business, and generally where they want to go, creating in the process no end of traffic tangles and even seriously endangering in life and limb those who still have to get about on their own feet.

Le Corbusier has built in France and other European countries machines for living in—machines also for doing business in. Whether these machines are, in fact, more efficient than the houses other architects build is a question which will not be argued here. But it is true that, at three years short of 50, he is more famous as the articulate voice of the new architecture than as the executant of its projects. He represents a vision of the future rather than a proved practice of the present.

* * *

MODERN architecture—that is, machine-made architecture—was born, as even its most ardent European advocates admit, in this country. The Europeans who have taken it up have made it much more "modern" than we have dared or cared to make it. Nevertheless, New York—the part of it, at least, which enjoys high visibility—is the creation on the greatest scale that the world knows of the new architecture which is our own. That architecture pierces the sky with pinnacles that lift the level of our rocky little island (which in a state of nature could not boast a really respectable hill) into rivalry with the lesser mountains.

Le Corbusier, from the deck of the giant liner Normandie, looked up the harbor and saw (as he says) afar off a dream city hanging in the blue sky above the horizon of the water—a vision of enchantment. He went below for déjeuner and came up again with the solid substance of the vision right on top of him. He was appalled by the brutality of the great masses—the "sauvagerie"—the wild barbarity of the stupendous, disorderly accumulation of towers, trampling the living city under their heavy feet, like a herd of mastodons.

As the ship moved up the river and he got the city broadside on, as the clutter of bunched towers of the stronghold of finance thinned out and other towers began to stand out separate, gleaming in the sunlight in the open space above their lowlier neighbors, his dispondency abated. Hope revived for the future which the first bright vision had seemed to embody. That vision might not, after all, be a mirage.

* * *

LATER, while touring the city in the company of the writer, he stood at the base of the steep sheer cliff of Raymond Hood's slat in Rockefeller Center and said that it was good, then began ruefully to rub the crick out of the back of his neck that was the result of trying to look up to the very top of anything so tall and uncompromisingly perpendicular.

He found the smaller buildings on the Fifth Avenue front—dedicated to France and the British Empire—out of scale, both with the upreared mass and the human beings walking about the central plaza. That plaza itself, all bare (as it is apt to be when the tourist season is on the wane), struck him as decidedly dull—in spite of Prometheus and his fountain.

Then he was shot in an elevator (at the rate of 1,200 feet a minute) to the very top of the big slat—the deck under which lurks the Rainbow Room—and looked out upon the map of the city, by that time half veiled in a soft gray mist, which cut off the horizons far short of the two extremes of our narrow island but revealed the bounding ribbons of water on either side.

North, south, east and west, the skyscrapers nevertheless stood out boldly. Now and again the sun thrust through the thin clouds and bathed their faces in a brief glory of high light or gilded the fancy tops which some of them have borrowed from all the styles—unimportant to M. Le Corbusier—that came before the steel skeleton revolutionized large-scale building. It was excellent theatre—spectacular drama.

* * *

BUT the modern architect was not particularly impressed. He was looking for architecture, not theatre, and shy, besides, of succumbing to drama so melodramatic. Moreover, he was looking for architecture in his own sense of the word—in this case, the city that is a machine for living in—not merely frightfully expensive scenery built to knock the beholder's eye out.

"They are too small," he said, looking straight at the Empire State Building, tallest in all the world of filing cases for men and standing on one of the biggest pieces of ground devoted to that purpose in the city.

Somebody pointed out a building with "modern" horizontal lines, belting continuous windows about it, down by the Hudson, and a building with "modern" vertical lines, stacking up windows in parallel slits, over toward the East River.

"I am not interested," said Le Corbusier, "in that sort of thing—both sets of lines are all right as expressing the idea of horizontal and vertical circulation respectively. But what counts is the actual existence in the building of the two kinds of circulation and their efficient coordination. That is the combination which creates adequate machines for business for swarms of people—human beehives—if it is joined, of course, with free circulation among the buildings."

The skyscrapers that thrust up

(Continued on Page 23)

New York Times Studios

Too Small?—Yes, Says Le Corbusier; Too Narrow for Free, Efficient Circulation.

© Andre Steiner

Le Corbusier Looks—Critically

Figure 4.2 H. I. Brock, 'Le Corbusier scans Gotham's towers', *New York Times Magazine*, 3 November 1935, p. 10. © 2005 by The New York Times Co. Reprinted with permission.

circulation', reports the *New York Times* (figure 4.2).[4] Headlines in the *New York Herald Tribune* announce: 'Finds American Skyscrapers "Much Too Small" / Skyscrapers Not Big Enough, Says Le Corbusier at First Sight . . . / Thinks They Should Be Huge and a Lot Farther Apart'.[5]

Le Corbusier nonetheless finds himself thrilled by aspects of the skyline, the skyscrapers and the views they afford. On a visit to an office on the fifty-sixth floor, he describes his awe at 'the vast nocturnal festival of New York' below. 'No one can imagine it who has not seen it,' he writes. 'It is a titanic mineral display, a prismatic stratification shot through with an infinite number of lights, from top to bottom, in depth, in a violent silhouette like a fever chart beside a sick bed. A diamond, incalculable diamonds.'[6] Over the two months of his visit to the United States, Le Corbusier will feel continually torn, assailed by a stormy debate in his mind involving both 'hate and love'. He despairs at the violence of New York, at its distances, its uproar, its slums. But he is also enthused and optimistic at what he terms its 'fairy splendour'. It is a constant debate for him 'through every minute in the midst of this stupefying city', and one that he returns to repeatedly in his account of his journey. 'A hundred times I have thought: New York is a catastrophe,' he notes, 'and fifty times: it is a beautiful catastrophe'. With regard to cities in the United States more generally he remarks: 'Hopeless cities and cities of hope at the same time'.[7] In making his assessments he refers back to his utopian dream of the Radiant City, published in book form in France that same year. But despite his elements of despair, what particularly inspires him about New York is its sense of promise as a vertical city under the sign of the new times. His initial impressions confirm his belief that 'today it is possible for the city of modern times, the happy city, the radiant city to be born'; and, as he informs his radio audience in his first broadcast, he feels that it is in America that his ideas for the Radiant City will find their 'natural home'.[8]

In March 1935 the surrealist André Breton travels east from Paris to Prague. He is drawn by his interest in the Czech surrealist group, which was founded the previous year. This is his first visit, for a lecture tour. Travelling with his wife Jacqueline Breton and the poet Paul Eluard, they are greeted enthusiastically and their visit generates much interest in the newspapers. In a letter written shortly after arriving Breton tells of their 'triumphant welcome', and a week later Eluard is effusive about their reception, referring to '[d]elirious admiration and affection'.[9] Meanwhile, the Czech Communist daily newspaper *Rude Pravo* welcomes the pair as the 'two greatest poets of present-day France' (figure 4.3).[10] On his third day in the city, Breton gives a lecture entitled 'Surrealist situation of the object', which he begins by referring to the 'legendary delights' of Prague. He describes it as 'one of those cities that electively pin down poetic thought, which is always more or less adrift in space'. With its 'towers that bristle like no others', when viewed from afar he suggests that it seems to be 'the magic capital of old Europe'. Despite not having known the city a couple of days before, he states that of all those he had not visited it 'was by far the least foreign to me', and he adds: 'By the very fact that it carefully incubates all the delights of the past for the imagination, it seems to me that it would be less difficult for me to make myself understood in this corner of the world than in any other.'[11]

The topic of the lecture is surrealist poetry and art. In his talk he too refers back to a dream space, although this time it is not an ideal city but an Ideal Palace. It is a structure found in the village of Hauterives, south of Lyons, in south-east France, constructed out of rocks and stones gathered from the region, out of quicklime, tufa, sandstone, fossils, shells and cement. Built single-handedly by a country postman, Ferdinand Cheval, over a period of thirty-three years between 1879 and 1912, it was initially inspired by a dream. Cheval had no training in architecture or construction but he worked on what he called his 'fairy palace' in the evenings and at night by candlelight after his postal rounds. The result is an extraordinary hybrid of sculpture and architecture around twenty-six metres in length and fourteen metres in width, that teems with figures, animals, organic forms, as well as pillars, columns, grottoes, galleries, temples, representations of different places and fragments of text (figure 4.4). The profusion of forms and elisions between them overloads attempts to catalogue, register and locate references. 'Where the dream becomes reality', states an inscription above one of the entrances. Another in verse form runs: 'Everything you can see, passer-by / Is the work of one peasant / Who, out of dream, created / The queen of the world.'[12] For Breton it is a 'marvellous construction' with its dream-like qualities and its passionate expression of an individual's untutored and imaginative vision, and he takes particular delight in its lack of utility for, as he notes, the structure has 'no place for anything except the wheelbarrow that [Cheval] had used to transport his materials'.[13]

This chapter is located between these two journeys; or, rather, it is located in tensions that might be traced in the spaces and geographical imaginations here invoked. 'To encompass both Breton and Le Corbusier,' wrote Walter Benjamin, 'that would mean drawing the spirit of contemporary France like

Figure 4.3 From left to right: Paul Eluard, Karel Teige, Jacqueline Breton and André Breton, returning from the International Exhibition of Surrealism in Prague, 1935.

Figure 4.4 Ferdinand Cheval, Ideal Palace, Hauterives, 1879–1912. North-east corner. Photograph by Marcus Schubert, Toronto.

a bow, with which knowledge shoots the moment in the heart.'[14] My primary intention is to explore issues raised in the encounters discussed above, to examine further the utopian spaces outlined in the previous chapter. Le Corbusier's account of his journey to New York speaks of complex minglings of desire and fear that are characteristic not only of his responses to the 'chaos' of modern cities but also of his proposals for their radical transformation. By attending to his reactions and ambivalences more closely, I want to examine aspects of his utopian call to order. But my aim is also to raise questions about this order and especially about its *stability* by reconnecting it to – and by allowing it to be shadowed by – other strands of contemporaneous thinking, in particular those of surrealism. Put briefly, my interest lies in disturbing or re-contaminating that which, in the name of modernist urbanism, has often been projected in pristine and soundly formed terms.

Something of the spirit of this enquiry is suggested by a cryptic remark once made in an interview by Henri Lefebvre. Looking back on his own involvement with Breton and the surrealist group in the 1920s, and more particularly on his friendship with Tristan Tzara shortly after the break-up of the dadaists, about whom he wrote his first article for the journal *Philosophies* in 1924, he made the following assertion: 'To the degree that the word modernity has a meaning, it is this: it carries within itself, from the beginning, a radical negativity, Dada, this event that took place in a Zurich café.'[15] In addressing utopian visions that have been important in informing dominant notions of modernist urbanism, and in focusing on their ordered and purely defined spaces, I want to remain mindful of this 'other' side of modernity. This is both as it appears in the ambivalences of the utopian urbanists themselves, in terms of their entanglements with subjects they sought to repress, and as it finds expression in the oppositional activities of other avant-gardes. For while these entanglements and oppositions may be seemingly erased in the landscapes of the urbanists' dreams, they nevertheless continued to haunt them.

White cathedrals: confronting New York

Le Corbusier first confronted New York City in the early and mid-1920s. It was then a struggle with images of New York as he appraised the city through photographs; or, rather, it was a struggle to manufacture an image of the city through the use of photographs, to construct New York as a site not of modernity but of congestion, to make it *an image of congestion*. The term 'CONGESTION' is the caption he gives to a pair of photographs reproduced in his book *The City of Tomorrow* of 1925, showing high views across skyscrapers and down a canyon street in Manhattan. Below another photograph of the city he writes: 'As for beauty, there is none at all. There is only confusion, chaos and upheaval.'[16] He insists in the book that New York is not a city of the machine age, not truly modern. This denigration of New York is crucial to his strategy because, as Rem Koolhaas notes, he needs to prove that the 'new city' toward which he is striving does not yet exist, to distance his own schemes from the messy reality across the Atlantic. Le Corbusier thus stays away from New York and constructs the city in negative terms from afar. His portrait of New York is likened by Koolhaas to a police 'identikit', to 'a purely speculative collage of its "criminal" features'. Manhattan's 'guilt' is repeatedly illustrated through a 'series of hasty paste-ups of grainy images' and 'fabricated mug shots', and he becomes like 'a paranoid detective who invents the victims . . . forges the likeness of the perpetrator and avoids the scene of the crime'.[17] Against this image of a non-modern or not-yet-modern New York, Le Corbusier sets his alternative: a Cartesian city, 'harmonious and lyrical'. The 'startling' juxtaposition creates a disjunction that aims to jolt the viewer into awareness of his message (figure 4.5).

When Le Corbusier finally makes it across the Atlantic to New York in 1935, he becomes caught up in the dramatic spectacle before him. The initial glimpse of the skyline strikes him powerfully as do the senses of movement and energy as he explores the city and contemplates the intoxicating views. He speaks highly of the machine-like rigour of the right-angle gridding, the smooth elevators and other urban elements. But at the same time he despairs. The city becomes to him a 'fairy catastrophe'. What is catastrophic in particular, in his view, is the disorder of New York that manifests itself in a number of ways: the skyscrapers, which appear like proclamations, banners in the sky, firework rockets, but not as proper elements in city planning; the congestion of the streets, caused by huge increases in traffic; the social divisions and slums, which he views as a symptom of the 'social machine' malfunctioning; and 'The Great Waste' – wastes of energy, time and money through inefficient spatial and social organisation – that threatens stagnation, an emptying of social life, even a death march. He associates the waste especially with urban sprawl whose wretchedness is revealed with particular clarity from an aeroplane. The result is portrayed as an illness, as a tumour or a case of encephalitis.[18]

Le Corbusier asserts that the 'true image of architecture' is '*a materially and spiritually superior putting-in-order*', and that urban planning is inseparable

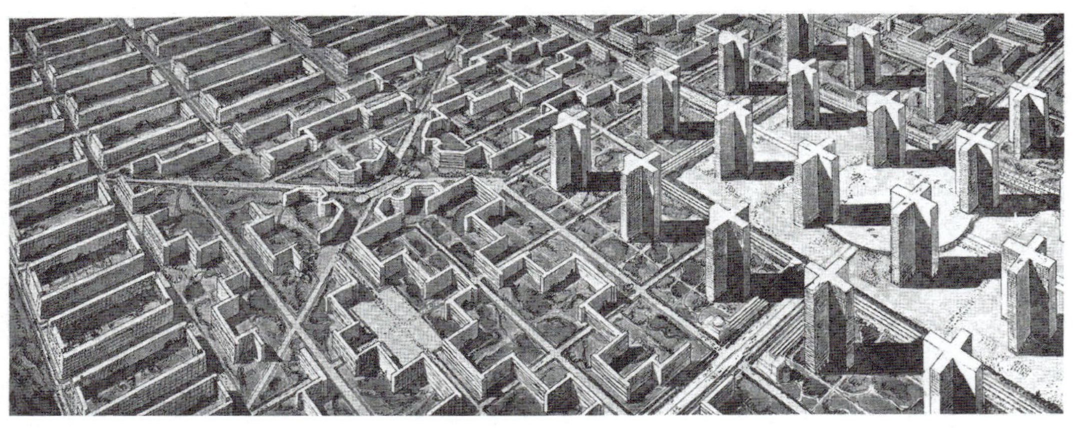

Figure 4.5 Photograph of Manhattan juxtaposed with a drawing of the centre of Le Corbusier's Contemporary City of Three Million People, 1922, shown to the same scale and seen from the same angle. © FLC/ADAGP, Paris and DACS, London 2004.

from this, involving a putting-in-order as 'the social organiser par excellence'.[19] The process takes a number of forms in relation to his alternative conception of New York. These include: constructing light-filled Cartesian skyscrapers that are larger and more widely spaced than at present, to concentrate population and restore ground in the centre; separating lines of traffic to keep apart pedestrians and motor cars; redistributing the open space of Central Park and multiplying it through the city; and eradicating sprawl and creating a Manhattan that is compact and dense with six million people (figures 4.6, 4.7). Addressing the problem of waste, Le Corbusier puts forward an essential guiding measure: the 'solar day'. He argues that the rhythms of the twenty-four hour daily cycle should be reorganised and restored to their equilibrium. He is inspired by a visit to a Ford factory in Detroit whose organisation provides fodder for his arguments about the importance of collaboration, a unity of purpose, and a combination of individual liberty and collective forces as a model of political participation. But his belief that a new age of synthesis and order is dawning is also suggested by the title of his account of his American journey, *When the Cathedrals Were White*. This is meant to compare the present to the great period of cathedral construction in Europe during the Middle Ages when a new world was opening up that was '[w]hite, limpid, joyous, clean, clear'. He states: 'The cathedrals of our own time have not yet been built. The cathedrals belong to other people – to the dead – they are black with grime and worn by centuries . . . Nevertheless, everything is potentially new, fresh, in the process of birth.'[20]

The call for white cathedrals relates to a further component of ordering for Le Corbusier during the 1920s, one that is so often taken to be a standard of modern architecture that it usually goes unsaid: the demand for white walls.[21] In his book *The Decorative Art of Today* from 1925, Le Corbusier presents what he calls 'the Law of Ripolin' based on a 'Coat of Whitewash'. This demands the replacement of hangings, wall-papers, stencils and the like with 'a plain coat of white ripolin'.[22] It involves clearing the home, cleaning up and purifying its spaces so that '[t]here are no more dirty, dark corners'. Rejecting the 'lie' of decoration and eliminating the equivocal, it allows attention to focus fully on objects. It is meant to create a space that encourages precision, accuracy, clear thinking, one that deters unnecessary hoarding and accumulation and that depends upon the efficient elimination of waste. With this banishment of shadows and darkness, '*Everything is shown as it is*.' Any dirt and dust shows up, any trace of muck or disturbance. 'On white ripolin walls these accretions of dead things from the past would be intolerable; they would leave a mark,' he

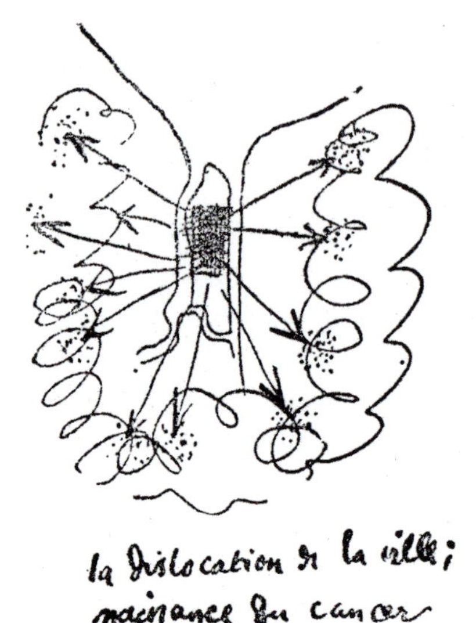

la dislocation de la ville;
naissance du cancer

Figure 4.6 'The dislocation of the city; the birth of cancer.' Drawing by Le Corbusier from *Quand les cathédrals étaient blanches* (1937). © FLC/ADAGP, Paris and DACS, London 2004.

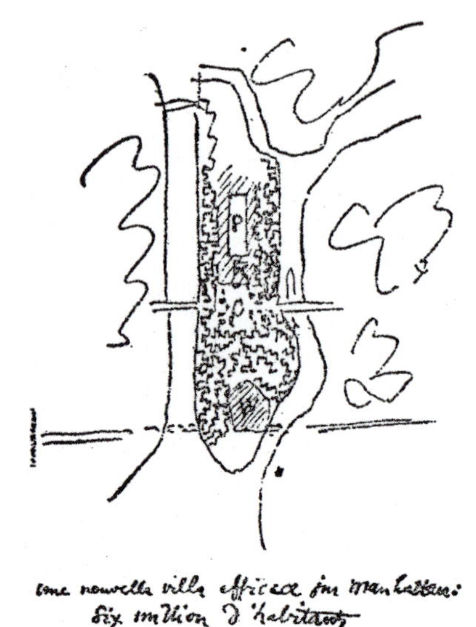

Figure 4.7 'A new efficient city on Manhattan; six million inhabitants.' Drawing by Le Corbusier from *Quand les cathédrals étaient blanches* (1937). © FLC/ADAGP, Paris and DACS, London 2004.

writes. Anything out of place 'hits you in the eye', and the whitewash becomes 'like an X-ray of beauty' or 'the eye of truth'.[23]

This 'Law of Ripolin' works through an association of whiteness with the concept of cleanliness, a hygiene symbolism that has informed its use in styles of clothing as well as on the walls of hospitals and other institutions. It seeks to create a hygienic space or, rather, what Mark Wigley terms 'a cleansing of the look, a hygiene of vision itself'.[24] It thus connects with the theme of panopticism in which the arrangement of space and light is essential for the presentation of bodies and materials for disciplining. Le Corbusier asserts that the 'Law of Ripolin' is 'extremely moral', a dimension that is based on a love of purity and productivity and that is supposed to lead to a 'mastery' of one's home and of oneself. He even suggests that whitewash could be applied as a disciplining action with implications for the policing of the city. 'Suppose there were a decree requiring all rooms in Paris to be given a coat of whitewash,' he writes. 'I maintain that would be a police task of real stature and a manifestation of high morality, the sign of a great people.'[25]

Given the importance Le Corbusier attaches to this 'law' in his writings, it is not surprising to find him returning to the theme when he confronts New York. But while he is in America he also finds something else he admires: an adherence to cleanliness as a 'national virtue'. Soon after arriving in the city, he relaxes in Radio City in the Rockefeller Centre and describes with interest the insides of this 'machine age temple' with its marble surfaces, clear mirrors, efficient elevators, conditioned air and silent walls that shelter him from the turmoil outside. Later he writes of the clean offices he encounters in the city, the bath tubs, the shops, the glistening hotels, the dazzling restaurants and bars, the impeccably varnished surface of a new car. He also points to the cleanliness of Grand Central station and its trains, to the buildings with immaculate personnel clad in shining white, to the food wrapped in bright cellophane. All these are noted as signs of a commendable cultural and ethical stance: 'No filth, no dust . . . everything is new and spotless.'[26] He continues: 'People who wash their shirts, paint their houses, clean the glass in their windows, have an ethic different from those who cultivate dust and filth . . . A true culture manifests itself in fresh colour, white linen, and clean art.'[27] Just as this desire for cleanliness is not neutral in Le Corbusier's thinking but depends upon active processes of clearing, repressing, eliminating – and on a hierarchical social structure divided along lines of class, gender and 'race' that provides the necessary labour – neither is the 'purity' he envisages for his own dream city, the one whose modern radiance and order in other respects he sets against the realities of New York, and promises can supersede it.

In constructing this vision of a city that will transcend the existing realities of New York, however, blackness also plays a significant role. It is not only that he depicts the old cathedrals as black and worn in contrast to the whiteness of the structures that are to be constructed afresh. The blackness of surfaces and clothes also represent a suppression of the architectural spirit that animates America, a 'funereal sadness' and melancholy amidst New York's power. The black marble entrance of the Empire State Building is itself described as 'funereal', set against the polychromy of the wax mannequins in the windows next door on Fifth Avenue, its hue symptomatic of a solemnity that is yet to come alive in a flowering of the machine age.[28] The contrast with colour as a sign of life, as modelled especially in relation to women's clothes, is reiterated through *When the Cathedrals Were White*. In a rich commentary on the colours of the book, Wigley suggests that it is 'not so much the promotion of white walls as it is the demotion of black ones', something that Wigley explores in relation to the sensuality and psychosexual charge that Le Corbusier accords to surfaces and colours, and to the repression of sensuality by the surface clothing that the architect finds predominant on his tour in America. What Le Corbusier seeks is a balanced and controlled surface that controls but does not repress the sensuous and allows the emergence of a mental order.[29]

An exception to this repression noted by Wigley where Le Corbusier does claim to find a connection between sensuality and the machine lies in his discussion of what he terms 'Negro music', which he describes as 'the melody of the soul joined with the rhythm of the machine'. Writing about jazz and experiences of listening to an awe-inspiring Louis Armstrong on Broadway and of visiting African American clubs in Harlem, Le Corbusier develops an image of a new architecture: 'Jazz, like the skyscrapers, is an *event* and not a deliberately conceived creation . . . If architecture were at the point reached by jazz, it would be an incredible spectacle.'[30] The complex associations of the passages on jazz and brilliantly performing bodies, with their references to an alluring spirit and sensuality, have been discussed by Mabel Wilson, who develops a critical analysis of how Le Corbusier imagines his Radiant City through tropes of 'blackness' in this book. The dances and music in the clubs are depicted by Le Corbusier as being akin to the skyscrapers of Manhattan, with an enthralling rawness and energy that represents the forces of the day: 'I repeat: Manhattan is hot jazz in stone and steel.'[31] Wilson argues that they become part of a metaphorical scripting of blackness as dynamic and energising but also as threatening, enacting a play between the desired and the feared. Le Corbusier's articulation of whiteness is thus presented as 'ordering a dynamic and unstable blackness', and shown to be indicative of a vision of racial patriarchal social order underpinning the Radiant City.[32]

Of monsters and organic life

In asserting conceptions of order during his confrontations with New York, Le Corbusier retains a sense of detachment. In spite of the tumult, he stands back or rises above the scenes before him, to judge the disorder as well as the possibilities for change: 'Clearly and coolly,' he assures the reader, 'I know that a proper plan can make New York the city par excellence of modern times.'[33] That, at least, is how he presents it. But what particularly interests me here are the moments when the detachment breaks down, when he becomes anxiously embroiled in the subject that he is seeking to distance and compose. His understanding of order is necessarily entwined with that of chaos and disorder. There is a continual struggle between them, each term defined in relation to its other. New York, writes Le Corbusier, is a 'titanic effort of organisation and discipline in the midst of a chaos brought about by the speed of accelerated times'. It is 'a kind of snorting monster, bursting with health, sprawled out at ease'.[34] The monstrous is a term that recurs in his account of his visit. Urban sprawl is denounced as a monstrous and disruptive growth, while the Manhattan skyscraper is depicted as a 'man-eating monster', sucking the life out of neighbouring areas.[35] Elsewhere the skyscraper is presented like 'a man undergoing a mysterious disturbance of his organic life: the torso remains normal, but his legs become ten or twenty times too long'.[36]

The figure of the monster appears in Le Corbusier's accounts of other cities. 'Monsters have appeared,' he warns, 'they are the spread cities, the cancer of our agglomerations.'[37] In *The Radiant City*, he writes: 'Paris has become a monster crouching over an entire region.' It is a 'monster of the most primitive sort: a protoplasm, a puddle'. Buenos Aires, too, has become 'gigantic, protoplasmic'.[38] Le Corbusier's language fails to retain a clinical detachment, its excessiveness caught up in the transgressions and loss of definition that he seeks to denounce. But why the employment of the monstrous and protoplasmic? The attempt to bring monsters under a scientific gaze with the founding of 'teratology' in the late eighteenth century by the biologist Geoffroy de Saint Hilaire is suggestive in this context, with his proposed classification system referring to an excess, lack or displacement of organs.[39] Le Corbusier's own employment of the term is rooted in his use of organic and biological metaphors discussed in the previous chapter, and in his fears about the consequences of unorganised growth causing the body of the city to lose its nature and to degenerate. He makes this clear in his discussion of the 'becoming-monstrous' of Buenos Aires where he argues that the city was once organic, having a spirit of order and organisation meaning that it '*could be policed*', but then feverish expansion caused it to lose this structure and it became 'perfectly amorphous, a primitive system of aggregation. It is no longer an organism, *it is no more than a protoplasm*.'[40]

Le Corbusier's interest in organic conceptions of urbanism became especially strong from the late 1920s when, along with his collaborators and friends Amédée Ozenfant and Fernand Léger, he sought a new balance between the geometrical and the natural, and the machine and the organic. A view from an aeroplane was once again significant, this time as he flew over parts of South America in the summer of 1929 and found the perspective revealed a fundamental 'biology' and 'organic life', leaving him enthralled by the curves and undulations of the landscape and '*the law of the meander*' that he deduced from the rivers.[41] The significance of his visits to South America and North Africa for reshaping his interest in nature and the curve has been discussed by Mary McLeod, who notes how it was complexly bound up with his renewed interest in the human figure in his drawings and paintings, especially in terms of women's bodies that feature prominently in his sketchbooks from those journeys.[42] His exoticisation of these figures can be seen as part of a process of cultural othering through which his appeal to a new lyricism was constructed, as has also been explored in critical writings on the themes of orientalism and colonialism in his work by Zeynep Çelik, especially through his proposals for Algiers.[43] Le Corbusier's urban plans in this period, as demonstrated in his Radiant City, increasingly drew on principles of organic growth and generation as he sought to reconcile contradictions and conflict through a city characterised by biological harmony. He argued that all architectural products and cities should be *organisms*, a word that he claimed 'immediately conveys a notion of character, of balance, of harmony, of symmetry'.[44]

The figure of the 'monstrous' city therefore emerged out of this nexus of concerns. It is freighted with powerful associations and works in a variety of ways but in terms of symbolic processes it is connected to Le Corbusier's biological conceptions of the urban and his drive to create a well-structured form. Specifically, the notion of the protoplasm works as a negative other to Le Corbusier's interest in the 'classical' body, which he reworks from its Vitruvian and humanist forebears into a significant referent in his schemes, from the analogy for the spatial form of the Radiant City to its use as an architectural measure in relation to the 'body modular' and regulating lines. Attention might be given to the ideals of the body that are presupposed by Le Corbusier in his appeals to such regulating devices.[45] Also important are how his invocations of the protoplasmic and becoming-monstrous work metaphorically as part of his concern with ordering. At the core of the problem for Le Corbusier is the issue of *formlessness*: the monstrous city arises out of a confrontation with that which defies notions of definition, regulation and form. The term speaks of a fear but also a fascination with the body of the city and its excess, part of a discourse in which the scientific and the fantasmatic intertwine. The idea of the monster as a figure of contradictory signification is indeed suggested by its Greek root *teras/teratos*, which, as Rosi Braidotti notes, is simultaneously holy and hellish, evoking both horror and fascination, and is characterised by mixing and ambiguity, being classically depicted in terms of the blurring of genres.[46]

The reference to monsters therefore stems from a fundamental urge to make separations between categories and to reject the unstructured and under-determined. The threatening coding of the monstrous and protoplasmic relates to anxieties surrounding a failure to make such clear definitions. In this sense Le Corbusier construes the monstrous in relation to other signifiers of mixing and defilement – dirt, filth, waste – that represent, in Mary Douglas's famous formulation of dirt, 'matter out of place'.[47] The anxieties about spatial disorder relate not only to the instability and impermanence that it appears to usher in but to the fundamental struggle against the 'scandal of ambivalence', and to the fear of failing to eradicate ambivalent states and to create a proper space. It can also productively be related to what Julia Kristeva calls the *abject*, being focused on things that do not fit, that are out of place, that blur clear boundaries. According to Kristeva, abjection is strongly associated with ambivalence, arising out of the unconscious and feelings relating to boundary maintenance. As David Sibley has shown in his discussions of space and purification, Kristeva's arguments help to highlight the feelings of anxiety as well as desire evident in commitments to spatial order and geometry, where the imposition of order depends upon the removal of elements considered to be abject.[48] They also draw attention to the constitutive role of passions and unconscious feelings within ostensibly rationalist planning schemes and discourses about urban culture.

These points give further insights into the fears discussed earlier about the lack of geometric order, the dark spaces, the pullulating crowds. In Le Corbusier's utopian spaces there is a revulsion to interminglings, ambivalences, violations of boundaries; to things that stagnate or rot, where decay presages an inversion of hierarchies; to the mass, the swarm, the 'primitive' cell; and to undifferentiated matter or unchannelled flow that threaten to swamp, sweep away, or bring about the dissolution of the individual. The threat of uncoded and unregulated movement is also registered through a negative scripting of the nomadic, as Le Corbusier describes Paris as a 'gypsy encampment' and sets his vision against free wandering and drift. In an argument that resonates with those of earlier social reformers who attacked the disruptive 'wandering tribes' of the nineteenth-century city and attempted to separate them socially and morally from the 'civilised tribes', Le Corbusier complains that the city's boundaries have today 'become a confused and stifling zone comparable only to a camp of roving gypsies, who may have plumped their overcrowded caravans down anywhere'.[49] The disgust apparent in Le Corbusier's writings becomes a basis upon which he attempts to differentiate, to eradicate disturbances, and to make a 'proper' environment. Hence his obsession with establishing classifications, boundaries and hierarchies, and with zoning functions to ensure 'non-contaminating' land-uses, the last being one of the most influential legacies of the utopian urbanism discussed in the previous two chapters, and enshrined in documents such as the Athens Charter established by CIAM (Congrès Internationaux d'Architecture Moderne) in 1933. Hence too the reference is to disciplining operations where discipline is seen after Michel Foucault as 'an anti-nomadic technique': 'it arrests or regulates movements; it clears up confusion; it dissipates compact groupings of individuals wandering about the country in unpredictable ways; it establishes calculated distributions . . . it must neutralise . . . anything that may establish horizontal conjunctions.'[50]

For Le Corbusier the dislocated city must therefore be cut back and reconnected; dizzying distances and waste must make way for a compact green city, as was seen in his arguments about Manhattan and as he reiterated elsewhere. Channels must be cleared for flow, not only for reasons of efficiency but also for the city's health. He asserts that a 'fundamental condition of health of a city is being traversed, irrigated, nourished from end to end, being free!'[51] Faced with a city's supposedly amorphous and inorganic mass, the task becomes how to construct an organism with a proper biological structure; or, as he puts it: 'How then insert in this protoplasm a cardiac system (aorta, arteries, and arterioles) indispensable to the circulation and the organisation of a modern city?' When Le Corbusier is confronted with the 'protoplasmic' Buenos Aires in 1929, he therefore reacts by turning to questions of flow: 'must open the channels vital to urgent urbanisation: waterway, railway; must reshape its cellular condition'.[52] In sketches made during his lectures in South America in 1929, he gives a key role to circulation, hygiene, surgery and the recovery of the ground as he indicates how to transform sprawling spaces into a green city with a 'machine age profile' (figure 4.8). Another drawing from around the same time shows the significance of circulation for Le Corbusier's conceptualisation of the home, which is portrayed as a cell raised high from the ground, connected to lines representing streams of gas, electricity, water and the telephone, and supplied with 'exact air' internally organised

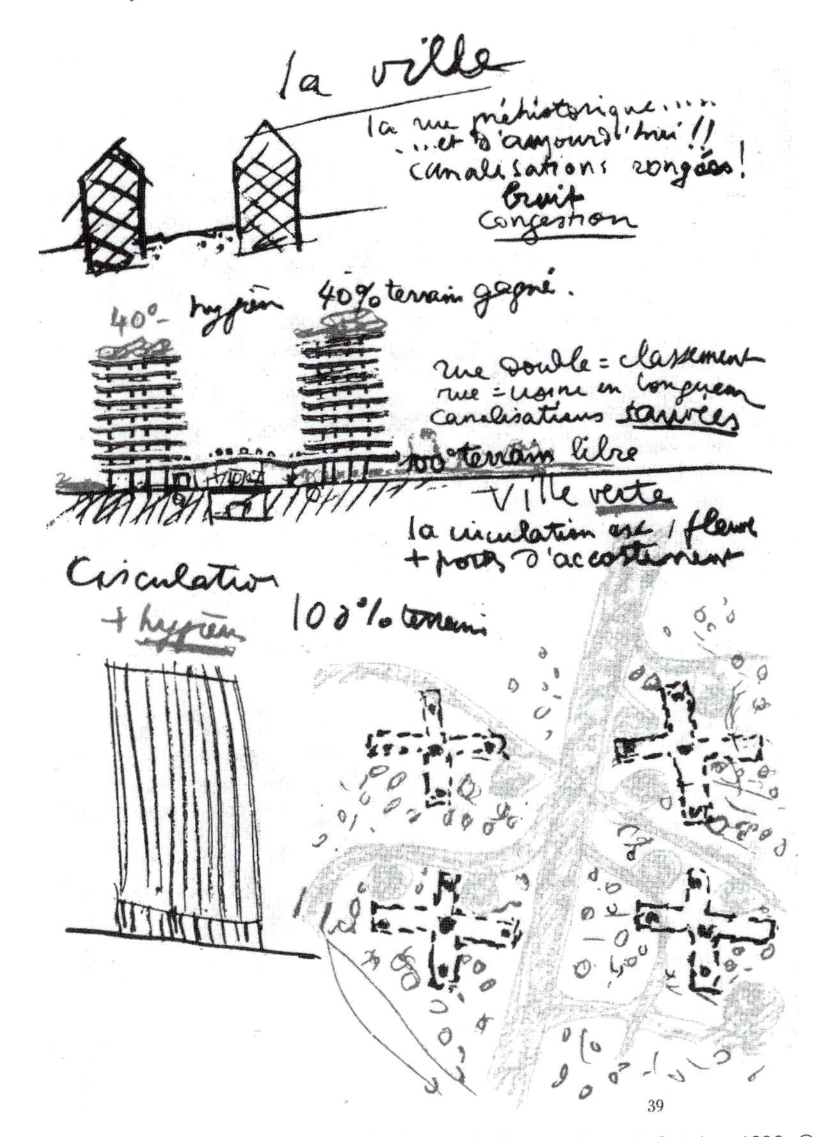

Figure 4.8 Sketch by Le Corbusier for lecture in Buenos Aires, 5 October 1929. © FLC/ADAGP, Paris and DACS, London 2004.

From the top:
the city, the prehistoric street and today's!! corroded drains!, noise, congestion
40% hygiene, 40% ground recovered
two-level street classification, street = factory alongside, drains conserved
100% ground free, green city, circulation is a river plus harbours for docking
circulation + hygiene, 100% ground

(as trans. in *Precisions*, 1987, p. 61)

through techniques of ventilation and heating (figure 4.9). The inhabitant is shown linked up to these flows, as a figure standing next to a giant eye on the outside of the cell at the window or glass wall. The depiction indicates the significance of the visual as an organising principle in Le Corbusier's architectural work and the way that the apartment frames the world as a view. It is not only the window that problematises notions of interior and exterior but, as the drawing makes clear, the connections to flows conceptualised in terms of the biological analogy of the cell.[53]

Through his desire for wholeness, harmony and the re-establishment of the healthy and soundly formed body, one of Le Corbusier's aims was to re-centre the family as the fundamental social element within which the new bodies would thrive. Although many of his schemes and 'machines for living in' might be seen as disrupting traditional notions of family life, they nevertheless placed considerable symbolic importance on a particular conception of the family and the hearth. They sought to restore the supposed balance of family life and gender relations that Le Corbusier argued had been shaken by industrialisation and urban sprawl. His efforts to attend to the physical conditions of urban inhabitants, and to reconcile the machine and the organic, also led him to reconnect with conceptions of the region, regional traditions and nature. Even the slogan 'the death of the street' was imbued with a desire to re-establish connections with the natural world and the soil, so that 'man' could be 'returned to his norm: he lives *on the earth*; when he walks, he walks with his feet on the ground.'[54] As Mary McLeod and Romy Golan have so lucidly argued, Le Corbusier's work thus connected with a wider discourse around a 'return to man' that was being developed within the syndicalist journals *Plans*, *Préludes* and *L'Homme réel* in the early 1930s, as the editors of these publications emphasised health, biology and athleticism as well as the ties between people and their region. Such discussions, particularly by a number of doctors that included Le Corbusier's friend Pierre Winter, at times carry disturbing connotations in the context of debates around social Darwinism, eugenics and an ideological concept of 'biological man'. This is especially in the light of the links between some of those writing in the journals and Italian fascism.[55] They also put a troubling perspective on Le Corbusier's own pathologising rhetoric and his construction of biological 'norms' through such notions as normal and abnormal, healthy and sick, productive and unproductive.

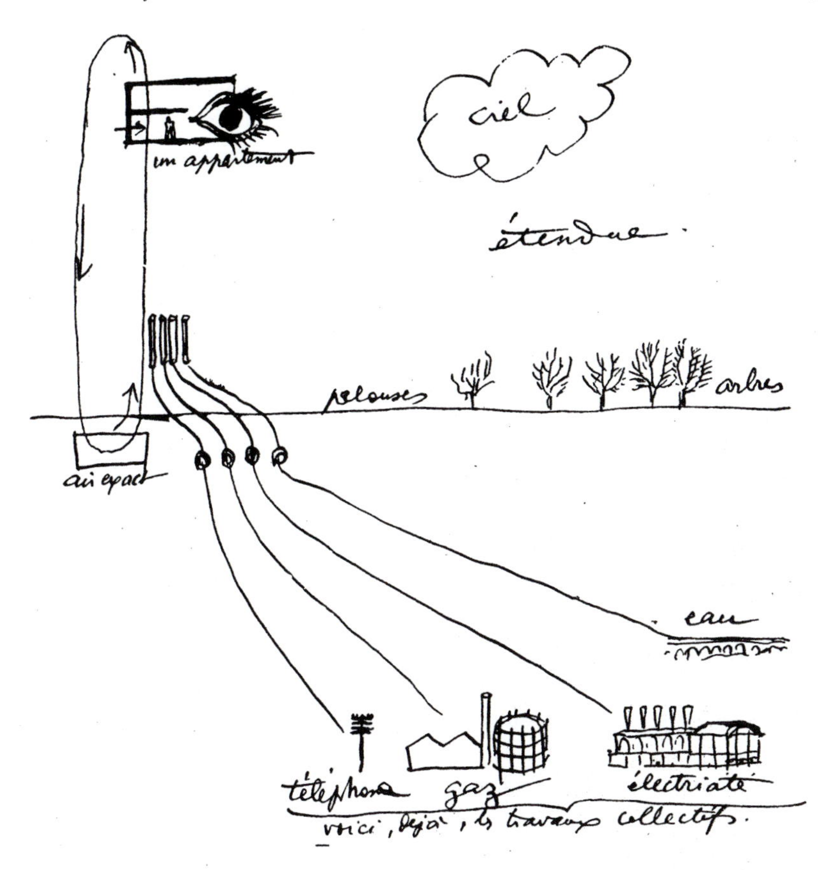

Figure 4.9 Drawing by Le Corbusier of a 'residential cell', connected to telephone, gas, electricity and water, and supplied with 'exact air'. From *The Radiant City* (1935). © FLC/ADAGP, Paris and DACS, London 2004.

Utopian regulation and authoritarianism

Neatly summarising the ambitions of his urbanism, Le Corbusier wrote of a space in which '[n]othing is contradictory any more' since 'everything is in its place, properly arranged in order and hierarchy.'[56] A central argument of the last three chapters has been that, by attending closely to the concern with ordering in utopian projects, other sides to their projected ideals become more visible. This opens perspectives on the desires, anxieties and fears that lie behind the projects, and on their politics beyond their consciously stated emancipatory intent. Specifically, it directs attention to the ways in which such utopianism functions as a regulatory regime that seeks to control spatial form along with the movements and presence of bodies in space or body space. While it bears repeating that the utopian traditions discussed here were addressing critical urban problems and they aimed to bring about radical improvements in those realms, critical studies have helped to bring the regulatory aspects of the utopian projects into focus, raising important questions about the *particularity* of the interests underlying the 'proper' space, and about the erasures and systems of regulation that their projection entails. These have included work drawing upon feminist theory, which has explored the gendered character of the anxieties underlying drives to order in urban planning, and the ways that their regulatory practices have centred on the working classes, ethnic minorities and women.

Noting the tendency of many utopian writers to view the city as a threatening space, a site to be tamed, even to be fled from, Elizabeth Wilson discusses how the presence of women in the city has been a particular point of anxiety for planners and social reformers, with women becoming constructed as 'an irruption in the city, a symptom of disorder, and a problem'. As the city became a place of increasing threat to men during the nineteenth century, she notes, the crowd was described 'as hysterical, or, in images of feminine instability and sexuality, as a flood or swamp'. In this context, utopian planning schemes sought to impose a new order and rigidity, to create dams and channels to protect against threatening fluidity and fragmentation, to fix women in their 'appropriate' place and control the female body.[57] Developing a related critique, Barbara Hooper suggests that the work of planners such as Le Corbusier may be viewed as 'poems of male desires, fantasies of control, written against the fears and urban upheavals of the nineteenth century that the female body comes to represent'. She draws attention to the binary logic of oppositions through which the planners constructed their order, and through which they presented planning itself as a creation of reason that is opposed to the bodily, so that the female/body is produced as that which must be disciplined to create (masculinist) order.[58] Her arguments can be connected to those of Braidotti to illuminate further the significance of the 'monstrous' in Le Corbusier's discourse. As Braidotti discusses, the term monstrous has been constructed within western scientific discourse as a negative pole, as a reference to a bodily incarnation of a difference from the established 'norm', one that through the binary logic of that discursive order has become structurally analogous with the feminine. In this way both monsters and bodily female subjects have functioned on the side of dissimilarity, as figures of devalued difference that must be controlled for order to prevail.[59]

In spite of their emancipatory aims, the utopian schemes have often been viewed more generally as authoritarian. They have appeared as an attempt to fix geography and freeze history in a regulated scheme. A fundamental reason lies not in their totalising vision as such but in their preoccupation with engineering a better future through the projection of an ideal spatial form. As David Harvey puts it, 'they in effect propose a fixed spatial order that ensures social stability by destroying the possibility of history and containing all processes within a fixed spatial frame.'[60] The privileging of spatial forms by Le Corbusier and other modernists is one that is shared with Ebenezer Howard along with many traditional utopian visions. In common, too, is their emphasis on categorising, sorting, expelling and regulating as well as on achieving wholeness and overcoming contradictions and antagonisms through the construction of a harmonious and 'pure' space. These processes of ordering, discussed in detail in these last chapters, recall an older argument made by Lewis Mumford about the connections between utopia and the city. He asserts that formal utopias, if they are to be realised, depend upon what he terms the 'machine'; that is, they demand the regimentation of the population into a machine-like mechanism, subservient to a higher authority whether it is a king, nation, science or the 'expert' (or the 'Invisible Machine', through which reality is reduced to the calculated and the controllable). Mumford traces this tendency back to the ancient world. He writes:

> Isolation, stratification, fixation, regimentation, standardization, militarization – one or more of these attributes enter into the conception of the utopian city, as expounded by the Greeks. And these same features remain, in open or more disguised form, even in the supposedly more democratic utopias of the nineteenth century, such as Bellamy's *Looking Backward*. In the end, utopia merges into the dystopia of the twentieth century: and one suddenly realizes that the distance between the positive ideal and the negative one was never so great as the advocates or admirers of utopia had professed.'[61]

From this there might seem plenty of justification for abandoning the utopian enterprise as inherently oppressive. Many critics have indeed done so. But what of those hauntings that I raised at the beginning of this chapter? What of those complications of the utopian schemes not only in terms of their entanglements with the subjects they sought to repress, but also in relation to the oppositional activities of other avant-gardes? This is the subject of the final sections of this chapter. By setting alongside these dreams of order the counter-spaces of other modernist and avant-garde groups, I raise further questions about the utopian schemes, and open up paths for a consideration of different utopian engagements with urban spaces.

Counter-spaces of the avant-garde

The dreams pursued by André Breton and the surrealists during the 1920s and 1930s refused to be shackled by such a logic of authority and took different lines of flight. The surrealist group contested the moralising *rappel à l'ordre* that was promulgated in France after the First World War and engaged in polemics with proponents of modernist architecture, including Le Corbusier. This was part of their wider commitment to revolution and to questioning established codes of space and time. Breton was initially involved with dada in Paris but severed ties with that group and published the first 'Manifesto of Surrealism' in 1924. He famously later highlighted the radical aspirations of the surrealists when he wrote: '"Transform the world", Marx said; "change life", Rimbaud said. These two watchwords are one for us.'[62] To return to where I began this chapter, Breton's reference to Cheval's Ideal Palace in his lecture in Prague celebrated an architecture of imagination, raw strangeness and 'outsider' creativity that challenged the protocols of formal artistic training. Breton and other surrealists came to eulogise the site, being among the first to proclaim its wider artistic significance. Breton first visited it in 1931. He reproduced a photograph of himself standing at an entrance to the structure shortly afterwards in his book *Communicating Vessels* (figure 4.10), and he made at least two more visits during his life, being particularly drawn by its dream-like spaces and praising Cheval as 'the undisputed master of mediumistic architecture and sculpture'.[63] Breton had been directed there by fellow surrealist Jacques Brunius, who published his own account of the palace in *Variétés* in June 1929. The latter discussed its 'feverish creations' and stated favourably that Cheval had established 'a monstrous system of imagined memories', with the palace itself being 'a monument to the imagination'.[64]

Three giants guard the palace on the eastern side, with two smaller druidesses positioned between them (figure 4.11). Staircases lead up to a terrace and to the Tower of Barbary, with an oasis and palm trees. Among many inscriptions is one on the western façade indicating 'Entrance to an

Figure 4.10 André Breton visiting the Ideal Palace, 1931. Photograph from *Les Vases communicants* (1932).

imaginary palace', which leads the visitor into an underground passage and chambers, featuring birds, animals, plants and mazes of sculptures. The palace's organic forms elide in an apparent process of exchange, metamorphosis, even flux, and the permeability of inside and outside further convey an impression of in-betweenness and flow (figure 4.12). Aspects

Figure 4.11 Three giants at the Ideal Palace, Hauterives. Photograph by Marcus Schubert, Toronto.

Figure 4.12 North detail at the Ideal Palace, Hauterives. Photograph by Marcus Schubert, Toronto.

recall the natural grottoes in the surrounding region of Drôme and the mountains of Vercors, while other elements draw on the postman's memories as well as images from illustrated magazines and readings, and experiences in Algeria, bringing together styles and scenes from around the world. The borrowings, associations and movements that characterise the palace are suggestive of the mechanisms of dreams and their forms of condensation and displacement. 'The visitor wonders whether he has been transported into a fantastic, chimerical dream that stretches beyond the confines of the imagination,' commented Cheval. 'Is he in India, the Orient, China or Switzerland? It is impossible to tell, as the styles of all lands and all ages are mingled and blended together.'[65] The west façade plays with a range of styles by including architectural models of, among other places, a Swiss chalet, a medieval castle, a Hindu temple, a mosque with minarets, the Maison Carrée in Algiers, and the White House in Washington, DC. There are also connections between stylistic aspects of his structure and the temples of Angkor Wat in Cambodia, a site that similarly fascinated the surrealists, and whose influence has been discerned in the paintings of Max Ernst after he visited Indochina in 1924.[66]

It is not surprising that the surrealists came to celebrate the Ideal Palace given the significance they attached to dream processes in their researches and activities and in their interrogations of reality, not only personally but also collectively and politically. The surrealists were attracted more generally to the work of marginalised figures and those situated outside the institutionalised spaces of art, and they asserted an affinity with the creativity of mediums, children, so-called 'naive' or 'primitive' artists, and those designated insane. Discussing this theme, Breton once wrote of being passionately summoned by the 'explosive disdain' of the work of Cheval and others, and by 'their self-generation entirely outside the cultural line assigned to an epoch'.[67] He further wrote a poem entitled 'Facteur Cheval' in 1932, and gave Cheval the honourary appellation of being surrealist '*in architecture*'.[68] Breton's reference to Cheval in his Prague lecture appeared alongside brief remarks about other architectural experiments and discoveries. They included art nouveau, a style that briefly gained considerable attention in Paris between around 1895 and 1904, including through Hector Guimard's designs for the entrances to the Métro stations. Breton describes how it fundamentally changed ideas about spatial construction and how it had recently been taken up with enthusiasm by Salvador Dalí, who refered to its delirious and essentially extra-plastic character. Dalí writes:

No collective effort has managed to create a world of dreams as pure and disturbing as these art nouveau buildings, which by themselves constitute, on the very fringe of architecture, true realizations of solidified desires, in which the most violent and cruel automatism painfully betrays a hatred of reality and a need for refuge in an ideal world similar to those in a childhood neurosis.[69]

In his personal accounts Dalí writes of art nouveau's 'terrifying and edible beauty', and of its metamorphoses and blendings of conventional categories, as in a time-space of dreams whereby 'Gothic becomes metamorphosed into Greek, into Far Eastern and even . . . into Renaissance'. He shows particular interest in Guimard's constructions and also the work of Antonio Gaudí in Barcelona, and suggests that art nouveau scandalises contemporary functionalism in architecture and art and serves only 'the "functioning of desires" (and the most troubled, disqualified and inadmissible ones at that)'.[70] The retreat from reality and the perversity of art nouveau are part of its appeal for Dalí, who associates its architecture with the unconscious and the expression of repressed desires, and who dwells particularly on its 'hysterical' and 'perverse' aspects, relating them to the repression enacted by the modernism of 'the functionalist ideal'.[71]

In his lecture, Breton sets this interest in a 'concrete irrationality' in architecture, as something breaking through the field's limits, against a modernist conception: specifically, his target is Le Corbusier's Swiss Pavilion of the Cité Universitaire in Paris, from 1930–2. The building, which has often been regarded as a prospective fragment of the Radiant City, is scathingly described by Breton as one that 'outwardly answers all the conditions of rationality and coldness that anyone could want in recent years'.[72] As Breton's comments indicate, there was a direct opposition to modernist dreams of urban order with surrealism. Many surrealists rejected technocratic and rationalist approaches to urban space, and in so doing pursued an architectural sensibility based on an inner-life of dreams and the psyche. The formal involvement of architects within surrealism was limited, with the group often focusing on 'discovered' architectures such as Cheval's palace and elements of art nouveau as well as various gothic castles or ruins. But among those envisioning architectural projects was Tristan Tzara, who argued that modern architecture 'as hygienic and stripped of ornaments as it wants to appear, has no chance of living' and who wrote instead of a sheltering, soft, tactile, 'intrauterine architecture' of the future that looked back to forms such as caves, grottos, irregular houses and 'prenatal desires'.[73] Related themes are apparent in the proposals by Roberto Matta Echaurren, known as Matta, who trained with Le Corbusier in 1934–6, and who published designs for an apartment in 1938 that struggled with the 'tyranny of right angles' by employing inflatable furniture, pliable surfaces, mirrors and 'walls like damp sheets which lose their shapes and wed our psychological fears'.[74]

Frederick Kiesler also became closely connected with some of the surrealists as he developed projects for an 'Endless Theatre' and the 'Endless House' from the mid-1920s. He proposed flexible, continuous living spaces and spheroid egg-shaped structures, whose planning was founded on 'our inner needs and processes rather than on the dictates of mechanics'.[75] Further significant activities included textual and visual creations of psychically charged interiors by Leonora Carrington and Max Ernst; the exhibition constructions involving among others Dalí, Marcel Duchamp, and Man Ray; and theoretical elaborations in Czech circles before Breton's visit to Prague, where Karel Teige had engaged in a critical debate with Le Corbusier in 1928–9 from a Marxist position between the poles of poetism and constructivism within the Devětsil group, before moving towards surrealism and becoming the main spokesperson of the Prague surrealist group soon after it was founded in 1934.[76] At the core of a range of surrealist ideas and practices was indeed an engagement with questions of space. Through their commitment to transforming everyday life and society, the surrealists contested in a variety of ways both the dominant socio-spatial order and the modern movement's conceptions of space as it was usually defined. Significant too were the urban practices of the surrealists around Breton that will be taken up in the next chapter, in terms of their wanders through cities and engagements with the geographies of what Walter Benjamin called 'the most dreamed-of of their objects', that is 'the city of Paris itself'.[77]

Perhaps surprisingly given the critical comments by Breton and others discussed above, surrealist elements are apparent in Le Corbusier's art works and architecture in the 1920s and 1930s. Recent critics have drawn attention, for example, to the confrontations in Le Corbusier's paintings between natural objects or what he called 'objects evoking a poetic reaction' – a term that resonates with Breton's positions – and to the interest that he shared with the surrealists in the paintings of Giorgio de Chirico. Alexander Gorlin in particular finds connections between Le Corbusier's early work and surrealism in the coincidence of the imagery, in the common interest in techniques of defamiliarisation and juxtaposition, and in the 'slightly sinister atmosphere' that pervades the ostensibly cleansed and hygienic spaces of Le Corbusier's architecture.[78] Others have often pointed to the oneiric qualities of some of Le Corbusier's architectural promenades and more specifically to the extraordinary entertainment spaces and contraptions of the penthouse that he designed for Charles de Beistégui on the Champs Élysées in Paris, in 1930–1, with its periscope, its electric moving walls and hedges, and its fireplace in a room with no ceiling. Charles Jencks describes the latter project as 'really a Surrealist apartment itself, designed with a Purist background', although he suggests that this was based on the architect's common strategy of appropriating 'another position through attack and transformation, criticism and juxtaposition'.[79] Breton may have been derogatory about Le Corbusier's surrealist-style inflections, but the criticisms were not one way. Although Le Corbusier rarely confronted the surrealists' ideas directly, and showed only sporadic interest in their journals,[80] he argued early on against the surrealists' approach to the object. In his view, the surrealists had failed to acknowledge the dependence of their poetic flights and dreams upon real objects produced through conscious effort, objects with a *function*, and hence upon a *realism* that was a product of the machine age.[81] Later, in his account of his trip to the United States in 1935, he described surrealism as 'a noble, elegant, artistic, funereal institution', before he launched into a dense attack:

> It was necessary to embalm and hide under flowers the remains of a dead society; chants and prayers were required . . . Dream! Freud! Phantoms in limbo! Almost spiritism. Spiritualism, stories, evocation. Literature. There are no bones in it any longer, but disjointed things, unearthly, passing over into stupefying and promiscuous combinations. Sensitive souls, lacking in solidity, occupy themselves with these precious, crepuscular decorations . . . What liturgy is this? What refined, moving, spectral ceremony? What appeal to the past?[82]

It is less the clash between perspectives as such that I want to focus on here, however, than the potential disruptions to the utopian dreams of urban order in the light of these counter-currents. For in their different ways the surrealists' activities – with their interest in interminglings, metamorphoses, the unconscious and the uncanny aspects of the urban – turn us towards elements that are rejected and repressed in the utopian urban schemes. As such, they not only pose a challenge to the dreams of order, although it is clear that at the same time they uphold some of their assumptions as well;[83] but they also raise questions about the stability of those dreams with their anxieties, suppressions and phobias. It is to these potential disruptions that I want to turn in the final section of this chapter.

Destabilising dreams of order

Alongside Le Corbusier's journey to New York and his aim to form 'the city par excellence of modern times' can be set the *de*-formations in Dalí's discussion of his own first visit to the city made the year before, in which he dwells in a 'paranoid-critical' mode on the morphology and metamorphoses of the city. From the deck of his ship the *Normandie*, Le Corbusier saw the city as 'distant, azure and mother-of-pearl, with its spires thrust up toward the sky'.[84] From the deck of the *Champlain*, Dalí views the skyline as 'verdigris, pink and creamy-white', adding: 'It looked like an immense Gothic Roquefort cheese. I love Roquefort . . .'[85] His early experiences in Manhattan lead him to assert, like Le Corbusier, that the city is not modern. But rather than understanding this as a case of *not yet*, Dalí treats it as a resistance to the idea of the modern, and especially to the vision of the 'modern and mechanical city' that 'the estheticians of the European advance guard, the apologists of the aseptic beauty of functionalism, had tried to impose upon us'. The day after arriving in the city he professes to find a number of manifestations of anti-modernism, citing as examples the use of candles in elevators, the heavy decorations of apartment interiors, and the deliberate projection of black smoke onto the façade of a building in Park Avenue to 'age' a new skyscraper. 'In Paris, on the other hand,' he comments, 'the modern architects *à la* Le Corbusier were racking their brains to find new and flashy, utterly anti-Parisian materials which would not turn black, so as to imitate the supposed "modern sparkle" of New York.' Against Le Corbusier's will to whiten, Dalí views New York as vivid red; and, reaching for his own biological conceptions to burst through the claims on the city's form made by other European modernists, and to disturb the serenity of the vision of Manhattan framed around sites such as the Rockefeller Centre, he states that the city's poetry is 'seething biology', it is 'calves' lungs', it is the poetry 'of a giant many-piped organ of red-ivory – it does not scrape the sky, it resounds in it, and it resounds in it with the compass of the systole and the diastole of the visceral canticles of elementary biology.'[86]

Provocative and disturbing though some of his images may be, however, and in passing it might be noted that Dalí's position within the surrealist group was highly contentious from around the time of that journey,[87] I want to press the question of destabilisation further by concentrating on that term that so haunts Le Corbusier, the *formless*. In particular, I want to follow it to a place 'at the side of surrealism'. Here differentiation, purification and systems of ordering are refused and instead the formless itself is valorised. The vertical that is so central to Le Corbusier's projects, its lines a regulating principle, its mark that of the morally upright stance, is brought down through a process of horizontalisation. The sun inscribing its arch through the sky, the 'sun our dictator' as Le Corbusier called it, an ennobling symbol of reason marking out the rhythm of the day, becomes also a 'rotten sun', one linked to self-destruction and sacrifice, a blinding presence for those who stare at it, its two sides indicated in the myth of Icarus where it not only illuminates his flight as an elevated goal, but also destroys his passage by melting the wax on his wings. The clearing of the look, the hygiene of vision, is disturbed by coverings of dust that obscure the transparency of glass, and the privileging of the eye is itself undermined through a variety of transgressions and denigrations. This line of thinking is associated with the dissident surrealist Georges Bataille, who described himself as the movement's 'old enemy from within'.[88]

Bataille's association with Breton and the surrealist group was tense after they met in 1925. Many written exchanges followed that highlighted the differences in their positions, although their polemical character also risks distracting from the complexities and importance of the relationship.[89] Bataille's interests lay in a base materialism and in issues of excess, expenditure and heterogeneity, alongside his concerns with the sacred, violence and eroticism. His work provides a vigorous repudiation of utopian schemes of ordering, one that sought to undo idealist conceptions and indeed exclude them altogether in asserting a materialism that resisted the distinction between form and matter and its attendant hierarchy of things, which he believed was founded on an obsession with an ideal form of matter even among most of those describing themselves as materialists. In a 'Critical dictionary' published in the journal *Documents* in 1929, Bataille provided a short entry for *informe* or 'formless'. He stressed that it is not only an adjective with a particular meaning but a term that performs a task: it declassifies, brings things down in the world. 'What it designates does not, in any sense whatever, possess rights, and everywhere gets crushed like a spider or an earthworm,' he wrote. He noted the desire of academics and philosophers to systematise and find pattern and shape in the universe, to fit what is 'into a frock-coat, a mathematical frock-coat'. But, in contrast, to affirm 'that the universe resembles nothing at all and is only *formless*, amounts to saying that the universe is something akin to a spider or a gob of spittle.'[90]

A questioning of form ran through the pages of *Documents*, which under Bataille's editorship brought together former surrealists with artists, sociologists and anthropologists in a review devoted to a subversive kind of ethnographic study. This ethnography examined, burrowed into, and sought to undermine prevailing categories, norms and hierarchies as it moved between the 'exotic' and the commonplace, and across lines between high and low culture, and took particular interest in impurities and displacements. Working especially through juxtaposition as a means of defamiliarising and disturbing notions of wholeness, and through a close focus on objects that were often magnified in photographs to disconcerting effect, the review created what James Clifford calls 'the order of an unfinished collage rather than that of a unified organism'.[91] When Bataille turned to the formless in this context, his interest lay not in advocating it as a positive value as such, but rather in its job (*besogne*), in its operation through disrupting and decomposing. His account of the term with its reference to the spider and spit brings us back to that which so horrified Le Corbusier – the 'protoplasmic', the 'puddle' – but in a way that, instead of demanding the institution of form, interrupts dreams of pure form and wholeness. In Bataille's view, base materialism and the formless fundamentally resist components of ordering. The matter they evoke is heterogeneous and refuses to be tamed or elevated through the use of concepts: it is defined by nonlogical difference.[92] This interest in the formless was characterised by a mistrust of the conventions of visual experience and optical clarity that have long been linked to notions of form, and it was part of Bataille's wider critique of ocularcentrism.[93] The concern with base matter and with countering the primacy of the visual was also linked by Bataille to a return to the body, as Martin Jay has noted, but it was a body that contrasted with Le Corbusier's ideal conception and contemporaneous discussions of a 'new man', being grotesque, open, with porous boundaries, and – after the image of a man adopted as the symbol for the 'Acéphale' secret society later established by Bataille – headless.[94]

What is particularly interesting in this context, however, is the significance Bataille assigned to architecture in both metaphorical and literal terms. His first entry of the 'Critical dictionary' was devoted to the subject where he addressed the role of architectural composition in systematisation, regulation and in asserting authority and social order. In his view, 'only society's ideal nature – that of authoritative command and prohibition – expresses itself in actual architectural construction.'[95] He believed that a taste for human or divine authority could be found in architectural construction as such, not only in monuments and spectacular buildings that 'speak to and impose silence on the crowds' but also in realms such as physiognomy, dress, music or painting.[96] Among his later dictionary entries were those addressing particular spaces. In an article on the 'Slaughterhouse', which was illustrated by photographs of the abattoir at La Villette by Eli Lotar, Bataille confronted the sublimatory practices involved in the homogenisation of space and the process, traditionally so important in utopian projects, by which elements of the city are hidden, parcelled away, structured as disorder to be repressed. Having suggested a connection between the slaughterhouse and the temple, he noted that today 'the slaughterhouse is cursed and quarantined like a plague-ridden ship'.[97] This constructed the space as one of repulsion, a force that functioned in relation to those of attraction at other sites in the city such as the case he discussed elsewhere of the 'Museum' (that was 'comparable to the lung of a great city' where 'every Sunday the throng flows into museum, like blood, and leaves it fresh and purified'.[98]) He argued that the act of quarantine was connected 'with an unhealthy need of cleanliness, with irascible meanness, and boredom'. Its effects led 'good folk' to 'vegetate as far as possible from the slaughterhouse, to exile themselves, out of propriety, to a flabby world in which nothing fearful remains and in which, subject to the ineradicable obsession of shame, they are reduced to eating cheese'.[99]

As Denis Hollier has shown, it was not by accident that the critical dictionary started with architecture, nor was it for alphabetical reasons, which the dictionary ignored; for Bataille's first published text was also on the subject, entitled *Notre-Dame de Rheims*. Dating probably from 1918 and before he distanced himself from Catholicism, the pamphlet meditated on the splendours of the cathedral and its recent burning during the war, and recalled a time when the cathedral was 'white', 'bathed in sunlight', and a 'vision as lovely as our dreams of paradise'.[100] It was never mentioned subsequently by Bataille but, according to Hollier, all his work can in some respects be read as a rewriting of that initial text, which he came to see as a result of 'the vast ideological system symbolised and maintained by architecture': it was an attempt to silence the white cathedral, to break up and loosen architectural construction, to open holes and gaps, to deconstruct the edifice, to lower hierarchies. Hollier presents Bataille's writings as anti-architectural, refusing and transgressing the imposition of form, where writing is 'antidiscursive' as it 'endlessly deforms and disguises itself, endlessly rids itself of form'.[101] Bataille provided an example of political contestation against architectural order in his text on 'Architecture', where he argued that the storming of the Bastille during the French Revolution was a mass movement that was fuelled by a popular hostility towards monuments. But Hollier's immensely suggestive reading also underlines the wider struggle introduced by Bataille in the article, a struggle that was pitched against what he identified as the 'common cause' made between human and architectural orders, where the latter was seen as a development of the former, meaning that 'an attack on architecture, whose monumental productions now truly dominate the whole earth, grouping the servile multitudes under their shadow, imposing admiration and wonder, order and constraint, is necessarily, as it were, an attack on man'. It was in these terms that Bataille commended the work of modernist painters in challenging the elegance of the human figure, and in tracing a path that 'opens toward bestial monstrosity, as if there were no other way of escaping the architectural straitjacket'.[102]

Thinking Bataille and Le Corbusier together not only brings out their oppositions and divergences, as discussed above, but can also lead to recognising points of connection. Their respective involvements in debates around *planisme* in France during the 1930s suggest that they had common associates. Although Bataille was opposed to authoritarianism and centralised forms of control, aspects of his arguments at the time especially around notions of expenditure were close to those pursued by Arnaud Dandieu and Robert Aron who founded the Ordre Nouveau group. They in turn became linked in 1931 with the group around the journal *Plans* that Le Corbusier contributed to and was involved in editing.[103] While connections between Bataille and Le Corbusier during that time are a matter of speculation, it is known that they later had direct contact. When Bataille developed an interest in *planisme* in terms of his theory of 'general economy' after the war in his book *The Accursed Share*, in 1949, he gave a copy to Le Corbusier dedicating it to him as 'a token of my admiration and sympathy'. This gift and Le Corbusier's apparently avid reading of the book is discussed by Nadir Lahiji, who argues that it was an important source for the symbol of the Open Hand at Chandigarh, and that it was influential on Le Corbusier's plans for that city generally, which were characterised by a shift away from his earlier pre-war conceptions of planning. Lahiji suggests that Bataille's notions of the gift and *potlatch*, which were developed from Marcel Mauss, were particularly influential on Le Corbusier, who seems to have read the book as he was starting work at Chandigarh.[104]

Out of the encounters and confrontations discussed in these last two sections, however, I want to conclude this chapter by tracing two general points in summary. First, my focus has been on exclusions and repressions involved in the constructions of the utopian spaces, and on how their regulatory practices were bound up with desires and fears about the spaces of the modern city. As I have discussed, their struggles for order could never be complete, always existing in relation to the disorders that they identified and opposed. The 'high' values of their utopian spaces were created through the exclusion of 'low' others, and through this process those low others became constitutive of their identity, included within them symbolically and often becoming a site of fascination as well as dread. This explains the charge surrounding boundaries and lines, and the disturbances created by transgressions and the failure of things to keep to their proper place. Whatever the supposed purity of the utopian space, there is always the threat of disruptions from within. By bringing the utopian projects back into contact with contemporaneous activities of the surrealists, questions about the formation of the utopian spaces and their instabilities return with particular force. This is especially the case in relation to Bataille's writings with their attacks on architectural order and their obsession with heterogeneous matter, waste and the abject. Bataille's defence of the 'formless' and his invocation of a 'bestial monstrosity' directly challenge the utopian schemes, just as they rewrite his own initial 'white cathedral'. His interest in horizontalisation and desublimation further suggests disruptions of their pure spaces from within, where the high is brought low, and where the drive towards homogenisation is displaced. A theme running through many of his early texts is that everything has a low use as well as a high use, and as one commentator puts it: 'It is the low use, its imperious affirmation, that fells the hot-air balloons of the ideal with one malevolent blow.'[105]

Second, the surrealists are part of a counter-current within modernism that not only resists utopian strategies of ordering that have informed dominant notions of the Concept City, but that also carves out other paths. As such, they challenge many orthodox readings of modernist urbanism. To begin with, the defence of the formless is itself part of a wider tradition within modernism that connects with figures beyond

Bataille, and that includes a range of oppositions against notions of formal purity and impositions of form. It constitutes what Jay has identified as 'a subordinate tendency in aesthetic modernism, which challenged the apotheosis and purification of form'. He suggests that this counter-impulse may be best understood as part of the avant-garde, following the definition of that term by Peter Bürger, for it 'calls into question the purity of the aesthetic realm, undermines the distinction between high art and base existence, and reunites vision with the other senses'.[106] Other critics have explored the 'use-value of "formless"' in more detail in relation to modernist and contemporary art practices, and have put it to work in remarkable ways with the suggestion that 'the formless designates an ensemble of operations by means of which modernism is here grasped against the grain'.[107] But in addition, the spatial practices of the surrealists trace alternative routes for intervening in urban spaces, again 'against the grain' of modernism, and again in ways that connect with the ideas and practices of other elements within the modern avant-garde. They are part of what the architect Bernard Tschumi has described as an 'irritant' that runs parallel to the stream of formalist ideas that are usually the subject of architectural discourses about modernism and postmodernism, forming a tradition that is typically written out of mainstream histories of the modernist urbanism.[108] These activities have their own problems and commentaries around them also now have their own limiting orthodoxies, but in the rest of this study I want to develop this notion of an 'irritant' or what Tschumi refers to elsewhere as a tradition of 'dissidence', in relation to utopian engagements with the geographies of the modern city by avant-garde groups in post-war western Europe.

My focus is on the Situationist International and on immediate predecessors, whose members draw on the legacy of dada and surrealism in the 1950s and 1960s and developed it into a far-reaching radical programme of their own. This was during a period when many cities were again undergoing rapid transformations, and when aspects of the utopian visions discussed over the last three chapters were being taken up by state administrations and employed in massive urban reconstruction programmes especially in Europe and North America. It was also at a time, especially during the 1960s, when these schemes were being met with increasing opposition. The situationists were among those contesting the new forms of capitalist urbanisation. Their targets included those earlier utopian dreams of urban order, which they believed were having a disastrous influence on cities. But despite the situationists' opposition to the earlier utopian spaces, they did not renounce the dream of changing the modern city altogether. Instead, their critique of human geography was driven by an alternative utopianism that looked towards the revolutionary transformation of urban space and society.

NOUVEAU THÉATRE D'OPÉRATIONS
DANS LA CULTURE

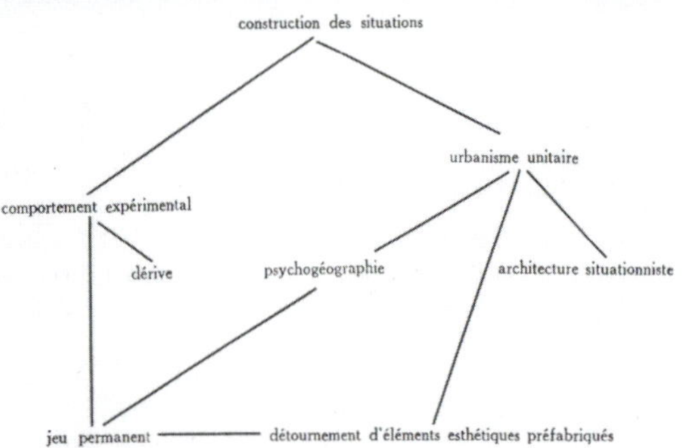

LA DISSOLUTION DES IDEES ANCIENNES VA DE PAIR AVEC LA DISSOLUTION DES ANCIENNES CONDITIONS D'EXISTENCE :

INTERNATIONALE
SITUATIONNISTE

Figure 5.1 'New theatre of operations within culture.' Tract by the French section of the Situationist International, 1958. Courtesy of Archivio Gallizio, Turin.

CHAPTER 5

Situationist adventures

The city expresses, concretely, the prevailing organisation of everyday life. The nightmare of the contemporary metropolis – space and time engineered to isolate, exhaust and abstract us – has driven the lesson home to everybody and its very pitilessness has begun to engender a new utopian consciousness.

The English section of the Situationist International[1]

We are only at the beginning of urban civilization; it is up to us to bring it about ourselves using the pre-existing conditions as our point of departure . . . The urbanists of the twentieth century will have to construct adventures.

Internationale situationniste[2]

To build the haçienda

'We are bored in the city, there is no longer any Temple of the Sun.' So declared Ivan Chtcheglov at the opening of his 'Formulary for a new urbanism' of 1953, the utopian text with which I introduced this book.[3] Writing two decades after many of the surrealist interventions discussed in the previous chapter, he argued that many of the earlier imaginings of such avant-garde groups were no longer possible. 'The poetry of the billboards lasted twenty years,' he stated. 'We are bored in the city, we really have to strain to still discover mysteries on the sidewalk billboards, the latest state of humour and poetry.' He followed this with a list of signs, sites and street names from Paris, referring to places that he and his colleagues in the Letterist International (LI) frequented through wanders in the streets and nights spent moving between bars. They were part of what Chtcheglov refers to as the 'geological' structure of the city, ascertained through explorations of urban atmospheres, legends and ghosts. 'We move within a *closed* landscape whose landmarks constantly draw us toward the past,' he noted. 'Certain *shifting* angles, certain *receding* perspectives, allow us to glimpse original conceptions of space, but this vision remains fragmentary.'[4] If a sense of loss hangs over the early part of his text, he sought alternative possibilities both in the existing city and through the construction of alternatives. He suggested some inspiration may also be found 'in the magical locales of fairy tales and surrealist writings: castles, endless walls, little forgotten bars, mammoth caverns, casino mirrors'. But while such 'dated images retain a small catalyzing power', he argued it was necessary to rework them by giving them new meaning. 'We propose to invent new, changeable decors,' he declared; 'You'll never see the hacienda. It doesn't exist. *The hacienda must be built.*'[5]

The Situationist International (SI) developed related criticisms of urbanism and attempts to realise alternatives after forming in 1957. As with many previous modernist and avant-garde movements, the situationists had an ambivalent attitude towards contemporary cities. They recognised cities to be key sites in the reproduction of social relations of domination as spaces of alienation and control. But at the same time they were concerned with the possibilities that lay embedded within these environments as they viewed cities as potential realms of freedom through which people could transcend alienation and create spaces in keeping with their own needs and desires, thereby realising their true selves as living subjects. In this sense the situationists resumed the progressive challenge posed by earlier modern movement architects and planners to transform capitalist urbanisation and to bring about better urban futures. But their commitment to changing urbanism as part of a revolutionary political project contrasted radically with the previous approaches of the modern movement. In 1958 the French section of the SI produced a tract that outlined their programme, illustrated by an aerial photograph of south-east Paris (figure 5.1). Unlike Le Corbusier, however, for whom aerial views were a means of rising above the city to reveal its 'horror' as a means of justifying planning surgery, the situationists had different intentions as suggested by the title above the image: 'New theatre of operations within culture'. This indicated their interest not in ordering the Concept City but rather in immersing themselves within its spaces. For them the city was a site of political struggle and they sought to investigate and change urban spaces through new forms of geographical research and action. Below the image was a conceptual map of terms they employed in this endeavour: 'construction of situations', 'psychogeography', 'permanent game', 'situationist architecture' and 'unitary urbanism'.

In the next three chapters I consider how the situationists and their avant-garde associates drew on such concepts in their attempts to transform urban spaces and society. Central to this account is the term unitary urbanism. The concept was not yet formulated when Chtcheglov was writing but his text anticipates its contours and influenced early investigations in this area. Unitary urbanism was not a doctrine of urbanism, the situationists repeatedly insisted, but a critique of urbanism. It was forged out of a revolutionary struggle to transform social space and everyday life. Its utopianism lay in both its visionary qualities in that it looked towards 'a terrain of experience for the *social space* of the cities of the future'. But it was also bound up with current experimentation and political struggle in the belief that it 'has already begun the moment it appears as a programme of research and development'.[6] The concept left behind modern movement ideals based on 'water-tight formulae' for urban ordering and related emphasis on permanence. The situationists declared that it was 'opposed to the temporal fixation of cities' and 'leads instead to the advocacy of a permanent transformation, an accelerated movement of the abandonment and reconstruction of the city in temporal and at times spatial terms'. They also asserted that it was 'opposed to the fixation of people at certain points of a city', and that it was 'the foundation for a civilization of leisure and play'.[7] They envisaged unitary urbanism as being dynamic, continually evolving, concerned with ambiences and situations, and the outcome of people's desires and actions. It would transcend the kinds of segmentations instituted through modern planning and would ultimately constitute 'a unitary human milieu in which separations such as work/leisure or public/private will finally be dissolved'.[8] Above all, it was opposed to the alienating conditions of the society of the spectacle and promoted as a project that was *collective* and *participatory*, one that would be 'lived' by its constructors. As such, it eschewed monumentalist architecture and privileged 'topological organisations commanding general participation', with the SI promising: '*We will play on topophobia and create a topophilia.*'[9]

In portraying unitary urbanism as a critique and not a doctrine of urbanism, the situationists distanced themselves from utopian planners who produced blueprints for the future city. The situationists did not present a spatial form as a means through which social hierarchies would be restored and processes channelled. Nevertheless they expressed utopian desire for radical change, a totalising claim for an other city and an other life that would transcend the present. As such their approach included attempts to imagine urban spaces otherwise, from Chtcheglov's visions of a new urbanism through to later situationist writings, maps, models, projects and actions. It also involved practices to intervene in the present so as to shatter contemporary illusions and open up possibilities. In this chapter I address how situationist visions of the city came out of the group's opposition to the conditions of cities at the time and to dominant forms of urbanism. This includes critiques of earlier utopian approaches associated in particular with the modern movement and Le Corbusier. In later sections of the chapter, I turn back to the formative years of the situationist project during the 1950s, including to the contributions of letterists who first formulated many aspects of this critique along with alternative ideas and practices about how cities could be used and what they might become. The following two chapters then trace out the utopianism of unitary urbanism.

Through this account, tensions and divisions will become apparent in the SI's approach to urbanism. Far from cohering as a singular perspective, it will be clear that situationist positions and priorities varied over time and between factions. Unitary urbanism's place as a central concern of the SI was strongest between 1957 and around 1961, from when the group's understanding of the term shifted markedly. This change was connected with a well-known source of controversy within the SI concerning the role of artists and artistic practices. Many of the first situationists had roots in artistic production and sought to take further the avant-garde aim of transgressing the boundaries between art and everyday space, and of changing life through the transcendence of art as a specialist category. As standard histories of the SI relate, however, most of the practising artists within the group had resigned or been expelled by mid-1962 and the group moved towards a more overtly political position, with the faction based around Debord assuming greater influence.[10] I discuss some of the tensions and splits involved later. But in starting with the situationists' critique of the spectacle and urbanism before moving back to consider earlier interventions, I also question orthodox views that have now built up around a schism between 'early' and 'late' periods within the SI. This is not least because the SI's early spatial concerns remain significant, being reworked rather than simply dropped from its agenda; such spatial concerns also have important implications for how the group's subsequent theorisations of capitalist society and the spectacle are understood, and vice versa.[11] Underlying these chapters is the situationists' belief that, despite the bleakness of present urban conditions, they contained within them the seeds of a radically different future. It is this *oppositional* and *transformative* utopianism and its framing as a critique of human geography that I draw out in what follows.

The critique of human geography

'The proletarian revolution,' wrote Debord, 'is that *critique of human geography* whereby individuals and communities must construct places and events commensurate with the appropriation, no longer just of their labour, but of their total history.'[12] Debord's understanding of revolution in spatial as well as social terms appears in his book *The Society of the Spectacle*, which was published in November 1967. His volume was published in the same month as Raoul Vaneigem's more flamboyant situationist text *Traité de savoir-vivre à l'usage des jeunes générations* (translated as *The Revolution of Everyday Life*).[13] While some critics depicted them as key texts of a new radical movement, few envisaged the role they would shortly play along with other situationist writings and activities as a theorisation and fuelling of political revolt as revolutionary actions and wildcat occupations spiralled through France in May 1968, temporarily transforming spaces and everyday life in Paris as part of wider insurrectionary movements shaking many other parts of the world. Contemporary urbanism and the production of space came under fierce attack in Debord's book, as he asserted the need for a spatialised revolutionary project. Considering the arguments of the book is important for positioning these attacks in terms of his critique of 'the society of the spectacle'.

Debord argued that the spectacle was the central organising principle of contemporary societies. We live in an image-saturated world, he asserted, where alienation is total. People are alienated from their labour, their surroundings, their desires and their true selves. Social life had been so occupied by the commodity and administrative techniques, so saturated in an accumulation of spectacles, that vision had become associated with a pseudo-world of illusion and people had become more like spectators than active agents, occupying roles assigned to them by others in a state of passive contemplation. Debord stressed that the spectacle cannot be understood as 'a collection of images', nor 'as a deliberate distortion of the visual world or as a product of the technology of the mass dissemination of images'; rather, 'it is a social relationship between people that is mediated by images', a 'world view transformed into an objective force'.[14] With everyday life riven with separations and dominated by the economy as a separate sphere, the spectacle becomes a means of unifying in terms of the image where it 'unites what is separate, but it unites it only in its *separateness*'.[15] This theorisation of the spectacle has associations with several strands of western Marxism. In particular it extends discussions of alienation and commodity fetishism within the Hegelian-Marxist tradition, tracing a lineage back to Marx's *Economic and Philosophic Manuscripts* of 1844. It is indeed important to underline his engagement with Marx's thought for this is in danger of getting obscured in recent appropriations of his ideas. The connection with Georg Lukács and his *History and Class Consciousness* of 1923 is especially significant as Debord took up questions of the totality, commodity fetishism and reification through his own critique of capitalist society. Parallels are also apparent between some of Debord's ideas and those explored by Jean-Paul Sartre as well as the Arguments group in France in the 1950s, although the situationists boycotted the latter group's journal in 1960. The situationists also had significant connections with the group *Socialisme ou Barbarie*, which Debord joined for several months in 1960–1.[16]

As the former situationists T. J. Clark and Donald Nicholson-Smith have argued, *The Society of the Spectacle* should be seen tactically as resisting attempts at the time to banish the concept of totality along with traces of Hegel from Marxist theory, as in Louis Althusser's reading of Marx's supposed 'epistemological break'. It should also be read alongside the situationists' other political analyses and specifically their opposition to the orthodox left, with much of the book being directed against Stalinism and its continuing reproduction in leftist circles.[17] An especially important precedent and parallel project involved Henri Lefebvre's analyses of everyday life in capitalist society, and his influential earlier attempts to re-orientate Marxist theory around notions of alienation and the struggle for the dis-alienation of society. Lefebvre had been involved with the surrealists and had been introduced to dialectical thought and to Hegel by André Breton in 1924, an encounter that led him to Marx.[18] Several decades on Lefebvre developed another mutually influential association and friendship with the situationists, especially Debord and Michèle Bernstein, before the group split acrimoniously with him in the early 1960s. Lefebvre never became a member of the SI, but he later recounted the intensity of the association, describing it as a 'love story' and a 'communion'.[19] Considering the encounters between Lefebvre and the SI sheds interesting light on their respective projects, especially in relation to their shared concerns with urbanism and the politics of space. In Lefebvre's case it underlines his embrace of utopian, heterodox and transgressive elements that have been downplayed in much of the rediscovery of his work in Anglophone academia since the 1980s and yet that are suggested by his reputation among some critics as a 'Marxist outlaw'[20] and as part of a band of 'wayward or renegade Marxists'.[21] For their part, in reply to the question 'are you Marxists?', the situationists stated in 1964: 'Just as much as Marx when he said, "I am not a Marxist."' As will be seen, their dissident attitudes too drift beyond the usual markers of western Marxism and bring them into contact with critical currents that include a 'Gothic Marxism', associated with the work of André Breton and the surrealists.[22]

Contact between the situationists and Lefebvre first came in the late 1950s as the latter's attempts to understand the impact of capitalism and administrative apparatuses on everyday life were deepening. Lefebvre's initial critique was marked by an interest in both the misery of everyday life, the conditions of which he believed were borne differently along class and gender lines, and the power of everyday life as a realm of struggle, adaptation and creativity that included residual elements that contrasted with current estrangements. Lefebvre pursued these themes from a position outside the Communist Party following his suspension in 1958, after which he decided to leave from the left rather than the right, as he later put it.[23] It was a period of immense personal upheaval and political ferment for him but one in which he also believed new possibilities were opening up as diverse revolutionary groups formed outside formal parties. He initially addressed these movements in 'Vers un romantisme révolutionnaire', in October 1957, where he stressed the significance of their revolutionary struggle over culture as well as economic structures in an essay that attracted the attention of the younger Debord and members of the SI, which had been formally constituted several months earlier.[24] Debord critically engaged with this text as he emphasised that the study of everyday life had to be explicitly for the purpose of transforming it, a point he made at a conference convened on the theme by Lefebvre for the 'Group for Research on Everyday Life' at the Centre National de Recherches Scientifiques (CNRS) in 1961.[25] Debord was thus committed to practices of disalienation and revolutionary change, which Lefebvre had previously figured in terms of the quest for totality through praxis that would allow the transcendence of 'economic man' of capitalist society and the realisation of 'total man'. But in addressing the organised poverty of the everyday and the reign of scarcity that he saw as being imposed and policed in an exploitative society, Debord introduced the notion of everyday life as 'a colonised sector'.[26] The situationists asserted that a revolutionary programme should aim for 'the complete decolonisation of everyday life' through a unitary critique.[27]

The colonisation of everyday life became an important concept for both the SI and Lefebvre, being employed in the latter's second volume of his

Critique of Everyday Life and in subsequent works.[28] The phrase had particular salience in the French context where a rapid state-led drive for modernisation brought abrupt changes in living conditions, urbanism and images of society between the mid-1950s and the mid-1960s. With the ending of the French empire being marked by struggles for independence as in the Algerian war, processes of decolonisation during this period were bound up with a shift towards a form of *interior* colonialism around 1960, so Lefebvre argued, as administrative techniques, capital and personnel turned to focus on new objects and spaces, including realms of consumption, leisure, private life as well as the built environment of cities. Urban spaces and the everyday became treated in a manner analogous to the treatment of colonial territories, with regions outside the centres of political and economic power being viewed as semi-colonies and with exploitation involving consumption as well as production.[29] The argument about interior colonisation is intrinsically geographical and directs attention to a concern shared by the situationists and Lefebvre within their critiques: the significance of geography and urban space in the reproduction of dominant social relations. These themes will be explored further in the next section.

Environments of abstraction

Debord argued that the spectacle 'corresponds to the historical moment at which the commodity completes its colonization of social life'. It speaks of a world where 'social space is continually being blanketed by stratum after stratum of commodities'.[30] The spectacle now dominated social life and space, he stated, homogenising and fracturing space, unifying and separating, and becoming 'the perfection of separation *within* human beings'. Debord assigned particular importance to urbanism in affecting separation. He argued that it provided a means 'of tackling the ongoing need to safeguard class power by ensuring the atomization of workers dangerously *massed together* by the conditions of urban production', since it allowed the capturing of isolated individuals as 'individuals *isolated together*' in factories, cultural centres, tourist resorts, housing complexes and other spaces (figure 5.2). Attempts by established powers to maintain order in the streets, bolstered by the demands of modern movement architects and planners, had led to the street's eventual suppression.[31] Debord's analysis built on the situationists' earlier understanding of class segmentation in spatial-temporal terms. They argued that the proletariat, far from declining in significance, had now expanded and included 'all people who have

Figure 5.2 'Social space of leisure consumption.' Sports stadium at Milwaukee where eighteen members of two baseball teams are surrounded by 43,000 spectators, who in turn are surrounded by their cars. Photograph and caption from *International situationniste* 4 (June 1960).

Figure 5.3 Sarcelles was the first grand ensemble to be built in the Paris region, with its population increasing from around 1,500 to 60,000 between 1954 and 1974. After considerable early criticism it became a focus for resident activism to improve living conditions; it also became a symbol among many Parisians of the new urban form, with the term 'la Sarcellite' being coined to characterise an associated malaise. Photograph from *Internationale situationniste* 9 (August 1964).

no possibility of altering the social space-time that society allots for its consumption'. The ruling class was in contrast constituted by 'those who organise this space-time, or who at least have a significant margin of personal choice'. This fundamental social polarisation was typically veiled by gradations of income and rank and by the workings of the leisure society, they noted, but once posed it left other differences in status 'secondary'.[32]

In developing their theorisation of the spectacle during the 1960s, the situationists therefore portrayed urbanism and planning as important factors in ensuring the reproduction of these class lines and understood urbanism as a significant component of spectacular society. As part of this critique, they denounced the role of planning in dispersing populations from former urban centres. They regarded the building of developments such as the *grands ensembles* in the case of France as the work of twentieth-century Baron Haussmanns, enabling the repressive management of urban areas in the interests of state and police power, and representing the partitioning of space in its purest form. The situationists therefore called for revolutionary criticism of the conditioning being imposed upon inhabitants in places such as Sarcelles, the first grand ensemble to be constructed in the Paris region from 1954 (figure 5.3), and the company new town of Mourenx, built rapidly in south-west France during the 1950s as part of the petrochemical plants of Lacq. In an essay on the 'Geopolitics of hibernation', the group drew lessons about such housing developments from the interest at the time in constructing nuclear shelters. Noting how ineffective these shelters would be in the event of a nuclear war, the situationists argued that 'protection' in this context was only a pretext for stimulating consumer demand and that the building of such structures demonstrated the ways in which people's interests could be manipulated, so that they would work for pseudo-needs that had never been desires. According to the situationists, the similarities between these shelters and the housing schemes were telling. 'The new habitation that is now taking shape with the large housing developments is not really distinct from the architecture of the shelters; it merely represents a lower level of that architecture,' they wrote. 'The concentration-camp organisation of the surface of the earth is the normal state of the present society in formation; its condensed subterranean version merely represents that society's pathological excess. This subterranean sickness reveals the real nature of the normal surface "health".'[33]

Utopian modernist planning projects in particular came under attack. These included Brasília, which was designed in the mid-1950s along Corbusier-influenced lines by Lúcio Costa and Oscar Niemeyer as a centre of bureaucratic power for Brazil. The SI depicted this city as 'the supreme expression of functionalist architecture';[34] or, as it put it elsewhere, as 'the architecture of functionaries, the instrument and microcosm of the bureaucratic *Weltanschauung*'.[35] No longer a positive dream, urbanism had become 'the most concrete and perfect fulfillment of a nightmare', according to the situationist Raoul Vaneigem. He argued that dominant utopian urban schemes were now a form of public relations, involving 'the projection in space of a social hierarchy without conflict'. As he put it: 'Roads, lawns, natural flowers, and artificial forests lubricate the machinery of subjection and make it enjoyable.'[36] Of concern too was the dominant role being accorded to the motor car within modern urban planning. Arguments that cities should be opened up more fully to traffic circulation, promoted so vigorously by modern movement architects and planners, now found a more receptive audience within many governments. In the Paris region the number of cars had continued to escalate since Le Corbusier's time, rising from around half a million in 1939 to more than one million by 1960, and to more than two million by 1965. To be truly modern, so it was often claimed, Paris had to embrace the motor car.[37] While the schemes of Le Corbusier among others gave a central place to the car as both destroyer and potential saviour of the city, the situationists Attila Kotányi and Raoul Vaneigem regarded traffic circulation in contrast as 'the organisation of universal isolation'. It was the 'opposite of encounter', in their view, since it 'absorbs the energies that could otherwise be devoted to encounters or to any sort of participation'.[38] Debord likewise contested the importance attached to motor cars and principles of circulation in planning discourses, as he promised: 'Revolutionary urbanists will not limit their concern to the circulation of things and of human beings trapped in a world of things. They will try to break these topological chains, paving the way with their experiments for a human journey through authentic life.'[39]

With Debord and many other situationists being based in Paris, the rapid transformation of that city from the 1950s was a process with which they were particularly concerned. Large-scale rebuilding works led to the demolition and reconstuction of an estimated twenty-four per cent of the surface area of the city between 1954 and 1974, and the expulsion of around 550,000 people from the city itself to the outskirts. The expulsions were centred along class and ethnic lines with the working-class population in the city during this period declining by forty-four per cent and the *cadres supérieurs* increasing by fifty-one per cent.[40] Certain changes took on a powerful symbolic significance. They included the closing of the old markets of Les Halles, in 1969, whose removal along with destruction of the widely celebrated metal and glass pavilions two years later represented for some critics the extraction of the very heart of the city.[41] Debord depicted the result as the sacking of the city. This was in an era which cities had 'exploded', he wrote, leading not to the transcendence of the country and the city but to their simultaneous collapse. Quoting Lewis Mumford's complaint about the 'formless masses' of urban debris now covering the countryside, he referred to how the fabric of urban areas was being dissolved and dispersed along highways and temporarily reconstituted in shopping centres – 'these temples of frenetic consumption' – before themselves being abandoned as spaces of consumption were restructured.[42] He argued that ideologies of urbanism were destroying cities and producing a new architecture for the poor that was shaped by modern means of mass construction and the interests of social control. He wrote: 'At the core of these conditions we naturally find an *authoritarian decision-making process* that abstractly develops any environment into an environment of abstraction.'[43]

Lefebvre's own interest in urban research was prompted by transformations in urbanisation during the 1950s and specifically by his witnessing, while studying rural issues for the CNRS, of the sudden building of Mourenx near to his home in the village of Navarrenx.[44] His critical response included questioning the impact of the town's 'machines for living in' and the ways in which projected onto the town was an analytic will to differentiate and separate zones, spheres and modes of behaviour as well as social groups. From its space could be read the kinds of paradoxes noted in relation to Debord's critique of the spectacle where, so Lefebvre suggested, dislocation and fragmentation were accompanied by an integration, a unification imposed from above that reduced differences though a process of homogenisation.[45] Lefebvre later argued that what could be 'read' from such new towns was not only the negation of the traditional city along with segregation and intense policing, but also the emergence of a new organisation of everyday life now carved up and being programmed. The result was a space itself 'strangely reminiscent of colonial or semi-colonial towns'.[46] The construction of the new towns followed what Lefebvre, like Debord, described as an explosion of the traditional city, or rather a double movement of 'implosion-explosion' produced by the double process of 'industrialisation-urbanisation'. This included the production of peripheries, suburbs, new satellite towns, spaces strung out along highways and sprouting beyond old city outskirts as forms of de-urbanised urbanisation, along with the expulsion and separation of the working class from the city as such and a dulling of the consciousness of urban reality.[47] It was further linked to new forms of state intervention in housing construction and the establishment of new governmental urbanism codes.

Lefebvre tackled the politics of these urban questions most explicitly through publications from around the mid- to late 1960s, following his association with the situationists. In these texts he considered 'official' urbanism as part of a programming of space that was itself part of the programming of everyday life, and understood social space in dialectical terms as a conflictive and contradictory medium through which the reproduction of the relations of production was attained. Addressing the space produced by modern capitalism Lefebvre came to use the term 'abstract space'. By this he meant a quantified space that is simultaneously commodified and bureaucratised, where use value is dominated by exchange value, where differences and diverse pasts are being erased, and whose extension and imposition is bound up with the disintegration of the city and the colonisation of everyday life. Stressing the complexities of abstract space, he argued that although it is homogenising it is not itself simply homogeneous but rather homogeneous and divided, fragmented and unified, continuous and cracked.[48] In particular, Lefebvre identified abstract space as geometric, visual and phallic. The visual formant referred to the power of the logic of visualisation that had come to dominate the other senses. Lefebvre acknowledged connections with the situationists' idea of the spectacle when he argued that this had both a metaphoric aspect, related to dependence on the written word, and a metonymic aspect that corresponded to 'spectacularization', a term that he linked to Debord and to the idea that 'the eye, the gaze, the thing seen, no longer mere details or parts, are now transformed into the totality'.[49] But he conceived of this approach as going beyond what he criticised as the 'sociologism' of Debord's book on the spectacle and as providing a wider analysis of visualisation in terms of the de-corporealisation of space. It is a process that subsumes spectacularisation and culminates in space having 'no social existence independently of an intense, aggressive and repressive visualization', whereby the visual realm 'overwhelms the whole body and usurps its role'.[50]

Bringing fuel to the fire

The criticisms by Lefebvre and the situationists connected with wider opposition to dominant utopian conceptions of urban planning that was mounting during the 1960s. In one of the most influential anti-modernist texts from the period, Jane Jacobs famously denounced what she called the 'sacking of cities'. Based in New York and focusing on American cities, she scorned 'the Radiant Garden City Beautiful', a composite term she used to characterise a disastrous amalgam of the work of Le Corbusier, Howard and the City Beautiful movement. Criticising its prescriptive ideals, she argued: 'there is a quality even meaner than outright ugliness or disorder, and this meaner quality is the dishonest mask of pretended order, achieved by ignoring or suppressing the real order that is struggling to exist and to be served.'[51] Her arguments helped to crystallise the anger and opposition that large numbers of people in New York and further afield were feeling towards grand modernist building works at the time, such as those works being driven by the planner Robert Moses as he sought to follow earlier expressway projects by 'hacking' another through lower Manhattan and destroying vibrant urban places in the process.[52] A range of critics shared Jacobs's attack on the authoritarianism of utopian planners, and similarly advocated grassroots action by urban citizens. While Richard Sennett rejected her anti-modernism and questioned her depiction of urban community, one that he found problematically enclosed, he too opposed utopian dreams of order as he advocated a more anarchistic attitude to the city that would lead to a 'disordered, unstable, direct social life'. He suggested that 'this disorder is *better* than dead, predetermined planning, which restricts effective social exploration', since it enables people to create their own lives more freely and to find ways of living with that freedom.[53]

Many people sympathetic to the original aims of the modern movement were also voicing doubts about its rationalistic plans. It is an often commented upon irony that, despite the radical emancipatory intentions of the modern movement proponents of the inter-war years such as the Bauhaus and Le Corbusier, elements of their projects became used in the post-war period to uphold and even to drive forward aspects of capitalist society they had opposed. Ideas that were intended to usher in a new space and way of life now became, through a tragic twist, a means to bolster the prestige of corporate and bureaucratic clients as well as to provide predominantly cheap and mass-produced solutions to meet pressing housing needs. Lefebvre notes that, although the Bauhaus may be seen as revolutionary and was closed down by the Nazis for its supposed subversiveness in 1933, it ironically emerged subsequently as formulating a programme that was 'tailor-made for the state'.[54] He argues that its members should be understood as '*practitioners* (architects and planners) and even *theoreticians* of so-called modern space, the space of "advanced" capitalism'.[55] David Harvey also remarks with respect to the modern movement more generally: 'It is easy in retrospect to argue that the architecture that resulted merely produced impeccable images of power and prestige for publicity-conscious corporations and governments, while producing modernist housing projects for the working class that became "symbols of alienation and dehumanization".'[56]

Resistance to high modernist orthodoxies included critiques from within the modern movement itself. These gained prominence after the ninth meeting of CIAM (Congrès Internationaux d'Architecture Moderne) in 1953 and the subsequent establishment of groups such as Team 10, which rejected earlier modernist vocabularies as inadequate for dealing with questions of the 'urban core' as well with other issues neglected in CIAM's Athens Charter such as neighbourhood, identity and complexity. These developments were not taking place in a vacuum, of course, but were embedded within changing economic and political conditions, and were bound up with oppositional voices being raised beyond the academy and outside institutions of architecture and planning especially in the 1960s. Versions of this story are often told as a preface to discussions of a sea-change in architecture and urban planning around the early 1970s, and the emergence of the 'postmodern'. This is often said to involve the rejection of utopian approaches, which are condemned as outmoded or dangerously authoritarian. Concentrating on the situationists, however, suggests a different narrative. For the group's activities represent a dissenting path within the post-war avant-garde that retains a utopian perspective and that takes up aspects of the surrealist counter-spaces introduced in the previous chapter. It is interesting to compare the situationists' approach with those of contemporaneous groups such as Team 10 and the Independent Group in the 1950s, which have also been gaining increasing attention in recent years, and which were based on a more positive reading of popular culture and consumption than that found within the SI. This serves to underline the heterogeneity of post-war modernist ideas about urbanism and the city as well as differing political commitments, with much remaining to be explored here.[57] My focus in what follows, however, is on the oppositional utopianism developed by the situationists and Lefebvre.

Lefebvre acknowledged that the power of abstract space suggests a solidity and oppressiveness that might seem destined to last for ever. In more hopeful mode, however, he emphasised the contradictions of abstract space that dialectical analysis was meant to reveal and stressed its contested character. Such contestation included adaptations of spaces such as those of a Corbusian housing scheme, in which the everyday practices of residents led to a 'differentiated social cluster'.[58] They also involved political struggles where he argued that space had become a terrain of 'a vast confrontation', which was 'none other than the shadow, filled with desire and expectation, that goes inseparably with the occupation of the world by economic growth, the market and the state (capitalist or socialist)'.[59] His interest in what was *possible* was rooted in such confrontations and in demands for the 'right to the city'. Behind this slogan was a vision of the city as a realm not of exchange value and abstract space but of use value, encounter, difference and play. It was on this basis that Lefebvre argued that abstract space contains within itself the potential for a new kind of space. The emergence of this 'differential space', he believed, would allow the opening up of differences while also restoring the unity of fragmented social practices.[60]

A utopian spirit was similarly prominent among the situationists. They too looked towards forms of resistance and political struggle, many of which involved the contestation of space. In a line that anticipated interest in urban social movements by radical sociologists and geographers, they argued: 'Each component of social space which is more and more directly shaped by alienated production and its planners thus becomes a new arena of struggle, from primary schools to public transport, to mental hospitals to prisons.'[61] The situationists celebrated outbreaks of autonomous revolt and spontaneous action, including the Watts uprising in Los Angeles in 1965 that led them to write of how 'real desires begin to be expressed in festival, in playful self-assertion, in the *potlatch* of destruction'[62] (figures 5.4, 5.5). In so doing, they stressed the need to connect resistance over specific 'local' issues to struggles against the roots of problems, which for them lay in the conditions of modern capitalism and the spectacle. One of SI's main aims was to make known, articulate and develop forms of contestation. As Debord later stated, 'We brought fuel to the fire.'[63] He saw the group's role in unitary terms, with these critical efforts being combined with its stance as an artistic avant-garde and with its own attempts to intervene in everyday spaces. Utopian dimensions of Lefebvre's urban thinking and especially the situationists' vision of unitary

Figure 5.4 'Critique of urbanism': uprisings in Watts, Los Angeles, August 1965. From *Internationale situationniste* 10 (March 1966).

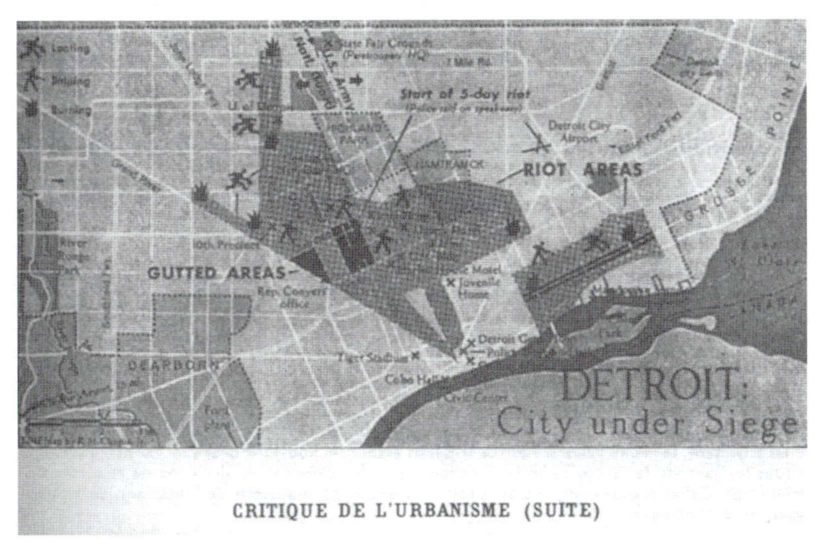

Figure 5.5 'Critique of urbanism': uprisings in Detroit, August 1967. From *Internationale situationniste* 11 (October 1967).

urbanism are explored further in the next chapters. In the rest of this chapter, however, I want to consider the oppositional culture out of which the situationists' utopian re-imagining of cities took place. This involves considering their resistance to the norms and values of capitalist society, their struggles against modernist planners and architects, and their explorations of the possibilities that lay buried within existing cities through the development of alternative geographical practices. It also means turning back to the early years of the SI when its manifestation as an artistic avant-garde was most apparent, and to its predecessors in the 1950s, especially the Letterist International (LI).

Never work

Of all the relics unearthed from the area of Saint-Germain-des-Prés in central Paris, the situationists once commented, one of the most important was an inscription that appeared in chalk on a wall of the rue de Seine in early 1953 that stated: 'Never work' (figure 5.6). For them it was 'a testament to the particular way of life that tried to affirm itself there', and they came to see it as 'the minimum programme of the situationist movement'.[64] Written by Debord, so he later noted,[65] the slogan echoed longer struggles against work that run through the surrealists and their cries of 'War on work!' in 1925, through other avant-gardes back to figures such as Arthur Rimbaud and Paul Lafargue who were part of the revolutionary culture of the Paris Commune of 1871. Lafargue was Marx's son-in-law and, after participating in the Commune and spending years in exile in London, he composed *The Right to Laziness* in 1880, an influential pamphlet that challenged boundaries between labour and leisure, and producer and consumer.[66] He wrote it against the idolising of work in revolutionary circles, and the moralising constructions of the 'good worker' on both left and right, as he emphasised the need for workers to break the conditioned demand for work that he claimed was at the root of suffering in capitalist society. Refusing to work in this context meant opposing the enchaining structure of waged labour as a trade, a specialism that was disconnected from the 'totally human' and that involved a disciplining relation to space-time. It was accompanied by a refusal of leisure since the latter was merely the other side of the same structure, gaining its meaning from the category of work and functioning as its effective support. Laziness thus constituted not leisure but what Kristin Ross calls 'a kind of third term outside the programmed dyad of labor and leisure'.[67] Such a critique of the categories of work and leisure and their disciplining of space-time, as well as efforts to open up and produce spaces for play and liberated activity, became central to situationist conceptions of unitary urbanism from the late 1950s. In the meantime it spoke of the values of a 'provisional micro-society' formed by the LI, which emerged in the summer of 1952 as a radical breakaway from the Letterist Movement, and which contained a number of people who would be influential in founding the SI.

The LI pursued an overtly political agenda through members that included Debord, Bernstein, Chtcheglov, Mohamed Dahou, Jacques Fillon and Gil J. Wolman. Their emphasis was on cultural and political action and on developing an aggressive revolutionary critique that they intended to live. Distancing themselves from dominant values and institutions, including the main channels of oppositional values, the letterists, like the situationists after them, aimed to contest rather than bolster the cultural edifices of the time. 'It must be understood that our business was not a literary school, a renewal of expression, a modernism,' Debord and Wolman wrote in the group's information bulletin *Potlatch*, in 1955. 'It is a question of a way of life that will come through explorations and provisional formulations, which tend themselves only to be exercised in a provisional way.' They added: 'We have a lot to learn, and we must experiment as far as possible with forms of architecture as well as with rules of conduct.'[68] An early manifesto signed by twelve members of the group

Figure 5.6 'Never work!' – 'minimum programme of the situationist movement'. Graffiti on a wall of the rue de Seine, Paris, in 1953. Photograph and caption from *Internationale situationniste* 8 (January 1963).

defended those people whose conscience told them 'one should absolutely never work'.[69] Former member Jean-Michel Mension recalls how the slogan 'never work' became 'our absolutely universal watchword' at the time, and how it was one of the first to resurface many years later during the May 1968 revolts.[70] The LI's attitudes cut against the stress on the dignity of labour in much of the utopian tradition as well as the orthodox political left. They clashed with the value attached to work by figures such as Howard and Le Corbusier, as well as in many utopian texts since Thomas More's *Utopia*, which depicted work as a duty, demanding that inhabitants must not waste their free time 'in roistering or sloth'.[71] More's text involved the 'rehabilitation of the idea of physical labour', something that according to two critics 'was a milestone in the history of utopian thought, and was incorporated into all socialist systems'.[72]

Images of the letterists' favourite bars and cafés around Saint-Germain-des-Prés as well as Les Halles at night and at dawn appeared in a film made by Debord in 1959, capturing aspects of the milieu through which their critical attitudes towards the geographies of the city were forged. In these settings, a male voice announces, 'a few people put into practice a systematic questioning of all the works and diversions of a society, a total critique of its notion of happiness.'[73] New forms of urbanism at the time were proferring images of new comforts, higher quality environments, a range of desirable goods. Their advocates spoke of a better future in which the masses of the population would reap the benefits of modernisation and the economic boom. Images of happiness covered the walls and billboards that Chtcheglov scoured vainly for inspiration, projecting messages that framed the roles of the spectacular society. The letterists invoked boredom as well as conceptions of happiness as they sought to turn urbanism's promises of happiness into points of critique. Developing his parallel discourse of everyday life not long afterwards, Lefebvre also raised questions about the problem of confronting boredom. He wrote of a 'sociology of modern boredom' that addressed the prevalence of repetition in contemporary society, its privatised spectacles, and the eradication of spontaneity and play in favour of the functional. This was particularly apparent in the new towns such as Mourenx, he believed, leading him to assert the need for small groups and political movements outside formal institutional structures to create a style, a way of living in which culture was directed towards the transformation of everyday life.[74] He later commented: 'The great positive minds will no doubt regard it as utterly utopian and unrealistic to introduce boredom into a theoretical and political discussion. For them, boredom doesn't count.' But a 'running sore' between happiness and boredom was how he described the problem in the context of a modernity where the tedium of the repetitive is masked by a pretended newness, and where the repeated is presented as new.[75] And in Mourenx itself he detected an agonising sense that 'boredom is pregnant with desires, frustrated frenzies, unrealized possibilities. A magnificent life is waiting just around the corner, and far, far away.'[76]

As a small group located outside formal institutions – one that was 'no longer expecting anything of the masses of known activities, individuals and institutions' and that declared that its members would 'show ourselves little'[77] – the letterists questioned such issues of happiness and boredom as they explored an alternative 'style' and 'way of living' in the city. The shape of the group's manifestations shifted continuously with new members joining and others being excluded. The group's approach to expelling members anticipated organisational features of the SI, which was later characterised by a carefully regulated membership, continual debates about the suitability or otherwise of making contacts with particular institutions and groups, and a rejection of the idea of 'followers' with the insistence on the need for total participation from members and the encouragement of autonomous action by others. In adopting the title 'Potlatch' for their bulletin, the letterists played on the associations of this Chinook word for a form of exchange and communication based on gift giving. As practised by certain north-west American Indian tribes, the potlatch was connected to festival, performance and to ceremonies involving escalating expenditure without return. It had been taken up by Georges Bataille, who used the term to develop his theory of a 'general economy' of excess and expenditure as opposed to the utilitarian logic and productive exchange of bourgeois society. In employing the concept themselves, the letterists and later situationists evoked ideas about abundance, sumptuous gift giving and generosity, and overcoming division and principles of exchange against the commercialised pursuits and programming of everyday life and space that they found in 1950s Paris. Debord once remarked with respect to the aims of the LI's bulletin itself: 'The non-marketable goods that such a free bulletin can distribute are unpublished desires and problems; and only their deepening by others can constitute a gift in return.'[78]

Among the desires and grievances aired in the bulletin were many scathing criticisms of the utopian urbanism and architecture of the modern movement during the mid-1950s. These at times erupted into virulent denunciations of individual figures, in particular Le Corbusier. André-Frank Conord attacked the 'official' state-sponsored means of addressing the housing crisis in 1954 as the 'construction of slums'. He argued that reinforced concrete was being used to build square boxes in a 'barracks' style, with the classic example being the Radiant City of the 'genius' Le Corbusier. He ended with the promise of an alternative: 'we will build passionate houses.'[79] Employing the abusive name 'Le Corbusier-Sing-Sing' in an article shortly afterwards, the letterists further denounced the connections between modern housing schemes and prisons. They singled out Le Corbusier as a key figure who was 'particularly repulsive' and 'clearly more on the side of law and order than most', as the builder of 'vertical ghettos' and 'morgues'. With a nod towards Haussmann's reconstruction of Paris, they noted that modern urban planning has 'always found inspiration in police directives'. But they highlighted the particularly repressive regulating ambitions of Le Corbusier's schemes and his concern to eradicate the street: 'His program? To divide life into closed, isolated units, into societies under perpetual surveillance; no more opportunities for uprisings or meaningful encounters; to enforce automatic resignation.'[80] Denying that this constituted a truly modern architecture, they asserted that it regressed to an old Christian morality: 'Cathedrals are no longer white. And we are glad of the fact.'[81]

At times the letterists pursued a more measured critique of modernism and functionalist architecture, proposing the need not so much for outright rejection as moving beyond its limitations. Debord criticised the reactionary social and ethical conceptions of functionalist theories of architecture but did so in terms that acknowledged 'the imperfect yet temporarily beneficial contributions of the first Bauhaus or the school of Le Corbusier'. This was even though 'an excessively retrograde notion of life and its scope' had now been smuggled into them.[82] Debord's arguments connected with positions developed by the other main group that contributed to the foundation of the situationists, the International Movement for an Imaginist Bauhaus (IMIB). Its members included its founder Asger Jorn, who had launched the IMIB in 1953 with the aim of promoting an integral revolutionary cultural attitude. The letterists published extracts about architecture from Jorn's writings in their bulletin in 1954.[83] Debord also collaborated with Jorn in 1957 to make the book *Fin de Copenhague*, which was marked by a critical engagement with urbanism along with advertising and consumerism. It was described at the time in an anonymous article in *The Architectural Review* as using 'the combined techniques of collage and action-painting to satirise *gemütlich* Europe in general, the author's native Copenhagen in particular, and Le Corbusier in passing'.

With its text culled from sources apparently picked up from a single visit to a news-stand and composed in one afternoon, the reviewer stated:

> [The book recalls] the propaganda for *la Ville Radieuse*; and Copenhagen is satirised not only as the seat of ancestral boredoms, and in other standard terms, but also for being a 'well-planned city', in the sense of making a pretty pattern of black and green in the planner's report – only in this case the pretty pattern is produced by applying place-names to patches of mechanical tint superimposed on (apparently) an action painting that has 'run'.[84]

Jorn's work and the critical spatial thinking that flowed through the Imaginist Bauhaus to contribute to ideas and practices of unitary urbanism will be returned to in the next chapter. As I will discuss, the members of the Imaginist Bauhaus and the LI shared many interests in revolutionary politics and spatial environments. In the remaining sections of this chapter, though, I address how the urban critique developed by the letterists and situationists involved an exploration of the possibilities of existing cities through critical geographical practices and specifically what they called 'psychogeography'. These spatial practices were highly significant in informing their visions of cities and their ideas about how they might be transformed, leading into what they saw in utopian terms as 'the great game to come'.

Unchaining the city

'We did not seek the formula for overturning the world in books,' noted Debord, 'but in wandering [*errant*].'[85] Since the principle of the spectacle was based on contemplation and nonintervention, the letterists and situationists sought to counter its powers by intervening in the city and experiencing its spaces directly as actors rather than spectators. They resisted dominant depictions of the city as a space of capital and traffic, and opposed restrictions on play. They attacked the way in which functionalist approaches to architecture and urbanism were seeking to eliminate play entirely, and mocked designers who implied that their schemes were being ruined by people's tendency to play.[86] The situationists further criticised the multiplication of 'pseudo-games' in cities – television was a frequent target, as was the recreation of the built environment into touristic spectacles and museumified zones – that enhanced passivity and isolation. The situationists sought to reclaim urban spaces in terms of desire, encounter and play with

Debord suggesting that situationist actions could be defined as 'the invention of games of an essentially new type'.[87] Through playful practices he and his colleagues intended 'to extend the nonmediocre part of life, to reduce the empty moments of life as much as possible' and to enhance the freedoms of cities. Their understanding of games was divested of those elements of competition and the separation from everyday life that characterised the classic conceptions of games, and took a stand 'in favour of what will ensure the future reign of freedom and play'.[88] In this way a ludic spirit ran through letterist and early situationist engagements with urban space. The groups' practices also had an agonistic dimension, through their critical and oppositional approach to existing norms and socio-spatial relations.[89]

A principle practice for the groups was the *dérive*, an experimental and critical drift through urban terrain. Initiated by the letterists, it was described by Debord as 'the practice of a passional journey out of the ordinary through rapidly changing ambiences'.[90] Usually undertaken in small groups of two or three people, on average for a day though the duration varied widely and could extend to weeks or even months, it privileged passage on foot, although taxis were on occasion also used to enable rapid displacements and arbitrary diversions.[91] The dérive involved an element of 'letting go' and aimless wandering, as participants put aside the practical motivations guiding movement through the city and allowed themselves to 'be drawn by the attractions of the terrain and the encounters they find there'.[92] Part of the interest lay in the act itself and what Debord termed its 'playful-constructive behavior'.[93] There was a utopian dimension to this experimentation towards a new mode of living and using the city, with Debord arguing that 'the application of this will to playful creation must be extended to all known forms of human relationships, so as to influence, for example, the historical evolution of sentiments like friendship and love.'[94] Just as the *flâneurs* of the nineteenth century had refused notions of a 'proper place' through continual wanders in the city, and of a 'proper time' through their disdain for the demands of time discipline, cocking a snook at those who measured efficiency in terms of the ticking hands of the clock, so those on the dérive refused the categories and rhythms of capitalist urban life and its demands for discipline and utility as determined by structures of work. Debord thus comments on how 'a loose lifestyle and even certain amusements considered dubious that have always been enjoyed among our entourage – slipping by night into houses undergoing demolition, hitchhiking nonstop and without destination through Paris during a transportation strike in the name of adding to the confusion, wandering in subterranean catacombs forbidden to the public, etc. – are expressions of a more general sensibility which is nothing other than that of the dérive.'[95] Drunkenness also characterised many drifts, which were frequently based around movements between bars.

The dérive therefore enacted the refusal of work that the letterists had announced in 1953. Debord often recalled the intensity of the period: 'Ceaselessly drifting for days on end, none resembling the one before.'[96] Chtcheglov too wrote of dérives lasting not just days but weeks, even months.[97] The defiance of these activities lay not simply in moving slowly, like the flâneurs for whom it apparently became briefly fashionable to parade through the arcades with a turtle on a leash around 1840 in a leisurely protest at the speed-up of circulation and time discipline, with the turtle setting the pace. ('If they had had their way,' notes Walter Benjamin, 'progress would have been obliged to accommodate itself to this pace.'[98]) Nor was it a case of refusing productive activity as such, so that the protest against the structure of work led only to inactivity, langour or indolence. Not that the last tendency was completely absent from the LI, with the group once boasting early on: 'Having spent a few years *doing nothing*, in the common sense of the term, we can speak of our social attitudes as avant-garde, because in a society still provisionally based in production, we have sought to devote outselves seriously only to leisure.'[99] This remark, however, was made in the context of identifying leisure as the 'real revolutionary question' in current circumstances, as a site of contestation in relation to which there was a need to take positions. A characteristic feature of the dérive was the way it allowed an undercutting of such categories of work/leisure with its sense of *dépaysé*, of being out of place according to the dictates of a city governed by principles of utility and efficient circulation. In one of their first discussions of the dérive published in June 1954, members of the LI wrote:

> The practice of displacement [*dépaysement*] and the choice of encounters, the sense of incompletion and passage, the love of speed transposed onto the plane of the mind, and inventiveness and oblivion are among the components of an *ethics of the dérive* that we have already begun to experiment with in the poverty of the cities of our time.[100]

Accounts of dérives often suggest slowness and a sense of drifting with currents. They also contain fugitive movement, willed drive and an intense sensation of the passage itself. This is at times combined with rapid shifts or accelerations to other zones. As such, practices of the dérive resonate in interesting ways with aspects of the earlier refusal to work and vagabondage that Kristin Ross explores through Rimbaud, Lafargue and the oppositional culture of the Paris Commune. In her brilliant reading of the poetry of Rimbaud, Ross notes how for him laziness combined both torpor and speed, where it paradoxically became registered as 'a kind of absolute motion, absolute speed that escapes from the pull of gravity'.[101] For Rimbaud the refusal to work similarly did not mean inactivity or leisure, but rather 'a qualitatively different activity, often very frenetic, and above all combative'. Laziness here becomes connected for him with a 'radical mobility', one that Ross associates with 'the impossible liberty of having exempted oneself from the organization of work in a society that expropriates the very body of the worker'.[102]

Alongside this oppositional mode of living in the city, the dérive had at the same time a more analytical, investigative side that distanced it further from standard notions of flânerie or strolling. This involved exploring cities in terms of their emotional contours, their powerful influences and the possibilities they contained. Thus the 'letting go' of the dérive was combined with what Debord called 'its necessary contradiction: the domination of psychogeographical variations by the knowledge and calculation of their possibilities'.[103] The letterists coined the term psychogeography to investigate different ambiences and zones in cities, and to attend to the relationships between social space and mental space and between urbanism and behaviour. But while they referenced the usefulness of academic texts in informing their studies, their concern was not with producing scholarly reports; rather, it was with scouting out urban areas with an activist agenda, including in terms of how they might be defended or changed, as they looked towards the mutual transformation of urbanism and ways of living.

Psychogeographical accounts therefore dwelled on the ambiences and potential uses of sites with an essay by Abdelhafid Khatib on Les Halles, for instance, discussing its distinctive qualities as a favourite area for the situationists and defending it against plans to 'clean up' its supposed 'unhygienic' and 'diseased' elements. He argued that the projected displacement of local population would present a 'new blow' to working-class Paris.[104] In line with Debord's assertion the year before that psychogeographical research should involve not only the 'active observation of present-day urban agglomerations' but also the 'development of hypotheses on the structure of a situationist city',[105] Khatib ended his essay with proposals for the transformation of the area that aimed to preserve it 'for the manifestations of a liberated collective life'. His ideas included replacing the existing pavilions with small easily modifiable 'architectural complexes'. These should give rise to 'perpetually changing labyrinths', he argued, which he valued for their potential contribution to constructional play and mobile urbanism as he looked forwards to the possibility of turning the area into 'an attraction park for the ludic education of the workers'.[106] His report was followed by a questionnaire that invited readers to submit their own findings about Les Halles. Questions included: 'What architectural changes seem desirable to you in Les Halles? In what zone, and in what directions, would you like to see an extension of this unity of ambience? Or, on the contrary, a destruction?'[107]

Traces of letterist spatial practices are found in Debord's films and publications from the time, especially in the book that he made in collaboration with Jorn, *Mémoires*, published in 1959.[108] Also significant are two psychogeographic maps of Paris produced by Debord in 1956–7, entitled 'The naked city' (figure 5.7) and 'Discours sur les passions de l'amour' (also known by its other title of 'Guide psychogéographique de Paris'). Based on dérives by the letterists, the maps are composed out of segments cut from existing maps of the city to show particular areas. Between these segments are red arrows that point towards some places, away from others, and that link or curl around locations. The maps disrupt cartographic discipline and order; their broken and fragmented appearance refuse the coherence imposed by the spectacle. They challenge urban meanings and the representational regimes by means of *détournement*, a term the letterists developed as a means of subversive diversion, reworking, hijacking. The maps also more positively depict 'unities of ambience' as well as tendencies, attractions, exclusions and routes that constitute what Debord called the 'psychogeographical relief' of the city.[109] By this last term he meant the influences that seem to shape the paths of dérives when people immerse themselves in the streets and put aside their usual goals. The arrows thus indicate what Jorn described as 'the spontaneous turns of orientation of a subject who is moving through this environment without the practical binds [*enchaînements practiques*] – in the form of work or leisure – that habitually govern his or her conduct'.[110]

One of the effects of these maps is to give a constrained sense of the city as they speak of movements channelled and freedoms restricted. Yet at the same time they suggest possibility, encounter and even a fluid city to be navigated as if at sea, as they indicate a loosening of daily binds and the flow of desire by breaking standard cartographic procedures and charting

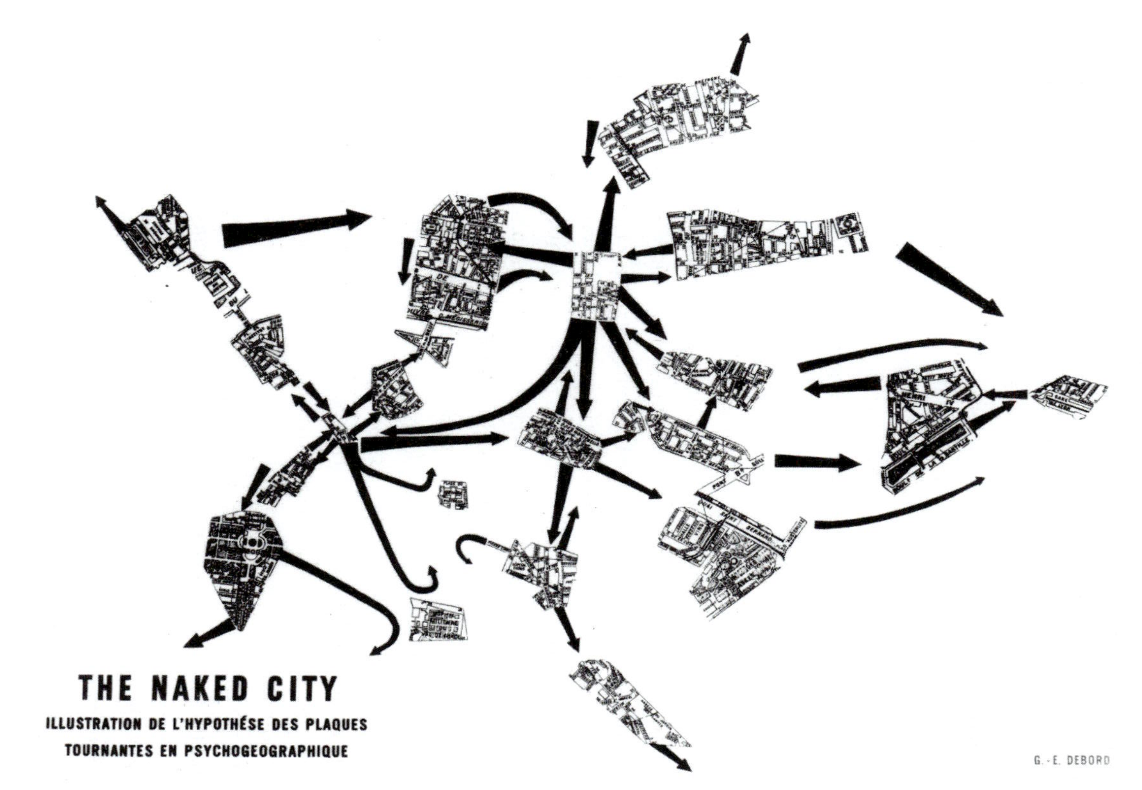

THE NAKED CITY
ILLUSTRATION DE L'HYPOTHÉSE DES PLAQUES
TOURNANTES EN PSYCHOGEOGRAPHIQUE
G.-E. DEBORD

Figure 5.7 Guy Debord, *The Naked City*, 1957. 33×47.5 cm.

other routes through urban space. What particularly interests me here is the sense of *unchaining* they register, and how this relates to the situationists' vision of cities. Debord was attentive to the constraints on daily mobility and argued that the 'difficulties of the dérive are those of freedom'.[111] Restrictions on mobility were rooted in the contemporary *un*freedom of the social organisation of space and time. In contrast, as noted above, the arrows on his own maps were supposed to indicate the movements of a subject who had put aside or been freed from the 'practical binds' that influence behaviour. However, his maps also imply a more active and conscious sense of contesting and breaking binds. The word *dériver* carries watery connotations of drifting, with its etymological roots lying in *rivus* or stream. It is also inflected by a more directed sense of the English word to 'drive'. It further contains within itself, as the letterists themselves noted, a forceful sense of '[to] undo what is riveted [*rivé*]'.[112] This 'undoing' is indicative of the politicised aspect of the practice whereby the hold of contemporary urbanism and the repressive organisation of space-time is to be loosened and even undone. It gains particular importance in light of the letterists and situationists' arguments about the petrifaction of the city and the fixing of space-time through dominant forms of urbanism, as suggested by their later description of urban planning as a 'geology of lies'[113] and urbanism as a 'freezing of life'.[114]

The theme of 'undoing' may be taken further through reference to the precedent of André Breton and surrealist strolls. The idea of unchaining as a social praxis was taken up by Breton when, as Margaret Cohen comments, he used the term *désenchaînement* to refer to tactical disruptions of components of social ordering and systems of meaning. He played on the polysemia of the French word *chaîne*, with its sense of both production line and chain, as a way of underlining the importance within revolutionary action of the revolt against work, and of the need for subjects to escape the defining hold of work to enact social transformation. His use of the term also has associations at a conceptual level as in the *enchaînement* of ideas, where again he and the surrealists aimed to break the hold of dominating and 'congealing' orders.[115] Cohen discusses how Breton's concept of unchaining appropriates from the Marxist language of liberation. But it does so in order to displace orthodox Marxist visions of the working class as agents of revolution. In his text *Nadja* of 1928, Breton responds to Nadja in the course of a discussion about the working class by contending that freedom is not created by 'the martyrdom one undergoes' through the burden of labour, but rather is 'a perpetual unfettering [*désenchaînement*]'.

He adds: 'it is also, and perhaps, in human terms, much more, the relatively long but marvelous series of steps which man may make unfettered . . . For myself, I admit such *steps* are everything. Where do they lead, that is the real question.'[116] Breton figures activities of unchaining in that book in terms of urban wanderings, and especially in relation to his encounters with the young woman Nadja and the steps they take through Paris. They connect with his aim to unlock the realm of the marvellous from within the everyday and with his poetic reading of the city that gives a central role to desire and unconscious associations in understanding spaces and events. In attending to urban spaces he gives particular significance to the kinds of coincidences, mysterious connections and encounters that thread through *Nadja* and his other writings, and to ghostly traces and historical layerings whose presence is conducted in relation to the psyche in uncanny ways.

Letterist and situationist engagements with urban space are in many ways different, with Debord being critical of surrealism's reliance on chance and on the notions of the unconscious. He also condemned that movement's decline as a revolutionary force after the initial period of experimentation around Breton in the 1920s and its slide into spiritualism and the occult. The dérive placed more emphasis on a conscious analytic subject, investigating and contesting terrain. If chance still played a significant role within dérives, Debord contended, then this was a mark of psychogeographical methodology being at an early stage. At times he thus imbued psychogeographical maps with a rhetoric of objectivity and scientific accuracy. Yet Debord also claimed that the surrealist project was 'much richer in constructive possibilities than is generally thought', especially in its assertions about 'the sovereignty of desire and surprise' and its propositions for 'a new use of life'.[117] There are clear resonances in the value that both the situationists and surrealists attach to unchaining at a material and conceptual level, and to their shared understandings of urban space and the street as a realm of possibility. The change, ambiguity and flux that the surrealists associated with the street were crucial to their perception of a 'soluble city'.[118] They played on such notions of fluidity in their search for a 'key' to the marvels that lay latent in the city's dreamscapes. A comparably evocative term for the situationists was 'passage' with its sense of movement, of transitoriness and of opening onto terrains. The lines on Debord's maps, along with the routes threading though his other reminiscences of the 1950s such as his *Mémoires*, trace out such passage as well as the attempt to open up new paths.

In this regard, the LI and SI frequently invoked the idea of the 'north-west passage'. In employing the term, they looked back to its use by Thomas De Quincey in his opium-fuelled rambles through early nineteenth-century London and his attempts to discover secret routes, as he sought 'ambitiously for a *north-west passage*, instead of circumnavigating all the capes and headlands I had doubled in my outward voyage'. They also cited the love between De Quincey and 'poor Ann', who had become separated from him by chance, and whom he sought daily. De Quincey remarks on how they were perhaps searching for each other at the same time 'through the mighty labyrinths of London; perhaps, even within a few feet of each other – a barrier no wider in a London street, often amounting in the end to a separation for eternity!'[119] The references surface amidst the fragments of found text and trails of paint in the book created by Debord and Jorn, *Mémoires*. As Greil Marcus comments, they stand in that book as a metaphor for the experiences of the dérive: they suggest the immense possibilities that the practice could open up, not only what could be lost but also what could be gained.[120]

In quest of new spaces

In opposing the remaking of cities by powerful interests from the 1950s, the letterists and situationists therefore sought alternative possibilities in what existed. Through practices such as the dérive and psychogeography, they attempted to 'undo' elements of the current socio-spatial order and to defend, articulate and promote other values. Not only did the LI and SI reject the utopian planning schemes of urbanists such as Howard and Le Corbusier, but their efforts to trace out different possibilities laid the path for a different kind of utopianism that drew sustenance from the street and everyday life. The impassioned will and desire that runs through this utopianism was at times envisaged in terms of the metaphor of the 'north-west passage'. It was also conceived as a kind of *quête du graal*. Discussing this in relation to surrealism, Octavia Paz notes how the Spanish word *querer* indicates the tone involved, its meaning having evolved historically from a relatively cool 'to seek' or 'to inquire' to signify a more passional, amorous search.[121] Roger Cardinal and Robert Short also comment on this theme, writing: 'Surrealism is best seen as an exemplary search in which the expectant journey itself, as in the quest for the Holy Grail, is somehow more significant that its destination.'[122] The LI and SI were wary of limiting notions of desire to the amorous and sexual, a danger they detected in surrealism. The letterists nevertheless likened their dérives to those of people seeking the Grail, remarking favourably on the latters' 'arbitrary strolls' and 'endless passion', as well as 'a great talent for losing themselves in play; the journey filled with wonder; a love of speed; a relative geography'. The group suggested that the religious make-up falls away in recognition of how the 'romance of the Quest for the Grail prefigures in several ways a very modern way of living.'[123]

Debord's maps of Paris can be read as both a record and a challenging part of this quest. Their scrambled insinuation of paths and movements counter the functional schemes of urban planners. At the same time they chart other routes and the search for alternative passages. It should be noted that in the maps and other accounts, Debord and his colleagues paid insufficient attention to the particularities of the subjects undertaking these actions. The routes through the city remain undifferentiated, seeming to universalise from particular experiences. Unlike traditional views of the flâneur where that figure is invariably male, not all the participants on the dérive were men, nor were they all white. But the maps risk collapsing perspectives in a way that relates to wider neglect of different axes of power within the situationist project, in particular its tendency to sideline issues of gender. Questions about the position of women and the feminine within the earlier activities of the surrealists have been the subject of considerable debate. This has been part of a wider concern with representations of woman by male surrealists and has included attempts to contextualise such views historically where, as Cohen notes, this can involve looking not only backwards but also forwards (including to how aspects of surrealism's legacy has nonetheless been taken up by French feminists such as Hélène Cixous in her interest in a disruptive unchaining).[124] The letterists and situationists for their parts rejected the unconscious fantasies favoured by the surrealists on which many of accusations of exploitation have centred. These discussions nevertheless highlight the need to think critically about the particularities of the former groups' engagements with cities on the dérive, including the problematic tendencies for drifts to be portrayed in terms of taking 'emotive possession' over the streets, where the city becomes figured in feminine terms;[125] or to be presented as venturing into 'unknown' lands, where the exoticisation of parts of the multicultural city has colonising connotations.[126] Also requiring attention are their own rhetorical constructions of heroic (often masculinist) 'adventure' and a questing spirit, especially in light of the LI and SI's small number of female members and the marginalisation of these members within their organisations and practices.[127]

In this respect it is important to stress the provisionality of Debord's maps along with that of situationist spatial practices more generally. Debord insisted on the continual need for experimentation and self-critique. Through the use of détournement, his maps embody a subversive attitude towards representations of the city, as things that work, that perform, that affect the ways in which urban spaces are conceived and lived. They have multiple entryways and are indicative of a mobile engagement with the city, an attempt to open up ways of seeing its spaces. Furthermore, as with psychogeography generally, the maps are not meant to remain at the level of the descriptive or explanatory-diagnostic in terms of present-day organisations of space. In challenging dominant representations, they look towards other imaginings and experiences. This includes questions of temporal orientation as well as spatial orientation for, rather than focusing solely on what exists, the maps have a retrospective element that refers to earlier activities by the LI; they also have a hypothetical element, which is turned towards the future and the possible.

The situationists believed that one of the purposes of psychogeographical maps was to assist in the drawing up of hypotheses for a new social space, and even to provide outlines and initial schemes for the construction of utopian spaces. This is suggested by Jorn's characterisation of psychogeography, cited by Khatib in his report on Les Halles, as being like 'the science fiction of urbanism'.[128] Ralph Rumney also noted in a psychogeographical report on Venice produced in 1958: 'Where there is sufficient documentation of psg [psychogeographical] phenomena we shall derive information for the creation of Situationnist [*sic*] cities.'[129] The aim was to go beyond the limitations imposed on present-day dérives and to fulfil the promise made by Debord: 'One day we will construct cities made for drifting.'[130] In the next two chapters I address the utopian spaces of the situationists and their immediate avant-garde predecessors more fully. I explore further how the ideas and practices of the oppositional culture discussed in this chapter informed a wider utopian vision of urban transformation. The critique of human geography at the heart of this demanded a revolutionary struggle through which dominant modes of urbanism and everyday life would be overturned. The quest for new routes and passageways, suggested by the lines on Debord's maps, here took a grand turn. It became a matter of discovering, and of opening up, a north-west passage towards a revolution in social and spatial relations.[131]

Figure 6.1 Constant, Ambience of a future city, 1958. The model was later rebuilt and entitled *Oranje construction* (Orange construction), 23×110×100 cm. From *Potlatch* (15 July 1959) and the catalogue *Constant* (1959). Photograph by Jan Versnel.

CHAPTER 6

The great game to come

From now on Utopia is not only an eminently practical project, it is a vitally necessary one . . . What does Utopia mean today? To create the real time and space within which all our desires can be realised and all of our reality desired . . . Utopia is the richest and most complex domain serving total creativity.

The English section of the Situationist International[1]

The world has long harboured the dream of something. Today if it merely becomes conscious of it, it can possess it really.

Karl Marx[2]

A science fiction of architecture

'The modern city is dead; it has fallen victim to utility', declared the Dutch artist Constant, in 1960. This conviction lay behind an experimental programme he had recently started to advance, which he described as 'a project for a city in which it is possible to live'.[3] He had earlier provided glimpses of what this might entail at the Stedelijk Museum in Amsterdam, where he exhibited thirty spatial models in May-June 1959. They included a large space-frame structure, open and loose-knit in appearance, almost appearing to float above the ground. Entitled 'Ambience of a future city', it was like an indeterminate web, connected together over the earth's surface, leaving the area below free for traffic and circulation (figure 6.1). Among other models were 'Ambience of play' (1956), a playground structure or game space made from copper and wood with painted shapes; and a variety of intricate spatial constructions such as the complex of spokes of 'Space circus' (1956), and 'Nébuleuse mécanique' (1958), with the latter case being made out of iron wire, aluminium, plexiglass and marble (figure 6.2). A report on the exhibition in *Potlatch* in July, unsigned but written by Guy Debord, identified the structures as models for a unitary urbanism. It acknowledged that they only posed the problem of unitary urbanism, being 'pre-situationist' experiments. It nonetheless suggested that, rather than being merchandise-objects to be simply looked at, they were project-objects whose 'complex appreciation calls for some sort of action, an action on a higher level having to do with the totality of life'.[4] In an essay in the same issue that was illustrated by the photograph of the model of the future city referred to above, Constant described the models as 'the science fiction of architecture'. They were part of his attempt to develop a dynamic and liberating vision of the city that was *not yet*, that clashed with dominant modes of urban thinking. The title of his essay conveyed a sense of this anticipatory-utopian consciousness and orientation towards the future: it was called 'Le grand jeu à venir' (The great game to come).[5]

In this chapter and the next I consider Constant's projects, which occupied him from the late 1950s to the early 1970s. I discuss his concern with the spatiality of social life and with establishing 'a new regard to social space'[6] through models, plans, paintings, drawings, photographs, films and writings, notably under the collective title of New Babylon. He insisted that these works were not primarily an urban planning project, nor a traditional work of art, nor an example of architectonic structure. Instead, they were meant to give material shape to a revolutionary understanding of urban space and to encourage, as well as to provide a medium for, a new approach to urban living. They were a proposal 'to maintain a creative game with an imaginary environment that is set in place of the inadequate, unsatisfying environment of contemporary life'.[7] I address his work in the context of utopian visions of the city associated with the Situationist International (SI) and its predecessors, especially through the concept of unitary urbanism. Constant related his early ideas directly to the psychogeographical interventions and the critique of everyday space that I discussed in the previous chapter. His projects represent the fullest attempt associated with the situationist movement to give graphic expression to utopian spaces and to imagine possible outlines for future cities, specifically 'cities for drifting'. The centrality of the latter theme was indeed made clear by Constant's provisional name for the projects, which was 'Dériville'. However, his approach was contentious within the group and other members pursued different paths. By exploring such debates, it is possible to draw out the tensions and ambiguities both within Constant's work and within the situationists' approach to utopian spaces.

When Constant exhibited his models at the Stedelijk in 1959, he was

Figure 6.2 Constant in his studio, Amsterdam, 1959. Photograph by Aart Klein. © 2005 Aart Klein/Nederlands fotomuseum.

a member of the SI. Internal disagreements soon reached breaking point and he resigned a year later. Given the difficult but revealing position of his urban projects within the history of the SI as well as their remarkable engagement with urban spaces in themselves, the lack of attention they received for so long in the literature on the situationists is surprising. They have nevertheless attracted increasing attention recently from a number of architectural historians and theorists in particular, being studied in relation to architectural culture and experimental design of the 1950s and 1960s, including situationist interest in architecture. This has done much to recover the often hidden influence of his work on architectural debates, both then and since, and to draw out the connections and differences between his projects and those of other architects and movements.[8] My own account explores further the utopianism of New Babylon in terms of the revolutionary desire to transform both space and society, in relation to the situationists as well as histories of utopian visions of cities. It centres on Constant's critical engagement with geographies of existing cities and his imagination of alternatives, where connections with other critical thinkers such as Henri Lefebvre are important. Before turning to Constant's projects more directly, I trace out aspects of unitary urbanism. In the next section of the chapter, I address unitary urbanism in relation to the situationist aim of 'constructing situations'. In the remaining sections, I then explore the earlier background and manifestations of unitary urbanism during the 1950s by focusing on utopian urban interests within Letterist International (LI), and within the International Movement for an Imaginist Bauhaus. With the merger of these two groups to found the SI in 1957, unitary urbanism was given a central role in their revolutionary endeavours and underpinned much of their artistic and political activity. In the following chapter, I turn to how this utopianism was subsequently taken up by Constant through his work on New Babylon, and how others within the SI developed different understandings of unitary urbanism as part of their critiques of human geography.

Unitary urbanism and the construction of situations

Early situationist thinking on unitary urbanism was brought together in 'The Amsterdam Declaration', signed jointly by Constant and Debord in November 1958. This document set out 'a minimum definition of Situationist action' and became a key reference point in group discussions.[9] Constant and Debord argued that unitary urbanism involved the continuous, conscious and collective recreation of the environment 'according to the most advanced conceptions in every domain', and in relation to questions of ambience and behaviour. Unitary urbanism was 'the fruit of a new type of collective creativity', and 'the development of this spirit of creation is the prior condition of unitary urbanism.' They suggested that an immediate task lay in creating ambiences favourable to its development. The task went beyond the specialism of architecture and, indeed, beyond every traditional aesthetic category. All artistic means were usable in this process so long as they involved a 'unitary action', acknowledged Constant and Debord, and they viewed the current 'decomposition' of individual arts as opening up opportunities for collective creativity as they rejected any attempts to renovate such arts.[10] Earlier Debord had referred to the need to embrace 'the creation of new forms and the détournement of previous forms of architecture, urbanism, poetry and cinema' as well to pay attention to the acoustic environment and to other factors such as food and drink.[11] He had also related unitary urbanism to activities of psychogeography and to another practice that had long been important to the letterists, that of the 'construction of situations'. At the end of their declaration, Constant and Debord returned to this last point in emphasising that the construction of situations and unitary urbanism were intertwined. 'A constructed situation is a means for unitary urbanism,' they wrote, 'just as unitary urbanism is the indispensable basis for the construction of situations as at once play and as seriousness in a freer society.'[12]

To construct a situation, for the LI and SI, meant to intervene at the level of everyday life and collectively transform its conditions. Debord defined the practice as 'the concrete construction of momentary ambiences of life and their transformation into a superior passional quality'.[13] It had long been important to letterist activities, with their references to the disruption and creation of situations appearing as early as Debord's first film *Howls for Sade* in 1952. The construction of situations could be understood at a simple and localised level of considering what combination of people, material means, events and interventions might produce a desired ambience. In this vein the letterists once flyposted Paris with copies of a tract entitled 'Construct yourselves a little situation without a future'. But it was ultimately meant to involve a total social and spatial transformation, where people would détourn and construct their own spaces and lives freely. It would be, as the letterists once declared, 'the continuous realisation of a great game that has been deliberately chosen'.[14] This idea of 'situation' is often linked to the existentialist Marxism of Jean-Paul Sartre and specifically to his emphasis on how the human subject is situated within the world, and on the choices and actions made by the subject in relation to that situation.[15] The situationists distanced themselves from Sartre and indeed most academic specialists, however, as they argued that 'existential passivity' must make way for activism. Reworking Marx's famous eleventh thesis on Feuerbach, they wrote: 'So far philosophers and artists have only interpreted situations; the point now is to transform them.'[16] The development of their ideas about situations and urbanism nevertheless involved discussions with, among others, Henri Lefebvre. In particular, they involved a critical engagement with Lefebvre's theory of 'moments', which he was exploring from around the mid-1950s.

Lefebvre's connections with the surrealists in the 1920s had left him with an abiding interest in the potential for transgressive cultural interventions and in the space-time of the city as a realm of encounters and possibilities. He recalled wandering through Paris at night with other members of the surrealist movement, and the importance of this experience for his thinking about space and time.[17] In the first volume of his *Critique of Everyday Life*, he was critical of the surrealists' 'poetic' critique of everyday life, where a turn to the marvellous had in his view led to a transcendental contempt for the real. But in a note to the foreword in the second edition of the book in 1958, he admitted that his assessment of the group had been partially unjust.[18] His reassessment was not only due to having the benefit of a longer perspective on his inter-war experiences; it also reflected shifts in his writings, which were now moving outside the strictures of French Communist Party officials. In thinking about changing everyday life, he employed a poetic language of his own as he wrote of 'moments' that puncture routine and that provide a glimpse of the limits and potential of one's situation. Among such moments were those of love, play, hate, surprise, struggle, delight, disgust. These were moments of 'presence' within everyday life yet whose authenticity is disalienating amid the diversions and commodified relations of modernity, and whose passing can reveal a range of possibilities. Lefebvre did not see these in individualistic terms but sought to connect them to the social totality, and criticised the conditions of modern capitalist society that made accomplishing such a connection so difficult.[19]

Lefebvre conceived of his theory of moments as being not separate from, but rather articulated along with his analysis of everydayness and combined with its critique. He developed the theory through a revision of the Marxist conception of praxis, which seemed to him too restrictive in its understanding of human experience in its focus on instrumental action and the productive process. He once demanded: 'Why must Marxism evacuate the symbolic, the dream and the imaginary and systematically eliminate the "poetic being", the *oeuvre?*'[20] Through attending to such matters Lefebvre deepened his critical concern with the disalienation of everyday life. He believed that it was a matter of emancipatory self-production, the restoration of wholeness, and life becoming a 'work' or an *oeuvre* through a transformed sense of creation. Hence his later declaration: 'Let everyday life become a work of art! Let every technical means be employed for the transformation of everyday life!'[21] However, he always rooted this idea of 'total man' in the real possibilities of society rather than in abstractions or distant fantasies. One of the consequences of his approach was a shift in the point of political intervention and utopian strategy. From this perspective, as two critics put it, it is 'in the midst of the utterly ordinary, in the space where the dominant relations of production are tirelessly and relentlessly reproduced, that we must look for utopian and political aspirations to crystallise.'[22]

The SI's focus on situations had similarities but it took a more spatial turn. It was also explicitly interventionist and characterised by a sense of intention, as it demanded the conscious construction of new situations. Whereas Lefebvre spoke of the 'moment of love', for example, the situationists believed that, in terms of constructing a moment, this should be understood in a less abstract manner as love for a certain person in particular circumstances. They stated:

> The 'moment' is mainly temporal, forming part of a zone of temporality, not pure but dominant. Articulated in relation to a given place, the situation is completely spatio-temporal . . . Moments constructed into 'situations' might be thought of as moments of rupture, of acceleration, *revolutions in individual everyday life.*[23]

During these debates the connections between Lefebvre and some of the situationists were strong. They travelled together and held discussions at Lefebvre's summer home in Navarrenx, at his new university base in Strasbourg, and at Michèle Bernstein and Guy Debord's tiny flat in Paris. It was 'more than communication, a communion', Lefebvre later recalled.[24] He even professed to have written an essay, never to be published, entitled 'You will all be situationists'.[25] Their thinking ran in parallel in a number of areas although they drew on different sources. Their mutual interest in moments and the construction of revolutionary situations came together in particular around their interpretation of the Paris Commune of 1871, which they declared to have been a 'festival'. This understanding was forged on a trip through the country that ended with a week spent writing and drinking at Lefebvre's house in the Pyrenees. For the situationists, it was part of their wider reassessment of the lessons to be learned from earlier workers' movements.

The situationists particularly wanted to reclaim the significance of political 'failures' such as the Commune, breaking such events out of the familiar teleological narratives in which they are usually embedded so as to attend to the powers and possibilities that they embodied. They acknowledged the ease with which the Commune can be presented as inevitably doomed and incapable of fulfilment by theoreticians who place themselves 'at the omniscient viewpoint of God' – its brutal suppression that left around twenty-five thousand people dead must, of course, be faced – but they underlined the different perspectives offered by those who lived it, for whom 'the fulfillment *was already there*.'[26] In their theses 'On the Commune' of March 1962, Debord, Kotányi and Vaneigem stated that the Commune was 'the biggest festival of the nineteenth century'.[27] They presented it as a participatory and anti-hierarchical struggle, one in which insurgents gained control over their own lives. In their view it represented '*the only realization of a revolutionary urbanism* to date – attacking on the spot the petrified signs of the dominant organization of life, understanding social space in political terms, refusing to accept the innocence of any monument'. Its horizontal or spatial movement was symbolised by the destruction of the Vendôme column (figure 6.3); and the measure of its inventiveness lay in 'the *interdependence* of all the prevailing banalities that it blasted to pieces'.[28] Michèle Bernstein exhibited a 'victory series' of plaster tableaux with toy figures and objects in 1963 that wrested such historical situations away from the dominant narratives of the victors and allowed speculation of what might have been, as she reconstructed the outcomes of struggles in works that included 'The Victory of the Commune of Paris', 'The Victory of the Spanish Republicans', 'The Victory of the Budapest Workers' Councils of 1956' and 'The Victory of the Great Jacquerie in 1358'. Their aim, according to fellow situationist Raoul Vaneigem, was to 'dereify historical events, to rescue them from artificial entombment in the past'. He added that they 'tended at once towards two goals: the rectification of the history of the workers' movement and the realisation of art'.[29]

Figure 6.3 Destruction of the Vendôme column during the Paris Commune, 1871. From *Internationale situationniste* 7 (April 1962).

Lefebvre was similarly enthusiastic about the rediscovery of the festival in cultural revolution, although it was something that he later tempered through his attention to the city and the production of space as he warned: 'A break with the everyday by means of festival – violent or peaceful – cannot endure. In order to change life, society, space, architecture, even the city must change.'[30] For this reason he too was fascinated by the Commune and his own studies of the festival of the Commune led to a full-length publication in 1965. In this book he tried to show how 'Paris lived its revolutionary passion' in a total festival that 'unfolded at first in magnificence and joy'. Through texts and documents from the revolution, he addressed how and why disparate people came together through the festival to become a 'community of actions' and a 'communion'. He also considered how people acclaimed the overcoming of alienation, and how a will to change the world burst through customary behaviours and opened up new possibilities. It was a time, he wrote, when 'free labour was to be born having become a game, a great game with arms, with life and death'.[31]

However, his discussions on the subject with the situationists were among the factors that precipitated their break-up. Shortly after the SI published its theses, Lefebvre published a nearly identical version in a short text under his own name in the journal *Arguments*, which had earlier been boycotted by the situationists. The situationists accused him of plagiarism and cut him off. The disagreement was combined with other complex disputes, involving ideological differences as well as personal relationships. The break was total. 'In the end it was a love story that ended badly, very badly,' remarked Lefebvre years later, still evidently troubled by the accusations and the split. 'There are love stories that begin well and end badly. And this was one of them.'[32]

The break came at a time when the SI's conception of unitary urbanism was changing. It was part of a shift that led to the group reworking earlier positions and distancing itself not only from Lefebvre but also from other former colleagues. These moves will be discussed in the next chapter. Before these events, however, the preceding years saw important attempts to develop and concretise unitary urbanism within the SI and its avant-garde predecessors. In the next two sections, I therefore turn back to earlier visions of cities and architecture that informed the initial situationist programme on unitary urbanism, focusing first on the utopianism of the Letterist International (LI), and second on the critical spatial thinking within the International Movement for an Imaginist Bauhaus. These discussions provide contextualisation for the statements on unitary urbanism and develop understandings in particular of the different positions of Constant and Debord, the two key figures of this story whose utopian paths will be explored more fully in the subsequent chapter.

Passionate environments

A text that constituted 'a decisive element of the new orientation by the experimental avant-garde', according to the situationists, was Ivan Chtcheglov's 'Formulary for a new urbanism' of 1953.[33] The year before, Chtcheglov produced an untitled 'métagraphie', which was based on a map of Paris. Superimposed onto the city were sections cut from maps of the world, among the fragments being areas of Alaska, the Northwest Territories of Canada, Greenland, Mexico, Japan, west Africa, Australia, and the islands of Novaya Zemlya in arctic northern Russia. With its sense of displacement, *dépaysement* and rediscovering urban space, the work is close in spirit to the psychogeographic détournements of existing maps of

Paris produced later by Debord. Its interest in challenging norms of geographical representation and evoking a sense of the 'exotic' and marvellous also recalls the playful map of the world published by the surrealists in the journal *Variétés*, in 1929, a cartographic subversion fuelled by that group's revolt against western codes of rationality and its anti-imperialist stance as it vastly expanded certain favoured regions of the world (among them the Pacific Islands, Alaska and Russia) and downplayed or even removed others (such as the United States and much of Europe, although Paris and Constantinople were marked). In Chtcheglov's reworked map, there is more specifically an intimation of the fantastical and delirious reimagining of urban space that he presented in written form the following year in his statement on a 'new urbanism'.

Movement and displacement were crucial to Chtcheglov's vision of the city. He called for continual experimentation with urban space through the invention of flexible and mobile 'architectural complexes', which could change according to the desires of their inhabitants. They could enable people to gain more control over their own environments, he argued, so that they could reclaim power from specialist planners and architects and begin to assemble buildings, spaces and even entire districts of cities according to their own interests and in line with the events of their lives. In this way architecture would become 'a means of *knowledge* and a *means of action*', bound up with changes in everyday life. Chtcheglov ultimately envisaged the establishment of 'cities for drifting'. These would be made up of distinct areas that inhabitants could wander through in a ludic search for adventure and pleasure on what he called a 'CONTINUOUS DÉRIVE'. He anticipated that 'the changing of landscapes from one hour to the next would result in complete disorientation', and each of these areas would have a distinct and powerful ambience, with his suggested examples including the 'Bizarre Quarter – Happy Quarter (specially reserved for habitation) – Noble and Tragic Quarter (for good children) – Historical Quarter (museums, schools) – Useful Quarter (hospital, tool shops) – Sinister Quarter, etc.'. He further noted that these would 'correspond to the whole spectrum of diverse feelings that one encounters *by chance* in everyday life'.[34]

A visionary element runs through many of the LI's other writings on architecture and urban space that followed Chtcheglov's text, as the group's critiques of contemporary urbanism were underwritten by demands for alternative possibilities. 'The great civilisation that is coming *will construct situations and adventures*,' promised the letterists in 1954. 'The adventurer is someone who makes adventures happen, more than someone to whom they happen.' They stressed that the use of architecture and urbanism alongside the 'science of relations and ambiences that we call psychogeography' were critical components of their endeavours to bring about a future society founded upon play.[35] When Debord and Jacques Fillon provided a summary of that year, they announced that 'Architecture must become *thrilling*. We cannot take more restrained building ventures into consideration.' They further viewed a 'new urbanism' as 'inseparable from economic and social upheavals, which are, happily, inevitable'.[36] In their demands for new architecture and cities, the letterists sought to undermine dominant understandings of urban space. They did so not only through the rhetoric of newness, a standard strategy of the avant-garde, but also through their emphasis on *desire*, the desire for a different and better way of living. Many of their claims may be understood in terms of one of the great functions of utopian writing: the education of desire. The theme recurs in letterist and situationist writings. Debord thus called in 1955 for 'the systematic provocative dissemination of a host of proposals tending to turn the whole of life into an exciting game'. He added: 'We need to work toward flooding the market – even if for the moment merely the intellectual market – with a mass of desires whose realization is not beyond the capacity of man's present means of action of the material world, but only beyond the capacity of the old social organization.'[37] In contrast to surrealist interest in the unconscious, the letterists and situationists stressed conscious desire. The SI later referred to this as a kind of politicised form of psychoanalysis where, unlike in Freudian approaches, 'each of the participants in this adventure would have to discover precise desires for ambiences *in order to realize them*. Each person must seek what he loves, what attracts him.'[38]

The letterists found inspiration in a number of existing sites and art works. Among their favourite locations was Facteur Cheval's Ideal Palace, previously also celebrated by the surrealists in the 1930s as discussed in Chapter 4. The letterists referred to what they called Cheval's 'inexplicable' creation in an early article in *Potlatch*, discussing it as an example of how 'a few disturbing pyramids resist the efforts of travel agencies to render them banal.' They described it as 'the first example of an architecture of *disorientation* [*dépaysement*]', and added:

In this baroque palace, which *détourns* the forms of certain exotic monuments and stone vegetation, one can only lose oneself. Its influence will soon be immense.

The life-work of a single, incredibly obstinate man cannot, of course, be appreciated in itself, as most visitors think, but instead reveals a strange and unarticulated passion.[39]

Like André Breton before him, Debord visited the palace in 1954 and was photographed standing under the inscription: 'Where the dream becomes reality' (figure 6.4). Fillon also appears in several photographs at the palace (figure 6.5). In a playful list of psychogeographical figures, one that echoed

Figure 6.4 Guy Debord visiting the Ideal Palace, 1954. Courtesy of the Silkeborg Kunstmuseum.

Figure 6.5 Jacques Fillon visiting the Ideal Palace, 1954. Courtesy of the Silkeborg Kunstmuseum.

Breton's own list of surrealist figures in his first Manifesto of Surrealism as well as his later nomination of Cheval as surrealist 'in architecture', Debord gave Cheval the accolade of being 'psychogeographical in architecture'. He placed him alongside others such as Piranesi as 'psychogeographical in the stairway', Arthur Cravan as 'psychogeographical in hurried drifting' and Breton himself as 'naively psychogeographical in encounters'.[40]

The letterists celebrated Cheval's Ideal Palace in opposition to dominant modernist conceptions of architecture, as had Breton before them. In this vein they mentioned further 'disturbing pyramids' that included the 'hallucinatory artificial castles' built by King Ludwig II of Bavaria. The letterists suggested that King Ludwig was struck by a similar desire to Cheval in giving form to his vision. Resisting the claims of 'riffraff psychiatrists' and 'paternalistic intellectuals' with their theories about naive art, and implicitly being critical of surrealist celebration of outsider creativity, the letterists argued that, in the cases of Cheval and Ludwig, 'the naivety is theirs' for they 'built the castles that they wanted to build, in accordance with a new human condition'.[41] In Debord's view they were among individuals who, while strikingly different in most respects, nevertheless shared approaches in modelling 'intentionally puzzling styles of architecture'.[42] He also referred in this context to the baroque character and 'integrated art' of the house constructed by Kurt Schwitters in Hanover from around 1923. This was based on the principle of artistic assemblage of Merz that Schwitters developed through his contacts with the dadaists, whereby he produced a continually evolving sculptural and architectural construction, an intermixing of life and art. The Merzbau employed an agglomeration of collages, found objects and the trash and detritus of urban living onto the walls and floors to form a monstrous growth of elements, continually bursting through boundaries around a variety of columns and grottoes that included the 'Cathedral of erotic misery', 'The gold grotto' and the 'Great grotto of love'. As Schwitters testified, the bewildering array of audio, visual and constructive elements were meant to involve not a synthesis of different genres as a total work of art or *Gesamtkunstwerk*, but instead involved a displacement of them, a shaking up of elements that one critic dubs a *Gesamtkunstmerz*.[43]

A further point of inspiration for the spatial imaginations of the LI came in the form of Giorgio de Chirico's paintings. The surrealists had previously been fascinated with his works, being drawn by their strangely haunting qualities and sense of expectancy, their enigmatic arrangements of objects and structures, and their striking and at times incongruous shadows with patterns cast from absent forms. The surrealists were also taken by Chirico's use of surprise and defamiliarisation enabling things to be seen with suddenness, as if for the first time. Louis Aragon even suggested creating a juxtaposition of Chirico's paintings 'from which one should be able to draw the plan of a whole city'.[44] Chtcheglov similarly wrote of their alluring qualities for a new urbanism, and in particular praised Chirico's works of the 'Arcade' period before 1918 as an architectural precursor in their attempts to explore absences and presences in time and space. 'It is easy to imagine the fantastic future possibilities of such an architecture and its influence on the masses,' he noted. 'Today we can have nothing but contempt for a century that relegates such *blueprints* to its so-called museums.'[45] Debord took up the theme about their potential for future construction, suggesting: 'Disquieting neighbourhoods of arcades could one day carry on and fulfil the allure of these works.'[46]

While the letterists believed that existing art works and sites could retain a catalysing power, however, they argued that they needed to be worked with and given new meanings if they were to be used in a symbolic urbanism. They had to be rejuvenated through the use of détournement.

This conviction informed how the letterists took to the streets. On psychogeographical wanders they were attracted to the atmospheres of places that carried a particular psychogeographical charge or interest. These places typically retained some distance from monumental vistas, modernising planning schemes, and the city of capital and spectacle. As such the letterists defended them against being destroyed by powerful interests. But their utopian interest in the possibilities for passionate environments also took the form of investigating how urban meanings, buildings and spaces could be reworked and détourned. Debord and Wolman commented on the promise of détournement for architectural construction in 1956, stating:

> To the extent that new architecture seems to have to begin with an experimental baroque stage, the *architectural complex* – which we conceive as the construction of a dynamic environment related to styles of behaviour – will probably détourn existing architectural forms, and in any case will make plastic and emotional use of all sorts of détourned objects: calculatedly arranged cranes or metal scaffolding replacing a defunct sculptural tradition. [47]

Given the letterists' recognition of the diverse ways in which power is exerted through the built environment, they believed that this détournement could be effective at a range of levels. These included in relation to street names where the group orchestrated a campaign to eliminate the use of the 'unpleasant' word 'Saint', contending that 'the Post Office, Telephone and Telegraph authorities will bow to the will of their customers.'[48] They also looked to graffiti and employed inscriptions of their own on city walls with the intention of creating a range of impressions in different areas, which ranged 'from psychogeographical insinuation to simple subversion'.[49]

The letterists further saw détournement as having potential for producing urban spaces, where elements from different buildings or even cities could be recomposed for dramatic effects. Among more concerted proposals were suggestions for reworking their favoured area of 'Continent' Contrescarpe in the fifth arrondissement. They suggested this could become a true example of a new urbanism through the judicious placement of architectural complexes as well as the blocking of a few streets.[50] As Thomas Levin notes, these ideas are remarkably prescient of the revolutionary street actions and détournements of May 1968, where such areas were transformed through the use of barricades and makeshift constructions along with the occupations.[51] A similar interest in reworking urban structures was apparent in the LI's ludic proposals for the 'rational embellishments for the city of Paris'. The group's counterpoint was the surrealists' experimental researches on the 'irrational embellishment of a city' in 1933, which included proposals for a number of sites such as the Arc de Triomphe ('Blow it up after burying it in a mountain of manure'), the Obelisk ('Remove it to the entrance of the Abattoir where it will be held by a woman's immense gloved hand'), and the Palace of Justice ('Raze it. Let the site be covered by a magnificent graffiti to be seen from an airplane').[52] The letterists' proposals ranged widely but for the most part were more practical. They included leaving open the underground and public parks at night; opening the rooftops of Paris to pedestrians for wandering, with the employment of fire escape ladders and catwalks where necessary; fitting street lamps with switches to allow people to modify lighting; abolishing cemeteries and museums, with art works being redistributed to bars; replacing monuments and statues where they are deemed to no longer have any use; and deliberately confusing travel information at train stations, including through broadcasts of announcements from other stations and ports, to enhance the station's aural environment as well as to promote the dérive.[53]

While some letterist proposals exhibited a classic avant-garde desire to break with the past, others worked with hidden or marginalised urban elements to reclaim alternative traditions. They were concerned to uncover histories and geographies in the city, including those suppressed by the authorities, or obscured through the discourses of planning and redevelopment, or subject to the forces of forgetting characteristic of the commodity system with its demands for the ever-new. In this spirit the situationists later revisited sites associated with the utopian tradition, for example studying and proposing to construct situations at the buildings designed by Claude-Nicolas Ledoux at Saline-de-Chaux.[54] They also reported a tribute to the utopian socialist Charles Fourier – a favoured figure within the LI and SI – in the form of the surreptitious installation of a replica of his statue at the Place Clichy in Paris by a group of 'commandos', on a plinth that had remained empty since the original had been removed by the Nazis (figure 6.6). The action was timed to coincide with the beginning of a general strike, on 10 March 1969, and included a plaque that announced: 'A tribute to Charles Fourier, from the barricaders of the rue Guy-Lussac'. The new statue did not last long, being guarded by the police the next day before being removed the day after.[55] The ultimate aim

Figure 6.6 Replica of a statue of Charles Fourier, as reinstated by 'commandos' at Place Clichy, Paris, on 10 March 1969. From *Internationale situationniste* 12 (September 1969).

of architectural détournements, however, was the transformation of social and spatial conditions, so as to enable people to construct their own situations. While the letterists often remained vague about what this might mean at the level of urbanism, these questions became central to their discussions with the International Movement for an Imaginist Bauhaus (IMIB) that led to the foundation of the SI. The letterists coined the term unitary urbanism in the summer of 1956 following the earlier discovery of its concerns, but it was formulated through a dialogue with the IMIB that had been developing over the two preceding years.

Living art of the Imaginist Bauhaus

The members of the IMIB were also critical of functionalist and rationalist ideas within modernist architecture but their roots lay in different artistic traditions. Asger Jorn launched the movement in Switzerland at the end of 1953. He announced his new group as 'the answer to the question WHERE AND HOW to find a justified place for artists in the machine age'. Its early activities confirmed his belief that 'experimental artists must get hold of industrial means and subject them to their own nonutilitarian ends.'[56] The group's definition was sharpened through Jorn's polemic with the architect Max Bill, after the latter rebuffed prospects for collaboration at a new Hochschule für Gestaltung in Ulm, a technological-oriented post-war version of the original Bauhaus that Bill was designing and then preparing to direct. Bill had trained at the Bauhaus in the late 1920s and his theory of 'good form' informed his conception of the new school as contributing to the needs of a mass industrial society. The school's prospectus emphasised that its 'underlying principle is the combination of a broad but thorough technical training with a sound general education on rational modern lines'.[57] Jorn outlined his objections to the school before its opening in an exchange of letters with Bill at the beginning of 1954, arguing that it should teach painting and not simply technical and productivist concerns, and that Bauhaus was the name of an 'artistic inspiration'. Having been rejected by Bill, Jorn wrote an essay that took its point of departure from this disagreement, in which he lamented the 'doctrinaire and conservative formalism' of the new school, whose 'purpose is only to bring order to already existing elements'. He argued instead that 'today we have need for a new, living Bauhaus, intense and fresh, which can reunite and fertilise the experiences of all the creative arts.'[58] When Bill resigned as director in 1956, the dispute ironically centred on the significance he attached to the creative artist in contrast to his replacement, Tomás Maldonado, who promoted a more scientific approach. The resignation was nevertheless recorded with pleasure by Mohamed Dahou on behalf of the letterists in Paris, although they noted that 'no truly progressive tendency has come to light in the Ulm school and we will continue to oppose it with a confidence strengthened by this notable victory.'[59]

Jorn was born as Asger Jørgensen in Denmark in 1914. He was a continual traveller and organiser who brought together diverse individuals through a remarkable range of groups. As a painter, he was gaining increasing recognition during the 1950s (he has recently been described by T. J. Clark, in some fascinating although tantalisingly brief comments on his work in relation to abstract expressionism, as 'the greatest painter' of that decade[60]). He was further an extraordinarily prolific writer whose books encompassed issues of art, aesthetics, architecture, urbanism, economics, along with a range of philosophical and theoretical problems. Debord later described Jorn's role in the SI as that of 'the permanent heretic of a movement which cannot admit orthodoxy', and stated 'no one contributed as much as Jorn did to the origin of this adventure.'[61] Jorn's influence was particularly important in the organisation of the SI as he drew on his artistic contacts across Europe to build the group in its early years. He also helped to pay for the SI's journal and other activities through the sale of his paintings, even after his own amicable resignation in April 1961 when he remained in friendly contact. Debord further praised Jorn's theoretical contributions and described him as 'one of the first to undertake a contemporary critique of that most recent form of repressive architecture, a form that to this day is like oil stains on "the frozen waters of egotistical calculation"'.[62]

Before the war, Jorn studied at Fernand Léger's academy after arriving in Paris from Denmark in 1936. He also worked under Le Corbusier, being employed in enlarging a child's drawing for a mural at the Pavillon des Temps Nouveaux the following year. He later described Léger as 'my old master and teacher'[63] and commented on the strict discipline of his training and his struggles to break free from its influence. He interpreted the tension he experienced in part in national terms, a theme to which he would often return, contrasting the rationalistic approaches to freedom of Léger and Le Corbusier with the more spontaneous idea of freedom that he associated with the Danish and Scandinavian tradition.[64] Gravitating towards surrealism, Jorn came to regard Breton and his circle as reactionaries, but he was drawn towards attempts to rekindle the flame of a politicised artistic practice after the war. This included through the Revolutionary Surrealists and then through the Cobra movement, which he founded in 1948 with, among others, the Belgian poet Christian Dotremont, and members of the Dutch Experimental Group that included Constant, Appel and Corneille. The name Cobra was taken from the first letters of their respective capital cities of Copenhagen, Brussels and Amsterdam.[65]

The interests of Jorn and Constant overlapped at many levels, including the theoretical and political where they both saw themselves as Marxists of an unorthodox and libertarian complexion, concerned with developing a materialist understanding of art. Constant was born in Amsterdam in 1920 and trained as a painter at the city's Beaux-Arts academy before the violent occupation of the Netherlands by Nazi Germany. After the war he devoted himself to painting and met Jorn in Paris in 1946. In his paintings from that period Constant deliberately avoided taking aesthetic standpoints and even spoke of the 'negation of style', but certain themes stand out. Figurative elements are often raw, vital and physical – masked faces and animals are common – as they provide an energetic and sometimes magical counter to modernist abstractions. In a manifesto from 1948, Constant stressed that the role of the creative artist was to be revolutionary and he called for the realisation of a 'new creativity' that stemmed from an experience of 'unfettered liberty'. He linked this to the aim of a revived living art that emphasised experimentation and research rather than the idealisation of art works, and that was opposed to the 'quasi-culture' and emptiness of the immediate post-war period, where virtually all sense of an avant-garde had disappeared. At a time when painters 'see themselves confronted by a world of stage decors and false façades in which all lines of communication have been cut and all belief vanished', he believed that salvation could only be gained by turning against the entire culture that made artistic expression impossible.[66] Constant took up these themes in another manifesto entitled 'Our own desires build the revolution', published in 1949. 'As a basic task we propose the liberation of social life, which will open the way to the new world,' he declared. Creativity in his view was inseparable from the struggle for liberty, and any truly creative activity must have its roots in revolution: 'Revolution alone will enable us to make known our desires.'[67] Along with several other members of Cobra, notably Dotremont, Constant was influenced by the first volume of Lefebvre's *Critique of Everyday Life* of 1947, especially by its critical Marxist engagement with alienation. Constant was further attracted by its utopian aspirations and its striving towards the possible and the qualitatively different, and it was not long before he gave these last terms a more spatial inflection.

Architectural and spatial interests were already being addressed within Cobra. In the first issue of the group's journal, Michel Colle argued in favour of a poetic and symbolically rich architecture, one that was capable of responding to the dream-life of cities and expressing the aspirations of its users. He rejected the functionalism that he associated with Perret, Le Corbusier and others. Instead of their straight lines and right-angles he favoured the curve, as he advocated an integrated approach concerned with the creation of the synthesis of 'city'.[68] Jorn was also developing his critique of functionalism, believing that its concern with order suppressed the spontaneity and vitality that were essential for a living art. In a series of articles in 1946–7 that drew on the writings of the Swedish architectural theorist Erik Lundberg, he outlined a fundamental cultural opposition between classical approaches to art and a materialist attitude, or between what he characterised generally as the rational Apollinarian principle and its vital opposition represented by Dionysus. He associated the Dionysian with the cultural values of those who are repressed in class society, and with the festival and play. But he believed that when it is brought under the control of Apollo, which he identified with the classical ruling class and with the wish-dream of the suppresser, it loses its spontaneous nature that he connected with life, fertility and movement.[69] He thus provided a politicised and Marxist-influenced reading of a clash between cultural perspectives, combined with a polemical claim about 'natural' values that informed his critique of functionalism as well as his advocacy of an alternative materialist approach. In a review published in *Cobra*, Michaell Ventris wrote: 'To the classical schism of form and content as construction and ideology, and to the functionalist rationalisation of construction *as* ideology, [Jorn] opposes the idea of spontaneous (surrealist) *simultaneity*; – of construction and *arabesque* developing freely together without compromise.'[70]

Although Jorn emphasised this opposition between Apollo and Dionysus, at the same time he aimed to critique the dualism and to work towards a dialectical solution. As Graham Birtwistle comments, he was not advocating a return to an 'old' Dionysus but rather the negation of the dualism and the unfolding of a 'new' role for Dionysian values.[71] This is significant for understanding his later interventions against functionalism as well as attitudes that were taken up within situationist ideas about unitary urbanism. In his essay 'Living ornament' of 1949, Jorn criticised the fragmentation and separations that he saw as at the heart of functionalist rationalist architecture where elements are cut up, isolated and enclosed. Instead, he stressed the importance of rethinking ideas about organic unity. He noted: 'The functionalists have defined urbanism as the creation of our framework of living. If this good idea is to be developed further we must substitute for a rationalistic framework an artistic way of working, in which all branches of art co-operate in an organic "art of unity".'[72] While Le Corbusier and others had employed organic principles for rationalist ends, Jorn thus aimed to work through and displace their approaches in his stress on freedom and richness.

Jorn's engagements with functionalism in the 1950s were marked by a number of changes, as he reworked his earlier understandings of organic unity. But he retained a polemical edge as he sought to go beyond current forms while preserving utilisable aspects as essential foundations for new projects. 'Usefulness and function remain the point of departure for any formal critique; it is simply a question of transforming the functionalist programme,' he stated. Among the issues that needed addressing in his view were poetic sensation, ambience and the psychological function of surroundings that were neglected by the functionalists, as well as a conception of the *dynamism* of forms in place of a static and ideal view based on precepts of standardisation.[73] Fascinated by spiral schemes in the 1950s as a form of re-ordering and providing coherence, he tried to rework traditional dialectics through the development of a method able to preserve dynamism, vitality and movement. In so doing, he increasingly employed 'third' positions rather than simple oppositions in an anticipation of what he called a 'triolectical' theory that he outlined during the 1960s.[74] An interesting comparison might be made with Lefebvre's own fascination with 'thirdings' and with what Edward Soja terms his 'trialectics' of spatiality, as outlined in philosophical writings in later years.[75] Situationist accounts of unitary urbanism contained a related critique of functionalism, where the group insisted that unitary urbanism was 'not a reaction to functionalism but rather a move past it'. While acknowledging the positive contributions of functionalists as an expression of current technological utilitarianism, they claimed these were now banalities that relied for their avant-garde pretensions on an outdated opposition. Functionalism had 'congealed into an inert doctrine', they argued, and now 'it is a matter of reaching – beyond the immediately utilitary – an enthralling functional environment.'[76]

Jorn remained a prolific painter through this time but Constant's own turn to architectural and urban questions, especially after the break-up of Cobra in 1951, took him away from painting and towards experimentation with architecture and urbanism. With former Cobra members dispersing, Constant travelled between cities, living in Paris and then London. His experiences of wandering through these cities had a significant impact on his views. He developed a method that he described as 'a mixture of adventure and observation, of mood and reflex', as he drifted through streets and saw 'people building and demolishing, removing, installing and widening roads'.[77] As traffic increased and people seemed to be disappearing, he believed he was witnessing 'a new phase of industrialisation, another industrial revolution' characterised by the emergence of 'mechanised technological environments'. But he was critical of the ways in which artists remained detached from these changes, producing work that was a defensive reaction on behalf of a 'lost individualism'. In his view the changing social conditions required artists to change their attitudes and even their cultural practices. He started to become 'more interested in the city as a construction, and in the agglomeration as an artistic medium'.[78] He began to believe that, as he later put it: 'The shaping of the material environment and the liberation and organisation of everyday life are the points of departure for new cultural forms.'[79]

In the autumn of 1952, Constant wrote to Jorn expressing his belief that he had broken with the artwork of the Cobra years.[80] His creative interests underwent a significant shift in this period, one that he contextualised in changing social and historical conditions. Returning to Amsterdam that year, Constant collaborated with the architect Aldo van Eyck on an exhibition entitled 'A space bounded by colour' at the Stedelijk Museum. Van Eyck had designed the Cobra exhibition at the Stedelijk in 1949, and he soon became a member of Team 10 and an influential critical voice from within CIAM (Congrès Internationaux d'Architecture Moderne). Constant described his 'space-colour experiment' with van Eyck as 'a spontaneous reaction to the passive role that colour has up to now played in modern architecture', and he employed within the exhibition one of his own paintings or 'compositions' that had recently taken a more abstract turn during his time in London.[81] Constant learned about architecture initially through books borrowed from van Eyck around that time, and he increasingly regarded himself as an ex-painter, devoted to experimental cultural activity and research. His focus was in particular on construction, which he later viewed as a response to the decline of individualism that was facing society and as an activity of a transitional period.[82] This led him to call for artists and architects to work together, not as separate specialists but across disciplinary boundaries. It involved collaborating with a number of other artists making similar moves, including Stephen Gilbert who had been a colleague in Cobra. Constant also played an active role in the Liga Nieuw Beelden (League for New Representation) after it was founded in 1954 as a forum in the Netherlands to connect across traditional divisions between artists and architects. These moves surprised others, though, such as the British painter Roger Hilton, who expressed his astonishment to Constant in 1953 'at the magnitude of the jump you have made'.[83]

Jorn had meanwhile moved to Albisola on the Ligurian coast of Italy, in 1954. He wrote to Constant in October of that year to express his excitement at the advanced state of architectural debate among contacts in Italy, one that he characterised as making a break with the principle of the right angle associated with Le Corbusier and Mondrian. The result, he suggested, was a striking conception of architecture that had a surprisingly close correspondence with Constant's own researches.[84] Through his IMIB group Jorn collaborated with a range of artists there including former colleagues from Cobra as well as Matta, with whom he had worked for Le Corbusier before the war, and Enrico Baj, Pinot Gallizio, Walter Olmo, Piero Simondo, Ettore Sottsass Jr. and Elena Verrone. A number of these artists later became founding situationists. The IMIB established an Experimental Laboratory in the nearby town of Alba, in September 1955, at Pinot Gallizio's studio in a medieval monastery. A period of concentrated collaborative work followed that was based on free artistic experimentation. Not only were the artistic practices in contrast to the approach adopted at Bill's industrial design-based and pedagogical version of the 'official' Bauhaus, but so was the setting, with the laboratory being a far cry from the modernist clean lines of the buildings at Ulm. Gallizio told of the laboratory's inspiring and haunting atmosphere, being housed in a building with halls and cellars that had been occupied by monks since the thirteenth century, where numerous tombs had been unearthed through digging, and where the walls were documents of past centuries and every night were 'ready to give birth to a ghost'.[85]

Jorn was by now in contact with the letterists, having received a copy of *Potlatch* in October 1954 via Baj. When Constant joined the Experimental Laboratory in 1956, the contacts with the letterists became particularly important for him as he found many common interests around urban and architectural questions.[86] These different threads lay behind the First World Congress of Liberated Artists at Alba, in September 1956, attended by representatives of both the IMIB and LI.[87] Jorn asserted the urgent need for an 'institute of artistic experiment and theory' and claimed that, in opposing the academicism of the fine arts, it was the assembled artists at the congress more than the Bauhaus at Ulm who were faithful to the original ideas of Gropius and Le Corbusier.[88] Unitary urbanism became the common platform, being projected by Gil Wolman, the representative of the LI, as 'the synthesis of art and technology that we call for'. Wolman contrasted this with Le Corbusier's attempt to establish a harmony based on a Christian and capitalist way of life that the latter had the 'impertinence' to consider immutable. Wolman recognised a need to incorporate certain elements of Le Corbusier's approach but argued that, since it was 'an illustration and a powerful means of action for the worst forces of repression', it 'will disappear completely'.[89] The resulting accord from the congress gave a central role to the integral construction of the environment by unitary urbanism through all artistic and modern technical means, and insisted that unitary urbanism was necessarily interdependent with a new way of living. The letterists regarded it as an element within a struggle for a new revolutionary sensibility that itself was part of the revolutionary resurgence of 1956 across Europe and north Africa.[90] Members of the IMIB and LI collaborated at an exhibition in Turin, in December, where they produced a tract that announced: 'The future of your children depends upon it – DEMONSTRATE IN FAVOUR OF UNITARY URBANISM.'[91] With the foundation of the SI the following year, the new group took practices of unitary urbanism further and in new directions. The period of the late 1950s and beginning of the 1960s was a critical hinge around which the situationists' engagement with utopian spaces turned. During these years intense artistic and political activity within the SI allowed a variety of approaches towards unitary urbanism to be kept in tense connection; after then, schisms between the original participants led to different paths being taken.

Games with machines

Debord visited Alba towards the end of 1956, and soon embarked on a particularly productive dialogue with Constant that led to the Amsterdam Declaration and beyond. Debord was committed to the principle that cultural activity should be an experimental method in the construction of daily life, arguing that: 'Art can cease to be a report on sensations and become a direct organization of higher sensations. It is a matter of producing ourselves, and not things that enslave us.'[92] As such he believed that traditional aesthetic categories were no longer relevant for their tasks, nor was traditional architectural thinking centred on buildings and forms. Although Constant came from a more artistic background, they found many shared concerns. By 1958 Constant had moved a considerable distance from his conceptions from the Cobra years. He now felt that 'all the Cobra ideals had been trampled upon – creativity, folk and art, mass art, collectivity – and several people from the Cobra movement started careers as geniuses, quite contrary to everything we had taken as our basic principles up to then.'[93] Rejecting a false opposition between individualist primitivism in painting and a supposedly 'cold' architecture and abstraction in the arts, he advocated new modes of research and action that were centred on unitary urbanism. He argued that Chtcheglov's earlier vision of a new urbanism, with its talk of everyone living in his or her own 'cathedral', to be 'chimerical' and too individualistic.[94] In contrast he emphasised the need for collective creation and an urbanism that would embody mass desires and creativity.

Constant's move away from painting put him increasingly at odds with others in the situationist movement that still adhered strongly to the practice, even if they were experimenting with different techniques. Jorn was starting to use forms of détournement in his kitsch paintings or 'Modifications'. These involved taking old canvases, found in flea markets or even people's homes, and overpainting them with drips and trails of paint as well as often playful forms, to give them new meanings and associations, or to disinvest them of old ones. Exhibited in 1959, they affected a devaluation of materials and also a revitalisation, with Jorn seeing the process in sacrificial terms. He followed these with his 'Luxury paintings' in 1961 and his 'New Disfigurations' in 1962.[95] Around the same time he was extending important theoretical investigations that included engaging critically with Marxist theory and questions of value, which led to several publications through the SI's press as well as extracts in the situationist journal.[96] During the same period, Gallizio was developing his remarkable experiments with painting and spatial settings. Gallizio was trained as a chemist and had interests in, among other fields, anthropology, botany, alchemy and nuclear physics. In becoming an artist, he drew on this diverse background. His work at the laboratory, where he was assisted by his son Giors Melanotte, consequently employed materials that included aniline substances mixed with sand and coal, and even explosives. This led to the production of 'industrial painting' through the use of simple machines to press oil paints and resins onto long strips of canvas. Gallizio described the paintings as 'a concrete expression of the painterly gesture' and the results were draped, hung or left partially rolled in galleries or at outdoor shows (figure 6.7). 'Painting is atomized, literally disintegrated,' he explained to René Drouin, describing in vivid detail the tactile and visual impact of the canvases that in the case of his 'Roll of industrial painting' in 1958 reached 74 metres in length.[97]

The following year Gallizio presented the 'Cavern of anti-matter' at the Galerie Drouin in Paris (figure 6.8). Made out of strips of his industrial paintings that were 145 metres long, it created an ambience through the additional employment of sounds, music, smells, the use of mirrors and the presence of female models themselves dressed in sections of painting. As well as being exhibited in various ways to create situations, his paintings could be cut up and sold to customers by the metre, allowing further opportunities for individual gesture and theatrical intervention (figure 6.9). The vast length of these creations was meant to swamp the art market, to undermine the art institutions' distributive and market apparatuses by unleashing inflation and precipitating a devaluation. This connected with Jorn's interest in devalorisation and was also in keeping with Debord's call in 1955 for the 'depreciation of all current diversions' in bourgeois society, where art was viewed not only as a significant case of such a diversion but an important element within the society of the spectacle.[98] Debord took a great interest in Gallizio and Melanotte's experiments, encouraging their

Figure 6.7 Pinot Gallizio and his son Giors Melanotte, working on an industrial painting at the Experimental Laboratory, Alba, 1959. Photograph courtesy of Archivio Gallizio, Turin.

development.[99] At Gallizio's first exhibition in Turin, in May 1958, Michèle Bernstein also wrote in praise of his industrial painting, placing it within the context of Italian painting and foreseeing it as delivering 'the final blow to the little glories of the easel':

It is hard to grasp all at once the myriad advantages of this astonishing invention. At random: no more problems of size – the canvas is cut before the eyes of the satisfied customer; no more bad periods – because of its shrewd mixture of chance and mechanics, the inspiration for industrial painting never defaults; no more metaphysical themes – industrial painting won't sustain them; no more doubtful

Figure 6.8 Pinot Gallizio with part of the *Caverna dell'Antimateria* (Cavern of anti-matter), Alba, 1959. He exhibited the Cavern that year at the Galerie Drouin in Paris. Photograph courtesy of Archivio Gallizio, Turin.

reproductions of eternal masterpieces; no more gala openings. And of course, soon, no more painters, even in Italy.[100]

The title of the 'Cavern of anti-matter' suggested a reversal of perspective, becoming a kind of black hole of the art market. When the industrial paintings initially enjoyed commercial success at Turin, Gallizio bumped up the price from 10,000 to 40,000 lire and made longer rolls.[101] At his exhibition at the Galerie van de Loo in Munich, coinciding with the SI conference in April 1959, he cut up canvases according to the intentionally provocative slogan of 'one metre of art for 40 to 70 deutschmarks'. He also emphasised their significance in intervening in everyday life and spaces, suggesting that sections could be worn, sat on or used in a myriad of different ways.

Gallizio effectively advocated a détournement of machines. 'Industrial painting has been the first successful attempt at a game with machines, and the immediate result has been the devaluation of the work of art,' he wrote. 'The giant bank-note called a painting, made according to the highest

Figure 6.9 Pinot Gallizio cuts a roll of industrial painting with Paolo Marinotti, Asger Jorn, Augusta Rivabella and Willhelm Sandberg, in Alba, 1960. Photograph courtesy of Archivio Gallizio, Turin.

profit, will no longer exist, only thousands of kilometres of paintings on sale in the streets and markets at a competitive price, which will appeal to thousands of people, encouraging them into other ways of arranging their environment.'[102] Using such procedures to create spaces and ambiences became one of his main interests, and he conceived of his cavern as a prototype for larger structures where rolls of canvas might envelop whole urban areas, even cities, as part of a festive and ludic transformation of the environment. The Italian section of the SI adopted the slogan: 'Down with independent art, down with industrious art, for an art applicable in the construction of ambiences.'[103] Gallizio's own rhetoric became wildly expansive with an air reminiscent of the futurist manifestos as he heralded the ending of the 'patented' society, and the movement towards a collective creativeness by 'the people'. He demanded machines to play with and declared:

> We will use these machines to paint the highways, to make the most fantastic and unique of fabrics, in which joyous throngs will dress themselves with artistic feeling for only an instant. Kilometres of printed paper, engraved, coloured, will sing hymns to the strangest and most enthusiastic follies. Houses of painted,

worked and lacquered leather, of metal and alloys, and of resins and vibrating cement will constitute on the earth an irregular, continuous moment of shock.[104]

Cinema and television will be wrested back from those who have used them to secure the reign of boredom and put to the collective use of the 'genius' of the people, he added. Meanwhile, the earth will transform itself into an immense Luna Park, creating new emotions and passions; and the new settings of this transformed world – ranging from ways of travelling, lighting, drinking and eating to issues of fabric, dwellings and experimental cities – will be 'unique, artistic, impossible to repeat'.[105]

Several themes signalled by Gallizio's proclamation connect with other situationist visions of urban space. Gallizio viewed automation as potentially allowing a movement beyond current senses of 'work' and 'recreation' and as promising free time for 'the liberation of anti-economic energies'. What was crucial, he stressed, was to reverse the situation whereby machines are a means for the domination of people. Instead, a liberated people must reclaim control of machines and use them for other ends. His was a vision of destroying 'the boredom and anguish created by the infernal machine, which is queen of the all-equivalent', and of commanding machines for 'the single, useless, anti-economic gesture in order to create a new society that is post-economic but super-poetic', and characterised by diversity and variation.[106] Such a movement beyond questions of utility, scarcity and capitalist economy, towards a realm of abundance and communal freedom was developed more fully in Constant's utopian projects, as will be seen. So, too, would another major theme present in Gallizio's vision, that of his emphasis on transitoriness and nomadism. Gallizio wrote of undermining the fixity of cultural forms and of urbanistic constructions that represent 'lugubrious ant-hills of armoured cement'. Against these he envisaged landscapes and habitats being continually remade and transformed. Rejecting the term '*immeubles*' (buildings, with connotations of real estate and also 'immovable'), he refered to '*meubles*' (as in furniture and 'movable' elements), where these would be 'momentary instruments of pleasure and play'.[107] Elsewhere he demanded scenes for camping and gypsy caravans.

A camp for nomads

Constant shared many interests with Jorn and Gallizio. However, he was critical of their positions as well as the individualism of much situationist artistic activity. He made some of his protests public in open letters to the SI in September 1958 that were published alongside a reply by the journal's editorial committee at the end of that year. Among Constant's charges was that Jorn's attitude to industrial culture was 'naive' and that his view of imagination was too closely tied to the 'isolated individual'. Setting out his agenda, Constant emphasised the indispensable role of the machine and industry. 'Those who scorn the machine and those who glorify it display the same inability to utilise it,' he argued. 'Machine work and mass production offer unheard of possibilities for creation, and those who know how to put these possibilities at the service of an audacious imagination will be the creators of tomorrow.'[108] He often criticised the hatred expressed by artists towards the machine, tracing this negativity back to William Morris and the arts and crafts movement, to art nouveau and Jugendstil, and on through modern movements such as surrealism and expressionism to certain current endeavours. The ideal of the garden city, too, he characterised as developing as 'a nineteenth-century reaction to mechanization, a manifestation of fear of the machine'. But at the same time he also resisted the conciliation with the machine that he associated with functionalism, and attached great importance to retaining the freedom of creative imagination.[109] A key task for creative people, he argued, was 'to prepare a new exciting reality based on the actual possibilities of technical production, instead of depicting and expressing the unsatisfying and stagnant reality that is about to be liquidated'.[110] In rejecting traditional ideas about painting he advocated the invention of new techniques involving light, sound and movement and any other means available to influence ambience across a range of domains, which could be united through the collective activity of unitary urbanism.

An important debate and correspondence between Constant and Debord developed following their meeting at Alba. Critics often mistakenly imply that the two figures were always at opposite ends of the group, inherently opposed through their positions as respectively an artist and a revolutionary theorist. But for a time they were close and admired each other's work. Many years later Constant recalled this friendship and their walks through Paris and other cities. He still thought very positively about Debord, remembering his intelligence and also his genial manner. He was struck by the clarity of Debord's views and by his remarkable ability to see things as a whole. Their admiration was mutual, and their discussions often centred on urbanism and architecture.[111] Constant regarded Debord as more philosophical in outlook than himself, and at the time less informed about urban questions. Debord meanwhile recognised the significance of Constant's developing ideas and practices in connection with his own interests in psychogeography, and gave Constant a copy of Chombart de Lauwe's book *Paris et l'agglomération parisienne* that had influenced his own thinking.[112] Quotations from the book subsequently found their way into the catalogue for Constant's exhibition in 1959.[113] Their correspondence became concentrated in 1958–60, as they criticised dominant forms of modernist urbanism and investigated the revolutionary possibilities of unitary urbanism and architecture, including the relevance of earlier approaches such as those of the constructivists. They also debated the significance that Debord attached to Cheval's Ideal Palace. Constant argued that the palace was based on a false notion of 'joy and luxury' that was incapable of being used to inform new conceptions according to their true needs.[114] In saying this he warned of the danger of nostalgia running through the avant-garde since Cobra and the surrealists. Debord tried to clarify his position, agreeing that the surrealist interpretation of the Palais was mistaken and reactionary, and asserting that generally he was against 'naive art'. However, he referred to the palace as a 'game in architecture' and suggested it retained an interest in relation to the need to develop 'a revolutionary conception of luxury', in opposition both to old forms of luxury and to its absence, with the latter being associated with the comfortable void of functionalist constructions.[115] Earlier Debord had connected the Ideal Palace with other sites containing elements of 'integrated art'. He had stressed they were valued as architectural manifestations not because of their relation to paternalistic notions of naive art but rather 'for their embodiment of the unexploited future potential of a discipline that is to an overwhelming extent economically beyond the reach of the "avant-garde"'.[116]

During this period Constant continued to worry about the influence of painters in the SI and the direction they were taking, frequently raising objections with Debord. Constant viewed much of their work as neo-Cobra and he reminded colleagues: 'Ten years separate us from Cobra, and the history of so-called experimental art demonstrates its errors to us.'[117] Among his concerns were the ways in which the situationists were being characterised in some art circles as a continuation of Cobra. This was not helped, he believed, by Debord contributing to the idea that Gallizio's work was 'situationist', nor by the decision to hold the third SI conference in van der Loo's gallery in Munich, in April 1959, immediately after an exhibition by Gallizio, whose work he saw as remaining 'in effect a by-product of grand pictorial art'.[118] Despite the common view among critics of Debord as an anti-artist theoretician and political strategist, having little sympathy with practicing artists within the group and supposedly always bent on removing them from its ranks, he supported a range of situationist activities and practices in the group's early years. He encouraged Constant to accept the risks involved in dealing with galleries as well as to find platforms to show his work, and also offered him texts for his catalogues when Constant decided to exhibit models.[119] No doubt Debord had Constant in mind when he wrote a few months before the foundation of the SI of how 'friends worry about a sudden numerical predominance of painters, whose work they inevitably judge insignificant and indissolubly linked with artistic commerce.' However, he argued that:

> We need to gather specialists from very varied fields, know the latest autonomous developments in those fields – without falling into the trap of ideological imperialism, whereby the reality of problems from a foreign discipline are ignored in favor of settling them from outside – and test out a unitary use of these presently dispersed means. We thus need to run the risk of regression, but we must also offer, as soon as possible, the means to supersede the contradictions of the present phase through a deepening of our general theory and through conducting experiments whose results are indisputable.[120]

Constant nevertheless became increasingly frustrated with the behaviour of other artists in the SI and the difficulties of pursuing his architectural and urban interests within the group. His sense of isolation was a key reason for his resignation, in June 1960. His move was also precipitated by more specific tensions and events, which will be discussed further in the next chapter, and which shed important light on changing positions towards architecture and urbanism among the situationists. Through the rest of the 1960s Constant developed New Babylon independently of the situationists, and in a manner increasingly shorn of the terminology of unitary urbanism that they had collectively developed. However, his association with Debord and the situationists still played a crucial role in the formation of his projects.

Discussions within the IMIB and LI in particular proved decisive in first encouraging Constant to devote his time to utopian spaces. A significant turn came when he stayed on at Alba after the congress there in 1956 and was introduced by Gallizio to a group of gypsies who regularly travelled through the town. Gallizio was a member of the municipal council and was defending the interests of the gypsies, having lent them grassland by the

Figure 6.10 Constant, *Ontwerp voor een Zigeunerkamp* (Design for a gypsy encampment), 1956. 130 cm diameter × 21 cm. Haags Gemeentemuseum. Photograph by Victor E. Nieuwenhuys. Courtesy of the artist.

river Tanaro to camp on after they had been banned from their usual practice of staying underneath the roof of the once-weekly livestock market. Visiting their temporary enclosure inspired Constant to design a scheme for a more permanent but flexible encampment. After he returned to Amsterdam he constructed a model entitled 'Design for a gypsy encampment', which proposed an overarching construction that included wire threads spiralling outwards in the manner of his earlier spiral constructions, representing flexible partitions that would allow the continual remodelling and reshaping of elements (figure 6.10). Constant dated the origin of New Babylon to these meetings and to the idea of constructing 'a camp for nomads on a planetary scale'.[121] Through subsequent models and art works he developed a vision commensurate with a sense of possibility he felt at the time of the Alba congress. 'For the first time in history, architecture has been able to become a veritable art of building,' he argued there. 'It is in poetry that life will reside.'[122] The next chapter explores this vision further in relation to Constant's New Babylon projects that occupied him through to the early 1970s. As already noted, they represented the fullest attempt associated with the situationists to imagine and elaborate a utopian vision of the city, as Constant sought to evoke an urbanism that would emerge through a future revolution. This vision took him on a path that both connected with, and later diverged from, that of the SI.

Figure 7.1 Constant, *Labyratoire* (Labyratory), 1962. Ink on paper, 48×69 cm. Haags Gemeentemuseum. Courtesy of the artist.

CHAPTER 7

Life will reside in poetry

We require adventure. Not finding it any longer on earth, there are those who want to look for it on the moon. We opt first to create situations here, new situations. We intend to break the laws that prevent the development of meaningful activities in life and culture. We find ourselves at the dawn of a new era, and we are already trying to outline the image of a happier life and a unitary urbanism – urbanism made to please.

Constant[1]

Welcome to New Babylon

'The world of plenty is New Babylon,' writes Constant, 'the world in which man no longer toils but plays; poetry as a way of life for the masses, "la poésie faite par tous et non par un" [poetry made by all and not by one].'[2] Constant's sketches for New Babylon evoke a sense of energy, movement and change. Lines clash and swirl, expressing a discontinuous and shifting spatial experience. In his drawings and graphics on the subject there is none of the geometric purity and order associated with the utopian plans of the modern movement architects. The emphasis is on motion, displacement and spatial transgression. Paths criss-cross or wander across the frame, sometimes forming a wheel, or tracks reminiscent of a railway line, or a ladder connecting different levels or elements, all of which had been common motifs in his earlier paintings from the Cobra years. In the drawing 'Labyratoire' of 1962, a red zone in the centre is framed by mobile walls and screens marked in black ink (figure 7.1). Movement is represented by arrows and thinner lines showing swirls of air currents, replete with curious mathematical notations. Passageways are indicated by the central ladder, linking up to other levels, and by a dark opening to the left of the centre, labelled as the 'obscenity zone'. In the foreground, vigorous and jagged scrawls are connected with atmospheric obstacles. To the left, an intense scramble of rounded and wheel-like shapes is marked as involving the use of mirrors. Far from being an abstract space to be appraised for its harmony and composition from a distance, the drawing conveys an intensification of space and senses characteristic of New Babylon. Even where there are straight lines in such depictions, as in one of the 'Labyrismen' series of lithographs from 1963 (figure 7.2), they are not the object of passive contemplation. Instead, they typically clash and cut across each other, in this case with bright red, blue and orange sectors pointing inwards. They recall the futurists' demand in the early years of the twentieth century for 'oblique and elliptical lines' as the basis for a dynamic, transient architecture for the modern city.

Constant developed his vision through a vast array of materials that include models, plans, maps, drawings, lithographs, paintings, photographs, photographic montages and films of his work. His writings on the subject also include manifestos, essays, catalogue texts, newsletters and a book manuscript. He worked on New Babylon until 1974 when it was shown almost in its entirety at the Haags Gemeentemuseum, in the Hague.[3] Constant argued that New Babylon was the '*experimental thought and play model* for the establishment of principles for a new and different culture'. He described it as 'the object of a mass creativity' that was based on 'the activation of the enormous creative potential which, now unused, is present in the masses'.[4] Given his arguments from his Cobra manifesto from 1949 that real creativity must be rooted in revolution, and that only the revolution will enable people to make known their desires, he unsurprisingly kept open the form that this mass creativity would take. It would emerge through post-revolutionary freedom, involving an unleashing of the creative potential of the whole population that was akin to Marx's early understanding of communism as the 'complete *emancipation* of all human senses and qualities'.[5] Constant was deeply influenced by Marx's early texts, especially the *German Ideology*, and he became committed to Marxism and to revolutionary perspectives.[6] In referring to poetry in this context, Constant therefore meant not individualistic expression but emancipated collective creativity and unalienated production. Poetry was understood akin to what Henri Lefebvre termed *poësis*, which embraces 'love, sensuality, the body, affect – a plethora of creative, emotive and imaginative practices';[7] such a vision works critically within the Marxist tradition, addressing elements beyond those traditionally incorporated into accounts of praxis and labour as it looks towards a city of freedom in terms of the realisation of desire and as an *œuvre* created by people themselves.

Figure 7.2 Constant, *New Babylon*, 1963. Lithograph from a series of ten, with texts by Simon Vinkenoog, 40×76 cm. Courtesy of the artist.

New Babylon was projected as a massive, interconnected urban space. Its main component was a giant space-frame, raised up from the ground by means of pilotis or as a suspended or self-bearing structure, so as to leave the ground below free for traffic or public meetings. The space frame provided the basis for the main units of the new city, the covered and horizontal units known as sectors. Constant sometimes indicated that the sectors might be around ten to thirty hectares in area, several stories high, and raised about fifteen or twenty metres above the ground. Functioning as macro-structures, they included service and technical centres and other facilities as well as social spaces and dwelling units. They were interconnected internally by stairs and lifts, and externally by fast transport. Within the sectors the emphasis was on maximising the volume and flexibility of public space with mobile walls, partitions, floors, bridges and the like. These internal spaces and micro-structures demanded the use of lightweight and easily transportable materials and were independent of the basic structure. Constant at first explored the potential structure of these sectors through models and related theoretical texts. The models were carefully constructed and often reworked over extended periods, with the help of an assistant. They were made out of various kinds of metal, wire, wood, plexiglass, oil paint and ink, and varied in size from around fifty centremetres in length and width to around two or three metres in the case of the largest (figures 7.3, 7.4). Their construction is still striking today in the field of architectural model-making, with Mark Wigley asserting their significance as 'extremely sophisticated architectural statements, which definitively establish many of the formal relationships that would be repeatedly rediscovered in the subsequent forty years of experimental design.' He adds that, given their long neglect in architectural history, 'the experience of architects when seeing these models today is typically one of shock, then confused admiration.'[8]

Despite the seeming fixity of the models themselves, they provided only a possible frame for the mobile activities of inhabitants. The emphasis was on allowing inhabitants continually to reshape their environments according to their needs and desires, in harmony with what Constant called their 'experimental life-play'.[9] The often fractured and complex internal sections of the models were therefore intended to be actualised by events and life itself, with an emphasis on the complete flexibility of all sections and components, and on technological systems that would be decentralised and put into the hands of the occupants to enable them to influence the quality of spaces and ambiences in terms of

Figure 7.3 Constant, detail of *Rode sector* (Red sector) model, 1958. 24×96.5×77.5 cm. Haags Gemeentemuseum, photograph by Victor E. Nieuwenhuys. Courtesy of the artist.

Figure 7.4 Constant, detail of *Grote gele sector* (Large yellow sector) model, 1967. Haags Gemeentemuseum, photograph by Victor E. Nieuwenhuys. Courtesy of the artist.

temperature, light, sound, smell and the like. Photography was another core medium through which Constant presented New Babylon, with images of models being exhibited alongside the models themselves as well as appearing in catalogues, magazines, journals and slides in lectures by the artist. The models were often photographed close up rather than contemplated from afar, so that the viewer was immersed within the spaces. A number of photographers therefore became important collaborators, including Bram Wisman, Jan Versnel and Constant's son Victor Nieuwenhuys, with the latter in particular employing methods of lighting and montage to convey a sense of being within a future city. Hy Hirsh and Carlheinz Caspari further collaborated in producing films of New Babylon that moved into and through its structures, again being used by Constant in presentations.

As Constant explored New Babylon further, he increasingly employed drawings and graphics in the 1960s. Initially this was to represent aspects of the existing models but later the drawings conveyed senses of movement, ambience and human life.[10] He further produced paintings on the theme of New Babylon, despite regarding himself as an ex-painter. His objection in texts such as the Amsterdam Declaration had not been to painting as such, however, but to attempts to renovate individual art forms in the context of current social changes;[11] and, especially towards the end of the project in the early 1970s, when he already thought of it as being essentially over, practices of painting again became an important means for developing different sides of the project. In various presentations of models and drawings, Constant adopted a raised or bird's-eye view to show how the sectors themselves would link together to form vast networks, stretching indefinitely across the landscape. He suggested that they would eventually form a raised extension or new skin to the earth's surface. In more totalising cartographic representations or in photographs of models from above, regions of New Babylon are shown with the sectors forming long chains, linked by lines depicting flows and movements to form a decentred city that could house millions (figure 7.5). Constant noted the inadequacy of standard forms of cartography to represent the multi-layered and transitory character of these spaces, something that led him to combine layered models with drawings, and to use symbolic notations on some of the graphics. He likened the notations to those in a ship's log to record unceasing topographical changes.[12] However, New Babylon was not simply a vision of new built forms, as already emphasised. It was an experimental proposal relating to a new space and society. It represented

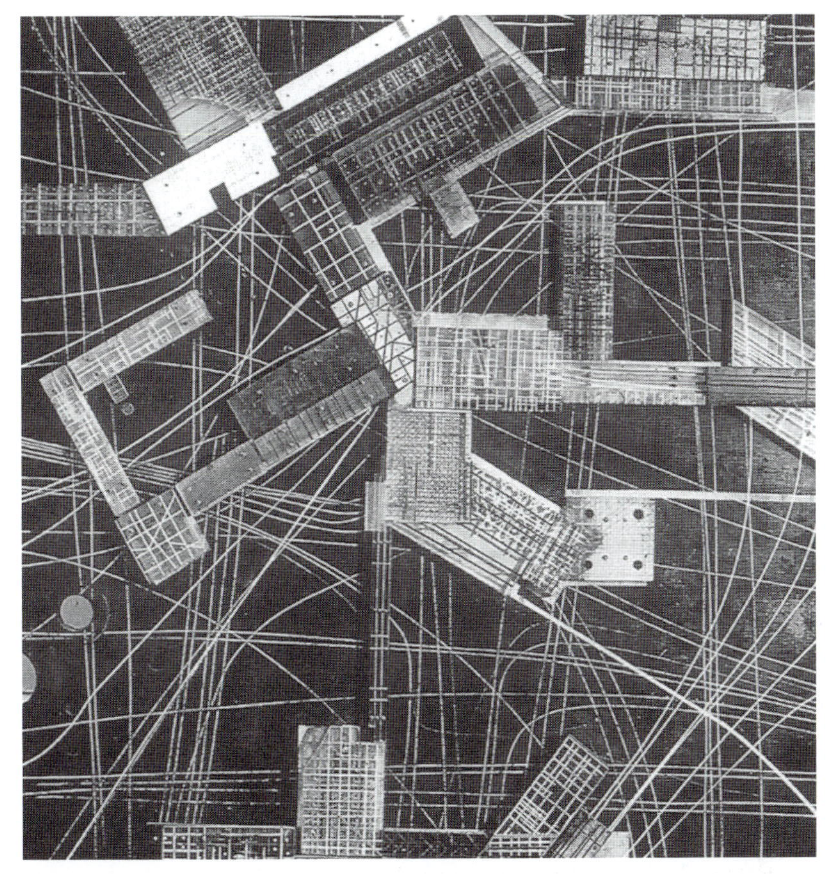

Figure 7.5 Constant, *Groep sectoren* (Group of sectors), 1959. 100×100×4.5 cm. Haags Gemeentemusuem, photograph by Victor E. Nieuwenhuys. Courtesy of the artist.

the medium for a new creativity that Constant believed would manifest itself in daily life. In considering this changed life and space, two interlinked themes can be emphasised: that social life and space in New Babylon would be *ludic* and *nomadic*.

Play structures

Ludic matters and concepts of play had long informed Constant's work. Along with other members of Cobra, he assigned great importance to play and spontaneity in art, exploring the theme particularly through ideas about childhood and the expressivity of children. Prior to social integration, he argued in 1948, the child 'knows of no law other than its spontaneous sensation of life and feels no need to express anything else'.[13] In response to an exhibition of children's art at the Stedelijk Museum in Amsterdam around the same time, he wrote that it 'showed once again what enormous creative forces slumber in people's nature'.[14] More generally Constant saw play and festivity as key elements of a radical art and politics. He had been influenced early on by Johan Huizinga's classic study of play, *Homo Ludens*, published originally in Dutch in 1938. Developing the theme in the late 1950s, Constant criticised the way that modern functionalist landscapes eradicated the play element in cities or confined it to demarcated times and places. Huizinga had pointed to the reduction and seclusion of play in European urban spaces since the beginning of the nineteenth century. 'Work and production became the ideal, then the idol, of the age,' he wrote. 'All Europe donned the boiler suit.'[15] But Constant argued that advances in technology and the automation of production were now opening up the potential for a radical change. Automation might be currently associated with causing unemployment and boredom for workers, he noted, but if the capacities of machines were seized for different ends they would allow the abolition of non-creative productive work, and the emancipation of creative capacities and the expansion of play.[16]

New Babylon thus became an attempt to envisage a space for this new ludic era. It was an environment for a new *homo ludens* (woman or man the player), who is free to create her or his own life, rather than *homo faber* (woman or man the maker). Unlike Huizinga, whose historical account presented homo ludens as an unusual and even isolated figure, who tended to come from the leisured propertied classes, and who stepped outside reality into an alternative 'reality', Constant looked towards the generalisation of homo ludens in a post-revolutionary and post-utilitarian society. This was based on the socialisation of the land and the means of production, and on the transformation of social and spatial relations. It was a classless society in which high production based on automated technology freed all people to develop their creativity through play. This grand expansion of ludic possibilities advanced the critiques of work that had long been important to the letterists and situationists as well as many avant-gardes before them, as discussed in Chapter 5. Constant believed that the revolutionary changes to come would sweep away categories of work and leisure as well as specialised trades of artist, architect and the like. Artists would no longer exist as such, since everyone in New Babylon would be creative in their everyday lives as they playfully and collectively constructed their own environments. Creativity would now be social rather than solitary, impacting immediately on the world and involving interaction and responses from others. This demanded rethinking the nature of cities and social space. As Constant put it in a lecture at the Institute of Contemporary Arts in London in 1963: 'it should be clear that the functional cities that have been erected during the long period of history in which human lives were consecrated to utility, would by no means suit the totally different needs of the creative race of the *homo ludens*.'[17] His emphasis was on collective social spaces that form around eighty per cent of urban space, where the ludic theme of New Babylon finds expression in its playground-like structures with their construction attuned to an 'adventurous and dynamic life'.[18] In Constant's models and drawings, automated production zones and energy supply points are often underground and less often addressed directly. As with many utopian thinkers considering the transformation of work, it is also notable that Constant does not refer to forms of social service, domestic labour or child-care.[19] Nor does he often discuss dwelling spaces, other than to liken them to a non-commercial hotel that would favour frequent changes in domicile.

That last point relates to the second main theme, which is that New Babylon is nomadic. With the automation of production and the creation of a ludic society, inhabitants are freed not only from the time discipline of work but also from fixity in place. They are unchained from the 'geology of lies' and leaden qualities that the situationists associated with contemporary urbanism. 'One can wander for prolonged periods through the interconnected sectors, entering into the adventure afforded by this unlimited labyrinth,' writes Constant.[20] This is not a case of urban space being opened up to circulation according to demands for efficiency, as in Le Corbusier's plans, nor of it being subordinated to pure flow and speed, as in Paul Virilio's more recent account of the 'overexposed city'.[21] Rather, the internal spaces are constructed for wanderings and dérives. The spaces themselves are continually being altered and re-created, with Constant demanding that all static and unalterable elements should be avoided. Not simply advocating movement per se, Constant addresses the qualities of movement, the relationship between the body and the ambiences and social spaces through which it moves. He seeks to counter the desensitisation of the body and the production of sterile spaces that he sees as characteristic of modern urbanism, where an emphasis on circulation has led to the detachment of bodies from spaces; and he envisages a heightened and expanded sensory engagement with spaces and other people based on continual change, in an environment conducive to fortuitous encounters and unforeseen games.[22] Constant writes: 'One crosses cool and dark spaces, hot, noisy, chequered, wet, windy spaces under the bare sky, obscure corridors and alleyways, perhaps a glass grotto, a labyrinth, a pond, a wind tunnel, but also rooms of cinematographic games, erotic games and rooms for isolation and rest.'[23]

In a reversal of the negative scripting of the nomadic found in the writings of many earlier urban critics, Constant therefore celebrates nomadic lines of flight, errant paths, resistance to the disciplining mechanisms of state power that aim to fix and to channel flows. His vision connects in interesting ways with discussions of 'nomadology' as well as recent politicised readings of the nomadic in poststructuralist theoretical discourses that have centred around its deterritorialisations and its interruptions of codes and ordering mechanisms.[24] In New Babylon, Constant argues, 'Life is an endless journey across a world which is changing so rapidly that it seems forever other.'[25] He develops the theme of nomadism through images showing figures entering and tracing paths through complex spaces of moveable walls, partitions and ladders. He also explores it through modes of 'joy riding', involving transport devoted primarily to the pleasures and sensory experience of movement. Following his discussions in 1956 with the gypsies at Alba that were a key inspiration for his projects, he continued to study spatial understandings within gypsy communities through the next decade, reading publications that he requested from the World Community of Gypsies in Paris and The Gypsy Lore Society in Liverpool. At a talk given at the opening of new buildings at Schiphol Airport in 1966, he suggested that elements of a new nomadism were already emerging in social spaces devoted to arriving and departing such as airports. The airport reflected aspects of the non-sedentary and playful life to come, he claimed, being an 'anticipatory image of the city of tomorrow, the playtown of homo ludens, the décor for a new mass culture'.[26]

Paradise on earth

What of the utopianism of Constant's New Babylon? What is its relation with other utopian visions of cities? As has been seen in earlier chapters, utopian visions of cities have traditionally been based on ordered spatial forms. These spatial forms provide the settings for ordered, harmonious societies, in which the ills of the present day are banished to another space or time. New Babylon sits critically within such a tradition. Constant ref-

Figure 7.6 Constant, *Mobile ladderlabyrint* (Mobile ladder labyrinth), 1967. Pencil and watercolour on paper, 99×110 cm. Haags Gemeentemuseum. Courtesy of the artist.

erences other classic utopian schemes and kept in his archive depictions of Campanella's 'City of the Sun', Victor Considérant's drawing of Charles Fourier's phalanstery from 1840, and Howard's diagrams of the garden city. They appear alongside images of Zion, Babylon, and Bosch's famous painting of 'The Tower of Babel'.[27] However, Constant subverts many aspects of the lineage of which earlier utopias are part. The name New Babylon itself carries a sense of challenging conventional expectations. The title was suggested by Debord at the end of 1959, and it replaced Constant's own previous suggestion of Dériville. The name Babylon has complex and varying associations and was often used in the middle ages as a metaphor for the luxurious or wicked city in contrast to its 'heavenly' counterpart. It was also frequently employed in the mid- to late nineteenth century to characterise the rapidly expanding cities of London and Paris, its ambivalence being part of its attraction for commentators. Associated with usage of the name are images made famous in the book of Revelation in the Bible of the great city that has fallen, of Babylon the great 'that was clothed in fine linen, and purple, and scarlet, and decked with gold, and precious stones, and pearls' and 'utterly burned with fire'.[28] There is also the connotation of a multiplicity of voices and confusion of tongues, connected with the diversity of the cities. Among the utopian thinkers that return to the legend of Babylon in the modern period are William Morris, who referred to the transformed London in his *News from Nowhere* as 'more like ancient Babylon now than the "modern" Babylon of the nineteenth century';[29] and Le Corbusier, who described the legend as a 'synonym for magnificence' and stated how 'We behold with enthusiasm the plan of Babylon.'[30] New Babylon was also the title of the film about the Paris Commune made in the Soviet Union by Gregorii Kosintsev and Loenid Trauberg in 1929, a more likely source for Debord.[31]

In employing the name Constant plays especially on the revolutionary connections as well as the associations of pleasure and luxury, of the glorious expenditure over and above the satisfaction of needs that defines his project. In an interview with the poet Simon Vinkenoog shown on Dutch television in 1962, he comments on the significance of the title. Noting that Babylon has a reputation among many Christians as 'the city of sin', compared with Zion as 'the city of God' where 'Prayer and Work' were the highest goals, he discusses how the former city has traditionally been depicted as being encircled by a snake, which appears to offer it as a forbidden fruit. But he argues that history reveals Babylon to have been a cultural centre, a cosmopolitan city of freedom where the first civil law was written, as well as a city famous for its terraces and hanging gardens. He suggests that the possibilities of the present era, where new freedoms and opportunities for generalised wealth in a post-scarcity society are beckoning, provide an opportunity to reclaim the name of Babylon as an image of freedom and luxury. 'Now, 2,500 years later, we live in an age of space and technology,' he states. 'We can play with a thought of a paradise on earth, a new Babylon, the city of the automised age.'[32] He contrasts this with previous urban utopias, specifically those of More and Campanella that he sees as typical ideal cities of the Renaissance, constructed as 'impregnable strongholds' with a population that is disciplined, well-drilled and militarised; and those of the early twentieth century by the likes of Tony Garnier, Sant'Elia and Le Corbusier that he characterises as 'cities of production', organised around trade, industry and housing for workers. In all cases their form and content reflect the material conditions of societies at the time. This, too, would be the case with his own city of play.

New Babylon's dreams of the liberation of humanity and the free creation of space need to be understood in their historical and geographical context. This includes not only the architectural and design debates, which have commanded the attention of most recent literature on the subject, but also strands of utopian thought and activism in western Europe and North America, especially those that contributed to what Fredric Jameson identifies as the 'reinvention of the question of Utopia' in the 1960s.[33] With the long post-war economic boom and other social and cultural shifts, many commentators looked towards the dawn of a new era, and Constant's belief in the growing potential for a new creative society of abundance had a number of counterparts. Among them were optimistic futurologists, heralding the advent of post-industrialism and envisaging technological progress as transforming the possibilities for urban planning and city construction.[34] They also included critical theorists and counter-cultural groups that were closer to his political perspectives. 'Utopian possibilities are inherent in the technical and technological forces of advanced capitalism and socialism,' argued the utopian Marxist Herbert Marcuse, in his book *An Essay on Liberation* at the end of the 1960s. In his view, 'the rational utilisation of these forces on a global scale would terminate poverty and scarcity within a very foreseeable future.' He stressed, however, that the rational and collective control of these forces by the 'immediate producers' would not by itself end domination and exploitation. Attention had to be paid to the possibilities for *qualitative* change relating to needs and satisfactions, one that had to extend to the 'nature' of people themselves and to possible forms of freedom where these were quite different from and beyond those envisaged at earlier stages.[35] Marcuse stressed the importance of imagination and art in negating the present and keeping alive and enabling the development of alternative futures. Through the concept of homo ludens and his presentation of possible urban futures, Constant similarly sought an opening up of what Marx called the 'realm of freedom' beyond the 'realm of necessity' and aimed to counter the hold of dominant urban imaginaries.[36]

Other radical social forces were also bursting onto the scene in this period that provided points of connection. In Constant's home city of Amsterdam, growing prosperity was paralleled by the rise of new forms of opposition and disaffection during the 1950s, including through teenage groups such as the so-called *nozems*. Constant interpreted their actions as part of a revolt against utilitarian society that would continue to find aggressive expression so long as the creative urge was not met with the realisation of a playful society. 'The world is now being confronted with the phenomenon of a generation which refuses to accept the existing order – "hipsters", "teddy boys", "rockers", "mods", "halbstarken", "blousons noirs", "beatniks", "sleazers", "stilyagi" or whatever they may be called – and which exerts an as yet largely ignored revolutionary influence,' he wrote in 1964.[37] He discussed how this revolt was spatial, being aimed mainly at 'the recovery of social space – the street – so that the contacts essential for play may be established'.[38] The following year saw the establishment of the anarchistic Provo movement in Amsterdam, its name derived from *provo*cateur. The group staged interventions, theatrical happenings and attempts to unmask the repressiveness of the current order. Its members drew inspiration from the situationists, although they were met with scepticism and often direct criticism from that group in return. Constant became something of a guru figure for the mainly younger members of the Provo movement, contributing writings on New Babylon to its magazine *Provo* and also being interviewed in the fourth issue.[39] He helped to shape their critical understandings of the city and their alternative urban plans, which included most famously their White Bike initiative to close off the centre of Amsterdam to motorised traffic and to provide free white bicycles for the population.

In developing his ideas Constant shared the concern of his situationist and later his Provo associates to critique capitalist urbanism, especially as exemplified in the changing urban landscapes of post-war Europe. In an article published in the situationist journal, Constant wrote of how the 'crisis of urbanism is worsening'. He attacked the degeneration of streets into highways, the commercialisation of leisure, and the oversimplified emphasis in mainstream planning on zoning functions that led to a 'dull and sterile environment'. With respect to new towns he asserted that 'cemeteries in reinforced concrete are being built where great masses of the population are condemned to die of boredom.'[40] In contrast, Constant's proposals for a multilayered covered city aimed to maximise arenas for social interaction and encounter with dense, complex and interconnected social spaces. He set his approach against the traditional urban quarter, where streets are only incidentally used as meeting places, and against the garden city, which reduces direct relations between people and emphasises traffic circulation (figure 7.7). While his use of the term garden city was directed in particular at modernist plans where 'circulation dominates everything', he argued elsewhere that the prerequisites for Ebenezer Howard's utopian vision – 'the wish to be near nature, a love of work, the

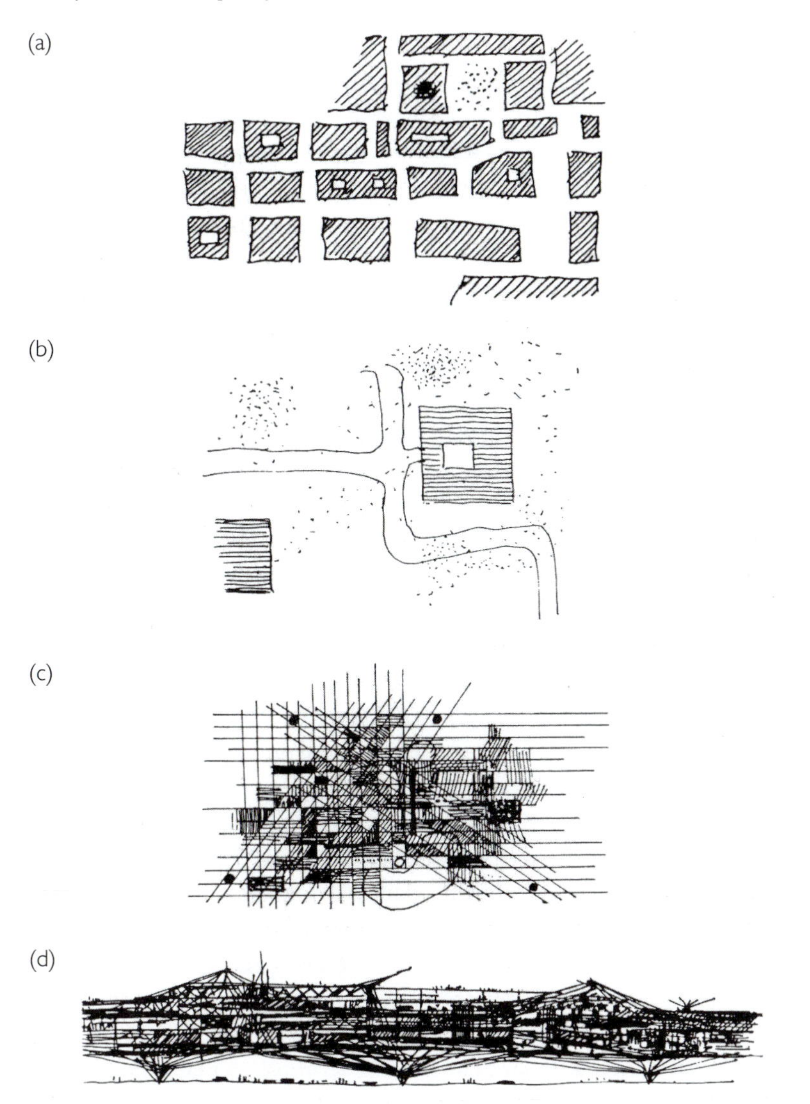

Figure 7.7 Drawings by Constant, from 'Une autre ville pour une autre vie', *Internationale situationniste* 3 (December 1959). Captions as trans. John Shepley, 'A different city for a different life'.
(a) Quarter in a traditional city. Quasi-social space: the street. The streets, laid out logically for circulation, are *incidentally* used as a meeting place.
(b) Garden city. Isolated dwelling units. Minimum social space: people meet only by chance and individually, in walkways or the park. Traffic circulation governs everything.
(c) Principle of a covered city. Spatial 'plan'. Suspended collective dwellings are spread over the whole city and separated from traffic, which passes above or below.
(d) Section view of covered city.

closeness of family ties' – were also no longer valid. He claimed that, far from bringing about socially progressive reform, plans based on this movement only constructed dormitory suburbs that worsened experiences of isolation.[41] In his view, 'the nineteenth-century rural garden city degenerated under the pressure of events into the traffic city, embellished with parks and trees, where social contacts become increasingly difficult, where human beings grow lonely.'[42]

The utopianism of Constant's critique lay in tracing out how cities and urban life could be radically different. In his essay 'The great game to come', published in *Potlatch* in 1959, Constant criticised professional urbanists who typically studied problems in isolation, stating: 'Our conception of urbanism is not limited to construction and its functions, but rather takes in all the uses that can be found, or even imagined, for it.'[43] A sense of utopianism is apparent in the title. It is evidently ambiguous: it refers to a potential future, to a 'great game' that is expected although not yet realised. But it also refers to the present situation, designating the great game that is now lacking, that is absent from what exists. This ambiguity is similar to that contained in Ernst Bloch's utopian concept of the Not Yet. The original German, *nocht nicht*, implies both something that is not *yet* (that is yet to come, but that is a real possibility, a future presence); and something that is still *not* (that is absent from the present situation).[44] One of the difficulties, however, came when Constant attempted to concretise his utopian vision in spatial terms. From some of his more technocratic looking models and plans, it might be construed that his focus was primarily urbanistic where his aim was to plan and implement a future spatial form. This would provide the frame within which social processes would be controlled, as with earlier utopias that he criticised so strongly. Some of the formal similarities between his spatial structures and more mainstream urban projects might seem to support such a view. The use of raised structures and pilotis were familiar from Le Corbusier's plans. Parallels to the space-frame approach can be found in contemporaneous and better known technological-based architectural projects such as the hangar designs of Konrad Wachsmann in the late 1950s, and the technologically-driven 'mobile urbanism' of Yona Friedman, with whom Constant corresponded and had a significant association. The schemes also relate to much emerging work on megastructures in the 1960s, where the emphasis was more on spatial construction than changing social relations. Constant's lecture at the ICA in London in 1963 seems to have been broadly received in that light, especially by attending members of the

British Archigram group.[45] However, there are also important ways in which New Babylon displaces assumptions of traditional urban utopias and disrupts attempts to view it as a settled urbanist plan or proposal, as the next sections will show.

Not yet: utopianism and games to come

Constant was uneasy with the description of New Babylon as utopian. He stressed that the changes he was envisaging were within reach, that they were based on possibilities opened up by new technical, economic and social conditions. In a lecture in Copenhagen in 1964, he stated that, given the decline currently facing urbanism and society, it 'would not be right to look at New-Babylon as a utopian project'. He claimed that 'from all the projects concerning the city of the future – to make such projects seems to become a kind of fashion – I may say that New-Babylon perhaps represents the only one that is based on the totally new social conditions that are offered by the complete mechanization of the production-labour.'[46] On occasions he acknowledged that it was a utopian project in the sense that it was imaginary, anticipatory and based on a radically different desired future. But he nevertheless preferred to call it 'realistic'.[47] Just as Howard and Le Corbusier had both presented their visions not for some distant future but for the current circumstances, so Constant insisted on the immediate relevance of his ideas. His denial of utopianism came from his understanding of utopia as 'a picture of society that ignores material conditions, an idealization of reality'. New Babylon was not a utopia according to this definition since it was based on material possibilities at the time connected with automation. Looking back on his project in 1980, Constant even ventured the proposal that utopia in its 'true sense' had ceased to exist, with the term now applying only to those ideal representations of societies that contravene 'the laws of science'.[48]

Constant's position was a means of countering those critics ready to dismiss his visions as necessarily unattainable and by extension irrelevant to the practicalities of urban development as conventionally understood. He wanted to confront people with the possibilities currently suppressed within technologically advanced societies as well as the potential creativity that he saw as dormant within the population. In effect his approach asks, whose interests are served by the insistence that such visions are impossible fantasies? On what grounds are lines between the possible and impossible being drawn? Why are certain mainstream fantasies deemed acceptable and even commonsensical, such as the idea that planners can build social harmony under current social and economic conditions, while others are disallowed and viewed as strictly off limits? The situationists shared Constant's attitude. 'Reality is superseding utopia,' they insisted. 'Everything we deal with is realizable, either immediately or in the short term.'[49] The stance chimes with Marcuse's discussion of 'The end of utopia' in a lecture in Berlin, in 1967. Far from using that phrase to discount prospects of radical social transformation like so many more recent critics, he retained a belief that such changes were possible as he looked specifically towards the abolition of alienated labour, and with it associated divisions between work and leisure. But his point was that these changes were now entirely feasible. He claimed that they were no longer in the strict sense 'utopian', where that term is understood as a historical concept referring to 'projects for social change that are considered impossible'. Making the argument later deployed by Constant, he therefore suggested that from now on the word utopian should be reserved for only those projects that contradict 'certain scientifically established laws' and are 'beyond history', although even that status might be open to challenge.[50]

To refer to New Babylon as utopian, in spite of these manoeuvres, therefore requires it to be made clear that its utopianism is of a distinctive kind. Aspects of this distinctiveness are suggested by the title of another essay that Constant contributed to a situationist journal while still a member in 1959: 'Une autre ville pour une autre vie' (Another city for another life). He originally drafted this text as 'Towards a new conception of urbanism', with an opening line that echoed the first sentence of Ivan Chtcheglov's earlier 'Formulary for a new urbanism': 'We are bored in cities of today.' However, the implied fixity in the title of a 'new conception of urbanism', with its overtones of modernist planning doctrine, gave way in subsequent versions. An interim draft title centred on 'ambience.' Constant sent this text to Debord for comments and, in reply, Debord suggested that the notion of ambience in the title was 'too restrictive' in this context and proposed as a possible alternative: 'Our aim is in the total construction of [either] life [or] milieu.'[51] In eventually settling for 'Another city for another life', Constant linked the transformation of city and the transformation of life. He called for not simply 'another' city and life, but more particularly for a city and life that would be 'other', that would be qualitatively different from the present.[52] New Babylon is utopian in its challenge to urban and social conditions and its attempt to trace out an other city and life. In presenting different worlds, though, Constant's art works and texts displace many common expectations of utopian schemes, and in what follows I want to draw out particular ways in which they do this.

Firstly, Constant's art works were never about planning out the otherness of the city to come in formal terms. Instead, from a basis in the present he sought to open up ways of envisaging urban space that reached towards that which is qualitatively different. In this sense Constant was always dealing with matters of the unknown and the not-yet. His approach was necessarily experimental since, as he had argued in his Cobra manifesto from 1949, the desires and needs that would give shape to an other city can not be known in advance of the radical break with the present that allows them to emerge, that *transfiguration* that Seyla Benhabib argues is characteristic of the utopian moment of critique.[53] As Constant put it in that manifesto:

> Experiment must always take the present state of knowledge as its point of departure. All that we already know is the raw material from which we draw hitherto unacknowledged possibilities. And once the new uses of this experience are found, a still broader range will be opened up to us, which will enable us to advance to still unimagined discoveries.[54]

Noting later that 'yesterday's world has come to an end, the world of tomorrow is still dim in outline', Constant argued that it was not the time for conclusive answers. 'By necessity [the creative person] continues to be the vague designer, the semi-player,' he wrote. 'He only suggests whereas he would like to give shape, he outlines only whereas he would like to be precise.'[55] Constant therefore always insisted that his project could never be a 'determined urbanist plan'.[56] He also acknowledged the difficulty of finding adequate means to explore a radically different world, since to speak of the different world to come requires deploying language and vocabulary bound up with present conditions. Facing this challenge, Constant emphasised the visual tools of art and the tensions that he negotiated in the process are striking in his works on New Babylon.

Constant provides a vast range of images and representations of a new regard to social space through different media. At the same time, though, he recognises the difficulties of doing so from within the restrictive and degraded conditions of the present. His constant stress on experimentation, flexibility and indeterminacy can be seen in part as an attempt to negotiate this dilemma. In constructing models he presents a vision of the future that could be seen – and, indeed, has been seen by many critics over the years – as fixing, constraining and technocratic in its implications. But he also undercuts this through his emphasis on openness and change. Such a shifting of perspectives is especially apparent in many of the drawings that proliferate from the beginning of the 1960s where the emphasis moves towards mobility and displacement, towards the dissolution of fixed reference points. The apparent solidity provided by the models recedes to become at times little more than a trace or shadow. In this sense it is possible to interpret a lithograph such as one from a series in 1963 (figure 7.8) as an evocation not only of the movement and nomadic qualities of life in New Babylon as discussed earlier, although it is certainly that with its rushing lines around partitions themselves in motion. It may also be seen as a testament to the very tension that is at issue here: namely, that tension common in utopian discourse between what Jameson refers to as 'description and narrative, between the effort of the text to establish the coordinates of a stable geographical entity, and its vocation as sheer movement and restless displacement, as itinerary and exploration and, ultimately, as event'.[57]

A second way in which New Babylon disturbs expectations of traditional urban utopias lies in the challenge it poses to their spatial forms and their dreams of order, harmony and fixity. It contests dominant visions of urban space, disrupting them through other projections and images. 'Above all, my project serves as a provocation,' states Constant.[58] The violently clashing lines, the kinetic quality of the sketches, the valorisation of disorientation and *dépaysement*, all displace assumptions about good city form and *deform* their ideal images. The 'reasoned disordering of all the senses', famously called for by Rimbaud and attractive to other avant-gardes such as the surrealists, here finds urbanistic expression.[59] The theme similarly characterises many situationist depictions of unitary urbanism, with the group declaring in a critique of functionalism: 'One must construct uninhabitable ambiences; construct the streets of real life, the scenery of daydreams.'[60] The need to construct ambiences that could shock was one the reasons why Constant initially rejected traditional arts such as painting while he was a member of the SI, and demanded the invention of new techniques in all domains including the visual, oral and psychological. In his art works this *dis*-ordering aims not only to envisage a medium for a new mass creativity but to encourage it. He seeks to undermine the passifying powers of the spectacle and to stimulate participatory

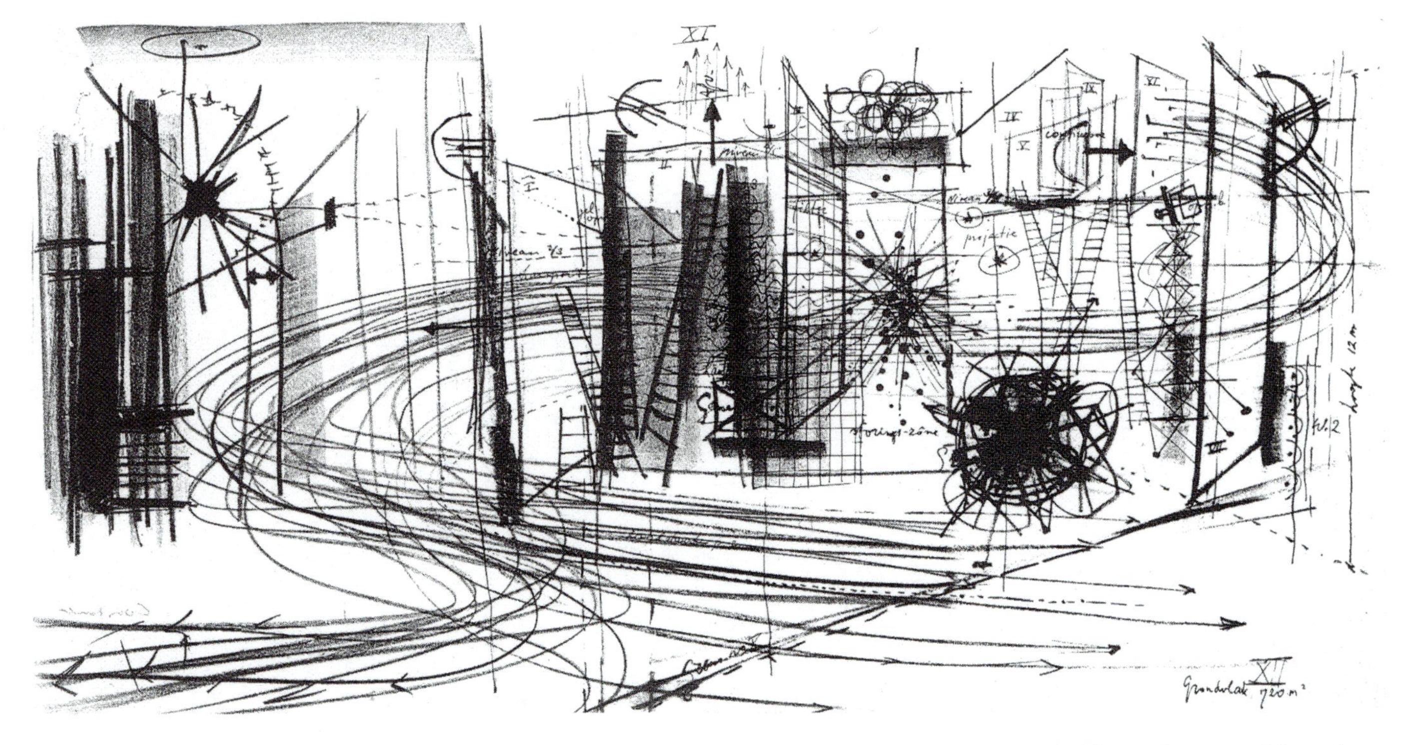

Figure 7.8 Constant, *New Babylon*, 1963. Lithograph from a series of ten, with texts by Simon Vinkenoog, 40×76 cm. Courtesy of the artist.

engagements with the creation of environments, where notions of exploration, dynamic states of becoming and creative change are privileged over dreams of order and harmony.

The aim of provocation was in keeping with Constant's earlier understanding of artistic practices. In his view art should awaken, it should stimulate a more participatory attitude towards creativity. The creative potential of the masses, he wrote in 1948, 'will be stimulated by an art which does not define but suggests, by the arousal of associations and the speculations which come forth from them, creating a new and fantastic way of seeing'. This emphasis on activating the urge to create meant that 'the creative act is more important than that which it creates.'[61] A similar aim was apparent in Constant's many lectures during the 1960s, often given in conjunction with exhibitions on New Babylon or while visiting architecture and art institutions across Europe. His talks on New Babylon were typically followed by a slide presentation of his models, and they were also often accompanied by a loud sound-tape, which he used to suggest forms of life, or on occasions films. When introducing his slides, Constant stressed his desire to avoid constructing a prescriptive vision. At a lecture in 1964, for instance, he stated that he only wanted to give 'a suggestion, like the painter and the poet used to suggest a world superior to the world they had to live in'. Far from trying to predict what the world will look like, he aimed 'to challenge the imagination of those who will have to prepare the construction of the future world, when labour will be abolished'.[62] As he prepared to plunge the audience into an intensive visual and audio experience, he asked them 'to look on these slides as if you were visiting a new and unknown city and to undergo its specific atmosphere, realising that this atmosphere is my personal interpretation of a world that will be altered every time another personality is involved'.[63] That was how he saw the task of the artist of the time. He believed that the critical artist had to struggle against the production of 'consolation-objects' in the form of traditional art works, and should aim to provoke things that happen, to intervene in the world and to change it. He argued later in the lecture:

> Artists are no longer trying to escape the reality of social life, but they want to change this reality. They are not satisfied any longer by a substitute reality on canvas or on written paper, they want to penetrate the real reality of their lives and of your lives, they want to influence people and to make them aware of their own creative possibilities, they want to wake up the creator that is slumbering in the mind of each individual.[64]

As part of this concern to stimulate and awaken, New Babylon therefore rejects utopian dreams of order in which all conflicts and ambiguities are resolved. When based on current social and spatial arrangements, goals of harmony are seen as part of the apparatus of dominant powers. Prominence is given instead to ambiguity, disruption and otherness. In place of the visual clarity of the modern movement with its aims of restoring a 'unified scopic regime', there are elements in New Babylon of a baroque fascination with the disorienting and the dazzling. Earlier interest by the letterists and the situationists in the baroque, manifested for example in their attitudes towards the constructions of Facteur Cheval and Kurt Schwitters, is taken in a different direction by Constant through technologically-informed means. His work explores themes associated with baroque visual culture more widely, its sense of change and time as well as its overloading of the visual apparatus and what Martin Jay refers to as a celebration of 'the confusing interplay of form and chaos, surface and depth, transparency and obscurity'.[65] Jay is drawing here on Christine Buci-Glucksmann's positive interpretation of baroque visual culture and its explorations of 'the madness of vision', which she seeks to reclaim for critical perspectives on modernity given its resistance to demands of essential form, to totalising views from above and to ocularcentric discourses.[66] It is especially apparent in some of Constant's models and photographs, which show interpenetrating spaces and dense layerings of wires, struts, frames and levels of plexiglass that are often scoured, treated, paint splattered and rendered opaque.

It must be acknowledged that the spaces of New Babylon are frequently unnerving, even disturbing. This is not surprising given their provocative stance. Constant argued that, as life is freed from utilitarian engagement, fixed life-patterns dissolve and life itself becomes a material of creation. But also dissolving amidst the swirls of the art works are any notions of solid ties, habits, customs and memories. The emphasis is entirely on the ephemeral and the transient. Constant suggests that the intensity of the moments of life can have 'the positive quality of brain-washing', with creators being so immersed in the exhilaration of the present moment that the creative imagination is released from the more stultifying influences of repetition, rootedness and past memories.[67] These themes are meant to express liberation from authoritarian restrictions, deadening habits and the conditioning of capitalist society. They nevertheless have a dark edge in some of the New Babylon drawings and paintings, as blurred shapes and anonymous figures make their way through vast labyrinths and a social space that are forever other. In an important commentary, Hilde Heynen discusses how perpetual drifting and freedom are bound up with more troubling aspects of 'groundlessness and indeterminacy'. As she notes, a feeling of unease accompanies the projection of total freedom, an unease that was contained in the models and writings but emerges into the frames of the art works.[68] The letterists and situationists had previously remarked themselves on the darker side of their promise of cities for continual drifting. Writing to Michèle Bernstein and Debord in 1963, Chtcheglov noted how 'the continual dérive is dangerous to the extent that the individual, having gone too far (not without bases, but . . .) without defences, is threatened with explosion, dissolution, dissociation, disintegration.' He therefore now retracted his earlier recommendations for an urbanism constructed for the continual dérive. 'Yes, continual like the poker game at Las Vegas,' he stated, 'but continual for a certain period, limited to a Sunday for some, to a week as a good average; a month, that's a lot. In 1953–54 we dérived for three or four months; that's the extreme limit, the critical point. It's a miracle it didn't kill us. We had a constitution – a bad constitution – of iron.'[69] In reply Debord concurred that the dérive is indeed a 'dangerous trade'.[70]

For another city and another life

The title of Constant's essay 'Another city for another life' indicates an additional theme that was central to his utopianism, and that placed it further in critical relation with much traditional utopian thought about cities. Along with numerous other visionaries, he connected the transformation of cities with the transformation of everyday life. He did not base this on a fixed spatial form, however, for the emphasis of New Babylon lay in envisaging the mutual transformation of space and society, so that another city and another life unfold together. Space on this basis is not as a static realm or container, waiting to be shaped according to some ideal scheme, but rather understood in social and political terms. As Constant put it: 'social space is truly the concrete space of meetings, of the contacts between beings. Spatiality is social. In New Babylon social space is social spatiality.'[71] Constant shared with the situationists the conviction that to change life it is necessary to change space, and vice versa. Constant's early development of New Babylon was in dialogue with, and attempted to provide an overarching framework or macro-structure for, the SI's psychogeographical interventions, constructions of situations and guerrilla-style actions. His initial models experimented with such a macro-structure, and with ways of making this flexible and mobile in spite of its grand scale. They were intended as a frame for games, desires and sensuous, playful activities to be realised.

Early on Constant rooted his project within the concept of unitary urbanism, oriented towards contesting and changing realities. In this sense it was avant-garde, even if that was another term along with utopian that he tended to avoid.[72] While a member of the SI, Constant insisted on working with present possibilities instead of postponing action to some distant and more favourable future. At the SI's conference in Munich in 1959, he stressed the need to connect theory and practice, and to find practical means of intervening in cities. Teams should be established to propose real projects, he asserted, so as to construct environments that are conducive to the propagation of unitary urbanism.[73] To this end the situationists agreed at the conference to found a Bureau of Research for Unitary Urbanism, based in Amsterdam and directed by Constant with the Dutch architects Armando, Har Oudejans and A. Alberts. The purpose of the Bureau was to develop ideas and practical activities of unitary urbanism, taking as its focus not formal architectural preoccupations – precisely what 'makes architecture today so boring', according to Constant[74] – but the collective creation of ambiences and situations. The Dutch recruits helped to develop architectural interests within the SI, including around questions of topology. With Constant their interventions included protesting against plans to renovate the Stock Exchange in Amsterdam as part of their campaign against turning the city centre into a museum, as they called for 'the demolition of the stock exchange and the redevelopment of the site as a playground for the area's population'.[75]

Amsterdam became a focus for many proposals concerning psychogeographical experimentation and urban construction. The most ambitious was an exhibition scheduled for the Stedelijk Museum in May 1960. Plans for this included holding continuous dérives for three days around central Amsterdam, conducted by teams of situationists in contact via walkie-talkies with Constant who would act as a director, and connected to events and 'micro-dérives' in a labyrinthine 'apartment-like' construction in the museum itself. The aim was to explore connections between different spatial scales, and to create an intense experience for participants instead of simply presenting them with representations of a future urbanism. The event collapsed, however, when the SI pulled out two months before the opening. Reasons for the cancellation have been the subject of much conjecture, with the report in the SI's journal blaming the director of the museum, Willem Sandberg, for suddenly introducing new stipulations about finance and fire regulations that compromised the group's plans and forced them to be beholden to external authorities. Constant in particular saw Sandberg's moves as driven by an underlying ideological opposition to the group.[76] Whatever the details of the wrangle, the Bureau of Research for Unitary Urbanism folded straight afterwards with the expulsion of the Dutch architects from the SI, followed by Constant's resignation in June 1960. In subsequent years Constant retreated from such direct interventions as he became increasingly disillusioned with the prospects of immediate effective action to enable the development of new forms of urbanism. New Babylon depended upon revolutionary social changes and, in elaborating on its worlds through the 1960s, Constant was driven by a feeling of being unable to participate in contemporary culture from any perspective other than one radically opposed to its current basis.

A number of elements of New Babylon nevertheless have close connections with practices of psychogeography, mapping and urban explorations that Constant pursued earlier with the situationists. A prominent example is the series of maps in which he showed sectors of New Babylon in coloured blocks forming long chains across maps of existing cities and regions that included Amsterdam, Paris, Cologne, Antwerp, Rotterdam, Barcelona, the Ruhr, and even a historical map of Middlesex. Like Chtcheglov's métagraphie or Debord's earlier maps of Paris, they used forms of cartographic subversion or détournement. For a map of Munich in 1963, for example, Constant altered and added to the index as well as overlaid sectors in red ink. He further employed détournement on a grander scale in his 'Symbolic representation of New Babylon' of 1969, in which he collaged fragments from a variety of city maps – among them Amsterdam, Lichtenberg, Altenburg and London – into sector-like blocks, which were set against a plain background with red lines flowing between them (figure 7.9). Based on neighbourhoods with distinct ambiences that he found interesting, this 'play model' invited speculation and the imagination to roam. One might be drifting through Bloomsbury and past Euston station in central London, for example, to find oneself suddenly beside a canal, yards away from the Amstel river, in Amsterdam. The map thus took up the challenge of urban détournement posed by Debord and Gil Wolman in 1956, when they wrote that 'not many people would remain unaffected by an exact reconstruction in one city of an entire neighbourhood of another'. They added provocatively: 'Life can never be too disorienting: détournements on this level would really make it beautiful.'[77]

The connections with psychogeography suggest that the maps were not founded on the idea of simply sweeping away old urban fabric, as with the tabula rasa demanded by Le Corbusier and other modernists. While there is undoubtedly an element of rejecting current cities and building anew, importance is also attached to articulating structures in relation to psychogeographical experiences of existing areas. Constant stated that a prefiguration of the sector spaces of New Babylon could be found in the 'acculturation zones' of historic cities, those typically marginalised spaces where people on the fringes of 'utilitarian society' gather together and which become centres for cultural activity. New Babylon would draw on such a spirit of creativity but also surpass it, he promised, becoming 'one uninterrupted immense acculturation zone', where the social contacts and

Figure 7.9 Constant, *Symboliese voorstelling van New Babylon* (Symbolic representation of New Babylon), 1969. Collage. Haags Gemeentemuseum. Courtesy of the artist.

activities would exceed those currently found in functional cities, which were for the most part hostile to it.[78] Connections with existing zones and activities are further suggested by the semi-transparent nature of the ink used to colour the sector blocks on most of the maps, allowing existing streets and spaces to show through, and the way that in the maps of Amsterdam and Paris the sectors are shown skirting the edges of the historic core. Tensions are nevertheless palpable in terms of how Constant envisages changing cities and life. They are particularly evident between his attempts to model and map future spaces, from the perspective of present conditions, and his commitment to the idea that New Babylon would only be realised through a revolution and therefore could not be known in advance.

Some commentators see Constant's work as imbued with a politics of architectural and urbanist determinism, as if it were primarily dealing with questions of architectural and spatial design. His work might suggest as much in places, such as where he presents a part of New Babylon through photographs and a plan along with an imaginary description of wandering through its spaces, referring to it as the first in a series of *Promenades in New Babylon*.[79] This guided tour approach relates to the device familiar from much utopian fiction where the narrator is shown around the already transformed space and reports back her or his experiences. Constant also more generally considered how different environments and zones shape moods, activities, impacting on the body and effectively conditioning responses. Along with the other situationists, he did not see conditioning as something necessarily negative; on the contrary, much of psychogeography was concerned with how geographical environments inspire and shape behaviour, and may therefore be manipulated to particular ends. However, Constant backed away from developing a 'guidebook' for New Babylon in recognition of the problems entailed. He realised that he would have been forced to describe the spaces more precisely and he deliberately wanted to retain a certain openness and vagueness. This was at a time when he was already being reproached by many critics for describing New Babylon as a space of the future towards which society was headed.[80] He further recognised in later years that, even if the models for him were an open-ended and tentative exploration, involving an ongoing experimentation, their seeming fixity and technical aesthetic often gave other impressions. He noted how they 'appeared to sow confusion instead of fostering understanding of my efforts to visualize a world that was so fundamentally different from the world in which we live or the worlds we know from history'. During the 1960s he therefore 'resorted once more to brush and paints as the most effective way of depicting the unknown'.[81] He even cut up and threw out one of the largest models when its technical cast seemed to get in the way.[82] The free movement of the drawings evoking life in New Babylon certainly exceeds prescription and control, as Constant reckons with the principle that the inhabitants are 'people who live so differently from ourselves' that 'we can neither dictate nor design their playful or inventive behavior in advance'.[83] As a key point Constant continually insisted that his projects were 'the foundations for a greater liberty', and that: 'The true builders of New Babylon will be the Newbabylonians themselves.' [84] He emphasised the non- or yet-to-be-determined character of the environment where space would take shape through people's actions.

Underlying the tensions involved is the idea of tracing out paths towards a life and a city that would be 'other'. This may be elaborated upon further by turning again to homo ludens, which was a crucial figure through which Constant sought to address a new mass creativity to come. Constant's painting 'Homo ludens', of 1964, is characterised by a riot of colour and a spontaneous energy (figure 7.10). The festive atmosphere does not hold back or respect boundaries but is rather an irrepressible crowd, a state of becoming, a molecular energy that will not be channelled and controlled. As with his references to homo ludens more widely, there is a sense of the transformation of the subject, one that does not involve the organisation and formation of coherent subjective identity so much as an intensification of energy, sensation and spontaneous mass creativity. In a collaboration with Constant for a series of New Babylon lithographs in 1963, Simon Vinkenoog suggests such a utopian transformation of the body: 'Look with your hands / Feel with your eyes / Hear with your nose / Smell with your tongue and / Taste with your ears'.[85] The New Babylonian is 'otherwise', he writes, a metamorphosis yet to come. Against the limitations on perception and freedoms imposed by current social relations, where the human subject has 'yet to discover his true countenance' and is someone 'who feels empty, who is empty, whose senses are still inadequate', the demands are total: 'everything will be different, everything will be possible / everything is different, everything is possible.'[86] There is something here of the call for a 'hypersensorial, more-than-human perception' that Kristin Ross finds in Rimbaud's 'reasoned disordering of all the senses'. To the socially produced dullness of the 'human' under capitalism and to the reduction of the body into a commodity-like 'thing', she notes how Rimbaud responds with 'the transformed utopian body of infinite sensation and libidinal possibility as figure for the perfected community, for associative or collective life'. In political terms she identifies the move with the term 'swarm', where this signals a radical atomisation that rejects identifying with work as the basis of community.[87]

In the case of New Babylon, Constant was wary of claims about the creation of a 'new' human being as evident in Vinkenoog's extravagant text. He felt that it was wrong to imagine a 'superior' type of human when addressing a culture based on collective creativity. In a letter to Sean Wellesley-Miller in 1966 he stressed that this creativity was currently 'still as fictive as space-travelling' and that 'all has to be prepared, to be invented, to be experienced'. Instead of thinking in terms of a new type of human being, he suggested it was better to think of this in terms of 'an organization of social life that will enable an outbreak of spontaneous energies, that were suppressed during the long period of human history in

Figure 7.10 Constant, *Homo Ludens*, 1964. Oil on canvas, 160×185 cm. Stedelijk Museum, Amsterdam. Courtesy of the artist.

which labour absorbed the almost entire energy of humanity'. He added: 'We have not arrived at this point yet and I foresee a long period of struggling and of destruction.'[88] Nevertheless, through his imagining of homo ludens and its spaces Constant suggests a transformation of human senses and capacities, one that depends upon the liberation from work and economic responsibility discussed earlier, and on the unleashing of creativity that it enables. He looks towards a realm of abundance and freedom that he believes to be within reach, and presents his schemes on that basis as a provocation against the emphasis on utility and control in dominant conceptions of capitalist space-time. It is an attempt to envisage spaces of creativity that go beyond previous categories such as work and leisure, something the situationists discussed elsewhere as 'a new surplus value, impossible to calculate in money terms because it cannot be reduced to the measurement of paid work';[89] or what Gallizio called 'a "potlatch" system of gifts that cannot be purchased, other than with other poetic experiences'.[90] Constant's arguments about the generalisation of the figure of homo ludens may be seen, moreover, as crucial to his effort to transcend the repressiveness of many utopian proposals where the freedom of elite social groups depends upon strict divisions of labour and the exploitation of others. New Babylon is an attempt to find means for inventions of the unknown. As I have argued, however, its utopian spaces are riven with tensions and it is clear that the new forms it presents are not meant to be settled, prescriptive or anything approaching compensatory.

A lived utopianism

Among the critics drawn to Constant's utopianism was Lefebvre. Looking back on his encounters with the situationists, Lefebvre discussed with affection his friendship and collaborations with Constant, whom he visited many times in Amsterdam after 1957. Constant for his part also recalled visiting Lefebvre in Paris and reading his books, and noted the influence of New Babylon for Lefebvre's own thinking. Remarking on Constant's experiments with spatial construction and the creation of ambience, emotion and situation, Lefebvre asserted that he 'recaptures and elevates a concept from the grand architectural tradition, according to which space arouses or creates something such as a gathering, a joy, a sadness, a submission'.[91] Lefebvre drew a connection with his own theory of moments and acknowledged his accord with the situationists when they put to the fore such issues of creation and the production of new situations.

Writing earlier on the subject of a new 'revolutionary romanticism' in his *Introduction to Modernity* of 1962, in a chapter that extended the arguments of his essay on that theme in 1957 that had initially attracted the SI's attention, he argued: 'the most brilliant Situationists are exploring and testing out a kind of *lived utopianism*, by seeking a consciousness and a constructive activity which will be *disalienating*, in contradistinction to the alienated structures and alienating situations which are rife within "modernity".'[92] Noting the importance they attached to the urban in this process, he stated that 'it is within the context of the urban milieu that the creative activity of situations, and thus of a style and a way of living, is best undertaken. Thus the group has concentrated its attention on describing towns, on urban space and its use for play, and on all the forms of participation which derive from it.'[93] He further compared them to other small radical groups and micro-societies that had emerged since 1956–7, and argued that along with others they imply 'a *philosophy of the possible*'. Lefebvre suggested: 'They are all in search of the *opening*, by which they may enter in a practical way into the "possible-impossible" dialectic.'[94]

Lefebvre believed that utopia was essential for critical thought and his conception of utopianism centred around the 'possible-impossible'. By aiming at what was impossible today, he asserted, it would become tomorrow's possibility. Contestation opened up this process, where its role was to embrace a dialectical analysis that allows the articulation of the real, the possible and the impossible so as to make possible that which seemed impossible. As this makes clear, his utopianism therefore did not involve abstract projections of the good society but focused on tracing out what *might be* within present conditions. Like Constant, he was drawn by the possibilities of a radical social transformation that would open up a post-scarcity realm characterised by full self-realisation and the free expression of desire. In later years his account of this potentiality had a dark edge. As he put it: 'On the one hand the growth of productive forces makes possible something that is absolutely new – enjoyment of the world through the automation of production. But at the same time reality, "the present", becomes more and more terrifying'.[95] In more positive scenarios, though, he employed the methods of 'transduction' to explore the potentiality of an 'urban society' that he saw as in gestation within the bureaucratic society of controlled consumption, an urban society that held out the promise for a liberation from the constraints of need and work as they were previously understood. Lefebvre's arguments for the 'right to the city' were part of this emphasis on the possible. The phrase was meant to include the right to participation, to appropriation and to the *œuvre*, to habitat and to inhabit. It was conjoined with the demand for the 'right to difference', and to the idea of a differential space that might emerge out of the abstract space of capitalist society.[96] He elaborated upon these concerns most fully around the late 1960s and early 1970s but elements are present in earlier writings, as his appreciation of the situationists and Constant make clear. Themes familiar from Constant's work thread into his considerations of urban futures, as when Lefebvre emphasises the significance of play, festival and spending without return, and when he writes of an ideal city that 'would involve the obsolescence of space: an accelerated change of abode, emplacements and prepared spaces. It would be the *ephemeral city*, the perpetual *oeuvre* of the inhabitants, themselves mobile and mobilized for and by this *oeuvre*.'[97]

As I have noted, however, Constant and Lefebvre both lost contact with the SI based around Debord from the early 1960s. In Lefebvre's case the break came acrimoniously amid accusations of plagiarism, as discussed in the previous chapter. In Constant's case, it followed a close involvement with the group and the manner of the break sheds interesting light on the significance of urbanism and architecture to the situationists at the time. Constant's willingness to be part of the SI depended upon the agreement that he had reached with Debord in the Amsterdam Declaration, in 1958. For a period this provided the basis for extensive dialogue, as Debord followed and encouraged the early development of New Babylon through regular correspondence. Debord was drawn by New Babylon's imaginative engagement with spatial construction, ambience and behaviour. He saw it as promising much in relation to the position he sketched out at the launch of the SI when he argued: 'Architecture must advance by taking emotionally moving situations, rather than emotionally moving forms, as the material it works with. And the experiments conducted with this material will lead to unknown forms.'[98] Nothing was fixed in this participatory understanding of architecture and space, with the immutable categories relied upon by modernist architects being in dissolution. 'Our situations will be ephemeral, without a future; passageways,' wrote Debord. 'The permanency of art or anything else does not enter into our considerations, which are serious.'[99] It was not long, however, before difficulties led to a break.

The reason for the break is often imputed to be the expulsion from the SI of the Dutch architects, Alberts and Oudejans, in March 1960. Their expulsion was supposedly for their agreement to construct a church in

Volendam as part of their private practice, an act by which, in the words of the situationist journal, they 'placed themselves immediately and without possible discussion outside the SI'.[100] Their transgression had come some months earlier, however, when they had infuriated Debord by reproducing two photographs of their church design alongside texts by Constant, Debord and others in an issue of the journal *Forum*, in August 1959.[101] That a church could be presented alongside the SI's revolutionary proposals and within the framework of unitary urbanism was an anathema to Debord. Yet, as Wigley shows in a detailed reading of how the scandal unfolded, no action was taken against the architects for some months, during which Debord continued to show interest in their ideas and to request contributions from them. It was only when the situationist event planned at the Stedelijk Museum fell through, in March 1960, and when the architects' immediate usefulness for that event ended, that the exclusion took place.[102] Debord wrote to Constant at the end of that month, stating that events showed the Bureau of Research for Unitary Urbanism to be 'unhappily premature' and referring to his Dutch colleagues as 'indifferent'.[103] Constant consented to the expulsion as a member of the editorial committee of the journal in which the announcement was made. He was angered, however, when Gallizio filled the newly vacant slot at the Stedelijk Museum with a personal art exhibition. That, more than the expulsion of the architects, was the decisive moment. No longer wanting to support such 'neo-Cobra' artistic events, and feeling more isolated and unable to pursue his ideas about unitary urbanism fully within the SI where the agreements forged by the Amsterdam Declaration seemed increasingly threadbare, Constant resigned from the group in June. Debord tried to keep Constant within the SI for several weeks after receiving his resignation letter, and asserted his continuing interest in Constant's research. But the decision was finally accepted.[104] 'I quit it because there were actually too many painters in this situationist movement,' recalled Constant many years later. He felt he had 'a choice whether to continue the already begun project, New Babylon, or to be a situationist, but theoretical'. He decided he would be better off outside the group if he wanted to continue with his project. It was a decision that he claims never to have regretted. 'Debord especially, he tried for a long time to get me back, and he wanted to keep contact with me. Actually, I didn't want this contact anymore, because I was continuing in my own way and it led me away from the situationists.'[105]

Re-appropriating cities: urban critique

The SI for its part soon distanced itself from Constant, as it did with almost all of its former members once they resigned or were expelled. With the departure of the Dutch members, the Bureau of Unitary Urbanism was transferred to Brussels and placed under the direction of Attila Kotányi in September 1960. A change of direction became clear from the new programme of the Bureau, issued by Kotányi and Raoul Vaneigem the following year. 'Urbanism doesn't exist; it is only an "ideology" in Marx's sense of the word,' they began. 'Architecture does really exist, like Coca-Cola: though coated with ideology, it is a real production, falsely satisfying a falsified need. Urbanism is comparable to the advertising propagated around Coca-Cola – pure spectacular ideology.'[106] The situationists increasingly turned their attention towards the critique of urbanism and to understanding its ideological function as part of the spectacle. Political and theoretical analyses came to dominate their interest in urban issues. They insisted that unitary urbanism had to be merged within a general revolutionary praxis and that anything representing a specialist and reformist urbanism project had to be rejected. Models and depictions of future urbanism were in danger of contributing to, rather than contesting, the repressive technologies of urban planning and cybernetic control. It was as a 'specialist' and 'technical' work that they now characterised Constant's New Babylon, as they claimed that he was acting as a '*public-relations man* for integrating the masses into capitalist technical civilization'.[107]

The SI's attacks on Constant were often vitriolic, strangely so given their earlier collaboration, although the tone was not out of keeping with the group's criticisms of many other former colleagues. Putting aside personal jibes, however, the situationists pointed to difficulties facing Constant's projects as well as wider utopian approaches to cities. These concern the place of urbanism within any revolutionary transformation, and the extent to which it is possible to outline future urban worlds from a position within the present where those worlds are necessarily unknown prior to the revolutionary changes that will transcend present conditions. The situationists also raised questions about whether projections of the future fed into current modes of conditioning and control, something they now claimed to be the case with Constant's 'technocratic' models. They emphasised the need for a negative critique of urbanism to be part of a generalised critique of the totality, a point they made in criticism of an essay by Lefebvre from 1961, entitled 'Experimental utopia: for a new urbanism'.

The title of the essay itself contained the key ambiguity, the situationists suggested, since the method of 'experimental utopia', in their understanding of the term, had to confront the totality, where 'its implementation ought not to lead to a "new urbanism" but to a new use of life, a new revolutionary praxis'.[108]

Lefebvre later commented on the change in Debord's approach around the beginning of the 1960s. He noted that Debord and other situationists moved from the idea of elaborating a unitary urbanism to adopting a thesis of urbanistic ideology. This was against a backdrop of dramatic changes in processes of urbanisation in France. '[B]y saying that all urbanism was a bourgeois ideology, they abandoned the problem of the city,' Lefebvre argued. 'They left it behind. They thought that the problem no longer interested them.' He contrasted this with his own position where he turned to explore a theory of the city and social space over the following decade.[109] But while Lefebvre rightly identified a significant shift in the SI's approach, he was wrong to suggest that the situationists abandoned the problem of the city. Instead they addressed unitary urbanism as a 'living critique' of the manipulation of cities and their inhabitants in the society of the spectacle. Détournement became a principal means of both struggling for disalienation against the 'bards of conditioning', and of reappropriating urban areas and establishing 'bases for an experimental life'. As with the modernist model of the enclave promoted by CIAM, whereby a new element was inserted into the fabric of the city so that it would radiate outwards and transform the surrounding spaces, the aim was for these sites to act 'as bridgeheads for an invasion of the whole of daily life'. But the idea of a separate activity of urbanism was denied, with Kotányi and Vaneigem insisting that their proposed architecture and urbanism 'cannot be realised without the revolution of everyday life'.[110]

In most histories of the SI, these changes are elided with the group's supposed rejection of art and its move towards a more political and theoretical stance. Again, there is some truth to this. A report by the SI in 1963 noted that 'of the 28 members of the SI who we have had to exclude so far, 23 personally had a recognised and increasingly profitable role as artists'.[111] Following the exclusion of Gallizio and the resignations of Constant and Jorn in 1960–1, among the most significant breaks was the split by six members of the SI in March 1962 (the so-called 'Nashists' after Jorn's brother, Jørgen Nash); this followed the exclusion the previous month of the German Gruppe Spur. A number of these individuals regrouped around the Movement for a Scandinavian Bauhaus Situationist that had originally been formed at the Drakabygget farmhouse in Hallandsåsen, Sweden, in September 1961, and around the title of the Second Situationist International, as well as the journal *The Situationist Times* edited by Jacqueline de Jong in Amsterdam. Jorn was a rare case of someone who continued to play a clandestine role in the SI after departing. That did not stop him from registering his disapproval at the group's direction, though, as he complained in 1963 that Debord 'reveals his mentality and his politico-Latin training in considering artists as pure specialists and, in the end, simply as an instrumental means'. Jorn was more open to the experimentation around the Second Situationist International and its interest in recentring visual art within a critical social framework. He asserted: 'That Debord – engaged as he is now – is returning strongly to conventional and convenient positions which are, in effect, those of the Parisian avant-garde, appears neither desirable nor possible to us.'[112]

The situationist practice of excluding members has often been derided by critics, both then and now, and the group's frequent denunciations of former associates and members certainly make for wearying reading. Less often discussed is how the exclusions were part of a serious attempt, whatever is made of the outcomes, to address the challenge of how to organise the group in response to threats and opportunities at the time. The SI was intent on retaining a distinctive stance in relation to dominant cultural and artistic milieux, and not being absorbed by them; it also sought to ensure the full and free participation of all members, without developing hierarchies or allowing its positions to congeal into an '-ism'. Members therefore debated internal positions and possible external collaborations with the aim of maximising the effectiveness of their interventions. The exclusions of artists ought to be understood in this context, in relation to the perceived need to work collectively while precluding certain activities and contacts.[113] Constant's case illustrates that these issues were often complex. Far from being effectively forced out as part of a general purge against artists as is often implied, he was in fact one of the most vocal opponents to the activities of painters such as Gallizio and Jorn, and Debord was reluctant to let him leave. The moves within the SI on questions of art and urbanism should therefore not be oversimplified. Instead of making a fundamental break, as is suggested in many historical accounts, the SI engaged in an important rethinking of art, architecture and urbanism during the 1960s. The group repeatedly insisted that its interest lay not in straightforwardly abandoning art or subordinating it to politics, but rather in the possibilities of its surpassing and its *realisation*.

T. J. Clark and Donald Nicholson-Smith emphasise the significance of the latter endeavour where 'art' is understood as 'those possibilities of representational and anti-representational action thrown up by fifty years of modernist experiment on the borders of the category'. They characterise this as 'the truly utopian dimension of SI activity', and argue: 'It was the "art" dimension, to put it crudely – the continual pressure put on the question of representational forms in politics and everyday life, and the refusal to foreclose on the issue of representation versus agency – that made their politics the deadly weapon it was for a while. And gave them the role they had in May 1968.'[114] Hence Debord's description, as he looked back on the early years of the LI, of the realisation of art as 'the "North West Passage" of the geography of real life which had so often been sought for more than a century'.[115]

As the SI redefined its positions on art and urbanism during the 1960s, it did so by positioning itself against many other experiments at the time. Among them was Constant's New Babylon, which was now frequently appearing in architectural magazines and journals as well as exhibitions. At the SI's seventh congress in 1966, Debord asserted: 'Both the ideas of unitary urbanism and the experience of the drift must today be understood in terms of their *struggle* with modern forms of utopian architecture, the Venice Biennales or "*happenings*".'[116] In pushing New Babylon away, it is often suggested that Debord and the SI retreated not only from art but also from a utopian engagement with urban spaces. Again, however, it was not so much a retreat as a reconsideration as the situationists took up and transformed many earlier ideas and practices in a critical appraisal of the spaces of the society of the spectacle. Unitary urbanism became largely a matter of critique, with the focus on re-appropriating cities and creating enclaves for the materialisation of freedom. That left the problem of how to project a wider utopian vision of which those enclaves could be specific figures. But if the SI now rejected attempts to map out positive visions of unitary urbanism, a continuing utopian thread remained. The situationists had earlier written of undermining current social and spatial conditions by raising 'at a few points the incendiary beacon heralding a *greater game*'.[117] They held that utopianism played an important role in this endeavour as it enabled the preservation, education and projection of desires. This was a point they asserted in defending the revolutionary value of Chtcheglov's proposals against Constant's charge that they were 'chimerical'.[118] Retaining a conception of what could be against the falsehoods and distortions of the times gave many of the SI's later practices their critical utopian edge. They sought to confront present social conditions with the possibilities that they harboured, whose suppression was required to maintain the status quo.

The situationists thus asserted in 1962 that, against the images propagated by dominant society, it was important to promote '*an economy of desires*, which can be formulated as: technological society plus the imagination of what could be done with it.'[119] They also argued in the same issue of the journal that the current '*absence of imagination*' could only be understood by attaining 'the *imagination of the absence*'. By this they meant a consciousness of 'what is missing, forbidden and hidden, and yet possible, in modern life.' In their view, this would help 'bring to light the only *positive project* that can overthrow the wall of sleep; and the measures of survival; and the doomsday bombs; and the megatons of architecture'.[120] The SI was well aware that sceptics among its readership might wonder about the basis of its more utopian claims. In response they emphasised their realism and wrote: 'What might appear to be audacious speculation in several of our assertions, we advance with the assurance that the future will bring their overwhelming and undeniable historical confirmation.'[121] The group quoted the line again several years later in their reports on the revolutionary events in Paris of May 1968. That month millions of people went on strike and took to the streets, occupied buildings, built barricades, and brought the everyday activities of the city and country to a halt. It was a time when the SI's emphasis on the possibilities that lay within present conditions found expression, including through slogans that materialised on the city's walls and the flowering of utopian demands. With the proliferation of actions across the country, around ten million workers stopped work in a general strike and France seemed to be on the verge of revolution.

Contestion opened up possibilities. Spontaneous action found space in the streets, a social space not occupied by institutions. It cut across hierarchies and left behind leaders, as it opposed the state as well as attempts by groups such as trade unions or the Communist Party to impose control. The aim for many participants became transforming life and self-management or *autogestion*. Lefebvre described how, for a time, 'Paris changed and was restored – the vistas, the streets, the Boulevard Saint-Michel which, rid of automobiles, again became a promenade and forum'.[122] Then a professor at Nanterre university, Lefebvre witnessed how the initial revolts by student *enragés* at that insitution, located at an alienating campus outside the city, soon spiralled much wider. He described how the Latin Quarter and Sorbonne were transformed as unfettered speech 'burst forth in the crowded lecture halls, courtyard, on the square, in the vast forum', and how a 'concrete utopia now proclaimed a unified culture transcending the division of labour and fragmented specializations'.[123] There were many clear differences from the Paris Commune of 1871 but Lefebvre pointed to parallels too. These were not least in their respective spatial claims for the right to the city. 'In March 1871 as in May 1968,' he wrote, 'the people come from the periphery, from the outside where they had been driven, where they found only a social vacuum, assembled and headed toward the urban centres in order to reconquer them.'[124]

The situationists for their part regarded the occupations movement as a generalised critique of all alienations, and as 'a festival, a game, a real presence of people and of time'. They wrote: 'The *recognised desire* for dialogue, for completely free expression, and the taste for real community found their terrain in the buildings transformed into open meeting places and in the common struggle.'[125] They were particularly delighted to see the return of the slogan 'Never work!' on the boulevard Port-Royal, some fifteen years after Debord had written it on the walls of the rue de Seine.[126] In the words of the situationist René Viénet: 'Capitalized time stopped. People strolled, dreamed, learned how to live.' He noted how the 'right to be lazy' was affirmed in the unleashing of playful activity, where the 'disappearance of forced labour necessarily coincided with the free flow of creativity in every sphere'.[127] As he put it:

> The critique of everyday life successfully began to modify the landscape of alienation. The Rue Gay-Lussac was named the Rue du 11 Mai, red and black flags gave a human appearance to the fronts of public buildings. The Haussmannian perspective of the boulevards was corrected and the green belts redistributed and closed to traffic. Everyone, in his own way, made his own critique of urbanism. As for the critique of the artistic project, it was not to be found among the travelling salesmen of the happenings or the cold leftovers of the avant garde, but in the streets, on the walls, and in the general movement of emancipation which carried within itself even the realization of art.[128]

The utopianism of the SI's oppositional geographical imaginary flared most brightly that spring month. The more permanent revolution in social and spatial relations that the group had hoped for did not materialise. Barricades were subsequently removed, traces of insurrection cleaned from the streets, and capitalised space and time safely restored. The world-wide struggles of 1968, of which the events in Paris were an iconic although specific part, also receded. Thousands of books, articles, memoires, television programmes, films and the like have since then offered their opinions on what the uprisings all meant. Looming large in many of them is what Michael Watts calls a 'death narrative' that closes down the profound significance of the political events, that rewrites their history as inevitably doomed, as a dead-end, as 'immature', as paving the way for the excessive individualism of later years. Above all it refuses to consider what the revolutionary movements and actions called into question and what they opened up. In this light, as Watts argues, there is a need to attend to those openings and to think about how they speak to ways of doing politics differently that are still significant today.[129] This is not about myth-making of another kind or denying the mistakes and tragedies involved, but rather entails reclaiming the moments and situations from the dead-end complacent narratives of the 'victors', and thinking about what other continuing stories they might enable. In the case of the situationists, it is worth reflecting on their own attempts to herald a greater game, and on how elements of their ideas and practices continued to glow into the future.

Figure 8.1 'Under the paving stones, the beach!': graffiti from Paris, May 1968. Photograph courtesy of Rebel Press.

CHAPTER 8

Partisans of possibilities

'Utopist!'
'And why not? For me this term has no pejorative connotations. Since I do not ratify compulsion, norms, rules and regulations; since I put all the emphasis on adaptation; since I refute "reality", and since for me what is possible is already partly real, I am indeed a utopian; you will observe that I do not say utopist; but a utopian, yes, a partisan of possibilities.'

Henri Lefebvre[1]

Benjamin insisted: 'We must wake up from the world of our parents.' But what can be demanded of a new generation, if its parents never dream at all?

Susan Buck-Morss[2]

Dark skies

What to make of the utopian spaces of the situationists today? How to approach them at a time when so many critics have been content to announce the 'end of utopia', to wave goodbye to dreams of radically transforming social spaces and societies? When Guy Debord looks back on the letterists and situationists in his film *In girum imus nocte et consumimur igni* of 1978, he conveys a sense of darkness falling, of possibilities closing down. 'We would soon have to leave it – this city which for us was so free but which was going to fall completely into the hands of our enemies,' he recalls. 'We would have to leave it, but not without having made an attempt to seize it by brute force.'[3] Through the film he figures the growing alienation of society, and the increasing grip of capitalism and the spectacle on all aspects of social life, in terms of the reshaping of urban space and specifically Paris. Tower blocks appear on the screen followed by other scenes from the city as he states: 'The landscape we are now traversing has been devastated by a war this society is waging against itself, against its own potentialities.' In his presentation of 'landscapes ravaged for the sake of commodity abundance', he notes the connections as well as fundamental differences between the positions of the situationists and those of dominant forces in society. He argues: 'We, more than anyone else, were the people of change in a changing time. The owners of society, in order to maintain their position, were obliged to strive for a change that was the opposite of ours. We wanted to rebuild everything and so did they, but in diametrically opposed directions. What they have done is a sufficient negative demonstration of the nature of our own project.'[4]

Does this represent for Debord a collapse of utopian dreams? Does it mark a retreat from the revolutionary approach towards urban space that he and his colleagues associated with the Situationist International (SI) had earlier articulated? There is, after all, a long tradition of nostalgic writings about old Paris, many of which embody an anti-modernist aesthetic and a reactionary stance on a supposed more coherent and structured life of the past. In Debord's case it can be seen as part a tragic narrative of urban decline. But it does not simply reflect a longing to return to the past, for it may also be seen in political terms as a case of urban resistance: an attempt to oppose the forces of capital and state planning that were remaking the urban landscape. Along with the other letterists and situationists, he protested against the destruction of favoured areas. Their resistance took hold in areas directly under threat, such as Les Halles in Paris or the Chinese Quarter in London, which had been designated as in need of 'modernisation' by developers and the state. It involved criticisms not only of wholesale reconstruction but also the reconstitution of areas according to cultural values promoted through heritage and gentrification schemes. Debord viewed the urban changes they were witnessing and the growing 'museumification' of central cities as symptomatic of the eradication of meanings and spatial differences except for those produced in terms of the spectacle. In his final film the camera thus becomes a denuciatory instrument as it tracks over monotonous tower blocks and complexes of 'neo-dwellings' in Paris, over territories of abstraction designed to house the poor and ghettoise them into selected zones far from the centre of the city, and as it presents 'neighborhoods where everything has now become so dismal'.[5]

Yet Debord's criticisms are cross-cut with references to the LI and SI's struggles for different futures and to political contestations that the groups sought to fuel. He speaks of 'a few glimmers of light' appearing in the midst of 'the setting sun of this city', by which he seems to have in mind in particular flames arising from political struggles: 'This is how, little by little, a new era of conflagrations was set ablaze, of which none of us alive at this moment will see the end. Obedience is dead.'[6] He also pays warm tribute to the efforts of many former comrades, including Ivan Chtcheglov. 'It might almost have been said that he transformed cities and life merely by looking at them,' Debord states. 'In a single year he discovered enough material for a century of demands; the depths and mysteries of urban space were his conquests.'[7] After the dissolution of the SI in 1972, utopian currents still thread through many of Debord's writings as he takes a dialectical view of the actions of the 'owners of society' as indicating the scope of the SI's own ambitions. He quotes Marx, writing to Arnold Ruge in May 1853: 'You won't say that I hold the present time in too much esteem; and yet if I don't despair of it, it is on account of its own desperate situation, which fills me with hope.'[8]

In 1979 Debord further claims to see the words that had been inscribed on the walls of ancient Babylon, the '*Mene, Tekel, Upharsin* which announces the inevitable fall of all cities of illusion.' He insists that a revolution to create a classless society will only triumph when it is extended spatially and socially. His utopianism fastens onto a particular urban image: 'Then we will see again an Athens or a Florence from whence no-one will be rejected, reaching to all corners of the world; and which, having brought down all its enemies, will at last be able to surrender itself joyously to the true divisions and never-ending confrontations of historical life.'[9] His appeal to those cities is another symptom of the nostalgic side to his demand for more authentic urbanity, one that he opposes to the 'cities of illusion' of the society of the spectacle. The image certainly contrasts with the technological and forward-looking vision of urbanism presented by Constant. But like the latter, Debord does not envisage utopia as a harmonious end point, as something that would abolish all conflicts and future change. Nor does he downplay the uncertainties and difficulties radical change entails. On the contrary, what most concerns him is the struggle and movement itself, the striving *towards* something other that is conveyed by his repeated use of the metaphors of journeys, quests and passageways. The proletarian revolution, he stated earlier, is a critique of human geography. As a result, 'the independence of places will be rediscovered without any new exclusive tie to the soil, and thus too the authentic *journey* will be restored to us, along with authentic life understood as a journey containing its whole meaning within itself.'[10]

For utopianism

At the beginning of this book I noted the incongruity in addressing such utopian perspectives on cities today when it has become common to speak of living in a post-utopian era, as well as to oppose the very concept of utopia. Debord's own positions became increasingly pessimistic during the 1980s as he wrote of the spectacle moving into an 'integrated' phase and where even the glimmers of hope of previous years seemed to be dwindling. He particularly elaborated on what he saw as one of the spectacle's most pernicious effects, that is the destruction of history and the management of an 'eternal present'. He now cherished historical remnants not completely transformed in terms of the spectacle; there was little of his old enthusiasm for breaking with aspects of the past as part of a group of 'people of change in a changing time'. Yet he retained his commitment to opposition and to finding alternatives, as he raged against present conditions and insisted that things could be otherwise.[11] A mood of utopian dreams turning bad, of dystopian images or imaginative collapse nevertheless pervades much more recent urban discourse. A sense of stasis and of horizons closing down has been much commented upon. 'We used to wonder about the future of the city in spatial terms,' writes Christine Boyer, articulating a common view; 'it was a place toward which we were progressing, full of hope and expectation that a better world might someday be accomplished. In the contemporary city, we have lost this hope and critical engagement and are offered no alternative to the flattened, absorbing present.'[12]

Boyer criticises claims that 'there is no utopia' by critics who advocate accepting many current conditions and social patterns as unavoidable, inevitable. Recent focus on the piecemeal renewal of the city's façades and tableaux not only leaves other needs unaddressed, she rightly stresses, but also helps to mask the spatial politics involved in the processes of restructuring, and fails to challenge the way that images and representations of the city have been colonised by private concerns. A key problem facing any attempt to confront this situation and defend utopianism in the present, however, lies with the fate of previous utopian visions and especially a prevailing suspicion about their negative consequences. As David Harvey put it, 'no one believes any more that we can build that city on a hill', since 'utopian visions have too often turned sour for that sort of thinking to go far'.[13] In this regard it should be acknowledged that the decline of certain kinds of utopianism may be welcomed. This is the case with schemes common to many of the dominant traditions of utopian thought about cities that seek to impose a fixed spatial and social order, and to shut out disorder, chance and spontaneity as immiscible to the task of building a 'perfect' state. Their demise allows a greater freedom in thinking about cities, a loosening of the hold of ideals and teleological notions of historical progress that were imposed externally or from above. An abandonment of the oppressive nature of these kinds of utopianism is a prerequisite for imagining emancipatory futures. However, this need not entail turning away from utopianism as such, and with it the anticipatory moment of critique that is aimed towards considering how things might be different. That abandonment has disquieting consequences. In its extreme form the turn against utopianism is symptomatic of a closing down of imaginative horizons and even a slide into a reactionary acquiescence to dominant understandings and representations of cities and to the injustices of existing conditions, akin to those 'end of history' arguments that claim that 'we [and an obvious question is who is this "we"?] cannot picture to ourselves a world that is *essentially* different from the present one, and at the same time better.'[14] In such cases there is not just acceptance but also often a trumpeting of the motto 'there is no alternative.'

An important reason for returning to previous currents of utopianism in this context, as I have argued, is to attend to their desires for other spaces and ways of living, to consider their struggles over what cities might be, with the aim of challenging closures frequently surrounding understandings of utopianism and urbanism. By focusing in later chapters on the situationists, my aim has not been to present their ideas and practices as forming a fully functioning model that can be mapped onto the present. Their perspectives need to be understood in their contexts, not as a transcendental theoretical critique. There are clearly problems with many of the positions taken by the SI when viewed from current perspectives. The situationists' faith in the onward expansion of productive forces and the overcoming of scarcity, along with the technological optimism shown in particular by Constant, jars with a less optimistic economic and political climate and with more ecologically informed positions since the 1960s.[15] Their engagement with issues of gender and sexuality was deficient, something that raises questions about their views on how exploitation would be abolished and alienation overcome through revolutionary struggle, as well as about the sexism of some of their practices. This relates to the wider failure within the group to address adequately a politics of difference and openness to the other, and how the city might be a space of 'togetherness in difference'.[16] Narratives of urban decline and laments about the loss of public space such as those developed by Debord and other situationists are important in highlighting dangerous trends of urban restructuring and restrictions on freedoms in cities, but they can also more problematically be based on a neglect of the exclusions – including those along lines of gender, sexuality and ethnicity – that have always been involved in the constitution of the public realm, for there was never a golden age in which public space was once 'whole'.

The individualised nature of some of the situationist engagements with urban space, as in Chtcheglov's call for a personal 'cathedral', have furthermore made them ripe for being taken up by those who would see utopia as something primarily in one's own head or body, to be approached through consumerist or psycho-chemical means, rather than as involving more collective changes of social and political life.[17] There is also the issue, which the situationists were always alive to themselves, of the recuperation of their positions and ideas so that they become fodder to smooth the wheels of spectacular society. The SI highlighted many cases of this itself. In the last issue of its journal, for example, the group reproduced a poster for a commercial film from autumn 1968 in which the revolutionary slogans of just a few months before – 'Take your desires for reality', 'Poetry in the streets', 'Contest the spectacle' – appeared as mocked up graffiti on a wall, already turned around in being used to sell a product. 'Vulgar recuperation' was the simple caption provided by the situationists.[18] One can only speculate what they might have made of more recent cases, such as the use of lines from Chtcheglov's manifesto for a new urbanism and references to the SI in a marketing brochure by developers in 2002 to promote 'stylish, luxury living' at the 'The Haçienda apartments' in Manchester, built on the site of the Haçienda nightclub that itself took its name from Chtcheglov's text when it opened twenty years earlier, and brandishing the new slogan 'now the party's over, you can come home.'[19] There is a need, then, for any contemporary 'return' to situationist ideas and practices to work critically with their positions, to address their own embeddedness in the society of the spectacle, and to consider them in their particular contexts as well as in relation to other critical perspectives concerned with different axes of power and forms of oppression, not only those of class.[20]

The utopianism of the SI's geographical imagination nevertheless has significant implications for critical spatial thought and practice and for understandings of the potential value of utopian approaches to cities. It raises questions about the operation of power through urban space and the ways in which cities are sites for the reproduction of powerful interests. Not only do situationist critiques resonate with many current debates about how urban spaces are imagined, represented and contested, as well as with interdisciplinary concern with the spatialisation of critical social theory. Their focus on contesting and reclaiming spaces further connects with a range of past and present political struggles and protests, which are particularly pertinent in the light of the current remaking of urban spaces by capitalist interests that are deepening forms of segregation, surveillance and control.[21] Along with wider movements of the time, the situationists contributed to an expansion and re-imagining of the political that was one of the most important legacies of 1968. In their case the situationists encouraged a radical politics that was nomadic, creative, outside formal channels, and concerned with self-realisation and the production of autonomous spaces. Their identification and encouragement of political struggles might seem to belie their characterisation of the spectacle as all-encompassing, but the group insisted on the necessity of resistance and of finding ways to intervene in everyday spaces. Through psychogeographical practices, they explored the nonsynchronous and multi-topical nature of capitalist socio-spatial relations, and looked to gaps and cracks in the space-times of developments for composing oppositional readings of urban space. Hence their interest in marginal and threatened spaces as they attempted to uncover hidden geographies and histories, to work with repressed elements and memories, and to *détourn* dominant representations of the city in the search for other possibilities.

The situationists articulated a utopianism that therefore contrasts with many traditional forms of utopian thought associated with abstract ideals and formal plans. The group emphasised potentialities in the present and realising desires through processes of social and spatial change. Their approach was based on the belief that another world is possible, and that the means to reach it are in the here and now through connecting with people's needs and desires, not in some distant time or place. Such a utopian spirit is conveyed vividly by the famous line from the walls of Paris in May '68: 'Under the paving stones, the beach!' (figure 8.1). It was also shared by Henri Lefebvre in his rethinking of the place of utopia within Marxism. Despite important differences between Lefebvre and the situationists, they emphasised issues of desire, pleasure, play, poetry and creativity in addressing how everyday life and space might be transformed. These themes are too often relegated in critical inquiries, and yet they are essential for understanding popular as well as avant-garde utopian aspirations that consider everyday life in terms of its prospects for transformation. The limitation in this respect of much of the orthodox left, with its focus on the productive process and a redemptive view of labour, and with its more ascetic attitude towards political organising, was something that the situationists and Lefebvre both confronted. They also entered in different ways the 'possible-impossible' dialectic as they sought to extend what is possible through demanding what has been deemed by dominant powers to be 'impossible'. Lefebvre indeed turned such dominant claims around when he asserted that the real impossibility was that of 'existing social relations being adhered to indefinitely'. The goal of a radical project, in his view, lay in finding out 'what this impossibility makes possible and, conversely, what the "real" obscures and blocks at present'.[22]

Rather than proposing an 'abstract utopia', to use Ernst Bloch's terminology for an approach that he identifies with a utopistic dreaming that is escapist and compensatory, Lefebvre and the situationists aimed more towards a 'concrete utopia' that addresses a possible future within the real. In this sense, as Michael Gardiner discusses, they may be connected with other contributors to a strand of French utopian thought concerned with everyday life and its transformation, a 'counter-tradition' that includes Charles Fourier, the surrealists and Michel de Certeau. Gardiner argues with respect to these different thinkers and groups:

> They aspire to locate the utopian impulse and the pervasive desire for social transformation in the rhythms and textures of everyday life; in, for example, the sensual and pleasure-seeking requirements of the body; the 'felt' needs of people as they interact within the lifeworld (Williams's 'structure of feeling'); the individual and collective aim of autonomy and self-realization; and the achievement of personal happiness. In particular, they strive to reconnect the aesthetic and the everyday realms and to introject the festival, the 'play impulse', and the logic of the 'gift' into every area of personal and social experience.[23]

Within these writings, according to Gardiner, there is also an underlying criticism of forms of utopianism that fail to connect with such issues of everyday life, and that are therefore viewed as 'a reification lacking any real content, and hence complicit with a hegemonic, instrumental rationality seeking to erase difference and particularity in the service of the globalization of capital'.[24] Referring to a 'counter-tradition' of utopianism along these lines should not, of course, downplay the differences between those involved. Several years after they had split, Lefebvre lambasted the situationists in 1967, arguing that they 'propose not a concrete utopia, but an abstract one.' He continued: 'Do they really imagine that one fine day or one decisive evening people will look at each other and say, "Enough! We're fed up with work and boredom! Let's put an end to them!" and that they will then proceed into the eternal Festival and the creation of situations?' While he noted that this had happened once before, at the start of the Paris Commune in 1871, he confidently asserted that it would not do so again. His words were quoted back at him with glee by the situationists when, not much more than six months later, Paris was again shaken by a revolutionary festival.[25] The situationists noted that Lefebvre was far from being the only intellectual whose assumptions were overturned by the events of May '68. For their part, they noted they had 'prophesised nothing' but simply pointed out the conditions that were behind new kinds of revolt as well as encouraged forces of opposition whose seeds were already present. 'What thus came to the light of consciousness in the spring of 1968,' they wrote, 'was nothing other than what had been sleeping in the night of the "spectacular society" whose spectacles showed nothing but an eternal positive façade.'[26]

Re-dreaming modernist urbanism

By setting the utopianism of the situationists and Lefebvre against earlier utopian visions of the city in twentieth-century western Europe, specifically the dreams of order of Ebenezer Howard and Le Corbusier, I have emphasised the contested character of utopian visions. My aim has been to develop critical accounts of the modes of socio-spatial ordering within modernist utopianism, and to unsettle and destabilise narratives about them so as to open up space for other imaginings. This approach relates to current 'insurgent planning histories', a term used by Leonie Sandercock and others in their critiques of dominant historical narratives of modernist planning that centre on the 'heroic' progress of planning and its practices.[27] Their critique has included rewriting histories by adding the contributions of groups and individuals that have been forgotten or excluded from mainstream accounts. More fundamentally it has involved reconceptualising the field of planning through employing the insights of recent cultural theory and the critical analysis of issues of gender, race and sexuality as well as class. Part of this requires re-reading historical texts that have been central to the modernist discourses of urban planning to uncover their 'noir' side, to make visible their forms of repression and discrimination through modes of regulation that have been centred around bodies, spaces and social order.

Questioning utopian dreams of urban order is of relevance not only for past projects but also for contemporary urban developments, given the hold that certain ways of imagining and understanding cities continue to exert. Kevin Robins suggests in this regard that perhaps what makes a figure such as Le Corbusier particularly significant is that he was so *unexceptionable*. He asks: 'Is it not the case that Le Corbusier's authoritarian rationalism was, and still is, implicit within the principles of modern urbanism generally?'[28] James Holston also comments on the continuing influence of approaches derived more widely from the doctrine of CIAM (Congrès Internationaux d'Architecture Moderne) on present conceptualisations of the urban landscape in architecture and planning, and on the spatial logic of the built environment in contemporary cities. This is even where that connection is not recognised and the social agenda of the earlier perspectives has been stripped out. But in opposing the authoritarianism of modernist utopias, he is also concerned about the tendency to react by ditching all utopian approaches to urbanism. As he asks: 'Is not the elimination of the desire for a different future as oppressive as the modernist perversion of it?'[29] Many writers therefore seek to go beyond the 'modernist paradigm' – specifically its 'anti-democratic' practices and its 'technical rationality providing order, coherence, regulation, homogeneity'[30] – with Holston and Sandercock in particular celebrating 'spaces of insurgent citizenship' that are rooted in civil society and activities of social movements. As part of this project they bring stories and activities from the past into dialogue with struggles today, so as to influence current thinking and to affect change, with Sandercock being explicit about her desire to strengthen the utopian impulse in the present.

In my own account I have returned to other oppositional utopian currents inside avant-garde movements as a means of loosening the hold of dominant modernist imaginaries from within, and also with the aim of revitalising utopian impulses. This is in recognition that, as Peter Wollen writes, modernism 'always contained currents that challenged the norms of Western culture'. He notes that the modern movement was 'a battlefield on which purists endlessly struggled to expel difference, excess, hybridity and polysemy from their brave new world'. Yet the works of the purists themselves was marked by these never-ending struggles and contained other openings. Counter-traditions also continually challenged the purist disciplining. Such different perspectives have been the subject of increasing attention in recent years, as critics have taken up the challenge 'to look back critically over the history of modernism and to pick up those threads which run counter to its orthodoxy'.[31] An important aspect of this critical re-viewing lies in opening up the field of modernist urbanism so that its heterogeneity and conflictual character is explored, including elements too often written out of historical accounts. The case of the situationists and their avant-garde predecessors is remarkable here given the ways in which, despite often being forgotten or marginalised in the past, they placed urban space and the transformation of the geographies of everyday life at their heart of their concerns.

Referring to the earlier utopian dreams from the first half of the century nevertheless leads me to raise two sets of questions before closing. The first relates to one of the most striking features of the utopian schemes promoted by the likes of Howard and Le Corbusier when considered today, and that is the dissipation of their social and political energies. Despite the continuing influence of aspects of their spatial imaginaries on conceptions of cities, their commitment to transforming urban spaces contrasts with the relative dearth of utopianism in more recent years. The difference between the worlds they promised and what their visions helped to construct in reality is also dramatic. To give a particular case, Evan McKenzie suggests: 'If Ebenezer Howard could awaken now, like Bellamy's protagonist Julian West, and look about him at the America in which his ideas have had so much impact, he might react with astonishment and disappointment.'[32] Howard's disappointment would be not only at the narrowing and instrumentalisation of the garden city vision where its social ideals have been sidelined, writes McKenzie, but also more specifically at the absorption of his vision in the United States into private housing initiatives and common-interest developments that McKenzie calls 'privatopias'. These spaces emphasise versions of community and citizenship, but they contradict Howard's social ideals. According to McKenzie: 'In place of Howard's utopia is privatopia, in which the dominant ideology is privatism, where contract law is the supreme authority; where property rights and property values are the forms of community life; and where homogeneity, exclusiveness, and exclusion are the foundation of social organization.'[33] Howard's ideas can further be seen as finding a distorted echo in other forms of 'utopic degeneration'. These include the classic case of Disneyland, which Michael Sorkin notes is indebted to the garden city movement for its strictly zoned spaces, and for its ordering of movement and circulation to ensure the operation of 'Taylorised fun'. The Disney zones in turn embody aspects of the new city that Sorkin suggests has been in emergence in America, in terms of 'the ageographia, the surveillance and control, the simulations without end'.[34]

Utopian images from the past are now frequently used only for aesthetic and commercial effects. They become disconnected from a progressive political project and treated as a source for stylistic pillaging, a practice that was associated with much 'postmodern' architecture and urbanism alongside its suspicion of the utopian itself. Susan Buck-Morss refers to a contemporary 'melange of neo-, post-, and retroforms that deny responsibility for present history'. These forms, she argues, 'reproduce the dream-image, but reject the dream'. They are part of a wider attitude:

> In this cynical time of the 'end of history', adults know better than to believe in social utopias of any kind – those of production or consumption. Utopian fantasy is quarantined, contained within the boundaries of theme parks and tourist preserves, like some ecologically threatened but nonetheless dangerous zoo animal. When it is allowed any expression at all, it takes on the look of children's toys – even in the case of sophisticated objects – as if to prove that utopias of social space can no longer be taken seriously; they are commercial ventures, nothing more.[35]

In such a situation where many of the social ideals of earlier modernist utopian schemes now lie in ruins, might not there be further significance in revisiting their dreams of transformation? While resisting the uses to which they were put, is there not value in recognising the desires for change that they embodied and their surplus utopian energies before they are completely forgotten in a supposedly 'post-utopian' present? Are there indeed ways in which these desires and energies could be rescued for other ends? Could they provide a critical means with which to confront present distortions and utopic degenerations that have become such a prominent legacy?[36]

A second set of questions has been alluded to through the book, but it finally needs to be aired directly. It relates to the connections between the utopian visions of Howard and Le Corbusier and those of avant-gardes that opposed them, such as the surrealists and situationists. I have presented these movements as locked in an antagonistic relationship, with the latter groups opening up different paths. But to what extent did they share common ground and even exhibit continuity with one another? And following on from this, to what extent have all these movements been complicit with the requirements of capitalist development? These questions are at the heart of the account of the modern movement by Manfredo Tafuri in his book *Architecture and Utopia*. His thesis on the 'unitary development' of modern architecture is derived from a Marxist understanding of ideological criticism, which situates the development of architecture in processes of capitalist modernisation and rationalisation. In particular he addresses the widespread concern in the early twentieth century with '*utopia as a project*'. He connects the projects of modern architecture and the avant-gardes to the significance attached across a number of fields at the time to the theme 'of a "rational" dominion of the future, of the elimination of the *risk* it brings with it'.[37] In the process he disputes the idea of fundamental divisions between different modernist and avant-garde perspectives on these issues, instead constructing a totalising narrative of their mutual interdependence and furthermore their collective significance in contributing positively to capitalist development. Far from undermining capitalist development and the power of the bourgeoisie, the avant-gardes in both their 'constructive' and 'destructive' guises are presented by Tafuri as collectively functioning as a means of educating and energising those dominant interests, naturalising the conditions of the industrial city and enabling the ever more effective modernisation of capitalist society. This was particularly through avant-garde confrontations with the negative and with change and unpredictability in the city, and through the ways in which the groups dealt with the shock of metropolitan experience, where that shock was absorbed to become a new principle of development. Tafuri argues that techniques such as montage, by which avant-garde groups addressed the challenges posed by new conditions, and the rapid turnover of avant-gardes themselves with their calls for negation and the new, are analogous to principles of the money economy and the law of capitalist production with its demand for incessant technical innovation.[38] T. J.Clark refers to this as the 'bad dream of modernism';[39] and it needs considering further.

Spaces and times of the avant-garde

Tafuri argues that modern architecture adopted a critical role in seeking to overcome crises and contradictions in capitalist development through a projection into the future by means of the plan. He suggests that, in so doing, it followed a path paved earlier by the historical avant-gardes as it responded to their demands, and specifically to their demonstration of the 'necessity of programed control of the new forces released by technology'.[40] Modern architecture took on the task of giving concrete form to the process of rationalisation, one that was beyond the capability of the avant-gardes themselves yet had been vividly indicated by them. Movements such as cubism, constructivism, futurism, *De Stijl* and surrealism together therefore enabled the projects of modernist architecture by demolishing old orders and values and throwing themselves 'into ideological anticipations, into *partial utopias* of the plan'.[41] The role of the Bauhaus became that of 'the decantation chamber of the avant-garde', according to Tafuri, as it tested out different interventions in terms of productive reality and tied them into the reorganisation of production. Even the negativity of dada is incorporated into Tafuri's story. He writes that it became 'a means of control for planning', as it 'demonstrated – without naming it – the necessity of a plan'. Viewed in its historical context, dada's anarchic and nihilistic approach converged and coalesced with, rather than simply opposed, the search for order and ideology of the plan exemplified by constructivist movements from 1922.[42]

Tafuri's critique of modernist utopias of the plan resonates with those developed earlier in this study, including through the surrealists, the situationists and Lefebvre. He advances the more troubling idea, however, that 'alternative' visions of the city – such as those by the surrealists or situationists – were at a fundamental level not really alternative at all and were themselves complicit with processes of capitalist development through their commitment to 'utopia as a project'. Although Tafuri does not address explicitly post-war avant-gardes such as the situationists, his general arguments about the illusory nature of a radical utopianism within the fields of architecture and art prior to revolutionary social change are clear. He opposes any approach that 'by means of the image alone, tries to anticipate the conditions of an architecture "for a liberated society"'. He asserts the limitations on all attempts to intervene politically in the present through art or architecture, something from which much of his reputation for pessimism is derived, as he argues that 'just as there cannot exist a class political economy, but only a class criticism of political economy, so too there cannot be founded a class aesthetic, art, or architecture, but only a class criticism of the aesthetic, of art, of architecture, of the city itself.'[43] In a thoughtful engagement with Tafuri's arguments, David Cunningham suggests that this rejection of the post-war 'neo-avant-gardes' may be connected to a critique of their continuation of characteristics of an earlier romanticism. He refers specifically to the attempt through artistic or architectural means to imagine a transfigured everyday life, where art is meant to provide a key form for addressing social transformation. In relation to this argument Cunningham points towards a shared ground between the modern movement and its post-war avant-garde opposition, such as the situationists, one that manifested itself in 'an explicitly "politically" informed desire for a futurally projected complete "aesthetic" reconstruction and management of urban space'. He further comments on Tafuri's resolute scepticism in particular at the idea that an avant-garde architecture or design could draw on earlier non-rationalist models, such as those found in surrealism or expressionism, to oppose the dominant rationalism of modernism and 'in any substantial way alter the course of architecture's complicity with capitalist development, (willing or otherwise), insofar as it continues to hold to the naïve belief that aesthetic "form" in itself may provide a model for the projection of revolutionary change'.[44]

The situationists were aware of their own entanglements with the modern movement. Their outright opposition was sometimes combined with more nuanced comments on their relationship, as has been shown in previous chapters. They were also alive to the way that they were treading a common path with capitalist utopias, which had their own revolutionary dynamics. Debord noted in a quotation above how the situationists were 'the people of change in a changing time' and that they shared the desire with those in power to 'rebuild everything', with the difference lying in the direction this would take. The situationists suggested elsewhere that they were pursuing a similar or even identical route to their 'enemies', meaning that there was need to differentiate themselves ever more clearly from those enemies.[45] Tom McDonough comments on the last reference as he raises the potential of a Tafuri-based critique of situationist positions himself as an invitation to further debate. His focus, however, is not on the more commonly discussed way in which the situationists drew on earlier avant-gardes to formulate non-rationalist perspectives; rather, it is on what he sees as rationalist and planning impulses within situationist utopianism that it shared with dominant rationalist utopias. He refers to a number of examples of the SI's 'call for the planification of the future', such as Debord's argument early on that the era demanded 'a superior organization of the world', and that there was a need to respond to 'the problem of the rational control of new productive forces, as well as the formulation of a civilization on a global scale'.[46] To these references could most obviously be added certain echoes of the earlier modern movement in Constant's New Babylon, notably its adoption of elements familiar from Le Corbusier's urbanism, such as the raised structures on pilotis, as well as its grand aims for urban construction. One critic even claims that Constant's urbanism finds its inspiration in Le Corbusier's '*pilotis*, his open plans, and his inclination to lay waste',[47] while another remarks on the 'megalomaniac' continuation of modernist ambitions of urbanism within the situationists.[48]

Exploring this side to the SI tempers the tendency to view the group primarily through the lens of the surrealist legacy, as McDonough notes. It brings into question what he posits to be a relatively neglected 'larger, rational utopia of a planned future' that underpinned much of their ambition and that co-existed with other (non-rationalist) tendencies.[49] It also highlights difficulties that the situationists to some extent negotiated and addressed themselves. From their experience of the fates of earlier avant-gardes, especially surrealism, they were all too aware of how avant-garde activities and anticipations of a 'liberated society' could be co-opted and lead to integration into processes of capitalist development. Concern about this process ran through many of their critical discussions of the historical avant-gardes and was also, as has been seen, one of their key contentions about Constant's New Babylon subsequent to his resignation from the group. The situationists long insisted that 'there can be no situationist painting or music [and by extension other cultural forms], but only a situtionist use of these means';[50] and their reworking of unitary urbanism in terms of the détournement of existing urban spaces and away from prefiguring alternatives through means of images was based on an increasing wariness of anything that might be construed as a doctrine of 'situationist urbanism'.

Wariness on such matters might seem justified when early situationist visions for a totally flexible and fluid unitary urbanism, of which New Babylon became the fullest expression, are considered in relation to later developments. To begin with, the most prominent architectural heirs to Constant's work were often very different in politics and social outlook. Anthony Vidler cites in particular 'the technologically utopian "moving cities" of Archigram', where demands for a festive space and new creativity 'resulted in a privileging of literally mobile architecture'.[51] The idea of the flexible and ludic megastructure that became current in the 1960s did not in itself match up to the socio-spatial critique initially promised by unitary urbanism, and the failure of much megastructuralist thinking to address a transformation of social relations has rightly been exposed by critics, who have discussed how it nullifies claims of freedom except where that term is understood in a narrowly consumerist understanding of 'choice'.[52] Moreover, from the perspective of recent changes in capitalist urbanisation, it is not hard to see in aspects of the situationist and New Babylon visions something strangely akin to the dreams of hypermobile and flexible capitalism. Situationist demands to revolutionise urban structures, their attacks on urban planning, and their opposition to temporal and spatial fixity through continual urban change certainly take on different connotations at a time when cities have been overturned and remade through processes of commodification; when planning has been undermined by neo-liberal advocacy of free markets; when capital itself requires high geographic mobility for 'flexible' and temporary workers; and when commercial logic dictates that office buildings favour neutral structures and a 'skin architecture' to allow easy reconfiguration of internal spaces to accommodate the needs of 'flexible' firms.[53] McDonough goes so far as to argue that, 'like the futurists and a long line of avant-gardes in their wake, New Babylon too may in retrospect appear more as a harbinger of our present that [*sic*] as a utopian projection.'[54]

Yet there are dangers with following a Tafurian line too closely. To begin with it should be remembered that Tafuri wrote his book in particular circumstances, in relation to issues facing Italian Marxism in the aftermath of 1968 and specifically to confront the institution of architecture as he targeted its role as an ideology.[55] To take away from it now a blanket renunciation of utopianism in all times and places would not seem to be the most productive way of reading its intervention. As a theoretical position it also depends upon a highly problematic view of capitalism as a 'total system', in which capital becomes determinant of all activities and there is little room to consider other lines of power and subject positions. A contrast might be drawn with an account of the survival of capitalism published in the same year by Lefebvre, who insisted in his analysis of the 'reproduction of the relations of production' that belief in a system or achieved totality was mistaken, and that there was only an attempt at systematisation that was marked by contradictions, conflicts and different elements. He argued that the 'total' concept of a closed system 'evacuates history', and he contrasted it with the perspective he found in Marx, 'which is to understand what is happening in order to transform it, to seize the "lived" in order to beat a path towards life'.[56] Hence his own interest in utopian perspectives that open up possible futures through proposing different ways of living, different conceptions of space and time, that aim to produce a difference and a horizon beyond that which already exists. It is necessary to remain mindful of the bad dream articulated by Tafuri, since it cannot be simply wished away, however much doing so might appeal, and it raises questions that deserve further critical reflection especially about the relationship between aesthetics and politics within situationist practices. But nor should it be allowed to stifle in advance the potentiality of other dreams emerging; and it is more in the spirit of Lefebvre that I want to resist too complete a closing down of the possibilities presented by the avant-gardes, and to trace out a more differentiated understanding of the political implications of utopian visions of cities.

Many such differences have been explored in the previous chapters. Particular attention has been given to questions of space where I have highlighted the ways in which the situationists and Constant approached urban space not as something to be shaped according to formal codes, but in relation to social and political contestation where new spaces emerge through social struggle. Their closeness for a time with Lefebvre is significant in this regard. The distinctiveness of their position in relation to those for whom utopianism is a matter of the plan, the implementation of which will fix space and history in a spatial form, has therefore been emphasised. While Constant's New Babylon is sometimes discussed as if it were projecting such a planned future, its primary concern was with the mutual transformation of everyday life and space, and with challenging dominant conceptualisations of urban space in exploring other possibilities. It takes on aspects of earlier modernism through certain structural components, but it also opens them to other non-utilitarian and ludic ends as its spaces of desire exceed rationalist planning formulae, and as it continually undercuts or shifts its own forms as soon as they appear too solid and fixed. Instead of total construction from a planning point of view, as implied by some of the analogies with Le Corbusier and other modernists, New Babylon envisages spaces and ambiences constructed by people themselves; it involves a proliferation of multiple, open-ended and continually renewed space-times. In spatial and temporal terms, there is therefore not the same attempt to tie in the future by implementing a spatial plan, as in Tafuri's argument about modern architecture's concern to exert 'a "rational" dominion of the future'. Through its images of a possible urbanism, New Babylon provides openings in both a spatial and temporal sense; its attempt to stimulate imaginations cannot be reduced to conceptions of the planification of the future.[57]

Challenges of utopia

The distinctive utopianism argued for here needs emphasising today, not least as a means of countering claims by those who proclaim the 'end of utopia' and yet who often have a very particular conception of the utopian in so doing. Exploring different utopian positions and their potentialities encourages a reconsideration of the value of utopianism in the present. Saying this is not, of course, to deny the many dangers of utopian approaches, including the risk of sounding a nostalgic note for singular pictures of the future or for supposedly stable and adequate representations of a 'good society', those 'dreams of unity' criticised by Rosalyn Deutsche for denying their partial and situated conditions of existence.[58] As recent debates in social and cultural thought have shown, it is imperative to recognise the partiality of theoretical and political positions as well as the multiplicities and radical uncertainties of possible futures. Yet one of the compelling features revealed by returning to the utopian visions associated with the situationists and especially Constant is the way in which they worked with the tensions and difficulties of opening up other spaces rather than assuming they could be fully worked out in an ideal form. This is put succinctly in a line that Debord cut out from another text and pasted into a page towards the end of the book *Mémoires* from 1959 that he made with Asger Jorn: 'It is not enough to want to create new cities so that, as a result, all problems are resolved.' Another fragment alongside casts this in a particular light, referring to 'the everyday struggle'.[59]

Some of the tensions apparent in situationist utopianism are symptomatic of those more widely within much utopian thought that takes space seriously. Challenges addressed by Constant's work in particular include: How to imagine and represent utopian spaces in ways that do not reproduce the restrictions, exclusions and stasis of those that they seek to surpass? How can utopian visions avoid settling into repressive forms that constrain and control, given the way that they must embody particular values and desires? How to suggest spaces that are not yet, while retaining a radical openness to different futures in recognition that the spaces would be constructed by people themselves through emancipation? There are also other difficulties that have been much commented upon in the utopian literature. They involve how to imagine alternatives from a position within the unsatisfactory conditions and value systems of the present that is itself to be transformed? How to trace out unrealised possibilities that are denied and even defined as impossible under existing conditions, through languages or visual means that have been shaped by those conditions? As Terry Eagleton expresses this last problem: 'Since we can speak of what transcends the present only in the language of the present, we risk cancelling out our imaginings in the very act of articulating them.' He therefore adds: 'The only real otherness would be that which we could not articulate at all.'[60] This relates to a tension in the very idea of transfiguration, which Seyla Benhabib identifies with utopianism as such, and which she differentiates from a progressivist model of change that constitutes the gradual fulfillment of potentialities already there. The former vision of emancipation involves a radical break with the present and aims to open up qualitatively new socio-spatial relations and modes of association and subjectivity. But unless it remains connected to conditions of the present and the realm of what can be, it loses its basis in a transformative politics that would make possible that which is supposedly impossible, and that would enable the movement towards a future that is as yet unknown.[61]

In her critical commentary on New Babylon, Hilde Heynen dwells on some of the difficulties apparent in Constant's work. She suggests that his paintings can be seen as a kind of 'reflection at a distance' and perhaps a commentary on his project, bringing out some of its contradictions. The later paintings in particular, made around 1970–3 after Constant felt he had finished the project, develop a darker side to his vision as traces and atmospheres of New Babylon remain but aspects of conflict, aggression and violence become apparent. This is clearly not a world in which history has ended and 'perfect' order reigns, nor one in which harmony has replaced all discord. A threatening undertow at times erupts within the canvas, with scenes of destruction and terrible carnage.[62] The shift might be seen in relation to contemporary political events, with the revolutionary hope of 1968 in Paris and beyond dissipating, and attention being drawn to the violence of political struggles and the reassertion of state power, as well as to that of the Vietnam War. Themes of terror and war had occupied Constant much earlier after the Second World War, as in his series of paintings from around 1950–1 that depicted agonies of the 'scorched earth' and the destruction of people and places. These themes reappear in paintings such as 'Le massacre de My Lai' of 1972. Heynen, however, reads the darker side of the images of New Babylon as suggesting more widely the 'tragic character of utopia', and as providing 'a multilayered commentary on the impossibility of giving utopia a concrete form'.[63] This could be taken as underlining my points made earlier about the disruptive and ambiguous spaces of New Babylon acting as a telling critique of earlier utopian dreams of harmony, which assume that contradictions, conflicts and history itself can be expunged though the perfect spatial order. But Heynen further finds within them an involuntary criticism of avant-garde and situationist positions, and especially of their aim of overcoming alienation through an attachment to concepts of 'authenticity'. She argues that the incommensurabilities of New Babylon are testament to the need to question the assumption that revolution will automatically abolish alienation, and to recognise the ultimate impossibility of achieving an authentic liberated utopian end-state.

Heynen's analysis is perceptive, especially in the way that she connects New Babylon to the antinomy identified by Adorno as being critical in art's commitment to utopia, where he states that 'art must be and wants to be utopia', and yet 'at the same time art may not be utopia in order not to betray it by providing semblance and consolation'.[64] What also needs emphasising, however, is that while New Babylon demonstrates the difficulties and even impossibility of depicting utopia as an ideal form, its power lies precisely in its continuing *utopian* desire over so many years and involving so much activity to displace dominant assumptions about urban and social futures, to imagine an other city and life, and to find ways of depicting those other spaces in spite of the problems of so doing. It is this extraordinary commitment to challenging the status quo and to provoking alternative understandings, and in the process working with tensions and difficulties rather than smoothing them away, that makes the project so striking today. Despite frequent criticism or incomprehension from others during the 1960s, Constant refused to give up. He only ended New Babylon when he felt he had completed what he needed to say. He also resisted the route of anti-art, rejecting the claim that artistic activity was best discarded under current social conditions in protest at its role in perpetuating oppressive structures and commodification. 'What threatens bourgeois society is not an abandonment of the creative spirit, but that spirit itself,' he argued. 'To change society one needs, above all, imagination.'[65] He was aware himself of the inadequacy of prescriptive plans that try to tie in the future and of their dangers of co-optation. Looking back on his project, he even noted how 'it is impossible and pointless to design a city for the future because we have no say in that future. What we can do is to predict or strive for changes in the way people live together, to take these into account when considering possible alternative urban forms.' Again, he emphasised the continuing need for utopian thought and practice:

> We build now for the present way of life, so we build wretchedly for a wretched life. For those who believe or think that another kind of society is possible, that, to paraphrase the eleventh thesis on Feuerbach, we must not interpret the world but change it, speculative representation is every bit as important as critical analysis.[66]

After ending his work on New Babylon, Constant returned fully to painting. He worked on compositions in oil and watercolours that took on diverse themes, from literary and classical sources to contemporary events and scenes. He now referred to how his earlier project was, somewhat ironically given its intended critical relation to the institution of art and its ambitions to change life, 'safely stored away in a museum, waiting for more favourable times when it will once again arouse interest among urban designers'.[67] One curator describes it as 'probably the last attempt in European art to provide a global revolutionary image of – and place for – society'. He follows the observation with the question, 'Why did the century begin so full of intentions to change the world, and end with a total absence of such perspectives?'[68] Recent years have nevertheless seen renewed interest in the historical trajectory of Constant's work, especially from within the field of architecture and urban design. This leads us to ask to what further projects do they now speak? And how might the utopianism of situationist ideas and practices more generally help to open up future paths?

Future paths

Discussion of Constant as well as the other letterists and situationists has included much interest in how the form of their proposals attack 'high modernism' in architecture, design and planning as it became defined after 1945, and how they anticipate later architectural and design ideas. Part of the reason for this emphasis lies in the influence accorded to the SI and especially to Constant by a number of architects and theorists, including Archigram, Paul Virilio, Bernard Tschumi, and Nigel Coates and the NATO group (Narrative Architecture Today). An interview with Constant by a young Rem Koolhaas in 1966 is also interesting in this regard.[69] Explorations of these lines of influence are helping to rewrite cultural histories of the recent past, something that is not only of interest for the historical record but also for questioning and displacing certain assumptions today. The utopian ideas and practices addressed in this study, however, also provide a significant resource for catalysing and rethinking the potential of utopian perspectives more widely. The understanding of urban space developed in particular by the situationists, Constant and Lefebvre in terms of appropriation and participation, as well as ideas about desire, pleasure and a possible ludic realm, remain important for attempts to re-imagine the city and to seek out what is possible within present geographies. Reconsidering such utopianism underlines the need to explore further dissident approaches to the transformation of everyday space, both within the avant-gardes and beyond, as well as to recognise forms of action and subversion that are already in play in the present and that challenge claims that utopianism is at an end.

Resonances and more direct influences may be traced between the practices of the situationists and the activities of many contemporary artists, architects, activists, cultural workers and writers concerned with the production and contestation of urban space, and with the emancipatory possibilities of cities. Such resonances are apparent with those seeking to develop new understandings of cities as well as different forms of practice to intervene in the production and reproduction of urban space. A number of situationist ideas and practices, especially around psychogeography, speak to contemporary interest in forms of molecular politics, including modes of association and sociality, and in subjectivity, affect, performance and the eroticism of the urban public realm as well as modes of dreaming and experiencing cities.[70] Certain shared concerns and tactics are also evident with many street actions, demonstrations, occupations and experiments in urban democracy associated in particular with the surge of creative protest and practice through the anti-capitalist or global justice movements in recent years. Those actions, indeed, provide an interesting lens through which to consider the potential legacies of the situationists and the wider political movements of 1968. This is especially in relation to the importance they attach to urban space for political struggle, as public space has been a significant medium through which demands have been made, political rights asserted, and social and economic values struggled over. In becoming the focal point of protest actions, streets in many cities around the world have recently witnessed creative spatial mobilisations by justice and peace activists asserting that 'another world is possible'. The actions include the staging of temporary parties and festive appropriations of public spaces, and the provocative reworking of those spaces to non-utilitarian and ludic ends.

What connects many of these approaches, and what makes drawing a connection with the situationists and Lefebvre suggestive, is the effort to root the utopian impulse in the contemporary situation, and to trace out possibilities from that situation. 'We must treat the city and its architecture as a "possibilities machine",' argue Iain Borden, Joe Kerr, Jane Rendell and Alicia Pivaro. By that they mean 'what Lefebvre refers to as an oeuvre – a place of artistic production in its widest sense, where the "texture" of the city is its creation of time-spaces through the appropriative activities of its inhabitants; a place of nonlabor, joy, and the fulfillment of desires rather than toil; a place of qualities, difference, relations in time and space, contradictory uses and encounters.'[71] This kind of utopian geographical imagination, always attuned to the possibilities contained within cities and urban life, has a significant role to play in resisting the closing down of future horizons and puncturing reactionary positions that acquiesce to dominant conceptualisations of urban space and to the injustices of existing conditions. A critical utopianism for today should not be afraid of demanding what has been deemed impossible so as to expand possibilities. It should also recognise the centrality of desire in utopian thought and action, the desire for a different and better life. 'Desire, the desire to be happy, creates the distance, the negation, that opens the space for criticism of what is', notes Iris Marion Young in relation to her utopian conception of urban life and social justice. In proposing ideals, she argues that they do not constitute goals to be implemented as such but insists that they are still significant. 'Ideals are a crucial step in emancipatory politics . . . because they dislodge our assumption that what is given is necessary,' she writes. 'They offer standpoints from which to criticise the given and inspiration for imagining alternatives.'[72]

In recent writings David Harvey also advocates the development of utopian visions as a means of countering the 'sclerosis' that reins in cities as well as in ways of imagining them, and to fuel an optimism of both will and intellect. He argues that 'we cannot do without utopian plans and ideals of justice. They are indispensable for motivation and for action.'[73] Harvey engages with Young's arguments among others in setting out what he calls a 'dialectical' or 'spatiotemporal utopianism', one that he distances from the 'dead' traditional utopias of spatial form. Instead, he embraces a 'living utopianism' of process, one that is 'rooted in our present possibilities at the same time as it points towards different trajectories for human uneven geographical developments.'[74] Harvey asserts his frustration, however, at visions that refuse to countenance closure and that keep choices endlessly open. Included is Lefebvre's position on the production of space, which he finds attractive for its devastating critique of the authoritarianism of traditional utopias of spatial form and absolute conceptions of space, but also disappointing in the way that its anti-authoritarianism leads to a refusal of specific recommendations. The result of such an approach, he complains, is that 'there is no way to define that port to which we might want to sail.'[75] Harvey makes surprisingly little of Lefebvre's demands for 'the right to the city' here, despite his own interest in rights as the basis for universal ideals upon which the imagination of alternative futures might be developed.[76] Harvey nevertheless insists that for utopianism to take spatial form and not to be forever deferred, choices have to be made that involve particular materialisations of spaces and institutions rather than others. He argues that if alternatives are to be realised, closure of some kind is necessary, whether temporary or more permanent, and this entails dealing with questions of authority. Evading these requirements through a utopianism of social process 'is to embrace an agonistic romanticism of perpetually unfulfilled longing and desire'.[77]

Harvey therefore favours a utopianism of process that confronts questions about spatialisation, materialisation and authority. In developing his thoughts on alternative possible worlds, he uses the figure of the architect. He chooses this figure primarily as a means of foregrounding the importance of spatial construction and the agency involved, as well as imaginative capacity and speculative activity. It also allows him to explore the demands posed by working under historical and geographical conditions not of one's own choosing, and through a particular socially constructed role, but where there is always still a moment of imaginative and creative play. However circumscribed the architect's role, there is always the possibility and indeed need to desire and think difference. Harvey emphasises these elements of imagination and speculation as he writes of being 'positioned as an insurgent architect, armed with a variety of resources and desires, some derived directly from the utopian tradition', a position from which one can 'aspire to be a subversive agent, a fifth columnist inside of the system, with one foot firmly planted in some alternative camp'.[78] It is a compelling image, one that recognises the constraints facing all forms of utopianism as they are forged within certain positions, while also striving for different spaces and futures. It takes us back to some of the difficulties common in utopian thought that were discussed above. And significantly, despite Harvey's insistence on making choices and defining a 'port' towards which one might sail, he returns to the fundamental recognition that the process of opening up alternatives has to deal with the unknown and as yet undefined. The 'risk' of an open future remains, for it is not removed through a utopia of the plan. He writes that the 'the leap from the present into some future is always constrained', yet it is necessary; it involves 'a speculative leap into the unknown and into the unknowable'.[79] Courage, a willingness to speculate, and an ability to face up to uncertainty and risk are therefore required in the effort to become active subjects capable of constructing other geographies and histories.

Utopias based on fixed urban forms may have appeal in this regard, as Harvey notes, since they provide secure pictures of the future through plans that rule out chance or uncertainty; as has also been argued, however, their attempt to lock in that future through closed schemes is dangerously restrictive. In developing more open and exploratory forms of utopianism, there is much to learn from other critical currents of utopian thinking that, despite the claims of 'endings' discussed earlier, have continued to challenge assumptions and to help reconfigure the utopian field. Among the strands of critical utopianism are those within feminism in Europe and North America since the 1970s that have been developing forms of utopian thought that are opposed to the closed, formal blueprints of traditional utopias. It is a utopianism that addresses the possibilities for shifts in consciousness and for radical change. But it is explicitly partial and accepts that struggle, conflict as well as ambiguity and flux are necessary and need to be acknowledged. Among its watchwords are process, dynamism, movement, open-endedness, transgression. It typically gives a central role to desire and reconceptualises the utopian in fluid terms as 'an *approach toward*, a movement beyond set limits into the realm of the not-yet-set'.[80] The challenge of drawing on such fluid conceptions of utopianism in attempts to transform cities and spaces is not easily resolved, hence Harvey's ambivalence about the openness involved. But its potential to inspire and transgress constraining norms is nevertheless considerable, as emphasised by among others Sandercock, who from within an urban planning context offers a 'Utopia in the becoming', a vision of 'cosmopolis' that is influenced by feminist and postcolonial theory. Her cosmopolis is a means of exploring what might be, as she conceives of utopia as a social project concerned with 'living together in difference' that is open to dialogue, change and contestation in contrast to utopia's traditional inability to deal with such issues.[81]

The particularities of these and other recent projects need discussion of their own. In cultivating critical utopian imaginations suitable for current circumstances, though, I have argued that there is also much to gain from exploring the geographies and histories of earlier urban utopianism, and from tracing out paths taken within European avant-gardes in relation to mainstream modernist currents. It is true that many of the more recent currents of utopian thinking, including in relation to feminist and postcolonial perspectives, raise sharp questions about the partiality and difficulties of earlier avant-garde positions as well as those of Lefebvre. These cannot be ignored in any attempts to extend their perspectives into the present. Furthermore, projects such as New Babylon will not satisfy those who seek from utopian thought a plan to guide the way into the future. Yet to demand from New Babylon the resolution of tensions and the presentation of a fixed goal would be to misconstrue its critical relation to traditional utopian proposals. To suggest that it failed on the grounds that it remained an imaginary project would similarly be to misunderstand its politics. New Babylon does not work through the logic of the spatial plan. It operates more along the lines of *interruption*, intervening in conceptions of urban space and time, and opening up opportunities for those spaces and times to be thought and lived otherwise. It has effects as a provocation, stimulating responses, and encouraging critical reflection and action.

Against dismissals of utopian visions of cities as irrelevant fantasies or compensatory distractions, or as being inherently authoritarian, it is important to retain this understanding that they can be open, dynamic and provocative. There is a continuing need for forms of critical utopianism that challenge the conditions of the present, that offer glimpses of other possibilities and that maintain a creative game with those conditions so as to figure alternatives. The visions of New Babylon as well as those associated with other avant-garde interventions provide no simple models, nor are they absolved of the problems that have long beset utopian visions of space and society, including their darker sides. Considering those earlier utopian visions today can nevertheless fuel conviction that things do not have to go on as they are. They can help to estrange taken-for-granted aspects of urbanism and city living, and to challenge common definitions about what is impossible and possible. Through connections with contemporary spatial thinking and forms of political practice, they may also serve to inspire new forms of critical utopianism intent on shaking up the imaginative terrain within which cities are thought about, conceived and lived, where the aim is to transform social and spatial relations. For all the risks associated with utopianism, its dreaming of alternatives remains indispensable in enabling critiques of human geography. It is vital part of being a 'partisan of possibilities'.

Notes

A note on references and translations

In the following notes I use existing translations in English where they are available. References to original language versions of selected primary sources are also provided in the first citation in each chapter, followed by the translation. Thereafter only the translation is cited. Where no translation is acknowledged, it is the responsibility of the author. All emphases in quotations are in the original unless otherwise indicated. Where original texts and translations have used gender-specific language, I have retained it in direct quotations but reworked it when paraphrasing or providing my own translations.

Chapter 1: Introduction

1. Henri Lefebvre, in Patricia Latour and Francis Combes, *Conversation avec Henri Lefebvre* (Paris: Messidor, 1991), pp. 18–19; from discussions held on 2–5 January 1991.
2. Henri Lefebvre *The Production of Space*, trans. Donald Nicholson-Smith (Oxford: Basil Blackwell, 1991), p. 59; originally published in French in 1974.
3. Gilles Ivain, 'Formulaire pour un urbanisme nouveau', *Internationale situationniste* 1 (June 1958), pp. 15–20, written under that pseudonym by Ivan Chtcheglov in October 1953, trans. as 'Formulary for a new urbanism' in Ken Knabb (ed. and trans.), *Situationist International Anthology* (Berkeley: Bureau of Public Secrets, 1981), pp. 1–4: pp. 3, 2, 3.
4. This is the name that members of the *Internationale Lettriste* adopted when referring to themselves in English.
5. Ivain (Chtcheglov), 'Formulary', p. 2
6. Ibid. p. 1.
7. Ibid. p. 2.
8. Ibid. p. 3.
9. Ibid. p. 2.
10. The journal ran for twelve issues between 1958 and 1969. It is reprinted in

facsimile editions as *Internationale situationniste, 1958–1969* (Amsterdam: Van Gennep, 1970; Paris: Champ Libre, 1975; and Arthème Fayard, 1997). References hereafter to *IS*.

11. See Gil J. Wolman, 'À la porte', in the LI's bulletin *Potlatch* 2 (29 June 1954), reprinted in *Potlatch (1954–1957)*, complete edition (Paris: Gallimard, 1996), pp. 21–2: p. 21. Chtcheglov was subsequently incarcerated in a psychiatric clinic and retained only intermittent contact with his former associates, corresponding with Debord and Bernstein in the 1960s.
12. Introductory note to Ivan Chtcheglov, 'Lettres de loin', *IS* 9 (August 1964), pp. 38–40, trans. in Knabb, *Anthology*, p. 371.
13. 'Problèmes preliminaires à la construction d'une situation', *IS* 1 (June 1958), pp. 11–13, trans. as 'Preliminary problems in constructing a situation', in Knabb, *Anthology*, pp. 43–5: p. 45.
14. See especially Guy Debord, *La société du spectacle* (Paris: Buchet-Chastel, 1967), trans. Donald Nicholson-Smith as *The Society of the Spectacle* (New York: Zone Books, 1994).
15. Guy Debord, 'Les situationnistes et les nouvelles formes d'action dans la politique ou l'art', in *Destruktion af RSG-6: En kollektiv manifestation af Situationistisk International* (Odense, Denmark: Galerie EXI, 1963), pp. 15–18, trans. Thomas Levin as 'The situationists and the new forms of action in politics or art', in Tom McDonough (ed.), *Guy Debord and the Situationist International: Texts and Documents* (Cambridge, MA: MIT Press, 2002), pp. 159–66: p. 159.
16. Guy Debord, *Rapport sur la construction des situations et sur les conditions de l'organisation et de l'action de la tendance situationniste internationale* (Paris, n.p., 1957), reprinted in Gérard Berreby (ed.), *Documents relatifs à la fondation de l'Internationale situationniste: 1948–1957* (Paris: Éditions Allia, 1985), pp. 607–19, excerpts trans. as 'Report on the construction of situations and on the International Situationist tendency's conditions of organization and action', in Knabb, *Anthology*, pp. 17–25.
17. 'Le détournement comme négation et comme prélude', *IS* 3 (December 1959), pp. 10–11, trans. as 'Detournement as negation and prelude', in Knabb, *Anthology*, pp. 55–6: p. 55.
18. Among them were Algeria, Belgium, Britain, Denmark, France, Germany, Italy, the Netherlands, Sweden, Tunisia and the United States. A list of those who participated along with a detailed chronology of the SI's history is contained in Jean-Jacques Raspaud and Jean-Pierre Voyer, *L'Internationale situationniste: chronologie/bibliographie/protagonistes (avec un index de noms insultés)* (Paris: Champ Libre, 1972).

19. 'L'aventure', *IS* 5 (December 1960), pp. 3–5, excerpts trans. as 'The adventure', in Knabb, *Anthology*, pp. 60–1: p. 60.
20. Perspectives on a range of understandings of 'utopia' in western culture are provided by John Carey (ed.), *The Faber Book of Utopias* (London: Faber, 1999); and Roland Schaer, Gregory Claeys and Lyman Tower Sargent (eds), *Utopia: The Search for the Ideal Society in the Western World* (Oxford: Oxford University Press, 2000). For a magnificiently illustrated history of 'ideal cities' over more than two millenia, see also Ruth Eaton, *Ideal Cities: Utopianism and the (Un)Built Environment* (London: Thames and Hudson, 2002).
21. Karl Mannheim, *Ideology and Utopia: An Introduction to the Sociology of Knowledge* (London: Routledge and Kegan Paul, 1979), pp. 176–7; originally published in German in 1929.
22. Edward Timms, 'Introduction: unreal city – theme and variations', in Edward Timms and David Kelley (eds), *Unreal City: Urban Experience in Modern European Literature and Art* (Manchester: Manchester University Press, 1985), pp. 1–12: p. 7.
23. See especially Marshall Berman's classic account in *All That is Solid Melts into Air: The Experience of Modernity* (London: Verso, 1983), which draws on Marx and other nineteenth-century writers in addressing these ambiguities of modernity.
24. Leonie Sandercock, *Cosmopolis II: Mongrel Cities in the 21st Century* (London: Continuum, 2003).
25. Sandercock discusses a range of challenges to 'official histories' drawing on critical theories since the 1970s, ibid. pp. 37–57. See also Leonie Sandercock (ed.), *Making the Invisible Visible: A Multicultural Planning History* (Berkeley: University of California Press, 1998).
26. Derek Gregory, *Geographical Imaginations* (Oxford: Blackwell, 1994), p. 216.
27. See, for example, John R. Gold, *The Experience of Modernism: Modern Architects and the Future City, 1928–1953* (London: Spon, 1997); Sarah Williams Goldhagen and Rjean Legault (eds), *Anxious Modernisms: Experimentation in Postwar Architectural Culture* (Cambridge, MA: MIT Press, 2001); and David Cunningham, Jon Goodbun and Karin Jaschke (eds), 'Post-war images', issue of *The Journal of Architecture* 6.2 (2001).
28. Leonie Sandercock makes this point forcefully in her *Cosmopolis II*, p. 41, in reply to Peter Hall's justification for focusing only on male planning visionaries in his *Cities of Tomorrow: An Intellectual History of Urban Planning and Design in the Twentieth Century* (Oxford: Blackwell, third edition, 2002), p. 7. Among many important feminist studies in this vein are those by Dolores

Hayden, such as *The Grand Domestic Revolution: A History of Feminist Designs for American Homes, Neighbourhoods, and Cities* (Cambridge, MA, MIT Press, 1981).

29. Peter Bürger, *Theory of the Avant-Garde*, trans. Michael Shaw (Minneapolis: University of Minnesota Press, 1984); an earlier version was published in German in 1974. In relation to avant-gardes in architecture, see Hilde Heynen, *Architecture and Modernity: A Critique* (Cambridge, MA: MIT Press, 1999), pp. 26–70.
30. David Cunningham, Jon Goodbun and Karin Jaschke, 'Introduction', *The Journal of Architecture* 6.2 (2001), pp. 107–12: p. 107.
31. Sadie Plant, 'The Situationist International: a case of spectacular neglect', *Radical Philosophy* 55 (1990), pp. 3–10. Her article appeared shortly after a travelling exhibition on the SI did much to raise its profile in 1989–90 by visiting Paris, London and Boston.
32. Tom McDonough, 'Introduction', in McDonough, *Guy Debord*, pp. ix-xx: p. xvii.
33. Erik Swyngedouw, 'The strange respectability of the situationist city in the society of the spectacle', *International Journal of Urban and Regional Research* 26.1 (2002), pp. 153–65. The literature on the SI is now too extensive to cite here but a bibliography of earlier texts published in 1972–92, mainly in English although including major publications in other languages, is Simon Ford, *The Realization and Suppression of the Situationist International: An Annotated Bibliography 1972–1992* (Edinburgh: AK Press, 1995).
34. Frank Manuel and Fritzie Manuel, *Utopian Thought in the Modern World* (Cambridge, MA: The Belknap Press, 1979).
35. Krishan Kumar, *Utopia and Anti-Utopia in Modern Times* (Oxford: Blackwell, 1987), p. 423.
36. Stephen Bann, 'Introduction', in Krishan Kumar and Stephen Bann (eds), *Utopias and the Millennium* (London: Reaktion Books, 1993) pp. 1–6: p. 1.
37. Susan Buck-Morss, *Dreamworld and Catastrophe: The Passing of Mass Utopia in East and West* (Cambridge, MA: MIT Press, 2000), p. ix.
38. David Harvey, 'Cities of dreams', *Guardian*, 15 October 1993, pp. 18–19: p. 18. The byline to the article was misprinted as David Harvie.
39. David Harvey, *Justice, Nature and the Geography of Difference* (Oxford: Blackwell, 1996), pp. 403–38: p. 404.
40. Anthony Cohen, 'Introduction', in Anthony Cohen and Katsuyoshi Fukui (eds), *Humanising the City? The Social Contexts of Urban Life at the Turn of the Millennium* (Edinburgh: Edinburgh University Press, 1993), pp. 1–18: p. 11.
41. David Harvey, *Spaces of Hope* (Edinburgh: Edinburgh University Press,

2000), p. 168. He takes the term from Louis Marin, *Utopics: The Semiological Play of Textual Spaces*, trans. Robert A. Vollrath (Atlantic Highlands, NJ: Humanities Press, 1984); originally published in French in 1972. See also Alastair Bonnett, 'Capitalist utopias: forever out of reach, always in your face', *Transgressions* 5 (2001), pp. 75–82.

42. Kevin Robins, 'Prisoners of the city: whatever could a postmodern city be?', *New Formations* 15 (1991), pp. 1–22: pp. 9, 11.
43. Andreas Huyssen, 'Memories of utopia', in his *Twilight Memories: Marking Time in a Culture of Amnesia* (London: Routledge, 1995), pp. 85–101: p. 85.
44. Fredric Jameson, *Postmodernism, or, The Cultural Logic of Late Capitalism* (London: Verso, 1991), p. xvi.
45. Henri Lefebvre, *Everyday Life in the Modern World*, trans. Sacha Rabinovitch (New Brunswick, NJ: Transaction Publishers, 1984), p. 75; originally published in French in 1968.
46. Thomas More, *Utopia*, ed. George M. Logan and Robert M. Adams (Cambridge: Cambridge University Press, 1989); first published in Latin in 1516, and in English in 1551.
47. My discussion of ways of defining utopia here draws especially on the useful scheme provided by Ruth Levitas, *The Concept of Utopia* (London: Philip Allan, 1990).
48. See Kumar, *Utopia and Anti-Utopia*; and Kumar, *Utopianism* (Buckingham: Open University Press, 1991). In the latter book Kumar states that utopia is 'first and foremost a work of imaginative fiction in which, unlike other such works, the central subject is the good society'; p. 27. However, he subsequently admits the difficulties of defining utopianism according to strictly literary criteria and leaves open the possibility for including social theory and other products of utopian imagination within the utopian canon.
49. Ernst Bloch's work includes his monumental three-volume study *The Principle of Hope*, trans. Neville Plaice, Stephen Plaice and Paul Knight (Oxford: Blackwell, 1986); volumes 1 and 2 were first published in German in 1955, and volume 3 in 1959.
50. Levitas, *The Concept of Utopia*, esp. Introduction and chapter 8. A similar argument for a 'new' and more open approach to utopianism is made in many feminist reconceptualisations of the field; see Lucy Sargisson, *Contemporary Feminist Utopianism* (London: Routledge, 1996), who also draws on Levitas in her book, and who bases her approach around a 'transgressive' utopianism that she identifies with feminist theory.
51. Colin Rowe, 'The architecture of Utopia', in his book *The Mathematics of the*

Ideal Villa and Other Essays (Cambridge, MA: MIT Press, 1976), pp. 206–23: p. 206; essay originally published in 1959.

52. Northrup Frye, 'Varieties of literary utopias', in Frank E. Manuel (ed.), *Utopias and Utopian Thought: A Timely Appraisal* (Boston: Beacon Press, 1967), pp. 25–50: p. 27.
53. Lewis Mumford, 'Utopia, the city and the machine', in Manuel, *Utopias and Utopian Thought*, pp. 3–24: p. 13.
54. More, *Utopia*, pp. 43, 45. Brian Goodey attempts to map the geography of the island and its cities based on More's descriptions, in his 'Mapping "Utopia": a comment on the geography of Sir Thomas More', *Geographical Review* 60 (1970), pp. 15–30. I am grateful to him for allowing me to reproduce two of his speculative maps in this chapter.
55. Bronislaw Baczko, *Utopian Lights: The Evolution of the Idea of Social Progress*, trans. Judith L. Greenberg (New York: Paragon House, 1989), p. 275.
56. More, *Utopia*, p. 60.
57. Anthony Vidler, *The Writing of the Walls: Architectural Theory in the Late Enlightenment* (Princeton: Princeton University Press, 1987), p. 41. See also his *Claude-Nicolas Ledoux: Architecture and Social Reform at the End of the Ancien Regime* (Cambridge, MA: MIT Press, 1990).
58. Kevin Lynch, *A Theory of Good City Form* (Cambridge, MA: MIT Press, 1981), p. 293.
59. Reyner Banham, *Megastructure: Urban Futures of the Recent Past* (London: Thames and Hudson, 1976), p. 80. Among commentators making this distinction is Kumar, who portrays philosophical traditions of the ideal city as one of the 'residues' feeding into modern utopian thought, contributing especially to the idea that the good society must be designed systematically; in his *Utopianism*, pp. 11–19.
60. Harvey, *Spaces of Hope*, p. 160.
61. See Tom McDonough, 'Rereading Debord, rereading the situationists', *October* 79 (1997), pp. 3–14. He refers to Sadie Plant's reading of Debord against 'postmodern theory' in this regard, in her *The Most Radical Gesture: The Situationist International in a Postmodern Age* (London: Routledge, 1992).
62. Donald Nicholson-Smith, 'Translator's preface', in Raoul Vaneigem, *The Revolution of Everyday Life* (London: Rebel Press and Left Bank Books, second edition 1994), pp. 5–6: p. 6.
63. George Robertson, 'The Situationist International: its penetration into British culture', *Block* 14 (1988), pp. 39–53: p. 40.
64. Already cognisant of the dangers at the time, the SI famously insisted that there was no such thing as 'situationism' as an ideology or body of theory,

only ideas and practices developed by situationists; in 'Définitions', *IS* 1 (June 1958), p. 13, trans. as 'Definitions', in Knabb, *Anthology*, p. 45. This does not seem to put off some commentators from still using the term.

65. Derek Gregory, 'Bloody theory', *Environment and Planning D: Society and Space* 11 (1993), pp. 253–4: p. 253.
66. Ibid. p. 254.
67. In this light I am also uneasy about the tone of some recent 'historicisation' of the situationists where reflection on the potential effects of such an encounter are downplayed in favour of a more narrowly conceived and detached interest in completing what Simon Sadler calls 'the autopsy and preservation of situationism'; in his *The Situationist City* (Cambridge, MA: MIT Press, 1998), p. 3; see also McDonough, 'Rereading Debord', p. 13. While I share many of the aims of this endeavour, which has been important in developing understandings of the SI, I want to insist that there is also more *life* to its ideas and practices than talk of autopsies implies, as well as more potential political significance in considering them today. Cf. Swyngedouw's critical discussion of 'The strange respectability of the situationist city in the society of the spectacle'; Andy Merrifield, 'The city of Marx and Coca-Cola', *Harvard Design Magazine* 12 (2000), pp. 72–5; and Merrifield, *Metromarxism: A Marxist Tale of the City* (London: Routledge, 2002).
68. Wohlfarth was originally referring to the work of Walter Benjamin, whose name I have substituted with that of the SI; in an essay based on a presentation at the opening of a conference marking the centenary of Benjamin's birth, entitled 'The measure of the possible, the weight of the real and the heat of the moment: Benjamin's actuality today', *New Formations* 20 (1993), pp. 1–20: p. 1.

Chapter 2: Restorative utopias

1. Ebenezer Howard, 'Common sense socialism', unpublished manuscript dated 1892, Howard Papers, Hertfordshire Archives and Local Studies (references hereafter to Howard Papers), D/EHo F10/8.
2. William Morris, 'News from nowhere, or an epoch of rest: being some chapters from a utopian romance', in his *News from Nowhere and Other Writings* (Harmondsworth: Penguin, 1993), pp. 41–228: p. 61.
3. Ibid. p. 62.
4. Ibid. p. 105.
5. William Morris, 'Ugly London', in Chris Miele (ed.), *William Morris on*

Architecture (Sheffield: Sheffield Academic Press, 1996), pp. 140–2: pp. 142, 141; the text was originally written in 1889,

6. William Morris, *The Earthly Paradise:* A *Poem*, 6 vols (London: F. S. Ellis, 1868–70).
7. Northrop Frye, 'Varieties of literary utopias', in Frank E. Manuel (ed.), *Utopias and Utopian Thought: A Timely Appraisal* (Boston: Beacon, 1967), pp. 260–80.
8. 'The city of dreadful night' was the title of a poem by James Thomson in 1880; see Peter Hall, *Cities of Tomorrow: An Intellectual History of Urban Planning and Design in the Twentieth Century* (Oxford: Blackwell, third edition 2002), pp. 14–47. On attitudes to cities in Europe and North America around this time, see also Andrew Lees, *Cities Perceived: Urban Society in European and American Thought, 1820–1940* (Manchester: Manchester University Press, 1985).
9. Lewis Mumford, 'The Garden City idea and modern planning', in Ebenezer Howard, *Garden Cities of To-Morrow*, ed. F. J. Osborn (London: Faber and Faber, 1946), pp. 29–40: p. 29. The original versions of Howard's book were published as: *To-Morrow: A Peaceful Path to Real Reform* (London: Swan Sonnenschein, 1898); and *Garden Cities of To-Morrow* (London: Swan Sonnenschein, 1902). All subsequent citations from the latter volume are from the 1946 edition.
10. Hall, *Cities of Tomorrow*, pp. 88, 8.
11. Howard, *Garden Cities*, pp. 145, 146.
12. Ibid. p. 145.
13. Lord Rosebery, speaking in March 1891, cited in ibid. p. 4.
14. Ebenezer Howard, untitled and unpublished text, Howard Papers, D/EHo F10/6.
15. Some of Morris's objections were set out in a review he wrote of Bellamy's book in *The Commonweal*, on 22 June 1889. He published the first part of his *News from Nowhere* in the same journal six months later.
16. Edward Bellamy, *Looking Backward: 2000–1887* (Boston: Ticknor and Co., 1888).
17. Ebenezer Howard, untitled and unpublished text for talk given at the celebration of the 'birthday' of Letchworth garden city, 1926, Howard Papers D/EHo F18.
18. Ebenezer Howard, untitled and unpublished text for talk to the Fabian Society, 1901, Howard Papers, D/EHo F3/5–7.
19. Ebenezer Howard, untitled and unpublished text for a talk, 22 August 1909, Howard Papers, D/EHo F3/10.

20. Ibid. Howard also refers in the same talk to Emile Zola's novel *Work* alongside the books by Bellamy and Morris. He finds in Zola's utopian tale of the establishment of a workers' co-operative in a small town steel mill an inspiring combination of the two methods 'of administrative machinery and personal initiatives', and he claims that Zola 'presents a story which may be truly prophetic of change which may come'. Zola's book was published in French as *Travail* (Paris: Fasquelle, 1901).
21. Howard, *Garden Cities*, pp. 145–46.
22. Ibid. p. 146.
23. Ibid. p. 138; see also pp. 128, 150.
24. Ibid. p. 111.
25. Ibid. p. 48.
26. On Howard's decision to adopt the title Garden City, see Robert Beevers, *The Garden City Utopia: A Critical Biography of Ebenezer Howard* (London: Macmillan, 1988), pp. 40–54; and Stephen Ward, 'The garden city introduced', in Stephen Ward (ed.), *The Garden City: Past, Present and Future* (London: Spon, 1992), pp. 1–27.
27. Ebenezer Howard, untitled and unpublished text, no date, Howard Papers, D/EHo F3/7.
28. Howard, *Garden Cities*, pp. 138–43: pp. 143, 142.
29. Ebenezer Howard, 'Spiritual influences towards social progress', *Light* (30 April 1910), pp. 195–208, cited in Beevers, *The Garden City Utopia*, pp. 17, 124.
30. Benjamin Ward Richardson, *Hygeia: A City of Health* (London: Macmillan, 1876), p. 24.
31. Beevers, *The Garden City Utopia*, p. 30.
32. James S. Buckingham, *National Evils and Practical Remedies with the Plan of a Model Town* (St Martin's Le Grand, London: Peter Jackson, Late Fisher, Son, and Co., 1849), pp. 151.
33. Ibid. p. 193.
34. Howard, *Garden Cities*, pp. 126, 127. Howard presented his views on drink in a talk called 'Licensing question', dated 'about 1907', Howard Papers, D/EHo F3/35.
35. Richardson, *Hygeia*, p. 47. For a discussion of the faith in spatial design as a means of reforming individuals in nineteenth-century social science, see Felix Driver, 'Moral geographies: social science and the urban environment in mid-nineteenth century England', *Transactions of the Institute of British Geographers* 13 (1988), pp. 275–87.
36. Howard, 'Common sense socialism'.

37. Ibid.
38. Howard, *Garden Cities*, p. 44. Howard originally intended to call his book 'The Master Key'; see Beevers, *The Garden City Utopia*, pp. 40–2.
39. See Frederick Aalen, 'English origins', in Ward, *The Garden City*, pp. 28–51.
40. Ebenezer Howard, untitled text for talk, 1926, Howard Papers, D/EHo F18. The article in the *Times* appeared on 19 October 1898.
41. Howard, *Garden Cities*, pp. 147–50.
42. Howard, 'Common sense socialism'.
43. Howard, 'Postscript', in the 1902 edition of *Garden Cities of To-Morrow*, p. 161.
44. Howard, *Garden Cities*, pp. 52–3, 51.
45. Ebenezer Howard, untitled text for talk, 1926, Howard Papers D/EHo F18.
46. Hall, *Cities of Tomorrow*, p. 88.
47. Raymond Unwin and Barry Parker, 'The art of building a home', in William Creese (ed.), *The Legacy of Raymond Unwin: A Human Pattern for Planning* (Cambridge, MA: MIT Press, 1967), pp. 47–54: p. 51. This is an extract from their book *The Art of Building a Home* (London: Longmans Green, 1901).
48. Unwin and Parker, 'The art of building a home', pp. 51–3.
49. Robert Fishman, *Urban Utopias in the Twentieth Century: Ebenezer Howard, Frank Lloyd Wright, and Le Corbusier* (Cambridge, MA: MIT Press, 1982), pp. 69, 70.
50. Standish Meacham, *Regaining Paradise: Englishness and the Early Garden City Movement* (New Haven and London: Yale University Press, 1999).
51. Ebenezer Howard, 'A new outlet for woman's energy', manuscript dated 1912; also relevant is 'Co-operative housekeeping and the new finance', unpublished text, no date, Howard Papers D/EHo F10/5. See Dolores Hayden, *The Grand Domestic Revolution: A History of Feminist Designs for American Homes, Neighbourhoods, and Cities* (Cambridge, MA: MIT Press, 1981), pp. 230–7.
52. On international influence in these countries, see Ward (ed.), *The Garden City*; on the United States specifically, see Stanley Buder, *Visionaries and Planners: The Garden City Movement and the Modern Community* (Oxford: Oxford University Press, 1990), chapters 10 and 11.
53. See Hall, *Cities of Tomorrow*, pp. 136–73.
54. Ebenezer Howard, letter to the *Daily Telegraph*, 21 June 1919, reprinted in Dugald MacFadyen (ed.), *Sir Ebenezer Howard and the Town Planning Movement* (Manchester: Manchester University Press, 1933), pp. 128, 129.
55. Fishman, *Urban Utopias*, p. 80.
56. Ward, 'The garden city introduced', p. 24; see also Dennis Hardy, *From*

Garden Cities to New Towns: Campaigning for Town and Country Planning, Vol. 1 1899–1946 (London: Spon, 1991).

57. See Hall, *Cities of Tomorrow*; Hardy, *From Garden Cities*; Ward, *The Garden City*; and Stephen V. Ward, 'The Howard legacy', in Kermit C. Parsons and David Schuyler (eds), *From Garden City to Green City: The Legacy of Ebenezer Howard* (Baltimore: The Johns Hopkins University Press, 2002), pp. 222–44.
58. Tristram Hunt, *Building Jerusalem: The Rise and Fall of the Victorian City* (London: Weidenfeld and Nicholson, 2004), p. 328.
59. David Harvey, *Spaces of Hope* (Edinburgh: Edinburgh University Press, 2000), p. 173. He explores related problems faced in this regard by the current 'new urbanism' movement. Like the garden city movement before it, this has had to 'embed its projects in a restrictive set of social processes' in order to realise its preferred urban forms. As with the garden city, too, the outcome has offered both positive and oppressive features.
60. Ebenezer Howard, untitled and unpublished text for talk in Edinburgh, 1908, Howard Papers, D/EHo F3/13.
61. Howard, *Garden Cities*, pp. 76–7.
62. Lewis Mumford, *The City in History: Its Origins, its Transformations, and its Prospects* (Harmondsworth: Penguin, 1966), pp. 587, 590.
63. Ibid. p. 621. Mumford developed related organic conceptions himself along with colleagues in the Regional Planning Association of America, especially through the influence of Patrick Geddes who trained as a biologist.
64. Ebenezer Howard, untitled and unpublished text, 1901, Howard Papers, D/EHo F3/5–7.
65. See Richard Sennett, *Flesh and Stone: The Body and the City in Western Civilization* (London: Faber and Faber, 1994), pp. 257–65.
66. Edwin Chadwick, *Report on the Sanitary Condition of the Labouring Population of Great Britain* (London: HMSO, 1842).
67. Richardson, *Hygeia*.
68. F. O. Ward, 'Circulation instead of stagnation', 1852, cited in Didier Gille, 'Maceration and purification', trans. Bruce Benderson, *Zone* 1/2 (1986), pp. 226–81: p. 237.
69. Gille, 'Maceration and purification'.
70. Wolfgang Schivelbusch, *The Railway Journey: The Industrialization of Time and Space in the Nineteenth Century* (Berkeley: University of California Press, 1986), p. 195.
71. Howard, 'Water supply', in *To-Morrow*, pp. 153–67: 165. For an interesting discussion of related concerns about energy and order as constructed through

regulated flow in geographical thinking in the early twentieth century, in particular in relation to the work of Patrick Geddes and Vaughan Cornish, see David Matless, 'A modern stream: water, landscape, modernism, and geography', *Environment and Planning D: Society and Space* 10 (1992), pp. 569–88.

72. This idea of physical beauty expressing moral qualities is also evident in earlier utopian texts, in particular Morris's *News from Nowhere*, where it applies in relation not only to the beauty of the architecture but also to the attractiveness of the inhabitants. For interesting critical comments on the ways in which women's beauty is presented in this regard and identified as a 'mere reflection of the harmonious utopian space', and on the gendered body in such utopian writings, see Jennifer Burwell, *Notes on Nowhere: Feminism, Utopian Logic, and Social Transformation* (Minneapolis: University of Minnesota Press, 1997), pp. 61–6.
73. Zygmunt Bauman, *Modernity and Ambivalence* (Cambridge: Polity, 1991), p. 34. The quotation from Wells is from his essay 'Socialism and the new world order', in his *Journalism and Prophecy, 1893–1946* (London: Bodley Head, 1984), pp. 278–9.
74. The power of the metaphor of 'weeds' within planning discourses as a botanical equivalent of dirt is discussed by Tim Cresswell, 'Weeds, plagues, and bodily secretions: a geographical interpretation of metaphors of displacement', *Annals of the Association of American Geographers* 87 (1997), pp. 330–45.
75. Dean Farrar, cited in Howard, *Garden Cities*, p. 43.
76. Anthony Wahl, *Endangered Lives: Public Health in Victorian Britain* (London: J. M. Dent and Sons, 1983), p. 337.
77. Mumford, 'The Garden City idea', p. 38.
78. *The Race-Builder*, 1906, cited in Hardy, *From Garden Cities*, p. 39.
79. See Wolfgang Voigt, 'The garden city as eugenic utopia', *Planning Perspectives* 4 (1989), pp. 295–312, who focuses particularly on eugenicists in the German garden city movement.
80. Jos Boys, Frances Bradshaw, Jane Darke, Benedicte Foo, Sue Francis, Barbara McFarlane, Marion Roberts, Susan Wiles, 'House design and women's roles', in Matrix (eds), *Making Space: Women and the Man Made Environment* (London: Pluto Press, 1984), pp. 55–80: pp. 69–71. See also Hayden, *The Grand Domestic Revolution*; and Marion Roberts, *Living in a Man-Made World: Gender Assumptions in Modern Housing Design* (London: Routledge, 1991), pp. 30–4.
81. Elizabeth Wilson, *The Sphinx in the City: Urban Life, the Control of Disorder, and Women* (London: Virago, 1991), p. 104.

82. Jane Jacobs, *The Death and Life of Great American Cities: The Failure of Town Planning* (Harmondsworth: Penguin, 1984), p. 27; originally published in 1961.
83. Burwell, *Notes on Nowhere*, pp. 48–54.
84. William Morris, 'Foreword to Utopia by Thomas More', in Morris, *News from Nowhere*, pp. 371–5: 374; the foreword was originally published in 1893.
85. William Morris, 1889, cited in Vincent Geoghegan, *Utopianism and Marxism* (London: Methuen, 1987), p. 64.
86. On Morris and the 'education of desire', see E. P. Thompson, *William Morris: Romantic to Revolutionary* (London: Merlin, 1977); and Ruth Levitas, *The Concept of Utopia* (London: Philip Allan, 1990), pp. 106–30.
87. Ebenezer Howard, draft of an autobiography, cited in Fishman, *Urban Utopias*, p. 37.
88. Harvey, *Spaces of Hope*, pp. 161–2, 182. The phrase is derived from Louis Marin, *Utopics: The Semiological Play of Textual Spaces*, trans. Robert A. Vollrath (Atlantic Highlands, NJ: Humanities Press, 1984).
89. Cf. Ward, 'The Howard legacy', pp. 232–44. For a discussion of Kropotkin's thought in relation to ideal cities and urbanism that includes brief references to Howard, see G. M. Horner, 'Kropotkin and the city: the socialist ideal in urbanism', *Antipode* 10/11 (1979), pp. 33–45.
90. Wilson, *The Sphinx in the City*, p. 9.
91. Chris Ferns, *Narrating Utopia* (Liverpool: Liverpool University Press, 1999), p. 153.
92. Ibid. p. 154.

Chapter 3: Modernist calls to order

1. Le Corbusier, *Vers une architecture* (Paris: Editions Vincent, Fréal and Cie, 1923), trans. Frederick Etchells as *Towards a New Architecture* (London: Architectural Press, 1946), p. 9.
2. Le Corbusier, *La Ville radieuse* (Boulogne-sur-Seine: Éditions de l'Architecture d'Aujourd'hui, 1935), trans. Pamela Knight, Eleanor Levieux and Derek Coltman as *The Radiant City* (London: Faber and Faber, 1967), p. 155.
3. Filippo Tommaso Marinetti, 'The founding and manifesto of futurism', trans. R. W. Flint in Umbro Apollonio (ed.), *Futurist Manifestos* (London: Thames and Hudson, 1973), pp. 19–24: p. 21; manifesto originally published in 1909.
4. Umberto Boccioni, Carlo Carrà, Luigi Russolo, Giacomo Balla, and Gino Severini, 'Manifesto of the futurist painters', trans. Robert Brain in

Apollonio, *Futurist Manifestos*, pp. 24–7: p. 25; manifesto orginally published in 1910.

5. Carlo Carrà, 'The painting of sounds, noises and smells', trans. Robert Brain in Apollonio, *Futurist Manifestos*, pp. 111–15: p. 113; manifesto originally published in 1913.
6. Antonio Sant'Elia, 'Manifesto of futurist architecture', trans. Caroline Tisdall in Apollonio, *Futurist Manifestos*, pp. 160–72: p. 172; manifesto originally published in 1914.
7. Ibid. p. 170
8. Ibid. p. 172. Although the manifesto is attributed to Sant'Elia, controversy has surrounded its authorship, due to passages that were added by Marinetti.
9. David Harvey, *The Condition of Postmodernity: An Enquiry into the Origins of Cultural Change* (Oxford: Blackwell, 1989), pp. 28–9.
10. Henri Lefebvre, *Introduction to Modernity*, trans. John Moore (London: Verso, 1995), pp. 178–83: p. 178; originally published in French in 1962.
11. Henri Lefebvre, *The Production of Space*, trans. Donald Nicholson-Smith (Oxford: Blackwell, 1991), p. 25; originally published in French in 1974. Derek Gregory provides an interesting discussion of Lefebvre's and Harvey's respective presentations of modernism in his *Geographical Imaginations* (Oxford: Blackwell, 1994), esp. pp. 392–400.
12. Dennis Sharp, 'Expressionist architecture today', in Shulamith Behr, David Fanning and Douglas Jarman (eds), *Expressionism Reassessed* (Manchester: Manchester University Press, 1993), pp. 80–90: pp. 83–4.
13. Marinetti, speaking in London, March 1910, cited in Caroline Tisdall and Angelo Bozzolla, *Futurism* (London: Thames and Hudson, 1977), p. 123.
14. Walter Gropius, 'Manifesto and programme of the Bauhaus', in Frank Whitford (ed.), *The Bauhaus: Masters and Students By Themselves* (London: Conran Octopus, 1992), pp. 38–41: p. 38; manifesto originally published in 1919.
15. Oskar Schlemmer, letter in June 1922, cited in Charles Jencks, *Modern Movements in Architecture* (Harmondsworth: Penguin, second edition, 1985), p. 117; and diary entry in June 1922, cited in Valerie Fletcher, *Dreams and Nightmares: Utopian Visions in Modern Art* (Washington, DC: Smithsonian Institution Press, 1983), p. 81.
16. Frank Whitford, 'The first years at Weimar, 1919–25', in Whitford, *The Bauhaus*, pp. 30–7: p. 36.
17. Lefebvre, *The Production of Space*, pp. 124–5.
18. Peter Hall, *Cities of Tomorrow: An Intellectual History of Urban Planning and*

Design in the Twentieth Century (Oxford: Blackwell, third edition, 2002), pp. 9, 219.

19. Le Corbusier, *Urbanisme* (Paris: Éditions Crès, 1925), trans. Frederick Etchells as *The City of Tomorrow and Its Planning* (London: Architectural Press, 1987), pp. xxiv, 25.
20. Ibid. pp. 253, 266, 96. A similar rhetoric characterised many CIAM pronouncements, as suggested by the title of José Luis Sert's publication based on discussions at CIAM IV in 1933, *Can Our Cities Survive?* (Cambridge, MA: Harvard University Press, 1942).
21. Le Corbusier, *Towards a New Architecture*, p. 289.
22. He adopted the name Le Corbusier from a maternal grandfather and initially used it alongside other pseudonyms, although he retained his original name for signing his paintings until 1928.
23. Stanislaus von Moos, *Le Corbusier: Elements of a Synthesis* (Cambridge, MA: MIT Press, 1979), p. 188.
24. As discussed in Norma Evenson, *Paris: A Century of Change, 1878–1978* (New Haven and London: Yale University Press, 1979), pp. 212–16.
25. Le Corbusier, *The City of Tomorrow*, pp. 5–12. To support these claims, Le Corbusier deployed a series of graphs and statistics showing increases in population, mechanical transport, motor car production and the like on pp. 107–26. It is estimated that there were approximately 150,000 cars in the Paris region in 1925; within five years the number rose to 300,000, and by 1939 it reached 500,000; figures from Evenson, *Paris*, p. 54.
26. Le Corbusier, *The Radiant City*, p. 92.
27. Le Corbusier, *The City of Tomorrow*, p. 191.
28. Ibid. p. 100.
29. Le Corbusier's early writings make frequent references to Taylorism although some of these are omitted in Etchells's translation of *Vers une architecture*. See Mary McLeod, 'Urbanism and Utopia: Le Corbusier from Regional Syndicalism to Vichy' (unpublished PhD dissertation, Princeton University, 1985), pp. 40–56; the quotation from his letter is from p. 46.
30. Fredric Jameson, 'Architecture and the critique of ideology', in his *The Ideologies of Theory: Essays 1971–1986* (London: Routledge, 1988), pp. 35–60: p. 51.
31. The last few lines draw upon James Holston's discussion of CIAM in his *The Modernist City: An Anthropological Critique of Brasília* (Chicago: Chicago University Press, 1989), pp. 52–8.
32. Hilde Heynen, '"Architecture or revolution?": Le Corbusier and the avant-garde', in Architecture Landscape Urbanism 9: *Le Corbusier and the*

Architecture of Reinvention (London: Architectural Association, 2003), pp. 40–57. See also Beatriz Colomina's discussion of the phrase 'architecture or revolution' in relation to the images of industrial society that appear alongside it in *Towards a New Architecture*, such as a centrifugal ventilator and turbine engines, which she reads as demonstrating his primary interest in the position of the architect in industrial society; in her *Privacy and Publicity: Modern Architecture as Mass Media* (Cambridge, MA: MIT Press, 1994), pp. 140–99.

33. Le Corbusier, *The City of Tomorrow*, p. 280.
34. Ibid. pp. 281, 287.
35. Kenneth Silver, 'Purism: straightening up after the Great War', *Artforum* (March 1977), pp. 56–63. The term *La Rappel à l'ordre* is often associated with Jean Cocteau, who used it as a title of a book in 1923.
36. Silver, 'Purism', p. 57.
37. Ibid. pp. 57–8.
38. Charles-Édouard Jeanneret and Amédée Ozenfant, 'Le Purisme', *L'Esprit Nouveau* (1920), pp. 369–86, trans. Robert L. Herbert as 'Purism', in Robert L. Herbert (ed.), *Modern Artists on Art* (Englewood Cliffs, NJ: Prentice-Hall, 1964), pp. 59–73.
39. Amédée Ozenfant and Charles-Édouard Jeanneret, 'L'angle droit', *L'Esprit Nouveau* 18 (no date), trans. Nadir Lahiji as 'The right angle', in Nadir Lahiji and D.S. Friedman (eds), *Plumbing: Sounding Modern Architecture* (New York: Princeton Architectural Press, 1997), pp. 20–31: p. 30.
40. Tisdall and Bozzolla, *Futurism*, p. 132.
41. Martin Jay, *Downcast Eyes: The Denigration of Vision in Twentieth Century French Thought* (Berkeley: University of California Press, 1993), p. 215.
42. Romy Golan, *Modernity and Nostalgia: Art and Politics in France Between the Wars* (New Haven and London: Yale University Press, 1995), chapter 2.
43. Le Corbusier, *The City of Tomorrow*, p. xxiii.
44. Marshall Berman, *All That is Solid Melts into Air: The Experience of Modernity* (London: Verso, 1983), pp. 165–70: 167. The citation from Le Corbusier is from *The City of Tomorrow*, p. 123.
45. Le Corbusier, *The City of Tomorrow*, pp. xxiii, xxiv.
46. Ibid. p. 164.
47. Le Corbusier, *The Radiant City*, pp. 100, 197.
48. Zygmunt Bauman, *Modernity and Ambivalence* (Cambridge: Polity Press, 1991), p. 15.
49. Le Corbusier, *The City of Tomorrow*, pp. 65, 15–25, 43–53.
50. Ibid. pp. 190, 190–1.

51. Karsten Harries, 'Building and the terror of time', *Perspecta: The Yale Architectural Journal* 19 (1982), pp. 59–69: p. 62.
52. Robert Fishman, 'Utopia in three dimensions: the ideal city and the origins of modern design', in Peter Alexander and Roger Gill (eds), *Utopias* (London: Duckworth, 1984), pp. 95–107: p. 106.
53. Le Corbusier, *The City of Tomorrow*, pp. 284–5.
54. Le Corbusier, *The Radiant City*, note added in 1964, p. 83; see also pp. 78–80. Anthony Vidler sets Le Corbusier's obsession with the aerial view into the wider context of French urbanism in his 'Photourbanism: planning the city from above and from below', in Gary Bridge and Sophie Watson (eds), *The Companion to the City* (Oxford: Blackwell, 2000), pp. 35–45.
55. Le Corbusier, *The City of Tomorrow*, p. 280.
56. Richard Sennett notes this 'destructive vision of time in space' in his *The Conscience of the Eye: The Design and Social Life of Cities* (London: Faber and Faber, 1990), pp. 173–4.
57. Michel Foucault, 'The eye of power', in his *Power/Knowledge: Selected Interviews and Other Writings 1972–1977*, ed. Colin Gordon (New York: Pantheon Books, 1980), pp. 146–65: p. 153.
58. Le Corbusier, 'The street', in Le Corbusier and Pierre Jeanneret, *Oeuvre complète de 1910–1929*, eds. W. Boesiger and O. Stonorov (Zurich: Les Éditions d'Architecture Erlenbach, fifth edition, 1948), pp. 118–19: p. 118. The essay was originally published in French in 1929.
59. Le Corbusier, *The Radiant City*, p. 94.
60. Anthony Vidler, 'Bodies in space/subjects in the city: psychopathologies of modern urbanism', *Differences: A Journal of Feminist Cultural Studies* 5 (1993), pp. 31–51: p. 36.
61. Felix Driver, 'Moral geographies: social science and the urban environment in mid-nineteenth century England', *Transactions of the Institute of British Geographers* 13 (1988), pp. 275–87: p. 281.
62. Anthony Vidler, 'Dark space', in his *The Architectural Uncanny: Essays in the Modern Unhomely* (Cambridge, MA: MIT Press, 1992), pp. 167–75: p. 172.
63. Michel de Certeau, *The Practice of Everyday Life*, trans. Steven Randall (Berkeley: University of California Press, 1984), p. 93; the book was first published in French in 1974. The significance of visualising the city was also taken up in critical ways by the situationists and Lefebvre, to be discussed in Chapter 5.
64. Ibid. pp. 92–5.
65. Christopher Prendergast, *Paris and the Nineteenth Century* (Oxford: Blackwell, 1992), p. 209.

66. Le Corbusier, *The City of Tomorrow*, pp. 298–301.
67. Ibid. pp. 7, 156, 267.
68. Ibid. pp. 255–6.
69. Susan Sontag, *Illness as a Metaphor* (London: Allen Lane, 1979), p. 84. She notes how the metaphor became especially prevalent in urban planning rhetoric by the 1950s, marking a shift away from earlier metaphors based around the idea of tuberculosis as a real or alleged threat.
70. Le Corbusier, *The City of Tomorrow*, p. 258; see also his *Précisions sur un état présent de l'architecture et de l'urbanisme* (Paris: Crès et Cie, 1930), trans. Edith Schreiber Aujame as *Precisions on the Present State of Architecture and City Planning* (Cambridge, MA: MIT Press, 1991), pp. 172–4.
71. Lefebvre, *The Production of Space*, p. 99.
72. Le Corbusier, *The Radiant City*, pp. 98, 99. Jean-Baptiste Colbert was Louis XIV's administrator, much admired by Le Corbusier along with Louis XIV and Baron Haussmann.
73. Lewis Mumford, *The City in History: Its Origins, its Transformations, and its Prospects* (Harmondsworth: Penguin, 1966), p. 638.
74. Moisei Ginzburg, letter to Le Corbusier, 23 September 1936, reprinted and translated in *ARSE: Architects for a Really Socialist Environment* 4 (May 1971), p. 6.
75. Le Corbusier, *Precisions*, pp. 212, 47.
76. Adolf Loos, 'Plumbers', trans. Harry Francis Mallgrave in Lahiji and Friedman, *Plumbing*, pp. 15–19: pp. 18, 19; essay originally published in 1898.
77. Matthew Gandy, 'Water, modernity and emancipatory urbanism', in Loretta Lees (ed.), *The Emancipatory City? Paradoxes and Possibilities* (London: Sage, 2004), pp. 178–91.
78. Le Corbusier, *The City of Tomorrow*, pp. 243–4.
79. Le Corbusier, *The Radiant City*, p. 80.
80. Ibid. p. 123; see also Le Corbusier, *Precisions*, pp. 60–2, 141–53, 182.
81. Le Corbusier, *Oeuvre complète de 1946–1952*, ed. W. Boesiger (Zurich: Éditions Girsberger, 1953), p. 95.
82. Le Corbusier, *The Radiant City*, p. 143.
83. Ibid. p. 302.
84. Dennis Crow, 'Le Corbusier's post-modern plan', in Dennis Crow (ed.), *Philosophical Streets: New Approaches to Urbanism* (Washington, DC: Maisonneuve Press, 1990), pp. 70–92: p. 82.
85. Ibid. p. 77.
86. See, for example, Kenneth Frampton, 'The other Le Corbusier: primitive

form and the linear city 1929–52', in Michael Raeburn and Victoria Wilson (eds), *Le Corbusier: Architect of the Century* (London: Arts Council of Great Britain, 1987), p. 29–34.

87. Le Corbusier, *Precisions*, p. 267.
88. An important discussion of these themes is Zeynep Çelik, 'Le Corbusier, orientalism, colonialism', *assemblage* 17 (1992), pp. 59–76.
89. Le Corbusier, *The Radiant City*, pp. 94, 149, 38, 57.
90. Evenson, *Paris*, pp. 220–6; and Jean Pierre Gaudin, 'The French garden city', in Stephen Ward (ed.), *The Garden City: Past, Present and Future* (London: Spon, 1992), pp. 52–68.
91. Le Corbusier, *The Radiant City*, p. 152.
92. Ibid. pp. 153, 154.
93. Ibid. pp. 94, frontispiece. An excellent account of the politics of Le Corbusier's architectural and social thought in the 1930s is McLeod, 'Urbanism and Utopia', chapters 3, 4. See also Robert Fishman, 'From the Radiant City to Vichy: Le Corbusier's plans and politics, 1928–1942', in Russell Walden (ed.), *The Open Hand: Essays on Le Corbusier* (Cambridge, MA: MIT Press, 1977), pp. 244–83; and Kenneth Frampton, *Le Corbusier* (London: Thames and Hudson, 2001), pp. 116–29.
94. Robert Fishman, *Urban Utopias in the Twentieth Century: Ebenezer Howard, Frank Lloyd Wright and Le Corbusier* (Cambrdge, MA: MIT Press, 1982), pp. 193–6, 234.
95. Le Corbusier, 'Commentary on the occasion of the reprinting of "The Radiant City"', in *The Radiant City*, p. 3, added for the republication of the book in 1964.
96. Ibid. frontispiece.
97. De Certeau, *The Practice of Everyday Life*, pp. 94–5.
98. Bauman, *Modernity and Ambivalence*, p. 4.
99. Ibid. p. 15.
100. See, for example, Timothy Mitchell, *Colonizing Egypt* (Cambridge: Cambridge University Press, 1988), chapter 3; and Derek Gregory, *The Colonial Present* (Oxford: Blackwell, 2004).
101. De Certeau, *The Practice of Everyday Life*, pp. 95, 94, 95.

Chapter 4: Dreams of cities and monsters

1. Louis Marin, 'The frontiers of utopia', in Krishan Kumar and Stephen Bann (eds), *Utopias and the Millennium* (London: Reaktion Books, 1993), pp. 7–16: p. 13.

2. Georges Bataille, 'Architecture', *Documents* 1.2 (May 1929), p. 117, trans. Dominic Faccini in Alastair Brotchie (ed.), *Encyclopaedia Acephalica* (London: Atlas Press, 1995), pp. 35–6: p. 35.
3. Le Corbusier, *Quand les cathédrals étaient blanches: voyage au pays des timides* (Paris: Plon, 1937), trans. Francis E. Hyslop as *When the Cathedrals Were White: A Journey to the Country of Timid People* (New York: Reynal & Hitchcock, 1947), p. 34.
4. H. I. Brock, 'Le Corbusier scans Gotham's Towers', *New York Times Magazine*, 3 November 1935, pp. 10, 23.
5. Joseph Alsop, 'Finds American skyscrapers "much too small"', *New York Herald Tribune*, 22 October 1935, p. 21.
6. Le Corbusier, *When the Cathedrals*, p. 42.
7. Ibid. pp. 40, 90, 43.
8. Ibid. pp. 34, 35.
9. André Breton, letter to Valentine Hugo, 30 March 1935; Paul Eluard, letter to Gala, 7 April 1935; cited in Mark Polizzotti, *Revolution of the Mind: The Life of André Breton* (London: Bloomsbury, 1995), pp. 413, 414.
10. As cited by the editor in André Breton, *What is Surrealism? Selected Writings*, ed. Franklin Rosemont (New York: Pathfinder, 1978), p. 141.
11. André Breton, 'Surrealist situation of the object', in his *Manifestoes of Surrealism*, trans. Richard Seaver and Helen R. Lane (Ann Arbor: University of Michigan Press, 1972), pp. 255–78: p. 255. The lecture was delivered on 29 March 1935 at the Mánes Union of Fine Arts.
12. Ferdinand Cheval, trans. in John Maizels, *Raw Creation: Outsider Art and Beyond* (London: Phaidon Press, 1996), p. 161.
13. Breton, 'Surrealist situation of the object', p. 261.
14. Walter Benjamin, *The Arcades Project*, trans. Howard Eiland and Kevin McLaughlin (Cambridge, MA: Harvard University Press, 1999), p. 495 [N1a, 5].
15. Henri Lefebvre, *Le temps des méprises* (Paris: Stock, 1975), pp. 39–40. The article mentioned was a review of Tzara's '7 Manifestes Dada', in *Philosophies* 4 (15 November 1924). Greil Marcus makes much of Lefebvre's line in his vivid and brilliantly written book that traces connections between punk, the situationists, dada and other voices of negation, entitled *Lipstick Traces: A Secret History of the Twentieth Century* (London: Secker and Warburg, 1989).
16. Le Corbusier, *Urbanisme* (Paris: Éditions Crès, 1925), trans. Frederick Etchells as *The City of Tomorrow and Its Planning* (London: Architectural Press, 1987), p. 45.
17. Rem Koolhaas, *Delirious New York: A Retroactive Manifesto for Manhattan*

(New York: The Monacelli Press, 1994) pp. 251–3: p. 253. The book was first published in 1978 and includes a remarkable discussion of Le Corbusier's attempt to 'conquer' New York. Mardge Bacon provides an exhaustively researched historical account of Le Corbusier's visit and the significance of the trans-Atlantic connections entailed in her *Le Corbusier in America: Travels in the Land of the Timid* (Cambridge, MA: MIT Press, 2001).

18. Le Corbusier, *When the Cathedrals*, pp. 80, 111.
19. Ibid. pp. 210, xix.
20. Ibid. pp. 4–5; 'The Great Waste' is discussed on pp. 171–8; and the Ford factory on pp. 167–70.
21. For a study that takes the 'strange invisibility' of the white walls of modern architecture as its starting point, along with the 'colour blindness' of dominant historiographies of the field, see Mark Wigley, *White Walls, Designer Dresses: The Fashioning of Modern Architecture* (Cambridge, MA: MIT Press, 1995).
22. Le Corbusier, *L'art décoratif d'aujourd'hui* (Paris: Éditions Crès, 1925), trans. James L. Dunnett as *The Decorative Art of Today* (London: Architectural Press, 1987), pp. 192, 188.
23. Ibid. pp. 188, 189, 190.
24. Wigley, *White Walls*, p. 5.
25. Le Corbusier, *The Decorative Art*, p. 192. This obsession was not applied in a blanket manner in his architectural practice, for he had returned to the use of colour in conjunction with white surfaces the year before, thus putting an intriguing angle on this demand for whiteness. See Wigley, *White Walls*, pp. 190–225, who notes how the colours in Ozenfant's atelier, an image of which is used to illustrate the chapter on 'The Law of Ripolin', are suppressed in the reproduction in the book to create the *effect* of a white space.
26. Le Corbusier, *When the Cathedrals*, pp. 33–4, 46, 168, 78–82.
27. Ibid. p. 46.
28. Ibid. pp. 108–10, 155.
29. Wigley, *White Walls*, pp. 284–99: p. 286.
30. Le Corbusier, *When the Cathedrals*, pp. 158, 161; Wigley, *White Walls*, p. 294.
31. Le Corbusier, *When the Cathedrals*, p. 161.
32. Mabel O. Wilson, 'Dancing in the dark: the inscription of blackness in Le Corbusier's Radiant City', in Heidi J. Nast and Steve Pile (eds), *Places Through the Body* (London: Routledge, 1998), pp. 133–52: p. 147. For wider contextualisation, see Bacon, *Le Corbusier in America*, pp. 221–8; and Petrine Archer-Straw, *Negrophilia: Avant-Garde Paris and Black Culture in the 1920s* (London: Thames and Hudson, 2000).

33. Le Corbusier, *When the Cathedrals*, p. 40.
34. Ibid. p. 111.
35. Ibid. p. 191.
36. Ibid. p. 89.
37. Le Corbusier, 'Preface to the second French printing of Precisions on the Present State of Architecture and City Planning', dated 4 June 1960, trans. Edith Schreiber Aujame, in Le Corbusier, *Precisions on the Present State of Architecture and City Planning* (Cambridge, MA: MIT Press, 1991), pp. vii-xii: p. ix.
38. Le Corbusier, *La Ville radieuse* (Boulogne-sur-Seine: Éditions de l'Architecture d'Aujourd'hui, 1935), trans. Pamela Knight, Eleanor Levieux and Derek Coltman as *The Radiant City* (London: Faber and Faber, 1967), pp. 202, 221.
39. See Rosi Braidotti, 'Signs of wonder and traces of doubt: on teratology and embodied differences', in Nina Lykke and Rosi Braidotti (eds), *Between Monsters, Goddesses and Cyborgs: Feminist Confrontations with Science, Medicine and Cyberspace* (London and New Jersey: Zed Books, 1996), pp. 135–52; and Marie-Hélène Huet, *Monstrous Imagination* (Cambridge, MA: Harvard University Press, 1993), pp. 108–9.
40. Le Corbusier, *Precisions*, pp. 210, 212.
41. Ibid. pp. 6, 5.
42. Mary McLeod, 'Urbanism and Utopia: Le Corbusier from Regional Syndicalism to Vichy' (unpublished PhD dissertation, Princeton University, 1985), chapter 6.
43. See Zeynep Çelik, 'Le Corbusier, orientalism, colonialism', *assemblage* 17 (1992), pp. 59–76; and Çelik, 'Gendered spaces in colonial Algiers', in Diana Agrest, Patricia Conway and Leslie Kane Weisman (eds), *The Sex of Architecture* (New York: Harry N. Abrams, 1999), pp. 127–40.
44. Le Corbusier, *The Radiant City*, p. 147.
45. Rob Imrie explores the decontextualised ideal of the body that is proposed in Le Corbusier's architecture, and the ways in which his attempts to establish an 'able-bodied' standard underpin disabled people's oppression in the built environment; in his 'The body, disability, and Le Corbusier's conception of the radiant environment', in Ruth Butler and Hester Parr (eds), *Mind and Body Spaces: Geographies of Disability, Illness and Impairment* (London: Routledge, 1999), pp. 25–45.
46. Braidotti, 'Signs of wonder and traces of doubt', pp. 136–7.
47. Mary Douglas, *Purity and Danger* (Andover: Routledge and Kegan Paul, 1966), p. 2.

48. David Sibley, 'Sensations and spatial science: gratification and anxiety in the production of ordered landscapes', *Environment and Planning* A 30 (1998), pp. 235–46; see also his *Geographies of Exclusion: Society and Difference in the West* (London: Routledge, 1995). Cf. Julia Kristeva, *The Powers of Horror: An Essay on Abjection*, trans. Leon S. Roudiez (New York: Columbia University Press, 1982).
49. Le Corbusier, *The City of Tomorrow*, pp. 25, 95. Cf. Sibley's discussion of the stigmatisation of the nomadic in his *Geographies of Exclusion*. The appearance of the nomad as a negative and disruptive symbol in texts by reformers such as William Mayhew, and in modernist thinking in the social sciences and cultural studies more widely, is also explored by Tim Cresswell, 'Imagining the nomad: mobility and the postmodern primitive', in Georges Benko and Ulf Strohmayer (eds), *Space and Social Theory: Interpreting Modernity and Postmodernity* (Oxford: Blackwell, 1997), pp. 360–79.
50. Michel Foucault, *Discipline and Punish: The Birth of the Prison*, trans. Alan Sheridan (Harmondsworth: Penguin, 1977) pp. 218, 219; originally published in French in 1975.
51. Le Corbusier, *When the Cathedrals*, p. 50.
52. Le Corbusier, *The Radiant City*, p. 221.
53. See Beatriz Colomina, *Privacy and Publicity: Modern Architecture as Mass Media* (Cambridge, MA: MIT Press, 1994), pp. 324–30.
54. Le Corbusier, *The Radiant City*, p. 126.
55. McLeod, 'Urbanism and Utopia', esp. chapter 3; and Romy Golan, *Modernity and Nostalgia: Art and Politics in France Between the Wars* (New Haven and London: Yale University Press, 1995), pp. 84–104.
56. Le Corbusier, *Manière de penser l'urbanisme* (Paris: Gonthier, 1946), p. 11; cited in François Choay, 'Urbanism in question', in Mark Gottdiener and Alexandros Ph. Lagopoulos (eds), *The City and the Sign* (New York: Columbia University Press, 1986), pp. 241–58: p. 250.
57. Elizabeth Wilson, *The Sphinx in the City: Urban Life, the Control of Disorder, and Women* (London: Virago, 1991), pp. 9, 7.
58. Barbara Hooper, 'The poem of male desires: female bodies, modernity, and "Paris, capital of the nineteenth century"', in Leonie Sandercock (ed.), *Making the Invisible Visible: A Multicultural Planning History* (Berkeley: University of California Press, 1998), pp. 227–54: p. 230. Hooper extends these arguments in her 'Urban space, modernity, and masculinist desire: the utopian imaginings of Le Corbusier', in Amy Bingaman, Lise Sanders and Rebecca Zorach (eds), *Embodied Utopias: Gender, Social Change and the Modern Metropolis* (London: Routledge, 2002), pp. 55–78.

59. Braidotti, 'Signs of wonder and traces of doubt'; and Braidotti, 'Mothers, monsters, and machines', in her *Nomadic Subjects: Embodiment and Sexual Difference in Contemporary Feminist Theory* (New York: Columbia University Press, 1994), pp. 75–94. The analogy has classical roots, with Aristotle positing an association between the monstrous and the female as deviations from a supposed 'norm' in his *Generation of Animals*; see Huet, *Monstrous Imagination*, pp. 3–4.
60. David Harvey, *Justice, Nature and the Geography of Difference* (Oxford: Blackwell, 1996), p. 419. See also his discussion of 'utopias of spatial form' in his *Spaces of Hope* (Edinburgh: Edinburgh University Press, 2000), pp. 159–73.
61. Lewis Mumford, 'Utopia, the city and the machine', in Frank E. Manuel (ed.), *Utopias and Utopian Thought: A Timely Appraisal* (Boston: Beacon Press, 1967), pp. 3–24: p. 9.
62. André Breton, 'Discours au Congrès des écrivains', June 1935, trans. as 'Speech to the Congress of Writers', in his *Manifestoes of Surrealism*, pp. 234–41: p. 241.
63. André Breton, 'Le message automatique', *Minotaure* (1933), trans. as 'The automatic message', in his *What is Surrealism?*, pp. 97–109: p. 103. Roger Cardinal suggests that three visits by Breton to the Ideal Palace seem fully authenticated in 1931, 1939 and 1953. While additional visits in 1932 and 1949 have been imputed by some commentators, he casts doubts on the evidence for these; personal communication, October 2004. I am grateful to him for allowing me to see his notes on the subject. The photograph appeared in André Breton, *Les Vases communicants* (Paris: Cahiers Libres, 1932).
64. Jacques Brunius, 'Palais idéal', trans. J. M. Richards, *The Architectural Review* LXXX (October 1936), pp. 147–50: p. 150.
65. Ferdinand Cheval, cited in Jean-Louis Ferrier, *Outsider Art*, trans. Murray Wyllie (Paris: Pierre Terrail Editions, 1998), p. 182.
66. See Robert McNab, *Ghost Ships: A Surrealist Love Triangle* (New Haven and London: Yale University Press, 2004). Ernst also painted a portrait of Facteur Cheval in 1932. For further discussion and illustrations of the Ideal Palace, see especially Pierre Jouve, Claude Prévost and Clovis Prévost, *Le Palais Idéal du Facteur Cheval: quand le songe devient la réalité* (Paris: Éditions du Moniteur, 1981).
67. André Breton, *Arcane 17* (New York: Brentano's, 1945), excerpted as 'Arcane 17' in his *What is Surrealism?*, pp. 248–53: p. 250.
68. André Breton, 'Surrealism yesterday, today, tomorrow', trans. Edward W. Titis, *This Quarter* II, 1 (September 1932).

69. Salvador Dalí, 'L'Ane pourri', *Le Surréalisme au service de la révolution* 1 (July 1930), pp. 9–12; cited in Breton, 'Surrealist situation of the object', p. 261.
70. Salvador Dalí, 'De la beauté terrifiante et comestible, de l'architecture modern'style', *Minotaure* 3–4 (December 1933), pp. 69–76, trans. as 'Art Nouveau architecture's terrifying and edible beauty', *Architectural Design* 48, 2–3 (1978), pp. 139–40: p. 139. In this regard it is interesting to note Brunius's claim that the detail of Cheval's construction can be described 'as a forecast of 1900 *art-nouveau* of the most confectionery-like variety'; 'Palais idéal', p. 147. The food theme is given a twist by Roger Cardinal, who suggests it is the 'half-digested' character of the palace's elements that make it so strange and interesting; in his *Outsider Art* (London: Studio Vista, 1972), p. 151.
71. Dalí, 'Art Nouveau architecture's terrifying and edible beauty', pp. 139–40. Here I am drawing on Hal Foster, *Compulsive Beauty* (Cambridge, MA: MIT Press, 1993), pp. 182–8.
72. Breton, 'Surrealist situation of the object', pp. 261–2.
73. Tristan Tzara, 'D'un certain automatisme du Goût', *Minotaure*, 3–4 (1933), pp. 81–4, trans. in Anthony Vidler, *The Architectural Uncanny: Essays in the Modern Unhomely* (Cambridge, MA: MIT Press, 1992), pp. 151–2.
74. Matta, 'Mathématique sensible – architecture du temps' (adapted by Georges Hugnet), *Minotaure* 11 (1938), trans. as 'Sensitive mathematics – architecture of time', in Mary Ann Caws (ed.), *Surrealism* (London: Phaidon, 2004), p. 279.
75. Frederick Keisler, cited in Thomas H. Creighton, 'Kiesler's pursuit of an idea', *Progressive Architecture* 42 (1961), p. 121.
76. For accounts of surrealism and architecture, see the essays in Dalibor Veseley (ed.), 'Surrealism and architecture', issue of *Architectural Design* 48, 2–3 (1978); and Thomas Mical (ed.), *Surrealism and Architecture* (London: Routledge, 2005).
77. Walter Benjamin, 'Surrealism: the last snapshot of the European intelligentsia', in his *One-Way Street and Other Writings*, trans. Edmund Jephcott and Kingsley Shorter (London: Verso, 1979), pp. 225–39: p. 230. The essay was first published in 1929.
78. Alexander Gorlin, 'The ghost in the machine', in Mical, *Surrealism and Architecture*, pp. 103–18: p. 103. Gorlin suggests that surrealist themes become more prominent in Le Corbusier's later architecture, such as at the chapel at Ronchamp in 1950–5.
79. Charles Jencks, *Le Corbusier and the Continual Revolution in Architecture* (New York: The Monacelli Press, 2000), p. 204. In contrast to Gorlin, Jencks

describes the Ronchamp chapel not in terms of surrealism but as a harbinger of post-modernism; pp. 262–75.

80. Christopher Green, 'The architect as artist', in Michael Raeburn and Victoria Wilson (eds), *Le Corbusier: Architect of the Century* (London: Arts Council of Great Britain, 1987), pp. 110–30: p. 125. Le Corbusier contributed one essay to a surrealist journal, his 'Louis Soutter, L'inconnu de la soixantaine', *Minotaure* 9 (October 1936), pp. 62–5.
81. Le Corbusier, *The Decorative Art*, pp. 187–8.
82. Le Corbusier, *When the Cathedrals*, p. 147.
83. This is particularly important to note in relation to the sexual politics of surrealism, where dominant gendered codings of spaces are often repeated and where, as Foster among others has discussed, there is a frequent association of the unconscious and repressed elements of modernism with the 'feminine'. Following from this are difficult questions about how surrealist understandings of the spatial may be appropriative and even masculinist, at the same time as they may subversively disrupt masculine identity and gender oppositions along with the spaces with which they are bound up; see Foster, *Compulsive Beauty*, esp. pp. 190–1, 193–206.
84. Le Corbusier, *When the Cathedrals*, pp. 186–7.
85. Salvador Dalí, *The Secret Life of Salvador Dalí*, trans. Haakon M. Chevalier (London: Vision Press, 1958), p. 331.
86. Ibid. pp. 333, 334, 336. Koolhaas presents Dalí's visit alongside that of Le Corbusier to remarkable effect in his *Delirious New York*, pp. 235–82.
87. That year the surrealist group called into question Dalí's interest in fascism and Hitler. Breton became increasingly angered by Dalí's desire for publicity and he referred retrospectively to 1935 as the date when the Dalí he had admired 'disappeared', although his expulsion did not come until 1939; Polizzotti, *Revolution of the Mind*, p. 471.
88. See Bataille's essays from 1929–30, trans. in his *Visions of Excess: Selected Writings, 1927–1939*, ed. Allan Stoekl, trans. Allan Stoekl with Carl R. Lovitt and Donald M. Leslie, Jr. (Minneapolis: University of Minnesota Press, 1985).
89. See Michael Richardson, 'Introduction', in Georges Bataille, *The Absence of Myth: Writings on Surrealism*, ed. and trans. Michael Richardson (London: Verso, 1994), pp. 1–27. In 1935 Bataille collaborated with Breton in constituting Contre-Attaque, a union of revolutionaries outside the Communist Party that aimed to combat fascism.
90. Georges Bataille, 'Informe', *Documents* 1.7 (December 1929) p. 382, trans. Iain White as 'Formless', in *Encyclopaedia Acephalica*, pp. 51–2: pp. 51, 52.

91. James Clifford, 'On ethnographic surrealism', in his *The Predicament of Culture: Twentieth-Century Ethnography, Literature, and Art* (Cambridge, MA: Harvard University Press, 1988), pp. 117–51: 133. The journal ran for seventeen issues in 1929–30, reprinted in facsimile as *Documents* (Paris: Éditions Jean-Michel Place, 1991).
92. The term 'nonlogical difference' comes from Bataille's essay 'La notion de dépense', *La Critique sociale* 7 (January 1933), trans. as 'The notion of expenditure' in Bataille, *Visions of Excess*, pp. 116–29. His discussions of materialism and abjection were an important source for Kristeva's influential concept of the abject in *The Powers of Horror*, but there are important differences especially in the philosophical and psychoanalytic roots of her term; see Rosalind Krauss, 'The destiny of the informe', in Yve-Alain Bois and Rosalind E. Krauss, *Formless: A User's Guide* (New York: Zone Books, 1997), pp. 235–52.
93. See Martin Jay, 'The disenchantment of the eye: Bataille and the surrealists', in his *Downcast Eyes: The Denigration of Vision in Twentieth-Century French Thought* (Berkeley: University of California Press, 1993), pp. 211–62; and Jay, 'Modernism and the retreat from form', in his *Force Fields: Between Intellectual History and Cultural Critique* (London: Routledge, 1993), pp. 147–57.
94. A drawing of the symbol by André Masson accompanied Bataille's text 'The sacred conspiracy', published in the first issue of the review *Acéphale* (June 1936), in which he wrote: 'Man has escaped from his head just as the condemned man has escaped from his prison'; trans. in Bataille, *Visions of Excess*, pp. 179–81: p. 181.
95. Bataille, 'Architecture', p. 35.
96. Ibid. p. 35.
97. Georges Bataille, 'Abattoir', *Documents* 1.6 (November 1929), pp. 328–30, trans. Annette Michelson as 'Slaughterhouse', in *Encyclopaedia Acephalica*, pp. 72–3: p. 73.
98. Georges Bataille, 'Musée' *Documents* 2.4 (1930), p. 330, trans. Annette Michelson as 'Museum', in *Encyclopaedia Acephalica*, p. 64.
99. Bataille, 'Slaughterhouse', p. 73. For a discussion, see Yve-Alain Bois, 'Abattoir', in Bois and Krauss, *Formless*, pp. 43–51; and Denis Hollier, *Against Architecture: The Writings of Georges Bataille*, trans. Betsy Wing (Cambridge, MA: MIT Press, 1989), pp. ix-xv. The latter book was originally published in French in 1974.
100. Georges Bataille, *Notre-Dame de Rheims*, pamphlet from about 1918 published in Saint-Flour, Cantal, and reproduced in Hollier, *Against Architecture*, pp. 15–19: p. 16.

101. Hollier, *Against Architecture*, pp. 23, 24.
102. Bataille, 'Architecture', p. 36.
103. Bataille's interest in *planisme* and Ordre Nouveau are discussed in Allan Stoekl, 'Truman's apotheosis: Bataille, "planisme", and headlessness', *Yale French Studies* 78 (1990), pp. 181–204.
104. Nadir Lahiji, 'The gift of the Open Hand: Le Corbusier reading Georges Bataille's La Part Maudite', *Journal of Architectural Education* 50.1 (1996), pp. 50–67. Lahiji argues: 'At Chandigarh, Le Corbusier transcends the *planisme* of the thirties and the authoritarianism of *Ville Radieuse*. The Chandigarh plan is clearly a plan without a head and free of a hierarchical distribution. It is a potlatch of an "excessive" expenditure of space; its structure is a disarticulated and disjunctive (de)composition'; p. 54. Bataille's book was published as *La Part maudite, essai d'économie general, la consumation* (Paris: Éditions Minuit, 1949), trans. Robert Hurley as *The Accursed Share* (New York: Zone Books, 1988).
105. Bois, 'Abattoir', p. 47.
106. Jay, 'Modernism and the retreat from form', pp. 147, 157. See Peter Bürger, *Theory of the Avant-Garde*, trans. Michael Shaw (Minneapolis: University of Minnesota Press, 1984).
107. Yves-Alain Bois, 'The use value of "formless"', in Bois and Krauss, *Formless*, pp. 13–40: pp. 24–5.
108. Bernard Tschumi, 'Architecture and its double', in his *Questions of Space* (London: Architectural Association, 1990), pp. 61–77: p. 77.

Chapter 5: Situationist adventures

1. The English section of the Situationist International: Tim Clark, Christopher Gray, Charles Radcliffe and Donald Nicholson-Smith, *The Revolution of Modern Art and the Modern Art of Revolution* (London: Chronos, 1994), p. 11; text written in 1967, previously unpublished.
2. 'L'urbanisme unitaire à la fin des années 50', *Internationale situationniste* (*IS*) 3 (December 1959), pp. 11–16, trans. Thomas Levin as 'Unitary urbanism at the end of the 1950s', in Elisabeth Sussman (ed.), *On the Passage of a Few People Through a Rather Brief Moment in Time: The Situationist International 1957–1972* (Cambridge, MA: MIT Press, 1989), pp. 143–7: p. 147.
3. Gilles Ivain (Ivan Chtcheglov), 'Formulaire pour un urbanisme nouveau', *IS* 1 (June 1958), pp. 15–20, text written in October 1953, trans. as 'Formulary for a new urbanism', in Ken Knabb (ed. and trans.), *Situationist International Anthology* (Berkeley: Bureau of Public Secrets, 1981), pp. 1–4: p. 1.

4. Ibid. p. 1.
5. Ibid. pp. 2, 1.
6. 'Unitary urbanism at the end of the 1950s', p. 143.
7. Ibid. p. 144.
8. Guy Debord, 'Positions situationnistes sur la circulation', *IS* 3 (December 1959), pp. 36–7, trans. as 'Situationist theses on traffic', in Knabb, *Anthology*, pp. 56–8: p. 57.
9. 'La frontière situationniste', *IS* 5 (December 1960), pp. 7–9, trans. Paul Hammond as 'The situationist frontier', in Libero Andreotti and Xavier Costa (eds), *Theory of the Dérive and Other Situationist Writings on the City* (Barcelona: Museu d'Art Contemporani de Barcelona/Actar, 1996), pp. 106–7: p. 107.
10. See, for example, Peter Wollen, 'The Situationist International', *New Left Review* 174 (1989), pp. 67–95; and Myriam D. Maayen, 'From aesthetic to political vanguard: the Situationist International, 1957–1968', *Arts Magazine* 65 (January 1989), pp. 49–53. Cf. Alastair Bonnett, 'Art, ideology and everyday space: subversive tendencies from Dada to postmodernism', *Environment and Planning D: Society and Space* 10 (1992), pp. 69–86.
11. This is in contrast to Simon Sadler in his *The Situationist City* (Cambridge, MA: MIT Press, 1998), who focuses on the initial period with the aim of taking 'perverse care in extracting situationist architectural theory from a revolutionary program', and of 'saving' that early theory 'from the obscurity to which it was later banished by the Situationist International'; pp. 3, 12. This portrays the SI's interest in architecture and design in too narrow terms, in my view, severing parts of the project too abruptly.
12. Guy Debord, *La société du spectacle* (Paris: Buchet-Chastel, 1967), trans. Donald Nicholson-Smith as *The Society of the Spectacle* (New York: Zone Books, 1994), thesis 178.
13. Raoul Vaneigem, *Traité de savoir-vivre à l'usage des jeunes générations* (Paris: Gallimard, 1967), trans. Donald Nicholson-Smith as *The Revolution of Everyday Life* (London: Left Bank Books and Rebel Press, second edition 1994).
14. Debord, *The Society of the Spectacle*, theses 4, 5.
15. Ibid. thesis 29.
16. The best of many accounts to date of Debord's critique of the spectacle is Anselm Jappe, *Guy Debord*, trans. Donald Nicholson-Smith (Berkeley: University of California Press, 1999). This is not least because he embeds it within the Hegelian-Marxist tradition.
17. T. J. Clark and Donald Nicholson-Smith, 'Why art can't kill the Situationist

International', in Tom McDonough (ed.), *Guy Debord and the Situationist International: Texts and Documents* (Cambridge, MA: MIT Press, 2002), pp. 467–88. Althusser's *Pour Marx* and his collection of essays written with Etienne Balibar, *Lire le Capital*, were both published in France in 1965.

18. Henri Lefebvre, *Le temps des méprises* (Paris: Stock, 1975), p. 49.
19. Ibid. p. 148.
20. Derek Gregory, *Geographical Imaginations* (Oxford: Blackwell, 1994), p. 219.
21. Kristin Ross, *The Emergence of Social Space: Rimbaud and the Paris Commune* (London: Macmillan, 1988), p. 8. Other recent studies of Lefebvre in English that take seriously the transgressiveness and complexity of his wide-ranging writings include Stuart Elden, *Understanding Henri Lefebvre* (London: Continuum, 2004); Rob Shields, *Lefebvre, Love and Struggle: Spatial Dialectics* (London: Routledge, 1999), and Andy Merrifield, *Metromarxism: A Marxist Tale of the City* (New York: Routledge, 2002).
22. 'Le questionnaire', *IS* 9 (August 1964), pp. 24–7, trans. as 'Questionnaire' in Knabb, *Anthology*, pp. 138–42: p. 141. On 'Gothic Marxism', see Margaret Cohen, *Profane Illumination: Walter Benjamin and the Paris of Surrealist Revolution* (Berkeley: University of California Press, 1993).
23. Lefebvre, *Le temps des méprises*, pp. 89–97: p. 92.
24. Lefebvre's essay appeared in *La Nouvelle Revue Française* 58 (October 1957), pp. 644–72.
25. Guy Debord, 'Perspectives de modifications conscientes dans la vie quotidienne', presented on 17 May 1961, *IS* 6 (August 1961), pp. 20–7, trans. as 'Perspectives for conscious alterations in everyday life', in Knabb, *Anthology*, pp. 68–75. Debord addressed Lefebvre's essay of 1957 in his 'Thèses sur la révolution culturelle', *IS* 1 (June 1958), pp. 20–1.
26. Debord, 'Perspectives', p. 70.
27. 'Définition minimum des organisations révolutionnaires', *IS* 11 (October 1967), p. 54, trans. as 'Minimum definition of revolutionary organizations', in Knabb, *Anthology*, p. 223.
28. Henri Lefebvre, *Critique of Everyday Life, Volume II: Foundations for a Sociology of the Everyday*, trans. John Moore (London: Verso, 2002), p. 11; originally published in French in 1961. See also Gregory, *Geographical Imaginations*, pp. 402–3, who notes the parallels but also differences with Jürgen Habermas's idea of the colonisation of the lifeworld by the system.
29. See Kristin Ross, *Fast Cars, Clean Bodies: Decolonization and the Reordering of French Culture* (Cambridge, MA: MIT Press, 1995).
30. Debord, *The Society of the Spectacle*, thesis 42.
31. Ibid. theses 20, 172.

32. 'Domination de la nature, ideologies et classes', *IS* 8 (January 1963), pp. 3–14, excerpts trans. as 'Ideologies, classes and the domination of nature', in Knabb, *Anthology*, pp. 101–9: p. 108.
33. 'Geopolitique de l'hibernation', *IS* 7 (April 1962), pp. 3–10, trans. as 'Geopolitics of hibernation', in Knabb, *Anthology*, pp. 76–82: pp. 78, 79.
34. Ibid. p. 80.
35. 'Critique de l'urbanisme', *IS* 6 (August 1961), pp. 5–11, trans. John Shepley as 'Critique of urbanism', in McDonough, *Guy Debord*, pp. 103–18: p. 111.
36. Raoul Vaneigem, 'Commentaires contre l'urbanisme', *IS* 6 (August 1961), pp. 33–7, trans. as 'Comments against urbanism', in McDonough, *Guy Debord*, pp. 119–28: pp. 120, 121.
37. Norma Evenson, *Paris: A Century of Change, 1878–1978* (New Haven and London: Yale University Press, 1979), pp. 54–5.
38. Attila Kotányi and Raoul Vaneigem, 'Programme élémentaire du bureau d'urbanisme unitaire', *IS* 6 (August 1961), pp. 16–19, trans. as 'Elementary program of the bureau of unitary urbanism', in Knabb, *Anthology*, pp. 65–7: p. 66.
39. Debord, 'Situationist theses on traffic', p. 58.
40. The figures are from Evenson, *Paris*, pp. 309–10, 238; and Claude Eveno and Pascale de Mezamat (eds), *Paris perdu: Quarante ans de bouleversements de la ville* (Paris: Éditions Carré, 1991), p. 159; cited in Ross, *Fast Cars*, p. 151.
41. See Louis Chevalier, *The Assassination of Paris*, trans. David P. Jordan (Chicago: Chicago University Press, 1994), p. 260; originally published in French in 1977.
42. Debord, *The Society of the Spectacle*, thesis 174.
43. Ibid. thesis 173.
44. 'An interview with Henri Lefebvre', trans. Eleonore Kofman, *Environment and Planning D: Society and Space* 5 (1987), pp. 27–38; originally published in 1983. See also Lefebvre, *Le temps des méprises*, pp. 222–3.
45. Henri Lefebvre, *Introduction to Modernity*, trans. John Moore (London: Verso, 1995), pp. 116–26; originally published in French in 1962.
46. Henri Lefebvre, *Everyday Life in the Modern World*, trans. Sacha Rabinovitch (New Brunswick, NJ: Transaction Publishers, 1984), p. 59; originally published in French in 1968.
47. Henri Lefebvre, 'Right to the city', in his *Writings on Cities*, ed. and trans. Eleonore Kofman and Elizabeth Lebas (Oxford: Blackwell, 1996), pp. 61–181: pp. 77–80, 123.
48. Henri Lefebvre, *The Production of Space*, trans. Donald Nicholson-Smith (Oxford: Blackwell, 1991), pp. 306–8, 355–6; originally published in French in 1974.

49. Ibid. p. 286.
50. Ibid. p. 75–6. Lefebvre's critical remarks on Debord's *The Society of the Spectacle* are from his *Le temps des méprises*, p. 161. On Lefebvre's concern with visualisation and the de-corporealisation of space, see Derek Gregory, *Geographical Imaginations*, chapter 6; and Steve Pile, *The Body and the City: Psychoanalysis, Space and Subjectivity* (London: Routledge, 1996).
51. Jane Jacobs, *The Death and Life of Great American Cities: The Failure of Town Planning* (Harmondsworth: Penguin, 1984), pp. 14, 25; first published in 1961.
52. Marshall Berman provides an impassioned account of resistance to the 'expressway world' that Robert Moses exemplifies in New York, in his *All That is Solid Melts into Air: The Experience of Modernity* (London: Verso, 1983). In the process he quotes Moses's famous maxim: 'When you operate in an overbuilt metropolis, you have to hack your way with a meat ax'; cited on p. 290.
53. Richard Sennett, *The Uses of Disorder: Personal Identity and City Life* (London: Allen Lane, 1970), pp. 166, 142.
54. Lefebvre, *The Production of Space*, p. 124.
55. Henri Lefebvre, 'Preface to the new edition of The Production of Space', trans. in his *Key Writings*, ed. Stuart Elden, Elizabeth Lebas and Eleonore Kofman (London: Continuum, 2003), pp. 206–13: p. 210; the preface was first published in French in 1986.
56. David Harvey, *The Condition of Postmodernity: An Enquiry into the Origins of Cultural Change* (Oxford: Blackwell, 1989), pp. 35–6.
57. Sadler provides a thoughtful discussion of some of these connections in his *The Situationist City*, pp. 15–43.
58. As commented upon by Lefebvre in his 'Preface' to Philippe Boudon, *Lived-in Architecture: Le Corbusier's Pessac Revisited* (London: Lund Humphries, 1972), no pagination.
59. Henri Lefebvre, *The Survival of Capitalism: Reproduction of the Relations of Production*, trans. Frank Bryant (London: Allison and Busby, 1976), p. 85; originally published in French in 1973.
60. Lefebvre, *The Production of Space*, p. 52.
61. Guy Debord and Gianfranco Sanguinetti, 'Thèses sur L'Internationale situationniste et son temps', in *La Véritable scission dans l'Internationale* (Paris: Champ Libre, 1972), trans. John McHale as 'Theses on the Situationist International and its time, 1972', in Situationist International, *The Real Split in the International* (London: Pluto, 2003), pp. 6–80: pp. 14–15.
62. *The Decline and Fall of the 'Spectacular' Commodity-Economy* (Paris:

Internationale situationniste, 1965), reprinted in Knabb, *Anthology*, pp. 153–60: p. 155.

63. Guy Debord, 'In girum imus nocte et consumimur igni', 1978, in his *Oeuvres cinématographiques complètes, 1952–1978* (Paris: Champ Libre, 1978), pp. 187–278, trans. under the same title in his *Complete Cinematic Works: Scripts, Stills, Documents*, ed. and trans. Ken Knabb (Edinburgh: AK Press, 2003), pp. 133–205: p. 173.
64. 'Programme préable au mouvement situationniste', *IS* 8 (January 1963), p. 42.
65. Guy Debord, 'Attestations', in Guy Debord and Asger Jorn, *Mémoires* (Paris: Jean-Jacques Pauvert aux Belles Lettres, 1993), no pagination. This book is a facsimile reprint of the original publication that appeared without the foreword by Debord as *Mémoires* (Copenhagen: Permild and Rosengreen, 1959).
66. See Ross, *The Emergence of Social Space*, pp. 69–71; and Paul Lafargue, *Le Droit à la paresse* (Paris: Maspero, 1965); the latter text was originally published in 1880.
67. Ross, *The Emergence of Social Space*, p. 161.
68. Guy Debord and Gil J. Wolman, 'Pourquoi le lettrisme?', *Potlatch* 22 (9 September 1955), reprinted in *Potlatch (1954–1957)*, complete edition (Paris: Gallimard, 1996), pp. 174–87: pp. 186–7.
69. 'Manifeste', *Internationale lettriste* 2 (February 1953), reprinted in Gérard Berreby (ed.), *Documents relatifs à la fondation de l'Internationale situationniste, 1948–1957* (Paris: Éditions Allia, 1985), pp. 154–5: p. 154.
70. Jean-Michel Mension, *La Tribu* (Paris: Éditions Allia, 1998), trans. Donald Nicholson-Smith as *The Tribe* (San Francisco: City Lights, 2001), p. 127.
71. Thomas More, *Utopia*, ed. George M. Logan and Robert M. Adams (Cambridge: Cambridge University Press, 1989), pp. 51–2.
72. Frank and Fritzie Manuel, *Utopian Thought in the Western World* (Cambridge, MA: Harvard University Press, 1979), p. 127.
73. Guy Debord, 'Sur le passage de quelques personnes à travers une assez courte unité de temps', 1959, in his *Oeuvres cinématographiques*, pp. 15–35; trans. as 'On the passage of a few persons through a rather brief unity of time', in his *Complete Cinematic Works*, pp. 13–27: p. 13.
74. Lefebvre, *Introduction to Modernity*, p. 231.
75. Lefebvre, *The Survival of Capitalism*, pp. 89, 34.
76. Lefebvre, *Introduction to Modernity*, p. 124.
77. Debord and Wolman, 'Pourquoi le lettrisme?', p. 186.
78. Guy Debord, 'Le rôle de Potlatch, autre-fois et maintenant', *Potlatch* 30 (15 July 1959), reprinted in *Potlatch (1954–1957)*, pp. 282–4: p. 283.

79. A.-F. Conord, 'Construction de taudis', *Potlatch* 3 (6 July 1954), reprinted in *Potlatch (1954–1957)*, pp. 25–6, trans. Gerardo Denís as 'Slum construction', in Andreotti and Costa, *Theory of the Dérive*, p. 43.
80. Internationale lettriste, 'Les gratte-ciels par la racine', *Potlatch* 5 (20 July 1954), reprinted in *Potlatch (1954–1957)*, pp. 37–9, trans. Gerardo Denís as 'Skyscrapers by the roots', in Andreotti and Costa, *Theory of the Dérive*, pp. 44–5: p. 44.
81. Ibid. p. 45.
82. Guy Debord, *Rapport sur la construction des situations et sur les conditions de l'organisation et de l'action de la tendance situationniste internationale* (Paris: n.p., 1957), reprinted in Berreby *Documents*, pp. 607–19, trans. Tom McDonough as 'Report on the construction of situations and on the terms of organization and action of the International Situationist tendency', in McDonough, *Guy Debord*, pp. 29–50: p. 38.
83. Asger Jorn, 'Une architecture de la vie', *Potlatch* 15 (22 December 1954), reprinted in *Potlatch (1954–1957)*, pp. 95–6, trans. Gerardo Denís as 'Architecture for life', in Andreotti and Costa, *Theory of the Dérive*, p. 51.
84. 'Jorn's Copenhagen', *The Architectural Review* 122 (September 1957), p. 223. The book was published as Asger Jorn and Guy Debord, *Fin de Copenhague* (Copenhagen: Permild and Rosengreen, 1957; reprinted in facsimile Paris: Editions Allia, 1985). Debord's contribution is credited as 'Conseiller technique pour le détournement'.
85. Debord, 'In girum', p. 172.
86. 'Problèmes preliminaires à la construction d'une situation', *IS* 1 (June 1958), pp. 11–13, trans. as 'Preliminary problems in constructing a situation', in Knabb, *Anthology*, p. 44.
87. Debord, 'Report on the construction of situations'; here and in subsequent citations I am following the trans. of excerpts of this text in Knabb, *Anthology*, pp. 17–25: p. 23.
88. Ibid. pp. 23–4, 24.
89. The terms 'agonistic' and 'ludic' to characterise these activities were suggested to me by Ralph Rumney, a founding member of the SI and previously member of the London Psychogeographical Association; letter to the author, 23 October 1991.
90. Debord, 'Report on the construction of situations', p. 24.
91. Guy Debord, 'Théorie de la dérive', *Les lèvres nues* 9 (November 1956), reprinted in Berreby, *Documents*, pp. 312–16. The essay was published without the final paragraph in *IS* 2 (December 1958), pp. 19–23, with the latter version translated as 'Theory of the dérive', in Knabb, *Anthology*, pp.

50–4: see p. 52. On the use of taxis, see Michèle Bernstein, 'La dérive au kilomètre', in *Potlatch* 9-10-11 (17–31 August 1954), reprinted in *Potlatch (1954–57)*, pp. 64–5, trans. Gerardo Denís as 'Dérive by the mile', in Andreotti and Costa, *Theory of the Dérive*, p. 47.

92. Debord, 'Theory of the dérive', p. 50.
93. Ibid.
94. Debord, 'Report on the construction of situations', p. 24.
95. Debord, 'Theory of the dérive', p. 53.
96. Debord, 'In girum', p. 172.
97. Ivan Chtcheglov, 'Lettres de loin', *IS* 9 (August 1964), pp. 38–40, excerpts trans. as 'Letters from afar', in Knabb, *Anthology*, p. 372.
98. Walter Benjamin, *Charles Baudelaire: A Lyric Poet in the Era of High Capitalism*, trans. Harry Zohn (London: Verso, 1983), p. 54.
99. Michèle Bernstein, André-Frank Conord, Mohamed Dahou, Guy Debord, Jacques Fillon, Véra and Gil J. Wolman, '. . . une idée neuve en Europe', *Potlatch* 7 (3 August 1954), reprinted in *Potlatch (1954–1957)*, pp. 50–1: p. 50; trans. Greil Marcus as '. . . a new idea in Europe', from http://www.cddc.vt.edu/sionline/presitu/potlatch7.html. Debord more critically once referred to an unnamed (and recently excluded) colleague who 'proclaimed himself in the forefront of the renunciation of writing, valuing our isolation and our idle purity so much that he reached the decision to refuse collaboration with the journal that, of them all, is the closest to our positions'; 'Un pas en arrière', *Potlatch* 28 (22 May 1957), reprinted in *Potlatch (1954–1957)*, pp. 262–6, trans. Tom McDonough as 'One step back', in McDonough, *Guy Debord*, pp. 25–7: p. 26.
100. Henry de Béarn, André Conord, Mohamed Dahou, Guy-Ernest Debord, Jacques Fillon, Patrick Straram, Gil J. Wolman, 'Réponse de l'Internationale lettriste à la question: "La pensée nous éclaire-t-elle, et nos actes, avec la même indifférence que le soleil, ou quel est notre espoir et quelle est sa valeur?"', 5 May 1954, in *La Carte d'après nature* (June 1954), copy in *Portfolio situationniste* vol. 2 (Paris: Éditions le lundi au soleil, 1993), no pagination.
101. Ross, *The Emergence of Social Space*, p. 54.
102. Ibid. pp. 59, 60.
103. Debord, 'Theory of the dérive', p. 50.
104. Abdelhafid Khatib, 'Essai de description psychogéographique des Halles', *IS* 2 (December 1958), pp. 13–18, trans. Paul Hammond as 'Attempt at a psychogeographical description of Les Halles', in Andreotti and Costa, *Theory of the Dérive*, pp. 73–6: p. 76. On wider prominence given to

discourses of hygiene and sanitation in urban redevelopment in France in this period, where hygiene was often used as a grounds of excluding certain social groups and especially immigrant populations from specific locations, see Ross, *Fast Cars*, pp. 151–6.

105. Debord, 'Report on the construction of situations', p. 23.
106. Khatib, 'Attempt at a psychogeographical description of Les Halles', p. 76.
107. 'Questionnaire', *IS* 2 (December 1958), p. 18.
108. Debord and Jorn prepared *Mémoires* in December 1957 and it was first published in 1959.
109. Debord, 'Theory of the dérive', p. 53.
110. Asger Jorn, 'Quatrième expérience du MIBI (plans psychogéographiques de Guy Debord)', originally published with 'The Naked City' and reprinted in Berreby, *Documents*, p. 535. For fuller discussions of the maps, see David Pinder, 'Subverting cartography: the situationists and maps of the city', *Environment and Planning* A 28 (1996), pp. 405–27; Tom McDonough, 'Situationist space', in his *Guy Debord*, pp. 241–65; and Sadler, *The Situationist City*, pp. 82–91.
111. Debord, 'Théorie de la dérive', quotation from the last paragraph of the original version of the essay that appeared in *Les lèvres nues* 9 (November 1956), reprinted in Berreby, *Documents*, p. 316.
112. 'Pour une lexique lettriste', *Potlatch* 26 (7 May 1956), reprinted in *Potlatch (1954–1957)*, p. 241, trans. Gerardo Denís as 'Towards a lettrist lexicon', in Andreotti and Costa, *Theory of the Dérive*, p. 60.
113. Kotányi and Vaneigem, 'Elementary program of the bureau of unitary urbanism', p. 67.
114. Debord, *The Society of the Spectacle*, thesis 170.
115. Cohen, *Profane Illumination*, pp. 106–8.
116. André Breton, *Nadja* (Paris: Gallimard, 1928), trans. Richard Howard as *Nadja* (New York: Grove Press, 1960), p. 69.
117. Debord, 'Report on the construction of situations', pp. 19, 20.
118. The phrase is from Roger Cardinal, 'Soluble city: the surrealist perception of Paris', *Architectural Design* 2–3 (1978), pp. 143–9.
119. Thomas De Quincey, 'Confessions of an English Opium-Eater', in his *Confessions of an English Opium-Eater and Other Writings* (Oxford: Oxford University Press, 1985), pp. 1–79: pp. 47, 34; originally published in 1821. Partly cited by the situationists in their 'Unitary urbanism at the end of the 1950s', p. 147.
120. Greil Marcus, 'Guy Debord's *Mémoires*: a situationist primer', in Sussman, *On the Passage*, pp. 124–31.

121. Octavia Paz, 'André Breton, or the search for the beginning', in his *On Poets and Others*, trans. Michael Schmidt (London: Paladin, 1992), pp. 66–78: p. 66.
122. Roger Cardinal and Robert Short, *Surrealism: Permanent Revelation* (London: Studio Vista, 1970), p. 151.
123. '36 rue des Morillons', *Potlatch* 8 (10 August 1954), reprinted in *Potlatch (1954–1957)*, pp. 60–1: p. 61.
124. Cohen, *Profane Illumination*, pp. 110–13.
125. See Sadler, *The Situationist City*, pp. 80–1.
126. Alastair Bonnett, for example, criticises the way that, in some accounts of letterist dérives, 'the colonial incursions of the avant-garde into everyday space are mapped onto a more familiar colonial experience of European fear of, and desire for, non-Europeans'; in his 'The transgressive geographies of daily life: socialist pathways within everyday spatial creativity', *Transgressions* 2/3 (1996), pp. 20–37.
127. Of the seventy people who became members of the SI during the fifteen years of its existence, only seven were women. Former member Ralph Rumney suggests that this marginalisation extended to the group being 'anti-feminist' in practice in terms of the division of labour within its organisation; interview with Stewart Home, in 'The Situationist International and its historification', *Arts Monthly* 127 (June 1989), pp. 3–4. Lucy Forsyth also comments on the absence of feminist politics within the practices as well as ideas of the situationist circle in her 'The supercession of the SI', in Andrew Hussey and Gavin Bowd (eds), *The Haçienda Must Be Built: On the Legacy of Situationist Revolt* (Universities of Manchester and Huddersfield: AURA, 1996), pp. 26–40: pp. 30–2. Such an absence is further suggested by the SI's reproduction of photographs of women within issues of its journal as 'spectacularised' images, as objectified within the spectacle but without any critical commentary.
128. Asger Jorn, cited by Khatib in his 'Attempt at a psychogeographical description of Les Halles', p. 72.
129. Ralph Rumney, 'The leaning tower of Venice', excerpts published in *ARK: The Journal of the Royal College of Art* 24 (1958), fold-out section on pp. vi-ix.
130. Debord, 'Théorie de la dérive', p. 316.
131. As announced in 'L'operation contre-situationniste dans divers pays', *IS* 8 (January 1963), pp. 23–9, excerpts trans. as 'The countersituationist campaign in various countries', in Knabb, *Anthology*, pp. 111–14: p. 113.

Chapter 6: The great game to come

1. The English section of the Situationist International: Tim Clark, Christopher Gray, Charles Radcliffe and Donald Nicholson-Smith, *The Revolution of Modern Art and the Modern Art of Revolution* (London: Chronos, 1994), pp. 11–12; text written in 1967 and previously unpublished.
2. Karl Marx, cited in ibid. p. 9; the quotation is from a letter from Marx to Arnold Ruge, in September 1843.
3. Constant, 'New Babylon', in *Constant.Amsterdam* (Bochum: Städtische Kunstgalerie, March/April, 1961), no pagination, excerpt trans. as 'New Babylon (1961)', in Ulrich Conrads (ed.), *Programmes and Manifestoes on 20th-Century Architecture* (Cambridge, MA: MIT Press, 1971), pp. 177–8: p. 177. His full name is Constant Anton Nieuwenhuys but he is usually known as Constant and signs his work as such.
4. 'Premières maquettes pour l'urbanisme nouveau', *Potlatch* 30 (15 July 1959), reprinted in *Potlatch (1954–1957)*, collected edition (Paris: Gallimard, 1996), pp. 289–91, and trans. Gerardo Denís as 'Preliminary models for a new urbanism', in Libero Andreotti and Xavier Costa (eds), *Theory of the Dérive and Other Situationist Writings on the City* (Barcelona: Museu d'Art Contemporani/Actar, 1996), p. 62. Debord's authorship of the text is revealed by the presence of a copy in his handwriting in the Constant archive at the Rijksbureau voor Kunsthistorische Documentatie (RKD), The Hague. The text has since been published alongside Debord's letters in Guy Debord, *Correspondance*, vol. 1, *Juin 1957–Août 1960* (Paris: Arthème Fayard, 1999), pp. 234–5.
5. Constant, 'Le grand jeu à venir', *Potlatch* 30 (15 July 1959), reprinted in *Potlatch (1954–1957)*, pp. 289–91, and trans. Gerardo Denís as 'The great game to come', in Andreotti and Costa, *Theory of the Dérive*, pp. 62–3.
6. Constant, 'New Babylon (1961)', p. 177.
7. Ibid.
8. New Babylon was the subject of a major exhibition at the Witte de With center for contemporary art in Rotterdam, in 1998–9; the lavishly illustrated and well documented associated publication is Mark Wigley (ed.), *Constant's New Babylon: The Hyper-Architecture of Desire* (Rotterdam: Witte de With center for contemporary art/010 Publishers, 1998). Two other recent exhibitions have also been significant for displaying aspects of New Babylon: on the SI at the Museu d'Art Contemporani in Barcelona, in 1996; and on the drawings and graphics of New Babylon at the Drawing Center in New York, in 1999. See respectively Libero Andreotti and Xavier Costa (eds),

Situacionistas: arte, política, urbanismo/Situationists: Art, Politics, Urbanism (Barcelona: Museu d'Art Contemporani/Actar, 1996); and Catherine de Zegher and Mark Wigley (eds), *The Activist Drawing: Retracing Situationist Architectures from Constant's New Babylon to Beyond* (New York: The Drawing Center and Cambridge, MA, MIT Press, 2001). For further publications, see also Jean-Clarence Lambert (ed.), *Constant/New Babylon. Art et utopie: textes situationnistes* (Paris: Cercle d'Art, 1997); and Simon Sadler, *The Situationist City* (Cambridge, MA: MIT Press, 1998).

9. Constant and Debord, 'La Déclaration d'Amsterdam', *Internationale situationniste (IS)* 2 (December 1958), pp. 31–2, dated 10 November 1958, and trans. Paul Hammond as 'The Amsterdam Declaration', in Andreotti and Costa, *Theory of the Dérive*, p. 80. The declaration was adopted at the Third Conference of the SI in Munich, in April 1959, with minor amendments published as 'Corrections pour adoption des onze points d'Amsterdam', *IS* 3 (December 1959), pp. 27–8, trans. Paul Hammond as 'Corrections to adopting the eleven points of Amsterdam', in Andreotti and Costa, *Theory of the Dérive*, p. 96.
10. Constant and Debord, 'The Amsterdam Declaration', p. 80.
11. Guy Debord, *Rapport sur la construction des situations et sur les conditions de l'organisation et de l'action de la tendance situationniste internationale* (Paris: n.p., 1957), reprinted in Gérard Berreby (ed.), *Documents relatifs à la fondation l'Internationale situationniste, 1948–1957* (Paris: Éditions Allia, 1985), pp. 607–19, excerpts trans. as 'Report on the construction of situations and on the International Situationist tendency's conditions of organization and action', in Ken Knabb (ed. and trans.), *Situationist International Anthology* (Berkeley: Bureau of Public Secrets, 1981), pp. 17–25: pp. 22, 23.
12. Constant and Debord, 'The Amsterdam Declaration', p. 80; I am here following the change of wording agreed by the SI in 'Corrections', p. 96.
13. Debord, 'Report on the construction of situations', pp. 22, 25.
14. Michèle Bernstein, André-Frank Conord, Mohamed Dahou, Guy-Ernest Debord, Jacques Fillon, Véra, Gil J. Wolman, '. . . une idée neuve en Europe', *Potlatch* 7 (3 August 1954), reprinted in *Potlatch (1954–1957)*, pp. 50–1: p. 51.
15. For example, Peter Wollen, 'The Situationist International', *New Left Review* 174 (1989), pp. 67–95: p. 73; and Sadie Plant, *The Most Radical Gesture: The Situationist International in a Postmodern Age* (London: Routledge, 1992), pp. 20–1.
16. 'Le questionnaire', *IS* 9 (August 1964), pp. 24–7, trans. as 'Questionnaire', in Knabb, *Anthology*, pp. 138–42: p. 138.

17. 'An interview with Henri Lefebvre', trans. Eleonore Kofman, *Environment and Planning D: Society and Space* 5 (1987), pp. 27–38: p. 33.
18. Henri Lefebvre, *Critique of Everyday Life, Volume I: Introduction*, trans. John Moore (London: Verso, 1991), pp. 110–17, and the note headed 'Autocritique' on p. 261 n. 49. The translation is from the second edition published in French in 1958; the first edition was in 1947.
19. Lefebvre advanced his theory of moments especially in his *La Somme et le reste*, 2 volumes (Paris: La Nef de Paris, 1959); and *Critique of Everyday Life, Volume II: Foundations for a Sociology of the Everyday*, trans. John Moore (London: Verso, 2002), pp. 340–58. The latter book was originally published in French in 1961. Among the English language commentators to draw out the political significance of these themes for Lefebvre are Greil Marcus in his *Lipstick Traces: A Secret History of the Twentieth Century* (London: Secker and Warburg, 1989), esp. pp. 144–6; and Rob Shields, *Lefebvre, Love and Struggle: Spatial Dialectics* (London: Routledge, 1999), pp. 58–64.
20. Henri Lefebvre, *De l'état*, 4 volumes (Paris: Union Générale d'Éditions, 1976–8), p. 270, cited in Eleonore Kofman and Elizabeth Lebas, 'Lost in transposition – time, space and the city', in Henri Lefebvre, *Writings on Cities*, ed. and trans. Eleonore Kofman and Elizabeth Lebas (Oxford: Blackwell, 1996), pp. 3–60: p. 23.
21. Henri Lefebvre, *Everyday Life in the Modern World*, trans. Sacha Rabinovitch (New Brunswick, NJ: Transaction Publishers, 1984), p. 204; originally published in French in 1968.
22. Alice Kaplan and Kristin Ross, 'Introduction', issue on 'Everyday Life', *Yale French Studies* 73 (Fall 1987), pp. 1–4: p. 3.
23. 'Théorie des moments et construction des situations', *IS* 4 (1960), pp. 10–11, trans. Paul Hammond as 'The theory of moments and the construction of situations', in Andreotti and Costa, *Theory of the Dérive*, pp. 100–1: p. 101.
24. Henri Lefebvre, *Le temps des méprises* (Paris: Stock, 1975), p. 158; see also his conversation with Kristin Ross in 1983, in 'Lefebvre on the situationists: an interview', in Tom McDonough (ed.), *Guy Debord and the Situationist International: Texts and Documents* (Cambridge, MA: MIT Press, 2002), pp. 267–83. Lefebvre's recollection of details regarding the SI in the latter interview, it should be noted, is not always accurate. For example he attaches significance to a text by Constant, entitled 'Pour une architecture de situation' from 1953, something he also references elsewhere as among the key influences on his book *Le retour de la dialectique: Douze mots clefs pour le monde moderne* (Paris: Messidor-Éditions Sociales, 1986), p. 13. This has since been repeated by other commentators on Lefebvre. But no record of such a text

seems to exist and it appears likely that Lefebvre is confusing it with Ivan Chtcheglov's 'Formulary for a new urbanism' from 1953, or possibly another later text by Constant.

25. Lefebvre comments on this essay, which he says was intended to help to replace the journal *Arguments* with *Internationale situationniste*, in 'Lefebvre on the situationists', p. 279.
26. Guy Debord, Attila Kotányi and Raoul Vaneigem, 'Sur la Commune', dated 18 March 1962, trans. as 'Theses on the Paris Commune', in Knabb, *Anthology*, pp. 314–17: p. 316.
27. Ibid. p. 314.
28. Ibid. pp. 315, 317.
29. Raoul Vaneigem, *Traité de savoir-vivre à l'usage des jeunes générations* (Paris: Gallimard, 1967), trans. Donald Nicholson-Smith as *The Revolution of Everyday Life* (London: Left Bank Books and Rebel Press, second edition 1994), p. 266. Bernstein's works were exhibited at the situationist exhibition 'Destruction of RSG-6' at Galerie EXI, Odense, Denmark, in June 1963.
30. Henri Lefebvre, 'The everyday and everydayness', trans. Christine Levich, with Alice Kaplan and Kristin Ross, *Yale French Studies* 73 (Fall 1987), pp. 7–11: p. 11. Cf. Lefebvre's comments on the festival and cultural revolution in his *Everyday Life in the Modern World*, p. 206.
31. Henri Lefebvre, *La Proclamation de la Commune* (Paris: Gallimard, 1965); citations from excerpts trans. as 'The style of the Commune', in his *Key Writings*, ed. Stuart Elden, Elizabeth Lebas and Eleonore Kofman (London: Continuum, 2003), pp. 188–9.
32. 'Lefebvre on the situationists', p. 69. He provides a frank personal account of some of these complications on pp. 77–80; and in his *Le temps des méprises*, pp. 158–9. Lefebvre's version of the article was published as 'La significance de la Commune', *Arguments* 27–8 (1962), pp. 11–19. The SI attacked Lefebvre's 'plagiarism' and the journal *Arguments* in its tract *Aux poubelles de l'histoire*, 21 February 1963; and reproduced his text alongside the group's own theses on the Commune in *IS* 12 (September 1969), pp. 108–11. The SI also responded to his book on the Commune in 'L'historien Lefebvre', *IS* 10 (March 1966), pp. 73–5. Lefebvre nevertheless remained close with Constant, who resigned from the SI in 1960, as will be discussed in the next chapter.
33. Editorial note following Gilles Ivain, 'Formulaire pour un urbanisme nouveau', *IS* 1 (June 1958), pp. 15–20: p. 20. The original text was written under that pseudonym by Ivan Chtcheglov in October 1953, and is trans.

(without the editorial note) as 'Formulary for a new urbanism' in Knabb, *Anthology*, pp. 1–4.

34. Ivain (Chtcheglov), 'Formulary for a new urbanism', pp. 2, 4. The situationists later referred to this latter aspect of the project as effectively corresponding to Lefebvre's 'moments' on an extended spatial and urban level; in their 'The theory of moments and the construction of situations', p. 101.
35. Henry de Béarn, André Conord, Mohamed Dahou, Guy Debord, Jacques Fillon, Patrick Straram, Gil J. Wolman, 'Réponse de l'Internationale lettriste à la question: "La pensée nous éclaire-t-elle, et nos actes, avec la même indifférence que le soleil, ou quel est notre espoir et quelle est sa valeur?"', dated 5 May 1954, in *La Carte d'après nature* (June 1954), reproduced in *Port-folio situationniste*, vol. 2 (Paris: Éditions le lundi au soleil, 1993), no pagination.
36. Guy Debord and Jacques Fillon, 'Résumé 1954', *Potlatch* 14 (30 November 1954), reprinted in *Potlatch (1954–1957)*, p. 91, trans. Gerardo Denís as 'Summary 1954', in Andreotti and Costa, *Theory of the Dérive*, p. 50.
37. Guy Debord, 'Introduction à une critique de la géographie urbaine', *Les lèvres nues* 6 (September 1955), reprinted in Berreby, *Documents*, pp. 288–92, and trans. as 'Introduction to a critique of urban geography', in Knabb, *Anthology*, pp. 5–8: p. 6.
38. 'Problèmes preliminaires à la construction d'une situation', *IS* 1 (June 1958), pp. 11–13, trans. as 'Preliminary problems in constructing a situation', in Knabb, *Anthology*, pp. 43–5: p. 43.
39. 'Prochaine planète', *Potlatch* 4 (13 July 1954), reprinted in *Potlatch (1954–1957)*, pp. 32–3, trans. as Gerardo Denís as 'Next planet', in Andreotti and Costa, *Theory of the Dérive*, p. 43.
40. Guy Debord, 'Exercice de la psychogéographie', *Potlatch* 2 (29 June 1954), reprinted in *Potlatch (1954–1957)*, p. 20, trans. Gerardo Denís as 'Exercise in psychogeography', in Andreotti and Costa, *Theory of the Dérive*, p. 42. Breton's original list is in the 'Manifesto of Surrealism', from 1924, in his *Manifestoes of Surrealism*, trans. Richard Seaver and Helen R. Lane (Ann Arbor: University of Michigan Press, 1972), pp. 1–47: pp. 26–7. Breton's reference to Cheval is from his 'Surrealism yesterday, today, tomorrow', trans. Edward W. Titis, *This Quarter* II, 1 (September 1932).
41. 'Next planet', p. 43.
42. Guy Debord, 'L'architecture et le jeu', *Potlatch* 20 (30 May 1955), reprinted in *Potlatch (1954–1957)*, pp. 155–8, trans. Gerardo Denís as 'Architecture and play', in Andreotti and Costa, *Theory of the Dérive*, pp. 53–4: p. 53.
43. William S. Rubin, *Dada and Surrealist Art* (London: Thames and Hudson, 1969), pp. 100–10; see also Elizabeth Burns Gamard, *Kurt Schwitters'*

Merzbau: The Cathedral of Erotic Misery (Princeton NJ: Princeton Architectural Press, 2000).

44. Louis Aragon, cited in Gaëtan Picon, *Surrealism 1919–1939*, trans. James Emmons (London: Macmillan, 1977), p. 54.
45. Ivain (Chtcheglov), 'Formulary for a new urbanism', p. 3.
46. Debord, 'Introduction to a critique of urban geography', p. 7.
47. Guy Debord and Gil J. Wolman, 'Mode d'emploi du détournement', *Les lèvres nues* 8 (May 1956), reprinted in Berreby, *Documents*, pp. 302–9, and trans. as 'Methods of detournement', in Knabb, *Anthology*, pp. 8–14: p. 13.
48. Nicolas Gogol, 'En attendant la fermeture des églises', *Potlatch* 9-10-11 (17–31 August 1954), reprinted in *Potlatch (1954–1957)*, p. 69, trans. Gerardo Denís as 'Waiting for the churches to close', in Andreotti and Costa, *Theory of the Dérive*, p. 48.
49. 'Du rôle de l'écriture', *Potlatch* 23 (13 October 1955), reprinted in *Potlatch (1954–1957)*, pp. 202–3, trans. Gerardo Denís as 'On the role of the written word', in Andreotti and Costa, *Theory of the Dérive*, p. 55.
50. Groupe de Recherche psychogéographique de l'Internationale lettriste, 'Position du Continent Contrescarpe', *Les lèvres nues* 9 (November 1956), reprinted in Berreby, *Documents*, pp. 324–6.
51. Thomas Y. Levin, 'Geopolitics of hibernation: the drift of situationist urbanism', in Andreotti and Costa, *Situationists*, pp. 110–46: p. 119.
52. André Breton, 'Recherches expérimentales: sur certaines possibilités d'embellissement irrationnel d'une ville', *Le Surréalisme au service de la révolution* 6 (May 1933), pp. 18–19, with contributions from Paul Eluard, Arthur Harfaux, Maurice Henry, Benjamin Péret, Tristan Tzara and Georges Wenstein; excerpts trans. as 'Experimental researches (on the irrational embellishment of a city)', in Breton's *What is Surrealism? Selected Writings*, ed. Franklin Rosemount (New York: Pathfinder, 1978), pp. 95–6.
53. 'Projet d'embellissements rationnels de la ville de Paris', *Potlatch* 23 (13 October 1955), reprinted in *Potlatch (1954–1957)*, pp. 203–7, and trans. Gerardo Denís as 'Plan for rational improvements to the city of Paris', in Andreotti and Costa, *Theory of the Dérive*, pp. 56–7.
54. 'Renseignments situationnistes', *IS* 2 (December 1958), p. 12.
55. 'Le retour de Charles Fourier', *Internationale situationniste* 12 (September 1969), pp. 97–8.
56. Asger Jorn, 'Notes sur la formation d'un Bauhaus Imaginiste', in his *Pour la forme: Ébauche d'une méthodologie des arts* (Paris: L'Internationale situationniste, 1958), reprinted in Berreby, *Documents*, pp. 428–9, and trans. as 'Notes

on the formation of an Imaginist Bauhaus', in Knabb, *Anthology*, pp. 16–17: p. 16.

57. Max Bill, 'Education and design', trans. in Joan Ockman (ed.), *Architecture Culture 1943–1968: A Documentary Anthology* (New York: Rizzoli, 1993), pp. 159–62: p. 162; text originally published in German in 1952.
58. Asger Jorn, *Immagine e forma 1* (Milan: Editoriale Periodici Italiani, 1954), excerpt trans. as 'Arguments apropos of the International Movement for an Imaginist Bauhaus, against an Imaginary Bauhaus, and its purpose today', in Ockman, *Architecture Culture 1943–1968*, pp. 173–5: p. 174.
59. Mohamed Dahou, 'La première pierre qui s'en va', *Potlatch* 26 (7 May 1956), reprinted in *Potlatch (1954–1957)*, pp. 235–6, trans. Gerardo Denís as 'The first stone falls', in Andreotti and Costa, *Theory of the Dérive*, p. 60. The school lasted until 1968, when funding was withdrawn.
60. T. J. Clark, *Farewell to an Idea: Episodes from a History of Modernism* (New Haven and London: Yale University Press, 1999), pp. 389–90.
61. Guy Debord, 'De l'architecture sauvage', September 1972, in Ezio Gribaudo, Alberico Sala and Guy Debord, *Le jardin d'Albisola* (Turin: Edizioni d'Arte Fratelli Pozzo, 1974), essay trans. Thomas Levin as 'On wild architecture', in Elisabeth Sussman (ed.), *On the Passage of a Few People Through a Rather Brief Moment in Time: The Situationist International 1957–1972* (Cambridge, MA: MIT Press, 1989), pp. 174–5: p. 174.
62. Ibid. p. 174.
63. Asger Jorn, 'The human animal', in Per Hofman Hansen (ed.), *A Bibliography of Asger Jorn's Writings* (Silkeborg: Silkeborg Kunstmuseum, 1988), pp. 39–42: p. 39.
64. See Guy Atkins (with the help of Troels Andersen), *Jorn in Scandinavia 1930–1953* (London: Lund Humphries, 1968), pp. 29–33.
65. On the history of Cobra, see Jean-Clarence Lambert, *Cobra*, trans. Roberta Bailey (New York: Abbeville Press, 1983); and Willemijn Stokvis, *Cobra: The Last Avant-Garde Movement of the Twentieth Century* (Aldershot: Lund Humphries, 2004).
66. Constant Nieuwenhuys, 'Manifest', *Reflex* 1 (September-October 1948), no pagination [pp. 2–7; for works with no pagination, page numbers in square brackets refer to my own counting of the pages], reprinted in Berreby, *Documents*, pp. 20–9, and trans. Leonard Bright as 'Manifesto', in Willemijn Stokvis, *Cobra: An International Movement in Art After the Second World War* (New York: Rizzoli, 1988), pp. 29–31. *Reflex* was the journal of the Dutch Experimental Group, which was founded in July 1948 and became part of Cobra.

67. Constant, 'C'est notre désir qui fait la révolution', *Cobra* 4 (1949), pp. 3–4, reprinted in *Cobra 1948–1951* (Paris: Éditions Jean-Michel Place, 1980), and trans. as 'Our own desires build the revolution', in Herschel B. Chipp (ed.), *Theories of Modern Art: A Source Book by Artists and Critics* (Berkeley: University of California Press, 1968), pp. 601–3: p. 601.
68. Michel Colle, 'Vers une architecture symbolique', *Cobra* 1 (1948), pp. 21–3.
69. Asger Jorn, 'Apollon eller Dionysos', *Byggmästaren* XXVI, 17 (1947), pp. 251–6, as discussed by Graham Birtwistle, *Living Art: Asger Jorn's Comprehensive Theory of Art Between Helhesten and Cobra (1946–1949)* (Utrecht: Reflex, 1986), p. 34. My discussion of Jorn's early work here draws substantially on Birtwistle's enormously rich study.
70. Michaell Ventris, 'Form and arabesque', *Cobra* 1 (1948), p. 18.
71. Birtwistle, *Living Art*, pp. 38–42.
72. Asger Jorn, 'Levend ornament', *Forum* IV, 4 (1949), pp. 137–47: p. 145, cited in Birtwistle, *Living Art*, p. 104.
73. Asger Jorn, 'A propos de la valeur actuelle de la conception fonctionnaliste', in his *Pour la forme*, reprinted in Berreby, *Documents*, p. 413, and trans. Paul Hammond as 'On the current value of the functionalist idea', in Andreotti and Costa, *Theory of the Dérive*, pp. 33–4: p. 33.
74. Graham Birtwistle, 'Looking for structure in Asger Jorn's theory', in Troels Andersen, Graham Birtwistle and Johannes Gachnang, *Asger Jorn 1914/1973* (Amsterdam: Stedelijk Museum, 1994), pp. 95–115.
75. See Edward Soja, *Thirdspace: Journeys to Los Angeles and Other Real-and-Imagined Places* (Oxford: Blackwell, 1996), pp. 53–82. Cf. Stuart Elden, *Understanding Henri Lefebvre: Theory and the Possible* (London: Continuum, 2004), pp. 36–7.
76. 'L'urbanisme unitaire à la fin des années 50', *IS* 3 (December 1959), pp. 11–16, trans. Thomas Levin as 'Unitary urbanism at the end of the 1950s', in Sussman, *On the Passage*, pp. 143–4.
77. Constant, cited in Hein van Haaren, *Constant*, trans. Max Schuchart (Amsterdam: J. M. Meulenhoff, 1966), p. 8.
78. Ibid. p. 8.
79. Constant, 'New Babylon (1961)', p. 177.
80. Marcel Hummelink, 'An animal, a night, a scream, a human being . . . unity and diversity in Constant's work', trans. Ruth Koenig, in *Constant: Schilderijen 1948–1998* (Amsterdam: Stedelijk Museum, 1995), pp. 27–40.
81. Constant and Aldo van Eyck, *Voor een Spatiaal Colorisme* (Amsterdam: Galerie Espace, 1953), p. 1.
82. See Constant, 'About the meaning of construction', in Anthony Hill (ed.),

DATA: *Directions in Art, Theory and Aesthetics. An Anthology* (London: Faber and Faber, 1968), pp. 175–9. The essay is reprinted in Wigley, *Constant's New Babylon*, p. 174.

83. Roger Hilton, letter to Constant, 1953; in Constant archive, RKD.
84. Asger Jorn, letter to Constant, 25 October 1954; in Constant archive, RKD.
85. Pinot Gallizio, letter to Renè Drouin, 9 December 1958; from http://www.essogallery.com/Pinot%20Gallizio/GallDrou.html, accessed November 2004.
86. Constant's archive contains almost the whole set of *Potlatch*. A number of texts are marked for attention, including Debord's 'Exercice de la psychogéographie', *Potlatch* 2 (29 June 1954), and the LI's attack on Le Corbusier in 'Les gratte-ciel par la racine', *Potlatch* 5 (20 July 1954).
87. See 'La plate-forme d'Alba' in *Potlatch* 27 (2 November 1956), reprinted in *Potlatch (1954–1957)*, pp. 246–9, trans. as 'The Alba platform', in Knabb, *Anthology*, pp. 14–15.
88. Asger Jorn, 'Discours d'overture du premier Congrès Modial des Artistes Libres', September 1956, in his *Pour la forme*, reprinted in Berreby, *Documents*, pp. 429–30, trans. Paul Hammond as 'Opening speech of the First World Congress of Free Artists', in Andreotti and Costa, *Theory of the Dérive*, pp. 37–8.
89. Gil J. Wolman, 'Intervention de Wolman, délégué de l'Internationale lettriste au Congrès d'Alba en Septembre 1956', reprinted in Berreby, *Documents*, pp. 596–98, 597; trans. Reuben Keehan, slightly modified, from http://www.cddc.vt.edu/sionline/presitu/wolman.html, accessed November 2004. Further statements from the congress by Pinot Gallizio, Constant and Ettore Sottsass, Jr. are reprinted on pp. 595–601.
90. 'The Alba platform', in Knabb, *Anthology*, p. 15.
91. 'Manifestate a favore dell'urbanesimo unitario', tract reproduced in Berreby, *Documents*, p. 605. Significant and well illustrated accounts of the situationists' artistic concerns around this time include Mirella Bandini, *L'estetico il politico: da Cobra all'Internazionale Situazionista, 1948–1957* (Rome: Officina Edizioni, 1977); and Roberto Ohrt, *Phantom Avantgarde: Eine Geschichte der Situationischen Internationale und der Modernen Kunst* (Hamburg: Edition Nautilus, 1990).
92. Guy Debord, 'Thèses sur la révolution culturelle', *IS* 1 (June 1958), pp. 20–1, trans. John Shepley as 'Theses on the cultural revolution', in McDonough, *Guy Debord*, pp. 61–5: p. 61.
93. Constant, in 'A talk with Constant' with Fanny Kelk, in *Constant: Schilderijen 1969–77* (Amsterdam: Stedelijk Museum, 1978), no pagination [pp. 2–7: p. 2].

94. Constant, 'Sur nos moyens et nos perspectives', *IS* 2 (December 1958), pp. 23–6, trans. Paul Hammond as 'On our means and our perspectives', in Andreotti and Costa, *Theory of the Dérive*, p. 77.
95. See Asger Jorn, 'Peinture détourné', in *Vingt peintures modifées par Asger Jorn* (Paris: Galerie Rive Gauche, 1959), trans. as 'Detourned painting', in Sussman, *On the Passage*, pp. 140–2. For a discussion of these works, see Claire Gilman, 'Asger Jorn's avant-garde archives', in McDonough, *Guy Debord*, pp. 189–212.
96. Among the books were *Pour la forme* in 1958, and *Critique de la politique economique suivie de la lutte finale* (Paris: L'Internationale situationniste, 1960).
97. Gallizio, letter to Drouin, 9 December 1958.
98. Debord, 'Introduction to a critique of urban geography', p. 6.
99. Gallizio referred to Debord as 'a reliable interpreter of mine', in his letter to Drouin, 9 December 1958. Gallizio and Debord corresponded extensively, with the latter's letters being published in his *Correspondance*, vol. 1.
100. Michèle Bernstein, 'Éloge de Pinot-Gallizio', text dated 1958, in Michèle Bernstein and Asger Jorn, *Pinot Gallizio* (Paris: Bibliothèque d'Alexandrie, 1960), trans. John Shepley as 'In praise of Pinot-Gallizio', in McDonough, *Guy Debord*, pp. 69–73: p. 70.
101. 'L'activité de la section italienne', *IS* 2 (December 1958), pp. 27–30.
102. Pinot Gallizio, 'Discours sur la peinture industrielle et sur un art unitaire applicable', *IS* 3 (December 1959), pp. 31–5: pp. 34–5. This text was originally published in a slightly longer version as 'Manifesto della pittura industriale – per un'arte unitaria applicabile', in *Notizie Arti Figurative* 9 (November 1959).
103. 'L'activité de la section italienne', p. 27.
104. Gallizio, 'Discours sur la peinture industrielle', pp. 32–3.
105. Ibid. p. 34.
106. Ibid. pp. 33, 32, 33.
107. Ibid. p. 34.
108. Constant, 'On our means and our perspectives', p. 77. In a reply to his formulation, the editorial committee of the journal in conjunction with Jorn gave its approval to this point but stressed the importance of not just utilising but also *transforming* the machine, an anticipation of future conflicts over the role of technology; p. 78.
109. Constant made these points in a lecture at a Conference for the Students Association at the Royal Academy of Copenhagen, 12 March 1964, unpublished text in Constant archive, RKD, no pagination [p. 1]. The quotation is from another lecture at the Stedelijk Museum in Amsterdam, on 20

December 1960, entitled 'Unitair urbanisme', manuscript trans. Robyn de Jong-Dalziel as 'Unitary urbanism', in Wigley, *Constant's New Babylon*, pp. 131–5: p. 131.

110. Constant, lecture at the Royal Academy of Copenhagen, [p. 6].
111. Their correspondence reveals the intensity of this exchange.
112. The book was first published as Paul-Henry Chombart de Lauwe, *Paris et l'agglomération parisienne*, 2 volumes (Paris: Presses Universitaires de France, 1952).
113. *Constant* (Paris: Bibliothèque d'Alexandrie, 1959).
114. Constant, letter to Debord, 26 February 1959; Constant archive, RKD.
115. Guy Debord, letter to Constant, 28 February 1959; published in Debord, *Correspondance*, vol. 1, pp. 194–7: p. 195.
116. Debord, 'Architecture and play', p. 54.
117. Constant, 'On our means', p. 77.
118. The quotation is from Constant's letter to Debord, 26 February 1959; objections were also raised in a letter from Constant to Debord, in September 1959; constant archive, RKD.
119. Debord's responses to Constant's models included a manuscript entitled 'Constant et la voie de l'urbanisme unitaire', written in 1959, extracts of which were published in German in *Constant. Konstruktionen und Modelle* (Essen: Galerie van de Loo, 1960). The original manuscript is trans. Brian Holmes as 'Constant and the path of unitary urbanism', in Wigley, *Constant's New Babylon*, pp. 95–6. One of the few critics to draw out the complex relationship between Constant and Debord over these issues, and hence to complicate the prevailing view of Debord mentioned here, is Mark Wigley in his important essay 'The hyper-architecture of desire', in Wigley, *Constant's New Babylon*, pp. 9–71; esp. pp. 30–9.
120. Guy Debord, 'Un pas en arrière', *Potlatch* 28 (22 May 1957), reprinted in *Potlatch (1954–1957)*, pp. 262–6, trans. Tom McDonough as 'One step back', in McDonough, *Guy Debord*, pp. 25–7: pp. 26–7.
121. Constant, 'Voorwoord', in J. L Locher (ed.) *New Babylon* (The Hague: Haags Gemeentemuseum, 1974), p. 27. This foreword and his text 'New Babylon, een schets voor een kultuur', from pp. 49–62, are trans. Paul Hammond as 'New Babylon' (1974), in Andreotti and Costa, *Theory of the Dérive*, pp. 154–69. The foreword begins with a quotation from Vaïda Voivod III: p. 154. the President of the World Community of Gypsies, in 1963: 'We are the living symbols of a world without frontiers, a world of freedom, without weapons, where each man may travel without let or hindrance . . .'.
122. Constant, 'Demain la poésie logera la vie', text dated 19 August 1956 and

presented in September 1956, reprinted in Berreby, *Documents*, pp. 595–6, and trans. Stephen Wright as 'Tomorrow life will reside in poetry', in Wigley, *Constant's New Babylon*, p. 78.

Chapter 7: Life will reside in poetry

1. Constant, 'Une autre ville pour une autre vie', *Internationale situationniste* (*IS*) 3 (December 1959), pp. 37–40, trans. John Shepley as 'A different city for a different life', in Tom McDonough (ed.), *Guy Debord and the Situationist International: Texts and Documents* (Cambridge. MA: MIT Press, 2002), pp. 95–101: pp. 95–6.
2. Constant, 'New Babylon, the world of Homo Ludens', in *De New Babylon Informatief* 4 (1966), p. 1. The quoted line is from Lautréamont, the nineteenth-century writer often cited favourably by the situationists.
3. The catalogue was published as J. L. Locher (ed.), *New Babylon* (The Hague: Haags Gemeentemuseum, 1974). Constant dates the end of the project to around 1970 when he returned to painting, although his paintings continued to address the theme for several more years.
4. Constant, 'New Babylon', in *Constant.Amsterdam* (Bochum: Städtische Kunstgalerie, March/April, 1961), no pagination, excerpt trans. as 'New Babylon (1961)', in Ulrich Conrads (ed.), *Programmes and Manifestoes on 20th-Century Architecture* (Cambridge, MA: MIT Press, 1971), p. 177.
5. Karl Marx, 'Economic and philosophic manuscripts of 1844', in Karl Marx and Frederick Engels, *Collected Works*, vol. 3: *Marx and Engels 1843–1844* (London: Lawrence and Wishart, 1975), pp. 229–346: p. 300.
6. Constant recently reaffirmed that he is still 'a Marxist in a philosophical way', in 'A conversation with Constant', with Benjamin Buchloh, 30 October 1999, in Catherine de Zegher and Mark Wigley (eds), *The Activist Drawing: Retracing Situationist Architectures from Constant's New Babylon to Beyond* (New York: Drawing Center and Cambridge, MA: MIT Press, 2001), pp. 15–25: p. 24.
7. Michael Gardiner, *Critiques of Everyday Life* (London: Routledge, 2000), p. 80. Lefebvre addresses this theme in his book *Métaphilosophie: Prolégomènes* (Paris: Les Éditions de Minuit, 1965).
8. Mark Wigley, 'Paper, scissors, blur', in de Zegher and Wigley, *The Activist Drawing*, pp. 26–56: p. 37.
9. Constant, 'New Babylon (1961)', p. 178.
10. Wigley discusses closely the significance of drawing in Constant's work, in 'Paper, scissors, blur'.

11. A point stressed retrospectively by Constant, in 'A talk with Constant' with Fanny Kelk, in *Constant: Schilderijen 1969–77* (Amsterdam: Stedelijk Museum, 1978), no pagination [pp. 2–7: p. 2].
12. Constant, 'New Babylon, een schets voor een kultuur', in Locher, *New Babylon*, pp. 49–62, trans. Paul Hammond as 'New Babylon' (1974), in Libero Andreotti and Xavier Costa (eds), *Theory of the Dérive and Other Situationist Writings on the City* (Barcelona: Museu d'Art Contemporani de Barcelona/Actar, 1996), pp. 154–69: p. 160.
13. Constant Nieuwenhuys, 'Manifest', *Reflex* 1 (September-October 1948), reprinted in Gérard Berreby (ed.), *Documents relatifs à la fondation l'Internationale situationniste, 1948–1957* (Paris: Éditions Allia, 1985), pp. 20–9, and trans. Leonard Bright as 'Manifesto', in Willemijn Stokvis, *Cobra: An International Movement in Art After the Second World War* (New York: Rizzoli, 1988), pp. 29–31: p. 30.
14. Constant, 'Cultuur en contra-cultuur', *Reflex* 2 (February 1949), reprinted in Berreby, *Documents*, pp. 41–2: p. 42.
15. Johan Huizinga, *Homo Ludens: A Study of the Play Element in Culture* (London: Temple Smith, 1970), p. 218; the first version of the book was published in Dutch in 1938.
16. Constant closely followed debates around technology, automation and computing, keeping numerous articles on these subjects; a number appear in the 'Automatie' file; Constant archive, RKD.
17. Constant, 'Lecture given at the Institute of Contemporary Arts, London', 7 November 1963, manuscript published in an attachment to the catalogue *Another City for Another Life: Constant's New Babylon* (New York: The Drawing Center, 1999), pp. a9–a13: p. a11. An abridged and edited version of this talk appeared as 'New Babylon/An urbanism of the future', *Architectural Design* 34 (June 1964), pp. 304–5.
18. Constant, 'New Babylon (1961)', p. 178.
19. This was a failing shared with others in the SI when they discussed automation and the abolition of work, and is a symptom of the absence of a feminist politics within the group discussed in Chapter 5. The wider neglect of such issues within 'radical utopian thought' is discussed by Filio Diamanti in 'The treatment of the "woman question" in radical utopian political thought', in Barbara Goodwin (ed.), *The Philosophy of Utopia* (London: Frank Cass, 2001), pp. 116–39.
20. Constant, 'New Babylon (1961)', p. 178.
21. Paul Virilio, *The Lost Dimension* (New York: Semiotext(e), 1991); originally published in French in 1984. Virilio's early work in architecture and urban-

ism was influenced by Constant's New Babylon, which became his route into encountering the situationists.

22. This relates to questions since taken up by Richard Sennett, who explores how urban design might counter the ways in which 'the modern mobile individual has suffered a kind of tactile crisis'; in his *Flesh and Stone: The Body and the City in Western Civilization* (London: Faber and Faber, 1994), p. 256.
23. Constant, cited in Hein van Haaren, *Constant*, trans. Max Schuchart (Amsterdam: J. M. Meulenhoff, 1966), p. 13.
24. See, for example, Gilles Deleuze and Félix Guattari, *A Thousand Plateaus: Capitalism and Schizophrenia*, trans. Brian Massumi (London: Athlone, 1988), esp. pp. 351–423; and Sadie Plant, 'Nomads and revolutionaries', *Journal of the British Society for Phenomenology* 24 (January 1993), pp. 88–101. Tim Cresswell presents a more critical view of the valorisation of the nomad in 'postmodern' theory in his 'Imagining the nomad: mobility and the postmodern primitive', in Georges Benko and Ulf Strohmayer (eds), *Space and Social Theory: Interpreting Modernity and Postmodernity* (Oxford: Blackwell, 1997), pp. 360–79.
25. Constant, 'New Babylon' (1974), p. 158.
26. Constant, 'Over het reizen', lecture to the BNA (Society of Dutch Architects), at opening of new Schipol Airport buildings, April 1966, published in Constant, *Opstand van de Homo Ludens* (Bussum: Paul Brand, 1969), and trans. as 'On traveling', in Mark Wigley (ed.), *Constant's New Babylon: The Hyper-Architecture of Desire* (Rotterdam: Witte de With centre for contemporary art/010 Publishers, 1998), pp. 200–1: p. 201.
27. From the 'Urbanisme teksten' file, Constant archive, RKD.
28. 'Revelation', *King James Bible*, 18: 16, 8.
29. William Morris, 'News from nowhere, or an epoch of rest', in his *News from Nowhere and Other Writings* (Harmondsworth: Penguin, 1993), pp. 41–228: p. 99; the text was first published in 1890.
30. Le Corbusier, *Urbanisme* (Paris: Editions Crès, 1925), trans. Frederick Etchells as *The City of Tomorrow and Its Planning* (London: Architectural Press, 1987), pp. 24, 39.
31. *New Babylon* was one of many classic films from which Debord used détourned materials in making his own film of *The Society of the Spectacle*, in 1973.
32. Transcript of 'Met Simon Vinkenoog naar het New Babylon van Constant', broadcast on VPRO television in the Netherlands on 2 April, 1962, as part of the series 'Atelierbezoek'.
33. Fredric Jameson, 'Of islands and trenches: neutralization and the production

of utopian discourse', in his *The Ideologies of Theory: Essays 1971–1986* (London, Routledge, 1988), pp. 75–101: p. 75.

34. For a discussion of futurology in this period and its relationship to thinking about urban futures, see John R. Gold, 'The city of the future and the future of the city', in Russell King (ed.), *Geographical Futures* (Sheffield: Geographical Association, 1985), pp. 92–101.
35. Herbert Marcuse, *An Essay on Liberation* (Boston: Beacon Press, 1969), pp. 4, 5.
36. Marx writes in a famous passage: 'In fact, the realm of freedom actually begins only when labour which is determined by necessity and mundane considerations ceases; thus in the very nature of things it lies beyond the sphere of actual material production'; *Capital*, vol. 3 (New York: International Publishers, 1967), p. 320.
37. Constant, 'Opkomst en ondergang van de Avant-garde', *Randstad* 8 (1964), pp. 16–35, trans. Dirk Verbiest as 'The rise and decline of the avant-garde', in *Another City for Another Life*, pp. a14–a28: p. a28.
38. Constant, 'Nieuw urbanisme', *Provo* 9 (12 May 1966), pp. 2–6, trans. as *New Urbanism* (New York: Friends of Malatesta, 1970), p. 6.
39. R. van Duyn, 'New Babylon. Gesprek met Constant', *Provo* 4 (28 October 1965).
40. Constant, 'A different city for a different life', p. 95.
41. Constant, *New Urbanism*, p. 5.
42. Constant, 'Unitair urbanisme', manuscript for lecture at the Stedelijk Museum in Amsterdam, on 20 December 1960, trans. Robyn de Jong-Dalziel as 'Unitary urbanism', in Wigley, *Constant's New Babylon*, pp. 131–5: p. 131.
43. Constant, 'Le grand jeu à venir', *Potlatch* 30 (15 July 1959), reprinted in *Potlatch (1954–1957)*, collected edition (Paris: Gallimard, 1996), pp. 289–91, and trans. Gerardo Denís as 'The great game to come', in Andreotti and Costa, *Theory of the Dérive*, pp. 62–3: p. 63.
44. See Ruth Levitas, *The Concept of Utopia* (London: Philip Allan, 1990), pp. 83–105.
45. These connections and others within the fields of architecture and design are discussed by Simon Sadler, *The Situationist City* (Cambridge, MA: MIT Press, 1998), pp. 127–38; and Mark Wigley, 'The hyper-architecture of desire', in Wigley, *Constant's New Babylon*, pp. 8–71.
46. Constant, unpublished manuscript for a lecture given to the Conference for the Students Association at the Royal Academy of Copenhagen, 12 March 1964, in the Constant archive, RKD, no pagination [p. 7].
47. Constant, 'Unitary urbanism', p. 132.

48. Constant, 'New Babylon – na tien jaren', manuscript for lecture at the University of Technology, Delft, Faculty of Architecture, on 23 May 1980, trans. Robyn de Jon-Dalziel as 'New Babylon – ten years on', in Wigley, *Constant's New Babylon*, pp. 232–6: p. 235.
49. 'Le questionnaire', *IS* 9 (August 1964), pp. 24–7, trans. as 'Questionnaire' in Ken Knabb (ed. and trans.), *Situationist International Anthology* (Berkeley: Bureau of Public Secrets, 1981), pp. 138–42: p. 140.
50. Herbert Marcuse, 'The end of utopia', *Five Lectures* (London: Allen Lane, 1970), p. 63. Marcuse's use of the concept of utopia is in fact often ambiguous. As Levitas notes, some of the ambiguities may be deliberate, to highlight the contested nature of utopia and to question notions of the possible and impossible, but shifts and inconsistencies are also apparent in his work; see Levitas, *The Concept of Utopia*, pp. 131–55.
51. Draft of essay in the Constant archive, RKD. Debord's comments were in a letter to Constant, undated (but written beginning of June 1959), published in his *Correspondance*, vol. 1, *Juin 1957– Août 1960* (Paris: Arthème Fayard, 1999), pp. 235–6.
52. This is conveyed by the rendering of the article's title by John Shepley as 'A different city for a different life' (full reference in note 1 in this chapter).
53. Seyla Benhabib, *Critique, Norm and Utopia: A Study of the Foundations of Critical Theory* (New York: Columbia University Press, 1986).
54. Constant, 'C'est notre désir qui fait la révolution', *Cobra* 4 (1949), pp. 3–4, reprinted in *Cobra 1948–1951* (Paris: Éditions Jean-Michel Place, 1980), and trans. as 'Our own desires build the revolution', in Herschel B. Chipp (ed.), *Theories of Modern Art: A Source Book by Artists and Critics* (Berkeley: University of California Press, 1968), pp. 601–3: p. 602.
55. Constant, 'New Babylon, the world of Homo Ludens', p. 1.
56. Constant, manuscript for lecture at the Royal Academy of Copenhagen [p. 7].
57. Jameson, 'Of islands and trenches', p. 95.
58. Constant, 'Autodialogue on New Babylon', *Opus International* 27 (September 1971), pp. 79–80: p. 80. Text originally also published in French in the same issue, pp. 29–31.
59. Constant uses the line in one of his essays to head a section on 'New Babylonian culture', in his 'New Babylon, een schets voor een kultuur', p. 57. The line does not appear in the translation as 'New Babylon' (1974).
60. 'L'urbanisme unitaire à la fin des années 50', *IS* 3 (December 1959), pp. 11–16, trans. Thomas Levin as 'Unitary urbanism at the end of the 1950s', in Elisabeth Sussman (ed.), *On the Passage of a Few People Through a Rather*

Brief Moment in Time: The Situationist International 1957–1972 (Cambridge, MA: MIT Press, 1989), pp. 143–7: p. 144.

61. Constant, 'Manifesto', p. 30.
62. Constant, manuscript for lecture at the Royal Academy of Copenhagen [p. 5].
63. Ibid. [p. 14]. One newspaper report on a lecture by Constant in Birmingham, in February 1968, complained that the slides were 'accompanied by a sound track of music, car and aeroplane engines and an assorted cacophony of other noises so painful to the ear that one could only hope that this was a row we should be escaping from and not going to'; Leslie Duckworth, 'Constant world of Homo ludens', *The Birmingham Post*, 27 February 1968, p. 1.
64. Constant, manuscript for lecture at the Royal Academy of Copenhagen [p. 8].
65. Martin Jay, *Downcast Eyes: The Denigration of Vision in Twentieth-Century French Thought* (Berkeley: University of California Press, 1993), pp. 48–9.
66. Christine Buci-Glucksmann, *Baroque Reason: The Aesthetics of Modernity*, trans. Patrick Camiller (London: Sage, 1994); originally published in French in 1984.
67. Constant, manuscript for lecture at the Royal Academy of Copenhagen [p. 5].
68. Hilde Heynen, *Architecture and Modernity: A Critique* (Cambridge, MA: MIT Press, 1999), p. 174.
69. Ivan Chtcheglov, 'Lettres de loin', *IS* 9 (August 1964), pp. 38–40: p. 38, excerpts apart from last sentence translated as 'Letters from afar', in Knabb, *Anthology*, p. 372, ellipsis in the original.
70. Guy Debord, letter to Ivan Chtcheglov, 30 April 1963, in his *Correspondance*, vol. 2, *Septembre 1960–Décembre 1964* (Paris: Arthème Fayard, 2001), pp. 218–20: p. 219.
71. Constant, 'New Babylon' (1974), p. 155.
72. See Constant, 'The rise and decline of the avant-garde'.
73. Constant, 'Rapport inaugural de la conference de Munich', *IS* 3 (December 1959), pp. 25–7.
74. Ibid. p. 26. See also 'La troisième conférence de l'I.S. à Munich', *IS* 3 (December 1959), pp. 19–22.
75. Resolution by the Dutch section of the SI, March 1959, cited in 'Renseignements situationnistes', *IS* 3 (December 1959), p. 16.
76. 'Die Welt als Labyrinth', *IS* 4 (June 1960), pp. 5–7. Asger Jorn gives a contrasting perspective on the dispute with Sandberg, in a previously unpublished document from the Silkeborg Kunstmuseum, trans. Peter Shield as 'The anti-situation of Amsterdam', *Transgressions* 5 (2001), pp. 15–19.

77. Guy Debord and Gil J. Wolman, 'Mode d'emploi du détournement', *Les lèvres nues* 8 (May 1956), reprinted in Berreby, *Documents*, pp. 302–9, and trans. as 'Methods of detournement', in Knabb, *Anthology*, pp. 8–14: p. 13.
78. Constant, manuscript for lecture at the Royal Academy of Copenhagen [p. 10].
79. Constant, 'Description de la zone jaune', *IS* 4 (June 1960), pp. 23–6, trans. Paul Hammond as 'Description of the yellow zone', in Andreotti and Costa, *Theory of the Dérive*, pp. 102–5.
80. No more instalments of *Promenades in New Babylon* appeared.
81. Constant, 'New Babylon – ten years on', p. 232.
82. Wigley, 'The hyper-architecture of desire', p. 51.
83. Constant, 'New Babylon- ten years on', p. 236.
84. Constant, 'Autodialogue on New Babylon', p. 80.
85. Simon Vinkenoog, 'Preamble to a new world', in Constant, *New Babylon*, a series of ten lithographs with accompanying text (Amsterdam: Galerie d'Eendt, 1963), p. 5.
86. Ibid. p. 5.
87. Kristin Ross, *The Emergence of Social Space: Rimbaud and the Paris Commune* (London: Macmillan, 1988), pp. 102, 120–1.
88. Constant, letter to Sean Wellesley-Miller, 8 August 1966; Constant archive, RKD.
89. 'Manifeste', 17 May 1960, published in *IS* 4 (June 1960), pp. 36–8, trans. as 'Manifesto', in Conrads, *Programs and Manifestoes*, pp. 172–4: p. 172.
90. Pinot Gallizio, 'Discours sur la peinture industrielle et sur un art unitaire applicable', *IS* 3 (December 1959), pp. 31–5: p. 32.
91. Henri Lefebvre, *Le temps des méprises* (Paris: Stock, 1975), pp. 156–7: p. 157.
92. Henri Lefebvre, *Introduction to Modernity*, trans. John Moore (London: Verso, 1995), p. 346; originally published in French in 1962.
93. Ibid. pp. 345–6.
94. Ibid. p. 348.
95. Henri Lefebvre, *The Survival of Capitalism: Reproduction of the Relations of Production*, trans. Frank Bryant (London: Allison and Busby, 1976), p. 104; originally published in French in 1973.
96. See Henri Lefebvre, 'Right to the city', in his *Writings on Cities*, ed. and trans. Eleonore Kofman and Elizabeth Lebas (Oxford: Blackwell, 1996), pp. 61–181; originally published in French as a book in 1968.
97. Ibid. pp. 172–3.
98. Guy Debord, *Rapport sur la construction des situations et sur les conditions de l'organisation et de l'action de la tendance situationniste internationale* (Paris:

n.p., 1957), reprinted in Berreby, *Documents*, pp. 607–19, excerpts trans. as 'Report on the construction of situations and on the International Situationist tendency's conditions of organization and action', in Knabb, *Anthology*, pp. 17–25: p. 23.

99. Ibid. p. 25.
100. 'Reneignements situationnistes', *IS* 4 (June 1960), p. 13.
101. Constant and the other members of the Bureau of Research for Unitary Urbanism played a leading role in guest editing this issue as part of the Liga Nieuw Beelden; the theme was 'Integration', *Forum* 14.6 (August 1959).
102. The exclusion of Alberts and Oudejans was reported in *IS* 4 (June 1960), p. 13. See Wigley, 'The hyper-architecture of desire', pp. 31–6, who traces the events through a careful reading of correspondence, mainly from Debord to Constant; Debord's letters have since been published in his *Correspondance*, vol. 1. On this matter see especially the letters on pp. 270–3, 273–5, 285–6, 308–9.
103. Debord, letter to Constant, 30 March 1960, in his *Correspondance*, vol. 1, pp. 325–6: p. 325; as cited in Wigley, 'The hyper-architecture of desire', p. 36, although he mistakenly gives the date as 30 May.
104. Constant's resignation was reported in *IS* 5 (December 1960), p. 10. The report also notes the exclusion of Pinot Gallizio and Giors Melanotte in June of that year.
105. Constant, 'A conversation with Constant', pp. 23, 24. His correspondence with Debord continued into August 1960. Constant recalls that Michèle Bernstein continued to send him situationist publications after his resignation, but he did not meet with Debord. He painted a watercolour portrait of Debord in 1989 that reveals a harder side to his former colleague.
106. Attila Kotányi and Raoul Vaneigem, 'Programme élémentaire du bureau d'urbanisme unitaire', *IS* 6 (August 1961) pp. 16–19, trans. as 'Elementary program of the bureau of unitary urbanism', in Knabb, *Anthology*, pp. 65–7: p. 65.
107. 'Critique de l'urbanisme', *IS* 6 (August 1961), pp. 3–11, trans. Paul Hammond as 'Critique of urbanism', in Andreotti and Costa, *Theory of the Dérive*, pp. 109–14: p. 109.
108. Ibid. p. 110. Lefebvre's essay was published as 'Utopie expérimentale: pour un nouvel urbanisme', *Revue française de sociologie* 2.3 (July-September 1961), pp. 191–8.
109. 'Lefebvre on the situationists: an interview', with Kristin Ross, in McDonough, *Guy Debord*, pp. 267–83: pp. 276–7; interview conducted in 1983.

110. Ibid. pp. 66, 67.
111. J. V. Martin, J. Strijbosch, R. Vaneigem and R. Viénet, 'Réponse à une enquête du centre d'art socio-expérimental', dated 6 December 1963, published in *IS* 9 (August 1964), pp. 40–4, and trans. as 'Response to a questionnaire from the center for socio-experimental art', in Knabb, *Anthology*, pp. 143–7: p. 146.
112. Asger Jorn, in Jorn, Glob, Gjessing, de Bouard, Réau, *Signes gravés sur les églises de l'Eure et du Calvados* (Copenhagen: Borgen, 1963), pp. 290, 291, cited in Peter Shield, *Comparative Vandalism: Asger Jorn and the Artistic Attitude to Life* (Aldershot: Ashgate, with Borgens, 1998), p. 7.
113. See, for example, the discussion in 'Instructions pour une prise d'armes', *IS* 6 (August 1961), pp. 3–5, trans. as 'Instructions for taking up arms', in Knabb, *Anthology*, pp. 63–5.
114. T. J. Clarke and Donald Nicholson-Smith, 'Why art can't kill the Situationist International', in McDonough, *Guy Debord*, pp. 467–88.
115. Guy Debord, *Preface à la quatrième édition italienne de 'La Société du Spectacle'* (Paris: Champ Libre, 1979), trans. Michel Prigent and Lucy Forsyth as *Preface to the Fourth Italian Edition of 'The Society of the Spectacle'* (London: Chronos, second edition 1983), p. 10.
116. 'Guy Debord's report to the seventh SI Conference in Paris [excerpts]', July 1966, trans. John McHale, in Situationist International, *The Real Split in the International* (London: Pluto, 2003), pp. 130–41: pp. 138–9.
117. 'Problèmes preliminaires à la construction d'une situation', *IS* 1 (June 1958), pp. 11–13, trans. as 'Preliminary problems in constructing a situation', in Knabb, *Anthology*, pp. 43–5: p. 44.
118. The SI argued that Chtcheglov's proposals were based on modern industrial production and so '[i]f they are chimerical it is to the extent that, concretely, we do not have at our disposal the technical means of today (or put another way, to the extent that no form of social organization is yet capable of making "artistic" experimental use of these means); not because these means do not exist or that we are unaware of them'; in 'Sur nos moyens et nos perspectives', *IS* 2 (December 1958), pp. 23–6, trans. Paul Hammond as 'On our means and our perspectives', in Andreotti and Costa, *Theory of the Dérive*, pp. 77–9: p. 78.
119. 'Les mauvais jours finiront', *IS* 7 (April 1962), pp. 10–17, trans. as 'The bad days will end', in Knabb, *Anthology*, pp. 82–7: p. 87.
120. 'Geopolitique de l'hibernation', *IS* 7 (April 1962), pp. 3–10, trans. as 'Geopolitics of hibernation', in Knabb, *Anthology*, pp. 76–82: pp. 81, 82.
121. 'Socialisme ou Planète', *IS* 10 (March 1966), pp. 77–9: p. 77. This is cited

again in 'Le commencement d'une époque', *IS* 12 (September 1969), pp. 3–34, trans. as 'The beginning of an era', in Knabb, *Anthology*, pp. 225–56: p. 227.

122. Henri Lefebvre, *The Explosion: Marxism and the French Revolution*, trans. Alfred Ehrenfeld (New York and London: Monthly Review Press, 1969), p. 118; originally published in French in 1968.
123. Ibid. pp. 119, 118.
124. Ibid. pp. 117–18.
125. 'The beginning of an era', p. 226.
126. As photographed in *IS* 12 (September 1969), p. 14.
127. René Viénet, *Enragés et situationnistes dans le mouvement des occupations* (Paris: Gallimard, 1968), trans. as *Enragés and Situationists in the Occupation Movement, France, May '68* (New York and London: Autonomedia and Rebel Press, 1992), pp. 77, 78–80.
128. Ibid. p. 82.
129. Michael Watts, '1968 and all that . . .', *Progress in Human Geography* 25 (2001), pp. 157–88; see also Kristin Ross, *May '68 and its Afterlives* (Chicago: University of Chicago Press, 2002).

Chapter 8: Partisans of possibilities

1. Henri Lefebvre, *Everyday Life in the Modern World*, trans. Sacha Rabinovitch (New Brunswick, NJ: Transaction Publishers, 1984), p. 192; originally published in French in 1968.
2. Susan Buck-Morss, 'The city as dreamworld and catastrophe', *October* 73 (1995), pp. 3–26: p. 26.
3. Guy Debord, *In girum imus nocte et consumimur igni*, 1978, text published in his *Oeuvres cinématographiques complètes, 1952–1978* (Paris: Champ Libre, 1978), pp. 187–278, and trans. as 'In girum imus nocte et consumimur igni', in his *Complete Cinematic Works: Scripts, Stills, Documents*, ed. and trans. Ken Knabb (Edinburgh: AK Press, 2003), pp. 133–205: p. 177. He is alluding here to May 1968.
4. Ibid. p. 190.
5. Ibid. p. 153.
6. Ibid. pp. 177, 169.
7. Ibid. p. 171. Debord earlier proposed making a film about Chtcheglov entitled *Portrait d'Ivan Chtcheglov*, as advertised on the back of his book *Contre le cinéma* (Aarhus, Denmark: Institut Scandinave de Vandalisme Comparé, 1964).

8. Cited in ibid. p. 192.
9. Guy Debord, *Preface à la quatrième édition italienne de 'La Société du Spectacle'* (Paris: Champ Libre, 1979), trans. Michel Prigent and Lucy Forsyth as *Preface to the Fourth Italian Edition of 'The Society of the Spectacle'* (London: Chronos, second edition 1983), p. 23.
10. Guy Debord, *La société du spectacle* (Paris: Buchet-Chastel, 1967), trans. Donald Nicholson-Smith as *The Society of the Spectacle* (New York: Zone Books, 1994), thesis 178.
11. Guy Debord, *Commentaires sur la société du spectacle* (Paris: Gérard Lebovici, 1988), trans. Malcolm Imrie as *Comments on the Society of the Spectacle* (London: Verso, 1990).
12. M. Christine Boyer, *The City of Collective Memory: Its Historical Imagery and Architectural Entertainments* (Cambridge, MA: MIT Press, 1994), p. 474.
13. David Harvey, 'Cities of dreams', *Guardian*, 15 October 1993, pp. 18–19: p. 18.
14. Francis Fukuyama, *The End of History and the Last Man* (London: Hamish Hamilton), p. 46.
15. Concerns about pollution and the global environment feature in a number of Debord's later works, though, including Guy Debord and Gianfranco Sanguinetti, *La Véritable scission dans l'Internationale* (Paris: Champ Libre, 1972), trans. John McHale as 'Theses on the Situationist International and its time', in *The Real Split in the International* (London: Pluto, 2003), pp. 6–80: p. 24; and his final film made in collaboration with Brigitte Cornand for Canal Plus, entitled *Guy Debord, son art et son temps* (1994).
16. The latter phrase is taken from Leonie Sandercock, *Cosmospolis II: Mongrel Cities in the 21st Century* (London: Continuum, 2003).
17. A critical point raised by one of the anonymous readers of this manuscript that would be worth exploring further.
18. *IS* 12 (September 1969), p. 103.
19. The marketing brochure by Crosby Homes was designed to mimic a 12-inch record sleeve, with a final line playing on Chtcheglov's words: 'You can see the Haçienda . . . it does exist.' The development was widely criticised in Manchester by former fans of the nightclub; as reported by David Ward, 'Hacienda fans rave at plan for luxury flats', *Guardian*, 29 August, 2002. The Haçienda club was opened in 1982 by Anthony Wilson and Rob Gretton, from Factory Records, with Gretton choosing the name from Chtcheglov's text. Wilson used to give his employees a copy of Christopher Gray's translation of situationist writings, *Leaving the Twentieth Century: The Incomplete Work of the Situationist International* (London: Free Fall Publications, 1974);

see Wilson's comments in the discussion with Mark E. Smith, Jon King and Stewart Home, 'Situationist fallout: punk rock, new wave and the end of the world', in Andrew Hussey and Gavin Bowd (eds), *The Haçienda Must Be Built: On the Legacy of Situationist Revolt* (Universities of Manchester and Huddersfield: AURA, 1996), no pagination.

20. On the need for any 'revival' of the situationists to be critical, see also Rosalyn Deutsche, 'Breaking and entering: drawing, situationism, activism', in Catherine de Zegher and Mark Wigley (eds), *The Activist Drawing: Retracing Situationist Architectures from Constant's New Babylon to Beyond* (New York: The Drawing Center and Cambridge, MA: MIT Press, 2001), pp. 75–81.
21. Here I am in agreement with Alastair Bonnett, when he argues that the group's most significant contemporary legacy lies in the struggle to transform everyday spaces and life; in his 'The situationist legacy', *Variant* (1991), pp. 29–33.
22. Henri Lefebvre, *The Survival of Capitalism: Reproduction of the Relations of Production*, trans. Frank Bryant (London: Allison and Busby, 1976), p. 36; originally published in 1973.
23. Michael Gardiner, 'Utopia and everyday life in French social thought', *Utopian Studies* 6.2 (1995), pp. 90–123: p. 116.
24. Ibid. p. 116.
25. Lefebvre's lines were quoted in 'Le commencement d'une epoque', *IS* 12 (September 1969), pp. 3–34, trans. as 'The beginning of an era', in Ken Knabb (ed. and trans.), *Situationist International Anthology* (Berkeley: Bureau of Public Secrets, 1981), pp. 225–56: pp. 227–8. They come from Henri Lefebvre, *Position: Contre les technocrates en finir avec l'humanité-fiction* (Paris: Gonthier, 1967).
26. 'The beginning of an era', p. 227.
27. Sandercock, *Cosmopolis II*; see also Sandercock (ed.), *Making the Invisible Visible: A Multicultural Planning History* (Berkeley: University of California Press, 1998). She derives the concept of insurgent planning in part from Holston's concept of 'insurgent citizenship', in his essay in the same volume entitled 'Spaces of insurgent citizenship', pp. 37–56.
28. Kevin Robins, 'Collective emotion and urban culture', in Patsy Healey, Stuart Cameron, Simin Davoudi, Stephen Graham, and Ali Madani-Pour (eds), *Managing Cities: The New Urban Context* (Chichester: Wiley, 1995), pp. 45–61: pp. 50, 51.
29. James Holston, 'Spaces of insurgent citizenship', in Sandercock, *Making the Invisible Visible*, pp. 37–56: p. 46. For an earlier important critique of the con-

tinuing malign influence of aspects of modern and rationalist urbanism, see also M. Christine Boyer, *Dreaming the Rational City* (Cambridge, MA: MIT Press, 1983).

30. Sandercock, *Cosmopolis II*, p. 2.
31. Peter Wollen, *Raiding the Icebox: Reflections on Twentieth-Century Culture* (London: Verso, 1993), pp. 205–6. In his view, postmodernism in the arts can be seen 'as a belated surfacing of subordinate aspects of modernism that had always been there. They had simply been written out of the orthodox version'; p. 206.
32. Evan McKenzie, *Privatopia: Homeowner Associations and the Rise of Residential Private Government* (New Haven and London: Yale University Press, 1994), p. 12.
33. Ibid. p. 177.
34. Michael Sorkin, 'See you in Disneyland', in Sorkin (ed.), *Variations on a Themepark: The New American City and the End of Public Space* (New York: The Noonday Press, 1992), pp. 205–32. The quotation is from his 'Introduction', pp. xi-xv: p. xv. For an account of the 'utopic degeneration' of Disneyland, see Louis Marin, *Utopics: The Semiological Play of Textual Spaces*, trans. Robert A. Vollrath (Atlantic Highlands, NJ: Humanities Press, 1984), pp. 239–57.
35. Buck-Morss, 'The city as dreamworld and catastophe', p. 26.
36. I have in mind the example of Buck-Morss's reading of the socialist dream-world of the Soviet Union, where she discusses how the gap between utopian promise and dystopian actuality can enable collective awakening. But she also argues that a political awakening further 'requires the "rescue" of the collective desires to which the socialist dream gave expression before they sink into the unconscious as forgotten'; ibid. p. 23. See also her remarkable book *Dreamworld and Catastrophe: The Passing of Mass Utopia in East and West* (Cambridge, MA: MIT Press, 2000).
37. Manfredo Tafuri, *Architecture and Utopia: Design and Capitalist Development*, trans. Barbara Luigia La Penta (Cambridge, MA: MIT Press, 1976), pp. 50, 52; originally published in Italian in 1973. I refer to Tafuri's 'thesis' since he makes clear that his argument is a 'only a prologue' and a 'framework for a hypothesis', inviting further development and argument; p. xi. A wider reading of his work would provide different perspectives.
38. Ibid. pp. 55–6, 84–9.
39. T. J. Clark, *Farewell to an Idea: Episodes from a History of Modernism* (New Haven and London: Yale University Press, 1999), p. 306. While Clark notes that this 'nightmare' has become commonplace, he imagines it particularly

through the voices of Tafuri and Michel Foucault, with 'the sardonic glumness of one alternating with the other's grim exaltation'. I have not considered Foucault in these last pages but his critiques of projects of liberation and ideas of an 'authentic' self have been another important source contributing to criticisms of utopian thought in recent years, and specifically to critiques of the kind of dialectical approach advocated by the situationists.

40. Tafuri, *Architecture and Utopia*, p. 96.
41. Ibid. p. 60.
42. Ibid. p. 93.
43. Ibid. p. 179.
44. David Cunningham, 'Architecture, Utopia and the futures of the avant-garde', *The Journal of Architecture* 6 (2001), pp. 169–82: p. 173.
45. 'Maintenant, l'I.S', *IS* 9 (August 1964), pp. 3–5, trans. as 'Now, the SI', in Knabb, *Anthology*, pp. 135–8.
46. Tom McDonough, 'Introduction', in McDonough (ed.), *Guy Debord and the Situationist International: Texts and Documents* (Cambridge, MA: MIT Press, 2002), pp. ix-xx: p. xiv. The quotation from Debord is from his *Rapport sur la construction des situations et sur les conditions de l'organisation et de l'action de la tendance situationniste internationale* (Paris: n.p., 1957), reprinted in Gérard Berreby (ed.), *Documents relatifs à la fondation l'Internationale situationniste, 1948–1957* (Paris: Éditions Allia, 1985), pp. 607–19, as trans. and cited by McDonough, 'Introduction', p. xv.
47. Bruno Fortier, 'L'animal situationniste', *Architecture d'Aujourd'hui* 312 (September 1997), p. 24, cited in Tom McDonough, 'Fluid spaces: Constant and the situationist critique of architecture', in de Zegher and Wigley, *The Activist Drawing*, pp. 93–104: p. 99.
48. Simon Sadler, *The Situationist City* (Cambridge, MA: MIT Press, 1998), p. 49.
49. McDonough, 'Introduction', p. xv.
50. 'Définitions', *IS* 1 (June 1958), pp. 13–14, trans. 'Definitions', in Knabb, *Anthology*, pp. 45–6.
51. Anthony Vidler, *The Architectural Uncanny: Essays in the Modern Unhomely* (Cambridge, MA: MIT Press, 1992), p. 213.
52. On this critique generally, see Reyner Banham, *Megastructure: Urban Futures of the Recent Past* (London: Thames and Hudson, 1976), p. 83.
53. On this context, see Richard Sennett, 'Cities without care or connection', *New Statesman*, 5 June 2000. He takes the term 'skin architecture' from the critic Ada Louise Huxtable.
54. McDonough, 'Fluid spaces', p. 102.

55. Anthony Vidler, 'Disenchanted history/negative theories: Tafuri's architectural dream book', paper circulated at the conference on 'Marx, architecture and modernity', University of Westminster, London, 28 May 2004.
56. Lefebvre, *The Survival of Capitalism*, p. 61. For further critical remarks on Tafuri's conception of a total system, see David Cunningham, 'Architecture in the age of global modernity: Tafuri, Jameson and enclave theory', in Esther Leslie and John Roberts et al. (eds), *Marxism and the Visual Arts Now* (London: Brill Press, forthcoming).
57. My argument connects here with Cunningham's interest in lessening the 'depressive impasse' associated with Tafuri. For Cunningham this centres on rethinking the temporal structure of the avant-garde and exploring possible differences with the avant-gardes in terms of their orientations to the future; 'Architecture, Utopia and the futures of the avant-garde'.
58. Rosalyn Deutsche, 'Boys town', in her *Evictions: Art and Spatial Politics* (Cambridge, MA: MIT Press, 1996), pp. 203–44.
59. Guy Debord and Asger Jorn, *Mémoires* (Paris: Jean-Jacques Pauvert aux Belles Lettres, 1993), no pagination; originally published in 1959.
60. Terry Eagleton, 'Utopia and its opposites', in Leon Panitch and Colin Leys (eds), 'Necessary and unnecessary utopias', *Socialist Register 2000* (Woodbridge: Merlin Press, 1999), pp. 31–40: p. 31.
61. Seyla Benhabib, *Critique, Norm and Utopia: A Study of the Foundations of Critical Theory* (New York: Columbia University Press, 1986), pp. 13, 41–2.
62. Hilde Heynen, *Architecture and Modernity: A Critique* (Cambridge, MA: MIT Press, 1999), p. 169.
63. Ibid. pp. 152, 174–5.
64. Theodor Adorno, *Aesthetic Theory*, trans. Robert Hullot-Kentor (Minneapolis: University of Minnesota Press, 1997), p. 32, cited in Heynen, *Architecture and Modernity*, p. 175. Adorno's book was first published in German in 1970.
65. Constant, 'Autodialogue on New Babylon', *Opus International* 27 (September 1971), pp. 79–80: p. 79. He later commented: 'For over half a century now, the world has been haunted by the spirit of dada. Seen from this perspective, New Babylon might perhaps be called a response to anti-art'; in his 'New Babylon – na tien jaren', lecture at the University of Technology, Delft, Faculty of Architecture, on 23 May 1980, trans. Robyn de Jon-Dalziel as 'New Babylon – ten years on', in Mark Wigley (ed.), *Constant's New Babylon: The Hyper-Architecture of Desire* (Rotterdam: Witte de With center for contemporary art/010 Publishers, 1998), pp. 232–6: p. 236.
66. Constant, 'New Babylon – ten years on', p. 236. The translation mistakenly

adds the word 'Freud's' to the eleventh thesis when of course it is Marx's; I have substituted the word 'the', following the Dutch version at http://www.vpro.nl/data/laat/010-map/materiaal-constant.shtml.

67. Ibid. p. 236.
68. Bartomeu Marí, 'Foreword', *From* 1 (September 1999), pp. 4–7: 6. This was in relation to the exhibition of New Babylon at the Witte de With center for contemporary art, Rotterdam, in 1998–9.
69. B. van Garrel and Rem Koolhaas, 'De stad van de toekomst. HP-gesprek met Constant over New Babylon', *Haagse Post* (6 August 1966), pp. 14–15. For some of these connections, see Sadler, *The Situationist City*; and Mark Wigley, 'The hyper-architecture of desire', in his *Constant's New Babylon*, pp. 8–71.
70. See, for example, James Donald, *Imagining the Modern City* (London: Athlone, 1999); Loretta Lees (ed.), *The Emancipatory City? Paradoxes and Possibilities* (London: Sage, 2004); and Steve Pile, *Real Cities: Modernity, Space and the Phantasmagorias of City Life* (London: Sage, 2005).
71. Iain Borden, Joe Kerr, Jane Rendell and Alicia Pivaro, 'Things, flows, filters, tactics', in their edited book *The Unknown City: Contesting Architecture and Social Space* (Cambridge, MA: MIT Press, 2001), pp. 1–27: p. 20.
72. Iris Marion Young, *Justice and the Politics of Difference* (Princeton, NJ: Princeton University Press, 1990), pp. 6, 256.
73. David Harvey, 'The right to the city', in Lees, *The Emancipatory City?*, pp. 236–9: p. 237. Harvey's turn to an explicit utopianism since the 1990s is interesting given his scant references to it in his earlier work. While Harvey had previously been committed to what he called the 'urbanisation of revolution', his own critique of capitalist urbanisation rarely led to explorations of other possible spaces and times. As Derek Gregory commented, 'Harvey offers fewer glimpses of a possible future than Lefebvre; by and large, his work fastens on an explanatory-diagnostic moment and rarely broaches the anticipatory-utopian moment that animates Lefebvre's project'; in his *Geographical Imaginations* (Oxford: Blackwell, 1994), p. 361.
74. David Harvey, *Spaces of Hope* (Edinburgh: Edinburgh University Press, 2000), p. 196.
75. Ibid. pp. 189, 183.
76. Cf. ibid. pp. 248–52; and Harvey, 'The right to the city'. Compare also with Don Mitchell, *The Right to the City: Social Justice and the Fight for Public Space* (New York: Guilford Press, 2003).
77. Harvey, *Spaces of Hope*, p. 183.
78. Ibid. p. 238. Harvey stresses that it is the *figure* of the architect with which he is concerned rather than the professional person; p. 200.

79. Ibid. p. 254.
80. Angelika Bammer, *Partial Visions: Feminism and Utopianism in the 1970s* (London: Routledge, 1991), p. 7. See also, for example, Lucy Sargisson, *Contemporary Feminist Utopianism* (London: Routledge, 1996).
81. Leonie Sandercock, *Towards Cosmopolis: Planning for Multicultural Cities* (London: Wiley, 1998), p. 8. See also the reworking of her positions in the extensively revised version of this book, *Cosmopolis II*, which emphasises her desire to '*practice utopia*, a city politics of possibility and of hope'; p. 2.

Select bibliography

Full references to all sources are given in the notes. The bibiliography therefore provides only a selection of references used, focusing mainly on primary sources with a number of additional materials. Texts contained within edited collections listed below are not referenced separately. Where texts have been translated into English, the translation only is given here with the date of original publication provided in square brackets.

Andersen, Troels, Birtwistle, Graham and Gachnang, Johannes 1994, *Asger Jorn 1914/1973*, Amsterdam: Stedelijk Museum.

Andreotti, Libero and Costa, Xavier (eds) 1996, *Theory of the Dérive and Other Situationist Writings on the City*, Barcelona: Museu d'Art Contemporani de Barcelona/Actar.

Andreotti, Libero and Costa, Xavier (eds) 1996, *Situacionistas: arte, política, urbanismo/Situationists: Art, Politics, Urbanism*, Barcelona: Museu d'Art Contemporani de Barcelona/Actar.

Apollonio, Umbro (ed.) 1973, *Futurist Manifestos*, London: Thames and Hudson.

Bacon, Mardge 2001, *Le Corbusier in America: Travels in the Land of the Timid*, Cambridge, MA: MIT Press.

Bandini, Mirella, 1977, *L'estetico il politico: da Cobra all'Internazionale Situazionista, 1948–1957*, Rome: Officina Edizioni.

Bataille, Georges 1985, *Visions of Excess: Selected Writings, 1927–1939*, ed. Allan Stoekl, trans. Allan Stoekl with Carl R. Lovitt and Donald M. Leslie, Jr., Minneapolis: University of Minnesota Press.

Bauman, Zygmunt 1991, *Modernity and Ambivalence*, Cambridge: Polity Press.

Beevers, Robert 1988, *The Garden City Utopia: A Critical Biography of Ebenezer Howard*, Basingstoke: Macmillan.

Bellamy, Edward 1888, *Looking Backward: 2000–1887*, Boston: Ticknor and Co.

Berman, Marshall 1983, *All That is Solid Melts into Air: The Experience of Modernity*, London: Verso.

Bernstein, Michèle and Jorn, Asger 1960, *Pinot Gallizio*, Paris: Bibliothèque d'Alexandrie.

Berreby, Gérard (ed.) 1985, *Documents relatifs à la fondation de l'Internationale situationniste: 1948–1957*, Paris: Éditions Allia.

Birtwistle, Graham 1986, *Living Art: Asger Jorn's Comprehensive Theory of Art Between Helhesten and Cobra (1946–1949)*, Utrecht: Reflex.

Bois, Yve-Alain and Krauss, Rosalind E. 1997, *Formless: A User's Guide*, New York: Zone Books.

Bonnett, Alastair 1991, 'The situationist legacy', *Variant* 9, 29–33.

Bonnett, Alastair 1992, 'Art, ideology and everyday space: subversive tendencies from Dada to postmodernism', *Environment and Planning D: Society and Space* 10, 69–86.

Bonnett, Alastair 1996, 'The transgressive geographies of daily life: socialist pathways within everyday urban spatial creativity', *Transgressions* 2/3, 20–37.

Borden, Iain, Kerr, Joe, Rendell, Jane and Pivaro, Alicia (eds) 2001, *The Unknown City: Contesting Architecture and Social Space*, Cambridge, MA: MIT Press.

Breton, André 1932, 'Surrealism yesterday, today, tomorrow', trans. Edward W. Titis, *This Quarter* II, 1 (September).

Breton, André 1960 [1928], *Nadja*, trans. Richard Howard, New York: Grove Press.

Breton, André 1972, *Manifestoes of Surrealism*, trans. Richard Seaver and Helen R. Lane, Ann Arbor: University of Michigan Press.

Breton, André 1978, *What is Surrealism? Selected Writings*, ed. Franklin Rosemont, New York: Pathfinder.

Breton, André 1990 [1932], *Communicating Vessels*, trans. Mary Ann Caws and Geoffrey T. Harris, Lincoln and London: University of Nebraska Press.

Breton, André 1993 [1952], *Conversations: The Autobiography of Surrealism*, trans. Mark Polizzotti, New York: Paragon House.

Brotchie, Alastair (ed.) 1995, *Encyclopaedia Acephalica*, London: Atlas Press.

Brunius, Jacques 1936, 'Palais idéal', trans. J. M. Richards, *The Architectural Review* 80 (October 1936), 147–50.

Buck-Morss, Susan 1995, 'The city as dreamworld and catastrophe', *October* 73, 3–26.

Buck-Morss, Susan 2000, *Dreamworld and Catastrophe: The Passing of Mass Utopia in East and West*, Cambridge, MA: MIT Press.

Bürger, Peter 1984, *Theory of the Avant-Garde*, trans. Michael Shaw, Minneapolis: University of Minnesota Press.

Burwell, Jennifer 1997, *Notes on Nowhere: Feminism, Utopian Logic, and Social Transformation*, Minneapolis: University of Minnesota Press.

Cardinal, Roger and Short, Robert 1970, *Surrealism: Permanent Revelation*, London: Studio Vista.

Certeau, Michel de 1984 [1974], *The Practice of Everyday Life*, trans. Steven Randall, Berkeley: University of California Press.

Clark, T. J. 1999, *Farewell to an Idea: Episodes from a History of Modernism*, New Haven and London: Yale University Press.

Cobra 1948–1951 1980, complete facsimile edition, Paris: Éditions Jean-Michel Place.

Cohen, Margaret 1993, *Profane Illumination: Walter Benjamin and the Paris of Surrealist Revolution*, Berkeley: University of California Press.

Conrads, Ulrich (ed.) 1971, *Programmes and Manifestoes on 20th-Century Architecture*, Cambridge, MA: MIT Press.

Constant 1959, *Constant*, Paris: Bibliothèque d'Alexandrie.

Constant 1961, *Constant.Amsterdam*, Bochum: Städtische Kunstgalerie.

Constant 1963, *New Babylon*, ten lithographs with an accompanying text by Simon Vinkenoog entitled 'Preamble to a new world', Amsterdam: Galerie d'Eendt.

Constant 1964, 'New Babylon/An urbanism of the future', *Architectural Design* 34, 304–5.

Constant 1965–6, *De New Babylon Informatief* 1–4.

Constant 1968 [1949], 'Our own desires build the revolution', in Herschel B. Chipp (ed.), *Theories of Modern Art: A Source Book by Artists and Critics*, Berkeley: University of California Press, pp. 601–3.

Constant 1968, 'About the meaning of construction', in Anthony Hill (ed.), *DATA: Directions in Art, Theory and Aesthetics. An Anthology*, London: Faber and Faber, pp. 175–9.

Constant 1970 [1966], *New Urbanism*, New York: Friends of Malatesta.

Constant 1970, *Constant, Schilderijen 1940–1980*, The Hague: Haags Gemeentemuseum.

Constant 1971, 'Autodialogue on New Babylon, *Opus International* 27 (September), 79–80.

Constant 1978, *Constant: Schilderijen 1969–77*, Amsterdam: Stedelijk Museum.

Constant Nieuwenhuys 1988 [1949], 'Manifesto', trans. Leonard Bright, in Willemijn Stokvis, *Cobra: An International Movement in Art After the Second World War*, New York: Rizzoli, pp. 29–31.

Constant 1999, 'The decomposition of the artist: five texts by Constant', attachment to *Another City for Another Life: Constant's New Babylon*, New York: The Drawing Center.

Constant and van Eyck, Aldo 1953, *Voor een Spatiaal Colorisme*, Amsterdam: Galerie Espace.

Cunningham, David 2001, 'Architecture, Utopia and the futures of the avant-garde', *The Journal of Architecture* 6, 169–82

Dalí, Salvador 1932 [1930], 'The stinking ass', trans. J. Bronowski, *This Quarter* 5.1 (September).

Dalí, Salvador 1958, *The Secret Life of Salvador Dalí*, trans. Haakon M. Chevalier, London: Vision Press.

Dalí, Salvador 1978 [1933], 'Art Nouveau architecture's terrifying and edible beauty', *Architectural Design* 48, 2–3, 139–40.

Debord, Guy 1957, *Rapport sur la construction des situations et sur les conditions de l'organisation et de l'action de la tendance situationniste international*, Paris: n.p.

Debord, Guy 1964, *Contre le cinéma*, Aarhus, Denmark: Institut Scandinave de Vandalisme Comparé.

Debord, Guy 1983 [1979], *Preface to the Fourth Italian Edition of 'The Society of the Spectacle'*, trans. Michel Prigent and Lucy Forsyth, London: Chronos, second edition.

Debord, Guy 1989 [1974], 'On wild architecture', trans. Thomas Y. Levin, in Elisabeth Sussman (ed.), *On the Passage of a few People Through a Rather Brief Moment in Time: The Situationist International 1957–1972*, Cambridge, MA: MIT Press, pp. 174–5.

Debord, Guy 1990 [1988], *Comments on the Society of the Spectacle*, trans. Malcolm Imrie, London: Verso.

Debord, Guy 1994 [1967], *The Society of the Spectacle*, trans. Donald Nicholson-Smith, New York: Zone Books.

Debord, Guy 1999, *Correspondance*, vol. 1, *Juin 1957–Août 1960*, Paris: Arthème Fayard.

Debord, Guy 2001, *Correspondance*, vol. 2, *Septembre 1960–Décembre 1964*, Paris: Arthème Fayard.

Debord, Guy 2003 [1978], *Complete Cinematic Works: Scripts, Stills, Documents*, ed. and trans. Ken Knabb, Edinburgh: AK Press.

Debord, Guy and Jorn, Asger 1959, *Mémoires*, Copenhagen: Permild and Rosengreen; facsimile reprint Paris: Jean-Jacques Pauvert aux Belles Lettres, 1993.

English section of the Situationist International (Tim Clark, Christopher Gray, Charles Radcliffe and Donald Nicholson-Smith) 1994, *The Revolution of Modern Art and the Modern Art of Revolution*, London: Chronos.

Fishman, Robert 1977, 'From the Radiant City to Vichy: Le Corbusier's plans and politics, 1928–1942', in Russell Walden (ed.), *The Open Hand: Essays on Le Corbusier*, Cambridge, MA: MIT Press.

Fishman, Robert 1982, *Urban Utopias in the Twentieth Century: Ebenezer Howard, Frank Lloyd Wright and Le Corbusier*, Cambridge, MA: MIT Press.

Fishman, Robert 1984, 'Utopia in three dimensions: the ideal city and the origins of modern design', in Peter Alexander and Roger Gill (eds), *Utopias*, London: Duckworth, pp. 95–107.

Ford, Simon 1995, *The Realization and Suppression of the Situationist International: An Annotated Bibliography 1972–1992*, Edinburgh: AK Press.

Gregory, Derek 1993, 'Bloody theory', *Environment and Planning D: Society and Space* 11, 253–4.

Gregory, Derek 1994, *Geographical Imaginations*, Oxford: Blackwell.

Haaren, Hein van 1966, *Constant*, trans. Max Schuchart, Amsterdam: J. M. Meulenhoff.

Hall, Peter 2002 [1988], *Cities of Tomorrow: An Intellectual History of Urban Planning and Design in the Twentieth Century*, Oxford: Blackwell, third edition.

Harvey, David 1989, *The Condition of Postmodernity: An Enquiry into the Origins of Cultural Change*, Oxford: Blackwell.

Harvey, David 1993, 'Cities of dreams', *Guardian*, 15 October, pp. 18–19.

Harvey, David 1996, *Justice, Nature and the Geography of Difference*, Oxford, Blackwell.

Harvey, David 2000, *Spaces of Hope*, Edinburgh: Edinburgh University Press.

Heynen, Hilde 1999, *Architecture and Modernity: A Critique*. Cambridge, MA: MIT Press.

Hollier, Denis 1989 [1974], *Against Architecture: The Writings of Georges Bataille*, trans. Betsy Wing, Cambridge, MA: MIT Press.

Howard, Ebenezer 1898, *To-Morrow: A Peaceful Path to Real Reform*, London: Swan Sonnenschein.

Howard, Ebenezer 1946 [1902], *Garden Cities of To-Morrow*, ed. F. J. Osborn, London: Faber and Faber.

Huizinga, Johan 1970 [1938], *Homo Ludens: A Study of the Play Element in Culture*, London: Temple Smith.

Internationale situationniste, 1958–1969 1997, complete facsimile edition, Paris: Arthème Fayard.

Hussey, Andrew and Bowd, Gavin (eds) 1996, *The Haçienda Must Be Built: On the Legacy of Situationist Revolt*, Universities of Manchester and Huddersfield: AURA.

Jacobs, Jane 1984 [1961], *The Death and Life of Great American Cities: The Failure of Town Planning*, Harmondsworth: Penguin.

Jappe, Anselm 1999, *Guy Debord*, trans. Donald Nicholson-Smith, Berkeley: University of California Press.

Jeanneret, Charles-Édouard and Ozenfant, Amédée 1964 [1920], 'Purism', in Robert L. Herbert (ed.), *Modern Artists on Art*, Englewood Cliffs, NJ: Prentice-Hall, pp. 59–73.

Jeanneret, Charles-Édouard and Ozenfant, Amédée 1997 [n.d.], 'The right angle', in Nadir Lahiji and D. S. Friedman (eds), *Plumbing: Sounding Modern Architecture*, New York: Princeton Architectural Press, pp. 20–31.

'Jorn's Copenhagen' 1957, *The Architectural Review* 122 (September), 223.

Jorn, Asger 1958, *Pour la forme: Ébauche d'une méthodologie des arts*, Paris: L'Internationale situationniste.

Jorn, Asger 2001, 'The anti-situation of Amsterdam', trans. Peter Shield, *Transgressions* 5, 15–19.

Jorn, Asger and Debord, Guy 1957, *Fin de Copenhague*, Copenhagen: Permild and Rosengreen; facsimile reprint Paris: Éditions Allia, 1985.

Knabb, Ken (ed. and trans.) 1981, *Situationist International Anthology*, Berkeley: Bureau of Public Secrets.

Koolhaas, Rem 1994 [1978], *Delirious New York: A Retroactive Manifesto for Manhattan*, New York: The Monacelli Press.

Lambert, Jean-Clarence (ed.) 1997, *Constant/New Babylon. Art et utopie: textes situationnistes*, Paris: Cercle d'Art.

Le Corbusier 1946 [1923], *Towards a New Architecture*, trans. Frederick Etchells, London: Architectural Press.

Le Corbusier 1947 [1937], *When the Cathedrals Were White: A Journey to the Country of Timid People*, trans. Francis E. Hyslop, New York: Reynal & Hitchcock.

Le Corbusier 1953, *Oeuvre complète de 1946–1952*, ed. W. Boesiger, Zurich: Éditions Girsberger.

Le Corbusier 1967 [1935], *The Radiant City*, trans. Pamela Knight, Eleanor Levieux and Derek Coltman, London: Faber and Faber.

Le Corbusier 1987 [1925], *The City of Tomorrow and Its Planning*, trans. Frederick Etchells, London: Architectural Press.

Le Corbusier 1987 [1925], *The Decorative Art of Today*, trans. James L. Dunnett, London: Architectural Press.

Le Corbusier 1991 [1930], *Precisions on the Present State of Architecture and City Planning*, trans. Edith Schreiber Aujame, Cambridge, MA: MIT Press.

Le Corbusier and Jeanneret, Pierre 1948, *Oeuvre complète de 1910–1929*, ed. W. Boesiger and O. Stonorov, Zurich: Les Éditions d'Architecture Erlenbach, fifth edition.

Le Corbusier and Jeanneret, Pierre 1964 [1935], *Oeuvre complète de 1929–1934*, ed. W. Boesiger, Zurich: Éditions Girsberger.

Lees, Loretta (ed.) 2004, *The Emancipatory City? Paradoxes and Possibilities*, London: Sage.

Lefebvre, Henri 1959, *La Somme et le reste*, 2 volumes, Paris: La Nef de Paris.

Lefebvre, Henri 1965, *La Proclamation de la Commune*, Paris: Gallimard.

Lefebvre, Henri 1969 [1968], *The Explosion: Marxism and the French Revolution*, trans. Alfred Ehrenfeld, New York and London: Monthly Review Press.

Lefebvre, Henri 1972, 'Preface' in Philippe Boudon, *Lived-in Architecture: Le Corbusier's Pessac Revisited*, London: Lund Humphries, no pagination.

Lefebvre, Henri 1975, *Le temps des méprises*. Paris: Stock.

Lefebvre, Henri 1976 [1973], *The Survival of Capitalism: Reproduction of the Relations of Production*, trans. Frank Bryant, London: Allison and Busby.

Lefebvre, Henri 1984 [1968], *Everyday Life in the Modern World*, trans. Sacha Rabinovitch, New Brunswick, NJ: Transaction Publishers.

Lefebvre, Henri 1986, *Le retour de la dialectique: Douze mots clefs pour le monde moderne*, Paris: Messidor-Éditions Sociales.

Lefebvre, Henri 1987 [1983], 'An interview with Henri Lefebvre', trans. Eleonore Kofman, *Environment and Planning D: Society and Space* 5, 27–38.

Lefebvre, Henri 1987, 'The everyday and everydayness', trans. Christine Levich with Alice Kaplan and Kristin Ross, *Yale French Studies* 73 (Fall), 7–11.

Lefebvre, Henri 1991 [1947/58], *Critique of Everyday Life, Volume I: Introduction*, trans. John Moore, London: Verso.

Lefebvre, Henri 1991 [1974], *The Production of Space*, trans. Donald Nicholson-Smith, Oxford: Blackwell.

Lefebvre, Henri 1995 [1962], *Introduction to Modernity*, trans. John Moore, London: Verso.

Lefebvre, Henri 1996, *Writings on Cities*, ed. and trans. Eleonore Kofman and Elizabeth Lebas, Oxford: Blackwell.

Lefebvre Henri 2002 [1961] *Critique of Everyday Life, Volume II: Foundations for a Sociology of the Everyday*, trans. John Moore, London: Verso.

Lefebvre, Henri 2003, *Key Writings*, ed. Stuart Elden, Elizabeth Lebas and Elenore Kofman, London: Continuum.

Levitas, Ruth 1990, *The Concept of Utopia*, London: Philip Allan.

Locher, J. L. (ed.) 1974, *New Babylon*, The Hague: Haags Gemeentemuseum.

McDonough, Tom (ed.) 2002, *Guy Debord and the Situationist International: Texts and Documents*, Cambridge, MA: MIT Press.

McDonough, Tom 1997, 'Rereading Debord, rereading the situationists', *October* 79, 3–14.

McLeod, Mary 1985, 'Urbanism and Utopia: Le Corbusier from Regional Syndicalism to Vichy', Unpublished PhD dissertation, Princeton University.

Marcus, Greil 1989, *Lipstick Traces: A Secret History of the Twentieth Century*, London: Secker and Warburg.

Marin, Louis 1984 [1972], *Utopics: The Semiological Play of Textual Spaces*, trans. Robert A. Vollrath, Atlantic Highlands, NJ: Humanities Press.

Mension, Jean-Michel 2001 [1998], *The Tribe*, trans. Donald Nicholson-Smith, San Francisco: City Lights.

Mical, Thomas (ed.) 2005, *Surrealism and Architecture*, London: Routledge.

More, Thomas 1989 [1516], *Utopia*, ed. George M. Logan and Robert M. Adams, Cambridge: Cambridge University Press.

Morris, William 1993 [1890], *News from Nowhere and Other Writings*, Harmondsworth: Penguin.

Mumford, Lewis 1966, *The City in History: Its Origins, its Transformations, and its Prospects*, Harmondsworth: Penguin.

Mumford, Lewis 1967, 'Utopia, the city and the machine', in Frank E. Manuel (ed.), *Utopias and Utopian Thought: A Timely Appraisal*, Boston: Beacon Press, pp. 3–24.

Ohrt, Roberto 1990, *Phantom Avantgarde: Eine Geschichte der Situationischen Internationale und der Modernen Kunst*, Hamburg: Edition Nautilus.

Pinder, David 1996, 'Subverting cartography: the situationists and maps of the city', *Environment and Planning* A 28, pp. 405–27.

Plant, Sadie 1992, *The Most Radical Gesture: The Situationist International in a Postmodern Age*, London: Routledge.

Port-folio situationniste 1993, vols 1 and 2, Paris: Éditions le lundi au soleil.

Potlatch (1954–1957) 1996, complete edition, introduced by Guy Debord, Paris: Gallimard.

Raspaud, Jean-Jacques and Voyer, Jean-Pierre 1972, *L'Internationale situationniste: chronologie/bibliographie/protagonistes (avec un index de noms insultés)*, Paris: Champ Libre.

Ross, Kristin 1988, *The Emergence of Social Space: Rimbaud and the Paris Commune*, London: Macmillan.

Ross, Kristin 1995, *Fast Cars, Clean Bodies: Decolonization and the Reordering of French Culture*, Cambridge, MA: MIT Press.

Ross, Kristin 2002, *May '68 and its Afterlives*, Chicago: University of Chicago Press.

Rumney, Ralph 1958, 'The leaning tower of Venice', excerpts in *ARK: The Journal of the Royal College of Art* 24, pp. vi-ix.

Sadler, Simon 1998, *The Situationist City*, Cambridge, MA: MIT Press.

Sandercock, Leonie (ed.) 1998, *Making the Invisible Visible: A Multicultural Planning History*, Berkeley: University of California Press.

Sandercock, Leonie 1998, *Towards Cosmopolis: Planning for Multicultural Cities*, London: Wiley.

Sandercock, Leonie 2003, *Cosmopolis II: Mongrel Cities in the 21st Century*, London: Continuum.

Shield, Peter 1998, *Comparative Vandalism: Asger Jorn and the Artistic Attitude to Life*, Aldershot: Ashgate, with Borgens.

Situationist International 2003 [1972], *The Real Split in the International*, trans. John McHale, London: Pluto.

Sussman, Elisabeth (ed.) 1989, *On the Passage of a Few People Through a Rather Brief Moment in Time: The Situationist International 1957–1972*, Cambridge, MA: MIT Press.

Swyngedouw, Erik 2002, 'The strange respectability of the situationist city in the society of the spectacle', *International Journal of Urban and Regional Research* 26.1, 153–65.

Tafuri, Manfredo 1976 [1973], *Architecture and Utopia: Design and Capitalist Development*, trans. Barbara Luigia La Penta, Cambridge, MA: MIT Press.

Vaneigem, Raoul 1994 [1967], *The Revolution of Everyday Life*, trans. Donald Nicholson-Smith, London: Left Bank Books and Rebel Press, second edition.

Veseley, Dalibor (ed.) 1978,'Surrealism and architecture', *Architectural Design* 48, 2–3.

Vidler, Anthony 1992, *The Architectural Uncanny: Essays in the Modern Unhomely*, Cambridge, MA: MIT Press.

Viénet, René 1992 [1968], *Enragés and Situationists in the Occupation Movement, France, May '68*, New York and London: Autonomedia and Rebel Press.

Ward, Stephen (ed.) 1992, *The Garden City: Past, Present and Future*, London: Spon.

Wigley, Mark 1995, *White Walls, Designer Dresses: The Fashioning of Modern Architecture*, Cambridge, MA: MIT Press.

Wigley, Mark (ed.) 1998, *Constant's New Babylon: The Hyper-Architecture of Desire*, Rotterdam: Witte de With centre for contemporary art/010 Publishers.

Wilson, Elizabeth 1991, *The Sphinx in the City: Urban Life, the Control of Disorder, and Women*, London: Virago.

Wollen, Peter 1989, 'The Situationist International', *New Left Review* 174, 67–95.

Wollen, Peter 1993, *Raiding the Icebox: Reflections on Twentieth-Century Culture*, London: Verso.

Zegher, Catherine de and Wigley, Mark (eds) 2001, *The Activist Drawing: Retracing Situationist Architectures from Constant's New Babylon to Beyond*, New York: The Drawing Center and Cambridge, MA: MIT Press.

Websites

In addition to the published collections above, situationist texts are now also widely available via websites. In particular, substantial collections of English language translations are currently (January 2005) available at:

Situationist International Online: http://www.cddc.vt.edu/sionline/

Situationist International text library: http://library.nothingness.org/articles/SI/all/

Not Bored Situationist International Archive: http://www.notbored.org/SI.

Not Bored Letterist International Archive: http://www.notbored.org/LI.

Bureau of Public Secrets (translations by Ken Knabb): http://www.bopsecrets.org/SI/

Index

Page references for illustrations are in italics.